DEATH, DYING and BEREAVEMENT

MW00353322

Hong Kong University Press thanks Xu Bing for writing the Press's name in his Square Word Calligraphy for the covers of its books. For further information, see p. iv.

The contributors to this volume are:

Philip Swan Lip BEH
Cecilia Lai Wan CHAN
Eddie Ho Chuen CHAN
Timothy Hang Yee CHAN
Kin Sang CHAN
Wallace Chi Ho CHAN
Grace Yee Kam Pau CHEUNG
Peter Ka Hing CHEUNG
Wing Shan CHEUNG
Amy Yin Man CHOW
Wai FU
Samuel Mun Yin HO
JING YIN
Brenda Wing Sze KOO
Elaine Wai Kwan KOO
Tracy Tak Ching KWAN
Carmen Yuek Yan LAI
Chi Tim LAI
Peter Wing Ho LEE
Sze Man LEE
Wendy Wai Yin LI
Yawen LI
Faith Chun Fong LIU
Jess Shuk Fun LO
Raymond See Kit LO
Vivian Wei Qun LOU
YvonneYi Wood MAK
Siu Man NG
Samantha Mei Che PANG
Michael Mau Kong SHAM
Agnes Fong TIN
Chun Yan TSE
Doris Man Wah TSE
Heung Sang TSE

DEATH, DYING and BEREAVEMENT
A Hong Kong Chinese Experience

Edited by

Cecilia Lai Wan Chan and Amy Yin Man Chow

香港大學出版社

HONG KONG UNIVERSITY PRESS

Hong Kong University Press
14/F Hing Wai Centre
7 Tin Wan Praya Road
Aberdeen
Hong Kong

© Hong Kong University Press 2006
First published 2006
Reprinted 2007

ISBN 978-962-209-787-2

Secure On-line Ordering
http://www.hkupress.org

British Library Cataloguing-in-Publication Data
A catalogue record for this book is available from the British Library.

Photograph on cover courtesy of Mr Timothy H. Y. Chan

Printed and bound by Condor Production Co. Ltd., in Hong Kong, China

Hong Kong University Press is honoured that Xu Bing, whose art explores
the complex themes of language across cultures, has written the Press's
name in his Square Word Calligraphy. This signals our commitment to
cross-cultural thinking and the distinctive nature of our English-language
books published in China.

"At first glance, Square Word Calligraphy appears to be nothing more
unusual than Chinese characters, but in fact it is a new way of rendering
English words in the format of a square so they resemble Chinese
characters. Chinese viewers expect to be able to read Square word
Calligraphy but cannot. Western viewers, however are surprised to find they
can read it. Delight erupts when meaning is unexpectedly revealed."

— Britta Erickson, *The Art of Xu Bing*

Contents

PART TWO   DYING

PART THREE BEREAVEMENT

Foreword

Robert A. NEIMEYER

Although death, dying, and bereavement are obviously universal phenomena, the meanings and practices with which people respond to them are intricately cultural and personal. This is perhaps most obviously true with respect to the immense diversity of secular and spiritual frameworks with which human communities conceptualize the state of death, but it is no less true of the variety of ways in which people engage the dying process and the ways survivors grieve in death's aftermath. This important book holds a magnifying lens over these three interwoven domains, taking as a case study the distinctive cultural matrix of Hong Kong, with its unique fusion of Eastern and Western practices. What emerges is a deeper understanding of both the universality of the human encounter with loss, and the specificity with which individuals, families and communities grapple with its inevitability, using an intriguing convergence of cultural resources.

My own fascination with a Chinese approach to death dates in some sense to an interest in Daoism, Confucianism and Buddhism some thirty years ago, an interest that was given fresh impetus as I began to offer workshops on meaning reconstruction and loss in Hong Kong three years ago. Certainly nothing in my naive, if earnest, study of these three rich traditions prepared me for their melding into a unique folk religion in the cultural crossroads the city represents, affording a set of practices with which many traditional families continue to confront the end of life and its wake. Nor could I have predicted the creativity with which leaders of Hong Kong's thanatology community (many of whom contribute to this volume) draw on these very traditions in constructing innovative rituals, therapeutic techniques, and even new terminology for responding to death in a contemporary context. Perhaps my overriding impression from visits to the area — aside from the unparalleled warmth and enthusiasm with which I was embraced — was that professionals engaging the dying and bereaved in Hong Kong are functioning as cultural revolutionaries in the best sense: preserving elements of China's rich traditions but also integrating them with cutting-edge Western theory and research to produce something unique that has relevance to a global community.

This volume reports the result of that work, carried out over a period of many years by many hands. The reader will find in these pages compellingly personal accounts of illness and healing, alongside probing reflections on problems arising in forensic labs, palliative care units, and bereavement services. Likewise, authors of various chapters mine the wealth of China's ancient spiritual and medical traditions to find resources of relevance to modern life — and death — and consider the special challenges of traumatic loss associated with suicide or the death of a child. Far from merely anthropological in intent, the book also offers a good deal of practical knowledge concerning end-of-life care and bereavement support, which, although rooted in the Hong Kong experience, has something to teach us all.

My hope is that you will find your engagement with a Hong Kong perspective on death, dying, and bereavement as rich and multi-dimensional as I have, and carry away something of value to you in the work you do, whatever your nationality or cultural background. Promoting a cross-fertilization of ideas, practices and traditions is at the heart of Hong Kong's culture, and becoming part of such exchange would honour its spirit and history.

Robert A. Neimeyer, PhD
Chair, International Work Group on
    Death, Dying and Bereavement
Memphis, TN, USA

Foreword

Che Hung LEONG

"Birth, aging, sickness and death" are integral parts of life. Each is inevitable that no one can avoid. It is also said that "birth follows death". The common saying "the king is dead, long live the king" is a vivid example of the philosophy that death begets life.

Yet the subject of death is such a taboo — a phenomenon that is associated not just with mystery, but with misery and fear. This feeling is global, irrespective of race or religion. "Death stalks the night" is something to shudder about. The Chinese are perhaps more sensitive to the issue. The mention of the word death 死 is sacrilegious and to be avoided — often replaced by "he has passed away" or "she is not here anymore". The fact remains that "生離死別" is such a sad and frightful thing.

But why should such everyday occurrences that have existed as long as humankind still produce such fear? Let us forget the emotion and analyse what goes on in the minds of the dying and their families once the pronouncement of death is made. To the dying person, the immediate reactions are: "Will there be any suffering or agony?"; "How should I tell my relatives so as not to alarm them?"; "There are so many things I want to tell my next of kin and I do not know how.". . . The same questions go through the minds of the relatives: "Will there be suffering?" "Should we comfort him and hide the fact?"; "Should we ask her what are the things she want us to do once she passes away?". . . All these are barriers to a closer relationship and bondage that the family should take every opportunity to enjoy in whatever time that is still available. This cloak-and-dagger attitude must be lifted so as to add life to days for families facing death; this is what hospice service is all about.

To the family of the deceased, death is by no means the end of the "injury". How do they deal with the body; how many bureaucracies do they have to go though to get the necessary documents and approval for the last ritual; how do they cope with the hassles of the funeral; when can they break down and let out their pent up feelings; and how can they get back into society and live. Hospice service is never complete without a proper bereavement with a heart!

Readers of this foreword may accuse me of being insensitive by trying to take emotions out of death and dying, or conclude that as a physician I probably see death and suffering as a common occurrence. This is far from the case. In presenting the facts, I hope to promote the needs of hospice and bereavement, something that both the society and government must take on board so that the reality of life can be contained with minimal grief and upset. The motto of hospice, "If we cannot add days to life, add life to days", should be put to good practice.

This book and the chapters written by Professor Cecilia Chan, Amy Chow and other experts will further analyse the philosophy of dying and death in Chinese culture, and will hopefully unveil the mystique surrounding a taboo buried in the thousands of years of our civilization.

Dr Che Hung Leong
Chairman
Elderly Commission
Hong Kong

Foreword

Vivian Taam WONG

My first encounter with bereavement counselling was during the 1970s when I was engaged in prenatal diagnosis and perinatology. I was struck by the strong sense of denial among Chinese parents such that practices borrowed from the West were not well received. Since then, the Tsan Yuk and Queen Mary Hospital perinatal team has developed a culturally sensitive programme for those undergoing the most traumatic experience of perinatal loss.

I am a firm believer of good death. While I was Hospital Chief Executive in Queen Mary Hospital, under the stewardship of Dr Jane Chan, we developed and piloted the "Do Not Resuscitate" protocol which was subsequently adopted and promulgated in all public hospitals under the Hospital Authority. That was the initial step in engaging patients and relatives in discussing the philosophy in relation to futility of treatment.

The choice to die peacefully and gracefully has been advocated in most developed countries. Under the chairmanship of the late Dr Chan Fu Luk, the Queen Mary Hospital Clinical Ethics Committee initiated the discussion on "Advance Directive" in Hong Kong, paving the way to the current deliberation by the Law Reform Commission. The observations in the following chapters may shed light on our community perspectives. This will enrich future intercourse in this arena.

Recently, the Hospital Authority has given due recognition to the importance of Palliative Care by forming a Central Committee to oversee its development, with emphasis on the psychological preparation and physical rehabilitation aspects starting from the earlier part of disease. The positive approach to chronic debilitating diseases conducted by a multi-disciplinary team with the help of volunteer patients and relatives with similar experience would help the whole family in the bereavement process eventually.

Over the past 30 years, we have witnessed the evolution of the coping behaviour of Chinese in Hong Kong when faced with death and dying. Yet for busy clinicians, training in the art of breaking bad news and bereavement counselling is still being relegated to the lower ranks of their priority list. This book contains insight and knowledge which could help initiated readers to reflect on their own belief and attitude towards life and death. In so doing, the daily experience with managing the dying and their beloved could be made much more fulfilling and gratifying. I commend the editors for this brave endeavour and look forward to another book on "life and living" in the near future.

Dr Vivian Taam Wong
Chief Executive
Hospital Authority
Hong Kong

Preface

"When days cannot be added to life, add life to days."
(Motto of the Society for the Promotion of Hospice Care in Hong Kong).

Both of us have a passion for helping people who are grieving, because we are terrified by the thought of the death of our loved ones. Through decades of serving patients confronting death, we have learnt so much, both from them and from their family members. Now, we are willing to accept the notion of "why not me?" and probably will not be stuck in the state of "why me?" for too long. As we serve patients living with a life-threatening illness, we want to help them to reach a state of bliss and acceptance of death.

Through our journey of service and education, we are impressed by the large number of professionals who are completely dedicated to helping patients in the dying and bereavement process. As a result of the contact with the IWG (International Work Group on Death, Dying and Bereavement), we realized that there is a vast amount of knowledge on death and dying that can be applied to our population. At the same time, there is a lot of interest in how traditional practices, Eastern philosophies and culture affect the way that Chinese people respond to death-related issues. The culturally sensitive practices that we have developed in Hong Kong were found to be relevant to an international audience.

As Chinese have become one of the largest migrant groups in contemporary society, health-care professionals all over the world are interested in understanding the reactions of Chinese patients upon diagnosis of an incurable illness and the risk as well as protective factors affecting their adjustment to the dying and bereavement process. The purpose of this book is for health-care professionals to share the Chinese experience of death, dying and bereavement in Hong Kong. It is hoped that the experiential synthesis of the authors can serve to increase the relevance of culturally sensitive practices, locally and internationally.

The process of editing this book was enlightening for us. The authors shared many touching stories of their personal and professional life, and it is a great privilege to read their work. The editing was enjoyable, and on many occasions we had tears in our eyes while reading the profound sharing of experiences and personal reflections.

As a result of discussion on good death and transformation through pain, we hope that death can be taken as a blessed ending to lifelong learning. With sadness, grief and fond memories of the deceased loved one, the bereaved can commit themselves to living a meaningful life, to serve and nurture. Death, dying and bereavement offer the most teachable moments and are beacons for those lost in the ocean of life.

After hearing of our work, acquaintances often say, "It must be sad to work with people who are dying and bereaved". It is true that there is grief in witnessing death, yet it is also the greatest privilege and honour to be working with people in their most precious moments at the end of life. If we can help dying and bereaved persons realize their dreams and review their life, they can proudly recognize their life contributions and the legacies they are leaving. There can be a great sense of peace, bliss and joy. Every encounter with death and bereavement is a reminder of our own mortality. Every suicide and accidental death alert us to the impermanence and unpredictability of life. It is a humbling process that grounds us in an appreciation of life and in living every day to the fullest.

Acknowledgements

We are indebted to all the contributors for sharing their enthusiasm, stimulating ideas and expert knowledge, thus making this book possible. Special thanks are due to Mr Dennis Cheung, our editor at Hong Kong University Press, and his team for their practical advice and efficient professional support. Other individuals provided valuable and indispensable assistance behind the scene, and they deserve recognition. Mr Timothy H.Y. Chan generously permits us to use a photograph taken by him on the book cover, and provides inspiration for the cover design. Dr Wing Wong, Ms Hilary Ho, Mr Wai Fu, and Ms Amy Choi devoted much time and effort in administrative work at various stages in the preparation of the book. We would like to express our gratitude to all of them.

Royalties from this book will be donated to the Society for the Promotion of Hospice Care in Hong Kong.

Cecilia L.W. Chan
Amy Y.M. Chow
December 2005

Contributors

Philip Swan Lip BEH, MBBS *HK,* DMJ *Lond,* FHKCPath, FHKAM (Pathology)

Dr Beh is currently a Clinical Associate Professor in forensic pathology in the Department of Pathology, Faculty of Medicine, University of Hong Kong. He graduated from the University of Hong Kong in 1981 and worked as a forensic pathologist with the Forensic Pathology Service, Department of Health from 1982 to 1995, before joining the Faculty of Medicine. He has been involved in over 10,000 coroner's cases, during which he interviewed family members in an effort to establish prior medical history and to inform them of the requirements for autopsies under the *Coroner's Ordinance.* He is frequently required to give expert medical evidence in death inquests, in civil cases involving injury and death and in criminal cases, particularly assault, rape and homicide.

Cecilia Lai Wan CHAN, BSocSc, MSocSc, PhD, RSW, JP

Professor Chan has been instrumental in the establishment of the Centre on Behavioral Health and the Centre of Suicide Research and Prevention of the University of Hong Kong. She served as director and associate director of the two centres respectively, and as a professor of the Department of Social Work and Social Administration. She is a committee member on various health-care societies and author of over 100 articles and book chapters on health, practice research, psychosocial oncology, bereavement and palliative care. She uses a strength-oriented approach in her work on empowerment of chronic patients, cancer patients, divorced women, bereaved family members and traumatized individuals. Her Eastern body-mind-spirit approach and culturally relevant practices have been widely adopted in the health care and social work field.

Eddie Ho Chuen CHAN, BSW, RSW

Mr Chan is the centre director of The Comfort Care Concern Group. He has over seven years of experience in serving people facing death and bereavement. He has conducted a number of in-house volunteer training workshops in various organizations related to the topic of care for the caregiver, emotional handling, volunteer befriending visitation training, etc. In recent years, Mr Chan has been interested in working with bereaved Chinese males.

Timothy Hang Yee CHAN, BCogSc

Mr Chan received his bachelor's degree in cognitive science from the University of Hong Kong in 2002. Currently, he is a research coordinator at the Centre on Behavioral Health, University of Hong Kong, working on research projects ranging from mindfulness and health, death attitudes, to post-traumatic meaning reconstruction.

Kin Sang CHAN, MBBS, MRCP *UK*, FRCP *Edin, Glas* and *Lond*, FHKCP, FHKAM

Dr Chan has been the chief of service of the Pulmonary and Palliative Care Unit of Haven of Hope Hospital since 1995. He is one the first group of five physicians accredited by the Hong Kong College of Physicians as a Specialist in Palliative Medicine in 1998. He graduated from the University of Hong Kong in 1981 and received post-graduate medical training at the United Christian Hospital of Hong Kong and in hospitals in the United States and the United Kingdom. His main interests include holistic care, psychological care, medical ethics and rehabilitation. He has been promoting palliative care through various professional societies and NGOs. Dr Chan is a contributing author in the second and third editions of *The Oxford Textbook of Palliative Medicine.*

Wallace Chi Ho CHAN, BSW, RSW

Mr Chan is currently a PhD candidate in the Department of Social Work and Social Administration, University of Hong Kong. His areas of interest include bereavement, death and dying, hospice care, logotherapy and existential psychology. In addition, Mr Chan is a registered social worker in Hong Kong. He is experienced in elderly service and medical social service. He is now a medical social worker and is responsible for working with patients and families of palliative care in the Ruttonjee Hospital.

Grace Yee Kam Pau CHEUNG, BSW, PhD, RSW

Dr Cheung is an Honorary Assistant Professor in the Department of Social Work and Social Administration, University of Hong Kong; and an Executive Committee member of the Centre on Behavioral Health in the same university. She has been engaged in social work practice as a marriage and family counsellor in Hong Kong for the past twenty-six years. Currently, she teaches the Satir model and family reconstruction to social work students in the University of Hong Kong, provides clinical consultation and supervision in the Satir model to workers in social agencies, runs a private practice in counselling, and conducts Satir workshops as well as life and death workshops for helping professionals and client groups.

Peter Ka Hing CHEUNG, Baccalaureatus and Prolytatus in Theology (University of Propaganda Fide, Rome), BSocSc, MA

Mr Cheung was chief editor of a weekly publication. He has also worked as a teacher, marriage counsellor, human rights organizer and researcher. He is currently a PhD candidate in the Department of Social Work and Social Administration, University of Hong Kong. His research area is the marital sexual experiences of husbands of women treated for breast cancer.

Wing Shan CHEUNG, BSocSc, MPhil

Ms Cheung started her investigation into Chinese perception of death as an undergraduate. Her research is widely accepted by international scholars and was published in the *Death Studies*, an international journal specifically focused on death research. Ms Cheung then extended her undergraduate research into a multi-cultural comparison study among adolescents, and obtained her MPhil degree in the University of Hong Kong. As a motivated young researcher, Ms Cheung had also participated actively in international research seminars and had won two research awards in international conferences.

Amy Yin Man CHOW, BSocSc, MSocSc, RSW, CT

Ms Chow is an Honorary Clinical Associate of the Centre on Behavioral Health, as well as an Assistant Professor in the Department of Social Work and Social Administration, University of Hong Kong. She is a registered social worker with a specialization in bereavement counselling. She has worked as a medical social worker, fieldwork instructor and centre-in-charge of the first community-based bereavement counselling centre in Hong Kong. She is certified in thanatology: death, dying and bereavement. In 2005, she received the cross-cultural paper award of ADEC (Association of Death Education and Counselling).

Wai FU, BSocSc (Gen), MPhil

Mr Fu is a research associate in the Centre on Behavioral Health, The University of Hong Kong. He is currently a PhD candidate in the Department of Social Work and Social Administration, University of Hong Kong, under the supervision of Professor Cecilia Chan. His major research interest includes analysis of narratives on the personal experience of cancer patients, the construction of health-related discourses, and the history of psychology in China and Hong Kong.

Samuel Mun Yin HO, BSocSc, MSocSc (Clin Psy), PhD *Melb*

Dr Ho is an Associate Professor in the Department of Psychology, University of Hong Kong. His research interests include clinical health psychology and indigenous psychotherapy. Dr Ho directs the Positive Psychology Laboratory of the Psychology Department and is doing research on positive changes after traumatic events such as life-threatening illnesses and bereavement. Dr Ho has published in prominent health and clinical psychology journals such as *Psycho-oncology* and the *Journal of Consulting and Clinical Psychology.*

JING YIN, MA, MPhil *Kelaniya,* PhD *Lond*

The Venerable Jing Yin obtained his PhD from the School of Oriental and African Studies, University of London, in 2001. He is the Director of the Centre of Buddhist Studies, University of Hong Kong. His research interests are Vinaya, Chinese Buddhism and the social application of Buddhism. In the more than twenty years since entering the Order in 1982, he has devoted some of his time to helping dying persons, to put them at ease. He founded the Buddhist Education Foundation in 1996 in the UK and edited two Buddhist texts for schoolchildren, with the intention to promote personal growth among young children.

Brenda Wing Sze KOO, BSW, MSocSc, RSW, CT

Ms Koo is a bereavement counsellor at the Jessie and Thomas Tam Centre for the Society for the Promotion of Hospice Care (SPHC). The Jessie and Thomas Tam Centre, one of the pioneer projects of the SPHC opened in 1997, is the first community bereavement counselling, education and resource centre in Hong Kong. She is specialized in providing individual and group counselling for various bereaved clients, including widows, widowers, bereaved children, bereaved elderly people, parents losing children and adult children losing parents.

Elaine Wai Kwan KOO, RN, RM

Ms Koo is a bereavement counsellor at the Jessie and Thomas Tam Centre for the Society for the Promotion of Hospice Care (SPHC). The Jessie and Thomas Tam Centre, one of the pioneer projects of the SPHC opened in 1997, is the first community bereavement counselling, education and resource centre in Hong Kong. She is specialized in providing individual and group counselling for various bereaved clients, including widows, widowers, bereaved children, bereaved elderly people, parents losing children and adult children losing parents.

Tracy Tak Ching KWAN, BSc (Nurs), RN *Can*

Ms Kwan received her BSc in Nursing from the University of Toronto. She has extensive experience working with physically and critically ill patients in the hospital setting. She is currently a research worker in the Department of Psychiatry, University of Hong Kong. She has participated in studies in the areas of clinical communication, mental illness and psycho-oncology.

Carmen Yuek Yan LAI, BScN (Hon), RN

Ms Lai has been a registered nurse since the 1990s, working in the medical ward and coronary care unit in an acute hospital. The increasing number of sudden deaths from heart attack and the admission of critically ill and dying patients had compelled Ms Lai and her supervisor to concentrate on the care of dying patients and the grieving family. They liased with several ward staff members and established a working group on bereavement care in 1999. They have gained valuable experience through the caring process and which has been shared with frontline nurses.

Chi Tim LAI, BA, BD (Hons), MA, PhD

Professor Tim is professor of Daoist studies at the Department of Cultural and Religious Studies, the Chinese University of Hong Kong, where he offers courses in history of Daoism, Six Dynasties Daoist Classics, Daoist ritual, and Hong Kong Daoism. He received his PhD from the University of Chicago Divinity School, specializing in Daoism and history of religions. His writings mainly cover Six Dynasties Daoism, and contemporary Guangdong and Hong Kong Daoism. He has published in the international journals of *T'oung Pao, China Quarterly, Asia Major* third series, *Numen, Journal of Chinese Culture* (Hong Kong), *Bulletin of the Institute of Modern History Academia Sinica, Bulletin of the Institute of History and Philology Academia Sinica,* and *Taiwan Journal for Religious Studies.* He is currently working on early Heavenly Master Daoism, Daoist ritual tradition, and histories of Hong Kong and Guangdong Daoism.

Peter Wing Ho LEE, BSocSc, MSocSc (Clin Psy), PhD

Professor Lee is professor in clinical health psychology in the Department of Psychiatry, University of Hong Kong. He has a long- standing interest in psychological treatments for physically ill patients, including cancer and end-of-life care. He is also interested in enhancing awareness and better emotional care for people who are physically ill, through working collaboratively with medical and allied health-care professionals.

Sze Man LEE, BSW, RSW

Ms Lee is a bereavement counsellor at the Jessie and Thomas Tam Centre for the Society for the Promotion of Hospice Care (SPHC). The Jessie and Thomas Tam Centre, one of the pioneer projects of the SPHC opened in 1997, is the first community bereavement counselling, education and resource centre in Hong Kong. She is specialized in providing individual and group counselling for various bereaved clients, including widows, widowers, bereaved children, bereaved elderly people, parents losing children and adult children losing parents.

Wendy Wai Yin LI, BN (Hon), RN

Ms Li has been working in the surgical unit for over twenty years. She is a Nursing Officer and a team member of bereavement support group in the hospital. She believes that bereavement service should be provided to all patients, and is committed to serving cancer patients in an acute surgical ward by spending time in caring, listening to, supporting and giving information to the cancer patients and their family members.

Yawen LI, MSW

Ms Li is now a doctoral student in the School of Social Work, University of Southern California. She was involved in a variety of studies when she worked at the Centre on Behavioral Health at the University of Hong Kong from 2002 to 2003. She studied the psychosocial well-being of cancer patients, death and dying, and bereavement, with a focus on culturally relevant practice.

Faith Chun Fong LIU, RN, RGN, BScN

Ms Liu is a pioneer in hospice care in Hong Kong. She is now working as a bereavement counsellor at Grantham Hospital. As a clinical nurse in the specialty for more than ten years, she has been very privileged to learn from her patients and their family members. They teach her to love, to forgive and to let go. The journey with those marvellous teachers is a way to grow in self-awareness, self-reflection and self-expansion.

Jess Shuk Fun LO, RN, RM, BN, MN

Ms Lo is an Advanced Practice Nurse of an adult intensive care unit of The Hong Kong Hospital Authority. Her major experience is in the areas of critical care nursing and clinical information system development. She has also been involved in the hospital bereavement support service working group. Her masters degree research was on death and bereavement perceptions among Chinese bereaved people who lost a loved one in the critical care unit.

Raymond See Kit LO, MBBS *Lond,* MD CUHK, MHA UNSW, MRCP *UK,* FRCP *Edin,* Dip Geri Med (RCPS *Glas*), Dip Palliat Med *Wales,* FHKCP, FHKAM

Dr Lo graduated from the United Medical School of Guy's and St Thomas Hospital in London and is currently Cluster Coordinator of Hospice and Palliative Care Services for New Territories East, Honorary Chief of Service of Bradbury Hospice, and Senior Medical Officer in the Department of Medicine and Geriatrics, Shatin Hospital. Dr Lo is accredited in the specialties of advanced internal medicine, geriatrics and in palliative medicine. He is also chairman of the quality assurance subcommittee of HA COC Palliative Care. He undertakes regular teaching for undergraduates and postgraduates in geriatrics, palliative care and ethical issues. His doctoral thesis is on quality of life in palliative care patients.

Vivian Wei Qun LOU, BEd *ECNU,* Med *ECNU,* MSW *HK,* PhD *HK,* RSW

Dr Lou is currently an assistant professor in the Department of Social Work, The Chinese University of Hong Kong. Dr Lou received her B.Ed. (Psychology) and M.Ed. (Psychology) from East China Normal University; and obtained her Master of Social Work and Ph.D. (Social Work) from The University of Hong Kong. Her research projects focus on the social adaptation and mental health of women and older adults. She also has a keen interest in practice research on factors that contribute to the enhancement of mental health status. Dr Lou is presently a member of the American Psychological Association and the Hong Kong Social Workers Association.

YvonneYi Wood MAK, MBBS *Lond,* DGM Lond, DRCOG *Lond,* MSc Wales

After qualifying at Guy's Hospital, London, Dr Mak embarked on general practice training with a particular interest in palliative medicine. Subsequently, she worked at Bradbury Hospice as a Medical Officer, during which time she completed the Diploma and Master Programs in Palliative Medicine at the University of Wales, receiving distinction for both modules. Her dissertation, "The meaning of desire for euthanasia in advanced cancer patients" received the 2001 UK Association of Palliative Medicine Award and the 2004 London

Royal Society of Medicine Innovative Research in Palliative Care Prize. She is involved in undergraduate education at the Chinese University of Hong Kong. As an honorary lecturer in palliative medicine at Cardiff University, Wales, she coordinates the postgraduate palliative care courses for Asia pacific. Since becoming a cancer patient, her mission has extended beyond the hospice walls and she serves as an honorary advisor for the Hong Kong Breast cancer Foundation. She aims to promote a positive attitude to living through education and creative writing.

Siu Man NG, BSc, BHSc, MSc

Mr Ng is an Assistant Professor and Clinical Coordinator at the Centre on Behavioral Health, University of Hong Kong. His research area is the application of Chinese medicine and traditional Chinese philosophies in mental health practice.

Samantha Mei Che PANG, RN, PhD

Dr Pang is a nurse by professional training, and a researcher in the field of health care and nursing ethics by scholarly endeavour. Dr Pang started her career as a nurse academic in 1990, when she took up a teaching post at the Hong Kong Polytechnic University, where she now serves as professor in the School of Nursing. Over the past ten years, she has taught, lectured, and published in the areas of nursing ethics, caring practices, and ethics in end-of-life care. She is on the editorial board of *Nursing Ethics, Chinese Journal of Nursing Education* and *Journal of Modern Nursing Education and Research.*

Michael Mau Kong SHAM, MBBS *HK,* FHKCP, FHKAM (Med), FRCP *Lond,* FRCP *Edin,* MHA *NSW*

Dr Sham, specialist and trainer in palliative medicine, is the consultant-in-charge of the Palliative Medical Unit, Grantham Hospital, Hong Kong. Dr Sham is also co-chairman of the Central Coordinating Committee (Palliative Care) of the Hong Kong Hospital Authority, and Honorary Clinical Associate Professor of the Department of Community Medicine and Unit for Behavioural Sciences, University of Hong Kong. Dr Sham also helps with palliative care service in Macau and mainland China, and is honorary consultant of the Hospice and Palliative Care Centre of Kiang Wu Hospital in Macau and honorary consultant (hospice) of the First Affiliated Hospital of Shantou University Medical College.

Agnes Fong TIN, MSW, RSW, CT

Ms Tin is a bereavement counsellor at the Jessie and Thomas Tam Centre for the Society for the Promotion of Hospice Care (SPHC). The Jessie and Thomas Tam Centre, one of the pioneer projects of the SPHC opened in 1997, is the first community bereavement counselling, education and resource centre in Hong Kong. She is specialized in providing individual and group counselling for various bereaved clients including widows, widowers, bereaved children, bereaved elderly people, parents losing children and adult children losing parents.

Chun Yan TSE, MBBS *HK,* FRCP, FHKCP, FHKAM (Med), MHA *NSW*

Dr Tse graduated from the University of Hong Kong in 1973. He became the consultant and head of the Department of Medicine of United Christian Hospital in 1984. He was a pioneer of the hospice movement in Hong Kong, and established the hospice service in the hospital in 1987. He became the Hospital Chief Executive of the hospital in 1994 and was the Cluster Chief Executive (Kowloon East) of the Hospital Authority in 2001 until his retirement in 2005. He led the Working Group in formulating the Guidelines on Life-sustaining Treatment of the Hospital Authority, in 2002.

Doris Man Wah TSE, MBBS *HK,* FHKCP, FHKAM (Med), FRCP *Lond,* FRCP *Edin*

Dr Tse is currently the Chief of Service of the Department of Medicine and Geriatrics and Intensive Care Unit of Caritas Medical Centre. She has also been the physician-in-charge of the Palliative Care Unit of Caritas Medical Centre since its establishment in 1992. Dr Tse is accredited in the specialty of advanced internal medicine, critical care medicine and palliative medicine of the Hong Kong College of Physicians. Dr Tse was the chair of the Hong Kong Society of Palliative Medicine from 2002 to 2005. Currently, she is the editor-in-chief of the newsletter of the Hong Kong Society of Palliative Medicine.

Heung Sang TSE, BSW, RSW

Mr Tse is an experienced social worker, particularly in hospice social work. He is keen on developing innovative services for terminal cancer patients and their families. He was in charge of the Medical Social Work Department of the former Nam Long Hospital. Currently Mr Tse is in charge of the Medical Social Work Department at Ruttonjee Hospital.

1

Introduction

Amy Yin Man CHOW and Cecilia Lai Wan CHAN

Chinese Culture and Death

Fear marks the boundary between the known and the unknown. Some Chinese people believe that talking about death will increase the likelihood of occurrence. Also, by talking about death, evil spirits will be attracted to haunt people.[1,2] In facing death, individual response is inevitably moulded by the values, attitudes, and beliefs of one's culture.[3,4] Despite the large Chinese emigrant population in major cities in the world, available material in English on death, dying and bereavement among Chinese people is scarce. Only recently has a book, Fielding and Chan's[5] *Psychosocial Oncology and Palliative Care in Hong Kong: The First Decade* addressed cancer deaths, psychosocial and palliative care, in English. Leung and Cheung's[6] book, *Viewing Death,* in Chinese, is a collection of papers presented at a 2002 conference on life and death. Bagley and Tse's[7] book is on suicide and bereavement of adolescents in Hong Kong. Other Chinese books on the topic of death and dying are translated works from the West [8–10] or from Japan.[11–13] There are a number of Chinese books on thanatology in Taiwan[14–18] and Hong Kong.[19, 20] However, Chinese people in different communities may hold very different beliefs and practices related to death and dying. For example, Chinese in Taiwan want to die at home,[2] whereas their counterparts in Hong Kong would prefer to die in a hospital.[21] As Hong Kong is a place where East meets West, most professionals working in the field of death, dying and bereavement adapt knowledge from the West to their practice with the Chinese population. The intention of this volume is to consolidate and disseminate valuable practical wisdom with professionals in the local and international communities who serve Chinese patients and their family members.

Death: A Chinese Experience

Chinese people are known for their inability to articulate their feelings and for commonly resorting to somatization in times of stress and emotional difficulties.[22] Grief and bereavement is even harder to articulate than are feelings, as death is seen as a curse in the Chinese culture.[1, 23] The intensity of the loss, pain, guilt and shame can be so acute that Chinese bereaved persons are unable to put their feelings into words. As well as somatizing their suffering, the pragmatic and action-oriented Chinese people focus on the performance of funeral and burial rituals, in the hope that such action can contribute to the smooth reincarnation of the diseased person. Thus, active participation in rituals and religious compliance to advice from authority are common. As a result of heavy reliance on experts and medical technology, ordinary people are excluded from taking a meaningful role in end-of-life decisions both for themselves and for their loved ones. What is left after death is a strong sense of helplessness, frustration and guilt among bereaved family members.

Disclosure of grief to non-family members might be perceived as inappropriate. Chinese family members are very close to each other. Discussing family matters in public would be disloyal to the family. Survivors should say only good things about the deceased family member. Sibling rivalry, interpersonal tensions or conflicts previously hidden may surface soon after a death in a family, as death is a stressful and traumatic event for everyone. There are also conflicting role expectations, alliances as well as questions of power and control, especially when it comes to the division of the estate and for rights over the items the deceased person has bequeathed.

Death Denial

Despite the knowledge that everyone dies, there is a general denial of death among the Chinese population. It is believed that death will come knocking if the word "death" is called or mentioned.[21] Even the thought of the word "death" would bring bad luck. As people do not talk about death, they do not prepare for it. When people die without preparing for it, they die with unfinished business. Such denial of death may result in deep regret and severe self-blame among the bereaved loved ones.[24]

Similar to saying "Your Excellency" or "Your Honour", people addressed the emperor in China as "Ten Thousand Years Old, Ten Thousand Years Old". Princes and princesses are "Thousand Years Old, Thousand Years Old", to signify that they are close to heavenly gods who are immortal. Death is not acceptable to those in power. The attending doctors who failed to heal the emperor would have to be buried with him, for their incompetence at curing disease. Enormous resources were invested in the construction of tombs for kings and emperors, even when they were young. The most scenic places in China are the tombs of ancient emperors. Most of the treasures recovered from tombs are now being turned over to heritage museums all over the world. The tombs at Xi'an are a good example of the magnificence of an emperor's tomb.

Talking about death is taboo in the Chinese culture. Words that sound like "death" are avoided as far as possible. For example, the number "four" (*xi*) sounds like "death" (*xi*) and so is avoided. Car registration numbers with the number four may invite accidental death. The numbers "fourteen" and "twenty-four" on car plates are worse, because fourteen sounds like sure (ten) death (four), and twenty-four like easy (two) death (four). Some car-owners will withdraw their randomly assigned plate number if it includes the number four, even at the expense of paying extra, to have another chance of a licence plate without four. The number "9413" will never appear, as it means nine out of ten will die (four), and only one out of ten will live (three). Flats on the fourth, fourteenth and subsequent floors ending in four in multistorey buildings in Hong Kong usually cost less than do flats on other floors. Some developers even deliberately omit all floors that end with the number four. More superstitious developers also remove the thirteenth floor from the numbering. Living on a floor that ends in the number four is seen as unlucky, as it can hasten death in the family, although there is no empirical evidence of this.

Death: A Failure to Care

In the midst of the rapid advancement of medical technology, people are given a false impression that modern medicine can cure all previously incurable diseases, and people do not have to die. Doctors see terminal illness as a "failure" of medical treatment, and family members see death as an "unsuccessful" cure. No matter how old the patients are, family members usually believe that their loved ones have died too young. This strong refusal to accept death reinforces prolonged grief among family members, because their loved ones continue to fight vigorously until the very last moment of life. When we get an injection, if we relax our arms and muscles, there is very little pain after the injection. If we are tense and tighten up, the insertion of the needle will bring greater and prolonged pain. The same phenomenon takes place in death and dying. If one is willing to accept death and relax, there is greater comfort and peace. If one fights death vigorously, the death can leave severe damage and suffering, not only on the deceased but also on the loved ones. Thus, if one is more willing to let go of life, one has more energy to live and die with peace of mind. A study on cancer patients found that fatalism and a fighting spirit is a continuous positive variable in the Chinese population. [25] Accepting fate can actually free up one's energy to cope more effectively with life-threatening illness and trauma.

Chinese family members are closely knit by a sophisticated web of mutual obligations and responsibilities.[26] The refusal to embrace death is also driven by a survivor's guilt at failure to fulfil filial obligations towards elderly parents, the duty of a husband to care for his wife, and the responsibility of parents to look after their children. For failure to protect loved ones from ill health and death, Chinese persons may indulge in self-blame, shame and guilt.[27]

The Case of a "Crazy" Doctor

Dick was a well-known TCM (traditional Chinese medicine) practitioner who had a very good relationship with his wife and mother. He lost both of them to cancer in one year. He felt that he was totally "useless", as he could not cure his mother and his wife. He closed his clinic and lived in self-blame. Ten years later, a community worker identified him as a "crazy herbalist" who was living on welfare in a slum and spending his time talking to insects.

Death: Isolation of Bereaved Family Members

According to old traditions, a white lantern is hung outside the house if someone in that family has died. Then, the neighbours and others in the community will know what has happened. People would come to mourn and offer their condolences to the family during the first two days. Then the corpse would be buried. The children, friends and relatives will stay awake in the house, burn paper money continuously and chat until the next day. Stories around the deceased person were told, and people felt the re-establishment of connections. In psycho-social-spiritual terms, such a ritual is a debriefing experience as well as an occasion for the living trying to pave the way for the deceased to move into the next world. Burning paper money is seen as a way to provide the deceased person with the necessary financial support so that he or she can buy his or her way through the guards and gods of the underworld, to ensure a good reincarnation in the subsequent life assignment. Daoists and Buddhists describe the elaborate punishments in hell for the various crimes one commits, as deterrents for the living to violate the social expectations of a good citizen.[#]

[#] Books and other publications on what punishments in hell are like can be obtained from temples in China, Taiwan and Hong Kong. Buddhists believe that, by promoting knowledge of karma (causes and consequences), one can accumulate credits in Heaven. Thus, they would sponsor books to be given out freely to temple visitors. Some of these books can also be found in vegetarian restaurants run by practising Buddhists.

After the burial, people will stop visiting. In fact, the house in which a person dies will be seen as a place that radiates bad energy (*qi*, 氣). It may be difficult to understand this from a Western viewpoint. Why do peers shy away when the family needs support most? In the old rural communities in China, a significant number of deaths might have been caused by infectious diseases. The bad *qi* around the family of someone who died might have been bacteria and virus that may spread infection and illness. Naturally, the community would tend to avoid going near that household.

Also because of the fear of infectious diseases, all clothes worn by the family members during the funeral and burial will have to be burnt. The family will have to eat a good meal after going to the burial, take a bath in hot water with herbs, and then burn all clothing. Although the original intention of such rituals was to stop infection, these measures reinforced the traditional concept that there is negative energy around death. Anything related to the funeral and burial rituals carry bad luck or evil energy and thus have to be destroyed. Therefore, for three months after the death, neighbours and friends will not visit a home where someone died. They have to walk over a burning fire before entering their own home, in order to burn away the "bad" or "toxic" energy that they might have picked up in the home of the deceased person. If we look at it from the perspective of modern medicine, these measures were performed for the prevention of the spread of epidemics in olden days.

Bereaved family members may not be able to concentrate and be accident-prone. If something goes wrong, the hypothesis that the bereaved person carried "bad luck" is confirmed. Without trying to find out the true reasons for cultural myths, the concepts of toxic energy and bad fate around bereaved family members continued into modern society. The fear of death and the reluctance to go near a house in which someone died are still very common, despite the fact that very few people actually die of infections in modern Chinese cities such as Hong Kong. The mass infection of SARS in Toronto during the SARS outbreak in 2003 reminded us of the possibility of infection at funeral services.

When friends are not willing to visit, the bereaved are left to grieve alone. Besides the loss of a loved one, bereaved persons have to bear social isolation from friends and peers. They are expected to stay away from happy celebrations such as weddings and birthday parties, because the bereaved will bring bad luck. It is a stressful experience to have someone die in the family, especially when the bereaved are seen as carrying negative energy around them.

Funerals and burial rituals give bereaved family members a sense of security, as it creates structure for the bereaved to hold on to. There are specific tasks to carry out during each day after death until the forty-ninth day, when the deceased is supposed to be reincarnated. Traditional Chinese mourning rituals last for three years, according to Confucius' teaching. Widows in traditional China are expected to mourn for the rest of their lives, because a woman can be married to only one man. Details of the Daoist rituals can be found in Chapter 4.

Death: The Great Teacher of Life

Death is often seen as a bad experience, yet there can be precious discoveries. The positive reaction to the book *Tuesdays with Morrie*[28] is a good example. Through the pain of facing death, we can appreciate the blessings in life. It is in the midst of the fear of death of our beloved family members that we treasure each and every one of them more dearly. In fact, death is not necessarily sad and miserable. Death can be a precious moment of completion, fulfillment and a perfect ending to lifelong learning. Our funeral is equivalent to our graduation ceremony to celebrate a life worth living and the legacies we leave. Awareness of death leads us to the appreciation of the vulnerability of life and life itself.

Life

Life is an opportunity, benefit from it.
Life is beauty, admire it.
Life is bliss, taste it.
Life is a dream, realize it.
Life is a challenge, meet it.
Life is a duty, complete it.
Life is a game, play it.
Life is love, enjoy it.
Life is mystery, know it.
Life is a promise, fulfil it.
Life is sorrow, overcome it.
Life is a song, sing it.
Life is a struggle, accept it.
Life is tragedy, confront it.
Life is an adventure, dare it.
Life is life, fight for it.

Author Unknown

If we replace the word "life" in the above verse with the word "death", most of the sentences in the passage still make sense. Death is part of life. Life is uncertain. The only certain promise in life is that all of us will die. According to Eastern philosophers, life is a difficult journey full of suffering. Infants start the journey by crying and end with a sense of relief when they die. Most people refuse to acknowledge the inevitability of death. As we become attached to people, to possessions, to power, to material comfort, it is hard to say goodbye to life.

Life and death, sickness and health, meeting and parting, love and hate, attachment and letting go, apathy and involvement, disengagement and integration, dependency and alienation are part of the reality of our existence. We have an impression that these facts of life are opposites, like the sun and the moon. In reality, we can always find the moon shining in the sky before the sunset. Life is interesting because of its impermanence and unpredictability. The processes of gain and loss can be both joyful and painful. For example, when a couple gets married, they are happy and joyful. Despite the wish to live happily ever after, one certain outcome of marriage is that it will end. In pre-marital classes, couples learn to handle matters of trust, intimacy, in-law relationships, family planning and asset management. However, there have yet to be offered anticipatory divorce or bereavement courses to help people prepare for the end of marriage, through spousal death or marital breakdown.

Death, Dying and Bereavement

In the first part of the book, we focus on the discussion of **death**. Chapter 2 is the recollections of our clinical experiences in the area of death, dying and bereavement. At times we witnessed the pain of the family when a family member faced death. Some patients isolated themselves or used all their energy to fight the unbeaten enemy — death. There are those who use their final days to attend to unfinished business, to reconcile and to forgive their loved ones as well as to realize their dreams. Those that can give the patient permission to die have an easier bereavement. Effective communication among family members seems to be a crucial step to restructure a mutually accepted way of facing the impending death.

In Chapter 3, Yvonne Mak shares her personal experience as a patient, a hospice physician, a researcher and a care-giver of her own family members with life threating illness. She affirms that death can be transformational. There can be growth through the process of confronting our death and end of life and that of our loved ones and the people we serve.

In addition to social workers and physicians, a professional actively involved in the area of death is the funeral director. The funeral arrangements in Hong Kong are quite different from those in the West. Usually, different rituals dominate funerals. Based on an interview with a funeral consultant in Hong Kong, personal reflections as well as literature review, Ka Hing Cheung and colleagues contribute the fourth chapter of this book, unveiling some of the mysteries around the Daoist funeral rituals in Hong Kong. Using the continuum of *letting go* and *holding on*, they analysed the meaning behind the different rituals and how they contributed to the adjustment to bereavement. Chapter 5 is also about funeral rituals, but from an academic point of view. Chi Tim Lai shares his reflections on Daoist funerary liturgy. A chapter by Jin Yin follows, on the Buddhist view of death, dying and bereavement.

Forensic pathologists deal with unnatural deaths such as suicide, homicide and accident. About thirty percent of deaths in Hong Kong involve pathologists in identifying the causes of death. Philip Beh, an experienced forensic pathologist, briefs us on the procedures in handling unnatural deaths, in Chapter 7. Facing the deep-rooted traditional belief of being buried whole, he shares the interaction and dynamics with family members on the negotiation of autopsies.

Wing Shan Cheung and Samuel Ho share their study on the personal meaning of death among Chinese, through the images or metaphors of death. The most common theme in the drawings of death among their respondents is "a separation from the loved one". The interpersonal nature of death and bereavement is obvious. Although the majority of the respondents used negative adjectives to describe death, as well as black and white to draw images of death, a substantial percentage of respondents used positive adjectives or bright colours. The perception of death among Chinese is not necessarily all negative. Wallace Chan and his colleagues reconsider the topics of good death through a historical review of traditional philosophy and public opinion studies. Physical and psychosocial well-being are the two key factors contributing to a good death.

The second section of our book is on the process of **dying**. About one-third of the deaths in Hong Kong are caused by cancer. Palliative hospice care is for those who have incurable cancer. Through home care and hospice beds, professionals address the physical, psychosocial, and spiritual needs of their patients through the last months, weeks and days of their lives. The Chinese name for hospice care has been translated as *xian zhong* (善終, literally, good ending). More recently, there has been a change in the use of term, because the public resents the concept of the hospice and equates it with death and the termination of life. New terms, such as *xian ning* (善寧, literally, good and peaceful), *ning yang* (寧養, peaceful and nurturing) and *shu huan* (紓緩, relax and relief) are being used in the name of service units instead of the old term of "good ending". Chinese in Hong Kong probably find the term "*zhong*" (終, ending) hard to accept. No matter what name is used, the professionals of palliative hospice care in Hong Kong are committed to providing quality care to all who are facing death. When we first shared our idea of editing this book, responses from the palliative care teams were very positive. Contributors of the second section of this book are from the palliative hospice care professionals in Hong Kong.

Michael Sham, Doris Tse, Kin Sang Chan and Raymond Lo are leaders of hospital and palliative care in Hong Kong. Their chapter, "Impact of Palliative Care on the Quality of Life of the Dying", succinctly describes the key concerns from the perspective of health care providers. With a rich historical review and detailed research findings, Chapter 10 guides us through a timeline of palliative care development in Hong Kong. Raymond Lo further elaborates on the medical and psycho-social-spiritual aspects of the final month of a dying patient. After discussing the problems faced by patients and families, he proposes strategies to relieve both the physical symptoms and psychosocial distresses.

Chinese people use the terms "euthanasia" and "palliative hospice care" interchangeably. The confusion lies in the similarities in their Chinese name and poor public knowledge of what death, euthanasia and palliative hospice care are about. Chun Yan Tse and Samantha Pang offer the term "euthanasia" from medical, legal and cultural points of view in Chapter 12. They further differentiate the term from "palliative care" and "forgoing life-sustaining treatment". Though forgoing life-sustaining treatment seems to be a patient's individual decision, such a decision is affects the whole family as well.

Nursing and community care are two significant components in palliative hospice care. Faith Liu, an experienced nurse specialist in palliative care, highlights the development of community palliative care in Hong Kong, in Chapter 13. Because of her extensive experience in caring for families with end-stage cancer, this chapter blends her expert knowledge and her devotion to promoting humanity. At the end of her chapter, she suggests practical tips that health-care professionals should note.

Despite the fact that Western medicine dominates the health-care delivery system in Hong Kong, patients pragmatically seek different sources of care, including Chinese medicine, when disease progresses. Siu Man Ng, a registered practitioner in Chinese medicine with rich experience in the field of mental health, describes the contribution of Chinese medicine to cancer palliative care, in Chapter 14. For those unfamiliar with the concepts of Chinese medicine, this chapter is an excellent start. Chinese medicine can be a complimentary treatment and helps to reduce undesirable side effects of chemotherapy, radiotherapy and surgery. Chinese medicine can also enhance the total well-being of the dying patients and increase the participation of family members, by helping them to accept the inevitability of death.

Human resources are the most important assets in the health-care system, especially in palliative care. Peter Lee and Tracy Kwan remind us of the importance of staff support in palliative care. Compared with other units in health care, palliative hospice care has the highest "death rate". In repeatedly confronting death, which might be taken as professional failure, health-care professionals respond with great emotional and spiritual pain. Lee and Kwan share their vision of how appropriate staff support can facilitate greater effectiveness in the delivery of palliative care.

Death can also be caused by illnesses other than cancer and can happen in wards other than hospice wards. Amy Chow and nurses in Kwong Wah Hospital describe ways of handling death in acute wards like medical, surgical and intensive care units, in Chapter 16. Strategies in working with patients and families facing death with little time to prepare for it are described through two case stories. A CDE model is introduced for working with families facing impending death.

Although the majority of deaths take place in late life, children and adolescents can die. In Chapter 17, Vivian Lou and Cecilia Chan discuss their study of grieving parents of children with cancer in Shanghai, where couples are allowed only one child. Thus the impending death of the only child may mean an end to their future as parents. The parents may spend all their money or even get themselves into heavy debt, as there is limited financial support for medical care in China. The parents grieve the loss of the child as well as the end of their dreams. It is hoped that this chapter can raise the concern of policy-makers on the establishment of proper medical insurance and protection for the population in mainland China.

The third section of this book focuses on **bereavement**, the loss of loved ones through death. In Chapter 18, we describe the development of bereavement care in Hong Kong. As there is no equivalent Chinese term for bereavement, we increase the awareness of the needs of bereaved persons and generate guiding principles in working with the Chinese population. These strategies have been well received by professionals all over the world and can be applied to Chinese who are migrants to other countries.

Agnes Tin, Brenda Koo, Elaine Koo, and See Man Lee of the Jessie and Thomas Tam Centre (JTTC), the community-based bereavement counselling centre in Hong Kong, contributed to Chapters 19 and 20. Chapter 19 integrates the traditional Eastern values and cultures into counselling models and offers practical guidelines in serving different bereaved groups of widows, widowers, parents, children and grandchildren. Chapter 20 discusses the theoretical background, design, application and implementation of structured therapeutic bereavement groups in Hong Kong. The authors introduce creative and culturally sensitive group activities as well as outcome evaluation on the effectiveness of these groups.

In addition to professional care, volunteers provide bereavement services. Eddie Chan, from the Comfort Care Concern Group, a volunteer-oriented organization in providing services for terminally ill and bereaved persons, shares his experience in using volunteers in bereavement care. Chan discusses the difficulties encountered in recruitment, selection, training and mobilizing volunteerism in the Chinese culture. Contrary to common beliefs that bereaved Chinese person is well supported by the family, Chan saw growing demand for volunteers in bereavement care as well as in guidance through funeral and burial rituals.

Suicide is considered a family shame. Along with guilt, shame, confusion, the traumatic scene of the suicide and the complicated criminal investigations before getting a death certificate, the pathway to recovery for the bereaved family of a suicide is often prolonged and difficult. In the last chapter, Chow portrays the pathway of the bereaved families of suicides in Hong Kong. A SUICIDE bereavement model is proposed as the intervention with this special target group.

We hope the rich cultural illustrations on a different temporal frame of death can help to paint an impressionist picture of death among Chinese, a forbidden and mysterious yet necessary path that we all have to take in our lifetime. Let's start the adventurous journey ...

PART ONE
DEATH

2

Our Memorial Quilt: Recollections of Observations from Clinical Practice on Death, Dying and Bereavement

Cecilia Lai Wan CHAN and Amy Yin Man CHOW

Introduction

In the West, a commonly used tool for dealing with grief is the memorial quilt, usually produced by sewing pieces of colourful cloth together. Each piece of cloth is prepared by an individual to commemorate a deceased loved one or a memorable experience.

In China, a similar tradition exists of sewing pieces of cloth together to make a quilt that is called the "cloth from 100 families" (*bai ja bu*, 百家布), but this quilt symbolizes a collection of blessings from families and friends to a newborn baby.

This chapter is our memorial quilt, a salute to the clients who are our teachers in life. It also brings blessings to those readers who share our path in this book.

The Chinese Experience

Traditionally, filial piety is regarded as the greatest virtue in Chinese culture. When parents are elderly or living with chronic illness, adult children are supposed to care for them. Not hearing a parent's last words or failing to witness the death is regarded as unfilial. Yet, because of increased business travel and migration to different parts of the world, it is becoming harder and harder to make sure the extended family is present when the death of a parent occurs. In addition, advancements in health care and medical technology allow people to live with life-threatening illnesses for prolonged periods. Compounding matters, dying today often takes place in hospitals, where family members are not necessarily allowed to be present all the time.

For these reasons, contemporary societal arrangements are in conflict with traditional belief systems when considering just what makes a good death. The trust in high-tech medical care has also given many people the illusion that all diseases can be cured. Consequently, many people refuse to face the fact that death is part of living and that there is an end to life.

Disengagement versus Integration

The final stage of Erikson's stages of development is integration, or disengagement. Are loved ones given permission to die and allowed to stop fighting to live? At what point in the treatment of incurable cancer do individuals come to terms with death? Should health-care professionals raise the issue of advanced care planning, upon the diagnosis of a life-threatening illness? Are living wills and/or advanced directives in order, so that family members know the preferred burial/funeral arrangements of their loved ones?

Those who can integrate life's meaning and purpose into their deaths will find peace and comfort in facing death, whereas those who are disengaged may be resentful, angry, or bitter until death. Whether or not to die is not our choice, yet we can choose whether to live every day fully and every moment happily.

The Refusal to Accept

It is quite common for dying patients to find themselves losing weight and not looking their best. Weight loss is particularly visible in patients with liver cancer. Some terminally ill patients may look very thin in their last days of life. The loss of their familiar appearance can be frightening to patients and family members alike. It can also be demoralizing and frustrating to look completely different. Some patients refuse to accept this and isolate themselves prematurely; but when patients allow friends to visit them, it makes an enormous difference in their quality of life and life-completion process.

A Case of Refusal to Accept Visitation

When Mr Lee was dying, he refused all visits from his friends, as he could not accept that he was losing weight and looking sick. Mr Lee had always been a very helpful and considerate person. He had many good friends. He was determined that his friends retain their image of him as a healthy, sporty, strong, and cheerful man. His friends felt very sorry after his death, as they could only talk to his picture in the funeral hall and hadn't been able to talk to him before he died.

The Problem of Avoidance

Many individuals avoid talking and thinking about their own death or the loss of their loved ones. These individuals die unprepared. Such avoidance and denial of death may lead to subsequent lifelong regrets, chronic self-blame, and unresolved guilt of the family members, as well as prolonged and pathological grief after bereavement.

A Case of Death Denial

Mr Cheung was in his early forties when he was diagnosed with terminal colon cancer with metastasis to the liver. He was willing to undergo very aggressive chemotherapy and treatments, as he desperately wanted to live. He went to a world-renowned medical centre in the United States to seek advanced treatment for "magical" cures that did not come, despite his spending large amounts of money. He returned to Hong Kong, and as he was dying, he experienced great physical, emotional, and spiritual pain. He refused to close his eyes in the last four days of his life and was in anger and despair when he died. His extended family was around him those four days when he was throwing temper tantrums and screaming because of his pain. He refused any pain control intervention, for fear the drugs would make him sleepy and he would not be able to fight death when it came.

As Mr Cheung absolutely refused to discuss death, Mrs Cheung had no idea what he would want at his funeral. She and their three children wanted to talk to him about their happy moments together and how much they appreciated him, but he refused to listen to them and instead yelled at them when they approached him. Because of a strong motivation to achieve that had made him successful in his career, Mr Cheung did not realize that his exceptional strength in fighting for his life would only made his "quality of dying" worse.

The last four days were hell for his family. Mr Cheung could not talk but could only scream. The family felt very guilty for not being able to reduce his pain, and it hurt them enormously to see him die in such a manner. In reality, it was Mr Cheung who pushed himself so much that he could not use his final moments to reconcile with life and death and the people around him.

When patients and family members refuse to accept the inevitability of death, any discussions related to palliative and hospice care, as well as end-of-life decisions such as advanced directives, are commonly refused. Instead, patients spend precious time and money looking for radical or alternative treatments for miracle cures. (People who accept death and forgo active treatment are likewise sometimes regarded as cowards who do not dare fight.) Some family members spend all their savings, borrow money, and remortgage their homes in order to finance continuous second-line, third-line, and even fourth-line chemotherapy, in order to maintain hope for a cure and extend the life of their loved one for as long as possible.

It is sad to witness families declaring bankruptcy before their loved one dies, but the option of dying at peace without continuous active treatment is often not considered. Instead, family members anxiously press the doctors for the next treatment. At the same time, the needs of these family members are frequently ignored while they attempt to provide unconditional care for their loved one.[1]

Interestingly, hospice and palliative care services are sometimes regarded as medical professionals giving up on their patients. At the same time, cultural myths against pain control drugs may account for the typical refusal of pain control among dying patients.[2] Whatever the reason, witnessing the severe pain of loved ones through their dying process can be great torture.

A Case of Protecting the Family from Bad News

Mrs Wong loved her family very much. She was diagnosed with terminal ovarian cancer and was given a prognosis of about four months to live. She had three adult children who were all doing well in their jobs; all of them were taking evening classes for further career advancement.

Mrs Wong decided on her own strategy of death preparation. She felt that it was cruel to have her husband and sons go through the process of her terminal illness and death. She then behaved in an unreasonable manner by throwing temper tantrums and making everyone at home think that she was a nuisance. She told the family that she needed more freedom and stormed out of her home. She rented a room in another place, to make sure her family could not find her. She felt that it was the best way to protect her family from the pain of bereavement.

She was admitted to a different hospital when she was terminal. She told her story to a social worker on her last day of life. She asked the social worker to arrange cremation and never to inform anyone. The hospital data were not computerized at that time. The social worker could only make arrangements according to Mrs Wong's last instructions.

Although Mrs Wong is an extreme case, requests from patients or family members not to let other family members know of their cancer diagnosis are common in Asian societies like Hong Kong, Singapore, Taiwan, and Japan.

Avoidance can take other forms, too. For example, some patients never ask questions about the progression of their disease or the prognosis. This type of avoidance is a common. Because of Chinese people's culturally strong habit of denying death, health-care professionals often find it hard to discuss end-of-life care. This is unfortunate, because most patients living with a life-threatening illness who give up active treatment can still enjoy a reasonable quality of life and a high degree of autonomy. Such individuals are typically at peace with death and have time to prepare for it and to attend to unfinished business. People who try to stay on radical treatments like chemotherapy may find that their precious last months and weeks are consumed in the hospital, leaving them no time to cope logistically, physically, and emotionally with their impending death.

The Changing Face of Traditional Rituals

Contemporary Hong Kong is influenced by rapid development and high expectations of efficiency. Many of the rituals and funerals of former days are being replaced by express types of service. The legitimate period of mourning now stops immediately after the funeral, and no formal support is offered to bereaved persons. In short, our modern metropolis allows no time for bereaved persons to grieve.

A Case of Policing Grief

Benny is a hospice nurse. When his wife died of chronic renal failure, he took a month's leave to mourn and to pack her books and clothes. He was sad, did not sleep very well, and cried easily. His colleagues were very worried about him and urged him to return to work instead of staying home to mourn. Benny felt that the quiet time on his own was necessary. He felt uncomfortable at the "policing" of grief by his colleagues.

Relatives and friends frequently volunteer advice on what to do for those who are grieving. Some of them have bereavement experience and some do not. Everyone feels he or she knows best and that his or her opinions should be respected. Although most of the traditional roots of rituals that were developed in a rural and agricultural society have lost their socio-medical meanings and pragmatic utility in today's modern cities, bereaved persons are frequently coerced into elaborate rituals that can be exhausting.

A Case of Exhaustion

When Barbara's husband died, she was made to go through bowing, kneeling, standing, kneeling, and bowing throughout the funeral. She was totally exhausted, and in addition to coping with her heartache, she had to lie in bed for a whole week after the funeral because of muscle aches all over her body. Then, she had to go through the elaborate procedures again on the seventh day and subsequent seven-day periods, until the seventh seven-day period.

The inability to hold a perfect funeral for a loved one can be a source of guilt for bereaved persons. The concept of continuing the bond and maintaining some form of connection with the deceased is highly valued. The interpersonal nature of death anxiety and death denial reinforce this guilt-driven culture in the decisions made during end-of-life care as well as the pattern of response towards bereavement and loss.

Good Deaths

"When I let go of what I am, I become what I might be." Lao-tzu

Touching stories of glorious death, death due to self-sacrifice, dignified death, and transforming death exist. If we are at peace with life and death, we will be overwhelmed with the wisdom of life and the compassion of humankind. By witnessing good death, we can grow emotionally and spiritually.

The Death of a Religious Leader

A religious leader died in a public hospital in Hong Kong. In his last week of life, lying on his sick bed, he was peaceful, calm, and wore a compassionate smile on his face. Although he was not able to speak very much, he sent greetings and blessings to people who visited him. When he died, the nurse in the room felt a ray of cheerful energy above the dead body. She thought that the soul of the religious leader was saying a very sweet goodbye to her.

We do not have a choice on how, where, and when we die; yet we can determine the quality of our life and our subjective feeling towards life until the moment of death. Living a meaningful life and dying with peace of mind are choices we can make. With constant reflection and good preparation, we can live and die well.

Coming to Terms with Terminal Illness

Dave, 42, was a very successful lawyer. He had liver cancer and was told he might not have much time to live. Upon receiving this bad news, he cried for a whole evening and was depressed for three days. As he regained some sense of hope and was ready to discuss his treatment with his doctor, a tumour was found in his lungs. As a person with a high emotional quotient (EQ), he collected himself after a week and started to give instructions on what he wanted at his funeral and tasks that he wanted to accomplish before he died. He could maintain a sense of optimism despite his physical deterioration. He could take short walks and listen to his favourite music until the last day of his life. As he was well prepared, he could discuss directly with the doctors what he wanted for pain control and end-of-life care.

Cecilia's mother told her about the "perfect death" of her neighbour when she was young: "An 85-year-old Catholic woman was saying a thanksgiving prayer before supper with her whole family around the dining table. When the others finished their prayers and opened their eyes, the grandmother did not. She died in the midst of prayers and surrounded by her loved ones." Culturally, it is a blessing to have one's extended family around during the moment of death.

What do we hope for in death? Many people hope they can die in their sleep, without awareness or pain. There is increasing evidence that there can be a good quality death with a high degree of independence, provided that individuals have good habits of physical activity and an acceptance of death.

The Case of an Elderly Man Who Passed Away in His Sleep

A 74-year-old man was staying in a home for elderly people and living with terminal cancer. As a very tidy and independent person, he got up and washed his face, brushed his teeth, and put the towel on the table covering his cups around 6:30 a.m. He then went to sleep again and was found dead at 7:30 a.m. The family was very pleased because he did not feel much pain or discomfort when he died. He enjoyed full mobility and was able to care for himself until the last day of his life. His was regarded as a dignified death.

Many people, physically active and positive about life, die in their sleep without obvious illness or symptoms. This explains why there is so much public education on the importance of physical activity. Those who live physically active lives tend to die good deaths.

Dying Persons Can Have Fun and Still Enjoy Life

Paradoxically, dying can even be joyful if there is a genuine acceptance of death in patients and their loved ones. Many dying patients go overseas or on local trips with their family members, try good restaurants and massage, participate in expressive art, and generally make full use of their remaining time to enjoy life and have fun. Hospice volunteers often take patients to parks, beaches, shopping malls, and to have dim sum.

One patient in a hospice said that the most important criterion of a good death is that one should not die hungry; otherwise, the person might be turned into a hungry ghost. This man enjoyed eating. One day, he had a big meal and went to bed. He died soon after. The other patients were very pleased to see his face full of contentment from the big meal.

A Case of a Happy Last Day of Life

Miss Poon was diagnosed with ovarian cancer when she was in her mid-thirties. She underwent treatment, returned to work, had a relapse, and continued treatment. Five years later, she was admitted to the hospital for her inoperable metastatic condition. Her good friend Elaine visited her on a Wednesday afternoon. They talked about their good old days in college, their trips to Europe, and their work, as well as their experience of advocacy projects to fight for more welfare for people who are underprivileged. They laughed over their jokes and good times together. The conversation was a brief review of Miss Poon's life. Elaine massaged Miss Poon's back and body. There were fond memories and a recollection of a life worth living. Miss Poon died in her sleep that evening, a smile on her face.

It is important for us to realize that death is not necessarily horrible, sad, and demoralizing. When handled properly, the process of death and dying can be manageable, with effective symptom control and room for joy and fun.

Preparing for Our Own Death

Ira Byock advocates five statements in death and dying. These five simple statements can serve as a reminder of life coming to a fulfilling closure. If we can say, "I love you," "Thank you," "I forgive you," "Please forgive me," and "Goodbye" to our loved ones every day before we go to bed, there will be no unfinished business if, for some reason, we die in the night. Let us take every day as the last day of our lives to treasure everyday the best we can.

When we see our loved ones in the morning, we can say "I love you", "I'm so proud to be your son/daughter/husband/wife", "I thank God for giving you to me as my parent/children/spouse", and "Let's start a day bringing peace and joy to the world". Every day is a gift, and a popular modern adage says that is why the "here and now" is called the "present." If we live every day as the "last" day of our lives, there is no time to waste on hatred, anger, envy, greed, blame, and guilt. The world would be a better place if we appreciated the sky, the weather, the sunshine, the rain, the people we met, and every human encounter as a blessing from heaven. So, take every "goodbye" as the last farewell. Share these goodbyes with love, appreciation, compassion, and blessings for a resilient mind and blissful soul.

Accepting Death

One of the core components of a good death is that the individual accepts death as it comes. We have to give ourselves permission to die. Those who are ready to detach, disengage, and let go of life can prepare for their death realistically and pragmatically. Those who stay in the emotions of denial, anger, frustration, and refusal to accept can make life very difficult for themselves and their family members.

A Case of Living a Full Life

Mr Ma had terminal lung cancer. He enjoyed his life every day. He went for his traditional Chinese medicine and daily walking qi-gong exercises, as well as actively participating in mutual help activities for cancer patients. He visited other dying cancer patients in the hospital and generated the following as wisdom in his life: "Those who accept death die in peace. Those who do not die in terrible conditions". He remained physically active despite the progression of his illness. On a Friday, he went to have roast goose in a famous restaurant in Sham Tseng, Hong Kong. On Saturday, he went lawn bowling with his friends from a cancer patient support group. On Sunday, he went to have dim sum with his family. He was admitted into the hospital on Monday morning and died on Tuesday afternoon. He died with peace of mind, for he had found his life worth living. He donated one-third of his savings to the cancer patient group and left two-thirds to his wife. His group members fondly remembered him.

Direct Communication

It is in the best interests of patient and the family members if there can be direct communication on end-of-life decisions, including what treatment regime to opt for, how to cope with discomfort and symptoms in the last days of life, how to take care of unfinished business, how to make arrangements for last rites and burial, how to manage practical matters of finance and care, and what sort of life the survivors should lead after bereavement.

It is also important to communicate directly with patients in a way that reinforces their importance.

A Case of Sharing Last Moments with Friends

Sonia was a 16-year-old girl who was dying. Her classmates visited her until the last day of her life. The day before she died, they held a small birthday party for her in her hospital ward. She tasted potato chips and a sip of soft drink, although she was not able to eat. They shared their jokes in school, talked about their good times together, and had a lot of fun and laughter. It is important, as we learn from the book by Mitch Albom, Tuesdays with Morrie, that we organize farewell parties and have fun even when we are dying.

Young people rarely witness death. Sonia served as an excellent role model who was able to share her experience of illness and death with her teachers and classmates. Although there were tears on the faces of her classmates when they walked out of her hospital room for the last time, they all felt they would treasure life more. Originally, the teenagers did not know how to interact with Sonia, who looked so thin and tired. With the help of the hospice nurse, they treated Sonia as one of them. A person who is dying is still the same person. The fond memories of this birthday and farewell party will stay with this group of teenagers, and in turn they contributed to Sonia's peaceful departure.

Giving Permission for Our Loved Ones to Die

There is so much that we cannot give up. It is hard to say goodbye. It hurts to see loved ones die. When our loved ones are sick and dying, it is crucial for us to express our appreciation of them, seeking pardon and forgiveness, and affirming that we shall live on with fond memories of them as well as giving permission for them to die.

If we "hold on", we may prolong the suffering of and induce guilt in the dying person. The person may tell him or herself, "I cannot die. I feel bad being a burden on my family, yet I have to live or my family members will collapse. I am better off dead, yet my death will hurt my family". Without open discussion and permission, dying is a very lonely process. It is painful to be silent about death.

A Case of a Young Couple's Final Goodbye

William was thirty-two years old when he was diagnosed with terminal lymphoma. His wife, Mary, was twenty-seven. Both of them felt very sad to lose one another. They tried to hide their tears in front of the other, thinking that the best thing they could do would be to hide their grief from the other. They refrained from discussing death, as both thought the other spouse might not be able to stand the pain of talking about death openly. This protective mentality of "I'll take all the burden" is actually a bad strategy. Avoidance and delay of the discussion of death arrangements can rob people of opportunities to say goodbye properly to each other.

The hospice nurse in the hospital encouraged William and Mary to share their true thoughts with each other. They allowed the nurse to videotape the session so that it could be used for the training of professionals. In the session, they shared their love for each other and their fears and anxieties about death and losing each other. William asked Mary to look for another man after his death. Mary told William that his love for her would keep her going, and she promised to live every day to the fullest and to her best ability.

We can provide reassurance to the dying person that his or her life has been a gift from heaven and that the *yuan* (pre-determined interpersonal relationships) and *fen* (recognized role in familial and intimate relationships) have been enriching and nourishing to the loved ones.

A Case of Healthy Dissociation

Ruth was a family therapist specializing in aging. When her mother was dying, Ruth invited her siblings and her mother's best friends to her house to say goodbye to her mother. When the guests left, Ruth put her mother to bed. Ruth wanted to hug her mother but her mother said, "No, don't do that. I do not need more love now. I need to go". Ruth did what she was told. The mother died peacefully the following day.

Ruth was diagnosed with terminal cancer ten years later. As she had actually learned about death from her mother, she decided that she would choose only hospice services and complimentary treatments that could provide her with a good quality of life. She quickly finished the book she was reading and started to complete her "wish list" of things that she would like to do before she lost her physical strength to do so.

> She went to visit friends and chose music for her funeral. When she was dying, she organized a farewell party in her home. Everyone shared stories and fun times they'd had together. Her friends provided Ruth with a lot of appreciation for her dedication and contributions. Laughter and tears were shared. Ruth died a few days after her farewell party.

The Chinese tend to ask their doctors to try to prolong life as long as possible. Death is clearly seen as an "inability" to prolong life. It is a "failure". As a result of this type of holding on and not letting go, people feel deeply hurt and guilty for witnessing the death of their loved ones. It is thus important for us to learn this concept of "giving permission" for our loved ones to die. We can assure them that their virtues and blessings will provide continuous strength for their surviving family members to live happy and fulfilling lives and that there will be "continuous bonding" between the living and the dead. This mutual love will fuel future activities for the betterment of humankind.

Taking Care of Unfinished Business

It is possible for family members to reassure the dying person of their appreciation, love, and thanks, in a life-completion ritual. We can encourage patients and family members to write down what they appreciate about each other and to share their love for each other. For those who are illiterate, a wide variety of expressive art techniques are available. Unfinished business can be shared, and ways can be sought to resolve past hurts and bring unresolved matters to an effective closure. Loose ends can also be tied up by forgiveness, conciliation, and mutual accommodation, thus turning pain into a beautiful knot and memoir.

> ### A Case of Seeking Pardon
>
> Madam Kam told the hospital nurse that she would like to apologize to her children and would like to go home and say goodbye to her husband, who was in a wheelchair and housebound after a stroke. As the five children accompanied Madam Kam home in an ambulance, the nurse encouraged Madam Kam to seek their pardon. Madam Kam could send only the eldest daughter to college, but the other four had to go without a university education. Although all of them had taken on professional jobs and were doing well, Madam Kam had felt guilty and blamed herself for not being able to earn enough money to provide all five of them with a university education.

All of the children were in tears and assured their mother of their love for her and told her that not going to the university was not her fault. They were all very proud to have her as their mother. Madam Kam had dinner at home with her husband and children. She went back to the hospital in the evening and died peacefully the next morning.

This is a beautiful story of life completion and closure. Madam Kam was able to say goodbye to her husband and children as well as to have a last supper at home.

Life Completion Exercise

Chinese people pay a lot of attention to relationships and rituals. Most unfinished business is related to those they love and care about. Seeing their children graduate from school, get married, and then have children are key milestones they don't want to miss. For this reason, hospitals and hospices run birthday parties, wedding rituals, and family conciliation ceremonies to help patients fulfil their last wishes.

A Case of Wish Fulfillment

Mr Hung was dying of terminal lung cancer. His son was to get married six months later. Mr Hung felt very sorry, as he was quite sure his health would not permit him to attend the wedding and give his blessing to the new couple. As his health deteriorated, the family discussed with the hospital staff what could be done to enable Mr Hung to bless the son's marriage. The hospital quickly vacated a side ward and turned it into a wedding hall. The family decorated the room with red paper (for a wedding) and arranged wedding gowns for the couple. An informal wedding ceremony was performed in the side ward on a Saturday morning. Mr Hung drank the tea offered by his daughter-in-law (a ritual to approve the marriage), and he offered the couple his blessings. He died two days later with a smile on his face.

Conciliation and Forgiveness

There are regrets in life. We might have been mean to people whom we love. We might have hurt them through our acts and words, intentional or otherwise. When life is coming to an end, most of us hope to grant forgiveness and seek pardon from our loved ones.

A Case of Reconciliation between Mother and Daughter

Veronica was in her late twenties when she was diagnosed with terminal lymphoma. She had left her family when she was fifteen and had had a baby girl with a boyfriend, who left her after the baby was born. Veronica later became a drug addict. She told the nurse that she would like to seek pardon from her mother, whom she had hurt so deeply through her unruly behaviour. The mother refused to come. Veronica's condition deteriorated, but the mother still would not come. The nurse finally visited the mother in her home and found that she actually felt very guilty for not providing Veronica with a supportive environment because of her own divorce. The nurse escorted her to the hospital and Veronica's tears streamed down her cheeks and she smiled at her mother before dying in her mother's arms. Although there was not a lot of verbal exchange, her mother holding her hands was an unspoken reconciliation. The mother thanked the nurse for encouraging her to visit Veronica before she died. Without this act of forgiveness, as well as the expression of pardon and mutual acceptance, the mother would have lived in guilt, shame, and self-blame for the rest of her life.

Forgiveness and conciliation can be verbal, symbolic, and metaphorical. When the person is not available, reconciliation can be in the form of thoughts, prayers, rituals, storytelling, and artwork. Opportunities to discuss happy moments, the meaning of events, important people, and regrets can be the greatest gift that health-care professionals can offer to patients during end-of-life care.

A Case of Conciliation with a Deceased Wife

Mr Chan had a stroke when he was in his seventies. He had lived in a home for elderly people for ten years. When he was dying and admitted to a hospital, he asked the medical social worker to convey to his wife how sorry he was for not being a responsible husband. The social worker tried to find his wife but to no avail. They found that his wife had died five years before. Mr Chan was encouraged to convey his thoughts through writing a letter to his wife, and the letter was burned so that the message could reach her in heaven. He was confident that his letter telling his wife that he would meet her in heaven would reach her. Mr Chan felt much better after performing this ritual of completion. He died a week later.

Bereavement

Although there is often open glorification of heroic deaths, suicide bombers in war-affected areas kill children and civilians in addition to killing themselves. During the tsunami in December 2004, more than 150,000 lives were taken in one day by the giant waves in South Asia. The dead bodies of many could not be found or identified. In the Chinese New Year holidays of February 2005, an estimated 6,000 car accidents killed more than 300 persons in Hong Kong. Millions of children in poor countries die annually of starvation, war, or infectious diseases due to a lack of safe water. Many find life not worth living and commit suicide. Increasing numbers of people in affluent societies die because of obesity. The number of deaths due to occupational hazards and poisoning in developing countries remains high. Irrespective of the cause of death, bereaved family members grieve.

Traditional Chinese culture endorses prolonged mourning. Widows are expected to grieve their whole life, and children are expected to mourn for three years. It is customary for the dying person to meet every loved one before his or her death. Many dying persons linger on in order to wait for the return of a family member. If the family member cannot return in time to meet the person who is dying, there is usually enormous guilt and self-blame.

Funerals and rituals are physically, emotionally, and financially demanding as well as exhausting. Bereaved persons are a high-risk group and must be offered easy access to psychosocial as well as legal and financial advice and support. By taking a public health approach to bereavement, we can reduce the morbidity and mortality of bereaved persons. This is the main reason that complicated grief will likely be included in the Diagnostic and Statistical Manual of Mental Disorder, fifth edition (DSM-V). It is to call professional attention to the vulnerability of those who are grieving as well as attention to the need for access to mental health support during this vulnerable period of bereavement.

Although funeral and mourning rituals are greatly simplified in contemporary societies like Hong Kong, most Chinese still hold on to traditional values and believe they should not allow themselves to be happy but instead should grieve for prolonged periods after the death of a loved one.

Deaths resulting from suicide, accident, or unanticipated health conditions such as SARS or a heart attack are the most devastating. "Why it happens?" is the question most commonly asked after an acute loss. Loved ones not only experience the pain of bereavement but also the loss of dreams for the family, disrupted goals and plans, and a dismantled future and disintegrated self-image. The guilt, shame, blame, and feeling of loss can lead family members to harm themselves or to commit suicide.

Like cigarettes, grief and trauma arising from bereavement can be hazardous to people's health. The morbidity and mortality rates of bereaved people are found to be higher than in non-bereaved persons. It is evident that preparation in anticipation of the death of a loved one can help to reduce the level of disruption in one's life, subsequent to the loss.

Conclusion: Death, Dying and Bereavement as Grace for Transformation

True acceptance of death can give patients and their family members a sense of peace and bliss. Adequate discussion of funeral arrangements and a review of life achievements can instil calmness, a sense of appreciation and fulfillment, and the feeling of having lived a worthwhile life. As death is part of living, we can educate ourselves about death in order to live full lives.[3]

Befriend death and do not avoid the pain of bereavement, as it is a catalyst for spiritual growth. Growth through death and bereavement often leads to a greater appreciation of life, to greater love of others, to greater appreciation for the beauty of simplicity, to a deep engagement with nature and its creator, and to transcendence into a dignified, honourable human being who has a broad mind replete with unlimited compassion and accommodation for differences.

More on the growth that can be discovered through the death, dying and bereavement process can be found in subsequent chapters.

3

A Personal Journey: The Physician, the Researcher, the Relative, and the Patient

Yvonne Yi Wood MAK

Introduction

Palliative care is not about dying, and bereavement is not about crying. Rather, they are about connecting, caring, and respecting — the essence of living. If you dare to add some passion, you might even be seduced by them, as I have been. Health-care professionals involved in palliative care often find their work rewarding and inspiring, whereas others not familiar with its beauty often comment, "It must be so depressing!" In reality, caring for people who are dying can be enriching because every patient narrative is an experience from which we can reflect and learn. Over time, care-givers acquire flexibility in their caring and communication, a healthy attitude to living and dying, and a creative frame of mind in facing challenges in life.

If we apply the art of palliative care to our lives, our everyday experiences, especially crises, can also become lessons. (Life, however, can become overwhelming if we take every experience too seriously.) The difficult part is that the "test" must come before the "lesson". We cannot prepare for the test beforehand, but we can reflect afterwards and learn experientially. We are fortunate compared to the terminally ill, who often have neither the time nor the energy to reflect thoroughly but can only undertake a brief life-review amid their physical and mental exhaustion. Thus, if we have the time and energy but choose not to learn from our experiences, we suffer in vain and deny ourselves opportunities for healing and personal growth. Then, suffering results in only negative experiences to which we say understandably, "Oh! It's too much; I'm better off dead!" or "If you have to suffer, you're better off dead!"

Although suffering is inevitable, we do not live to suffer; we suffer in order to learn to live. I consider myself fortunate to be a palliative care physician and researcher, and not that unfortunate having been bereaved, a relative of cancer patients, and now a cancer patient. This journey could be perceived as cruel. As my professor once said to me, "How much more is God going to torture this poor girl?" It has been bearable so far, though intolerable at times. It has been an invaluable experience, full of very thought-provoking and soul-searching times. I have pondered, "Is it fair to be afflicted with calamities sooner rather than later?"

I think the answer is "Yes", since observing and personally experiencing cancer and loss have moulded me gradually to become more authentic in my living. I have learned to appreciate family, friends, colleagues, and the "taken for granted" in my daily experiences, to grasp some understanding about both the meaning and meaninglessness in life. Over the years, this journey of suffering has transcended into a journey of healing, in which I have finally found courage, following many inspirational examples of my patients, to face my own wounds. Such experiences have transformed me into a human "being" instead of "doing".

This chapter aims to give you a personal perspective to understanding palliative care through experiential learning, reflective practice, and creative writing.[1] I have written my journey as a narrative, expressing my internal communication with my inner self; my external communication with my family, friends, patients and colleagues; and my eternal connection with God. These writings include excerpts from my diary, letters, lectures, and non-medical literature as a way to describe and interpret my journey. I hope this chapter helps you to experience the mystery and meaning hidden within our daily experiences, which we would otherwise overlook.

> I want to take you on a journey up the hills and into the valleys. But I must warn you: there will be storms. We'll get soaked but we'll look for shelter. Sometimes we'll roar, sometimes soar ... At other times, we'll need to be silent and absolutely still. But after each storm, we will search for that silver lining. At the end, I hope you will say, "It was worth it! Despite the storm, we enjoyed the scenery. And despite the rain, we remembered that rainbow. And that rock! It created the most beautiful waterfall."
>
> My diary, December 2003

Learning Palliative Care: Becoming a Wounded Healer

We all have wounds. Paradoxically, wounds can become instruments of healing, enabling us to understand the wounds of others. As we come to understand the suffering of others, we may find our wounds healed and ourselves becoming wounded healers.

Being wounded

My grief began with two consecutive miscarriages. Accustomed to having control over life, as patients had often said to me, "Doctor, my life is in your hands", the possibility of losing a life inside me never crossed my mind. These losses brought a sudden realisation about the illusion of control, for no matter how still I stayed, life disappeared inside me. I could not hold on to that life, however hard I tried.

The first miscarriage hurt but the second wounded me. I felt vulnerable, fragile, and worthless as a female, having been deprived of motherhood. Negative thoughts overwhelmed me and those grieving times were lonely, depressing, and seemingly never-ending. No one seemed to understand what I was going through; it was as if no one knew how to comfort me. I grieved in isolation and, so preoccupied with self-pity, I had no awareness that my husband could also be grieving. I demanded support but never thought about giving it. I did not know how to cope with loss, but living had to continue as usual.

Miraculously, subsequent births of Samuel and Katherine remedied my yearning for motherhood. But those wounds remained and my grief was unresolved. I lived in fear, wondering if something dreadful might happen to my children, knowing that life was out of my control.

Becoming immersed in the suffering of others and searching for healing together

Stepping into Bradbury Hospice as a physician was like the beginning of my grief therapy. Initially, I was unfamiliar with psychosocial care. It was better to say as little as possible, rely on non-verbal communication and smile. Dreading that I might say something wrong that would upset my patients, I focused on symptom control, which seemed the safest thing to do. Not knowing how to deal with their emotions, I tended to leave those issues to the psychologist or social workers. I could not, however, ignore my patients' psycho-spiritual concerns because it was impossible to separate palliative care into clear physical, social, psychological, and spiritual domains.

So I listened and gradually I learned to really listen. I noted that, if I asked questions like a doctor, patients reported only symptoms; but if I listened, patients told me stories about their lives. I became their student and they my teachers on the meaning of life. Instead of focusing on symptoms and signs, I began listening to the verbal, observing the non-verbal and, very naturally, patients led me to areas that needed immediate attention, whether physical or metaphysical. I learned that the art of palliative care is to sit down with no pre-set agenda, allowing my patients to lead the way rather than conforming to a rigid medical history taking. That way, they could express their needs and concerns spontaneously.

As patients shared their stories about life — its meaning, values, their hopes and dreams — they also expressed their suffering, losses, meaninglessness, hopelessness, worthlessness, and depreciation of what they had once valued. Such private dialogues were possible in a place like Bradbury. The environment was warm and comforting, but most importantly it provided a safe place to contain suffering: it was safe to cry, safe to share secrets, and safe to confess without being condemned. There was time to listen and time to spare. There was touch, understanding, and acceptance.

As I listened more attentively, I became immersed in my patients' suffering and began to "suffer with them"; I got close enough and felt vulnerable enough to cry with them. I began to identify similar negative feelings that I had hidden somewhere out of my consciousness for years. But my vulnerabilities brought them healing; their faces started to smile and their eyes sparkle.

How could this be? Somehow, my wounds enabled me to respond better to my patients — to understand and suffer with them. Immersed in their suffering, I no longer felt alone in my suffering. And understanding their grief enabled me to address my own grief in a gradual and gentle manner. So my wounds facilitated their healing process and their wounds mine; it was as if we were searching for healing together. As my wounds were healed, they equipped me to become empathic and compassionate. Thus my wounds made me a wounded healer. Perhaps the healing care-givers receive as they give is the beauty of palliative care that many come to appreciate over time.

There were other beautiful moments, when memories of my patients' last days, last hours and last few breaths live on.

> An elderly lady was very breathless and frail during her last few remaining days. Yet she made every effort to thank and appreciate us individually. When it was my turn, she told me, "Have patience with your children". She taught me how to be a nurturing mother — like a grandmother saying her last words to her daughter. I couldn't hold back my tears. She never stopped caring, not even during her last few breaths.
>
> My research journal, October 2000

> As I drove to work, the nurse phoned and urged me to hurry to the ward. "She's dying and she's been staring at the door, waiting for you!" My patient was young and beautiful. She was prepared for her departure and had put on her favourite. As I rushed to the ward, she was drowsy but could still hear. I spoke to her, and her mother replied for her, saying, "She wanted to say goodbye and she wanted me to tell you that she knew it hurt you more than it did her, when you put that needle into her arm". The ward felt warm, as the girl's sweetness and her mother's loving presence filled the room. Through the sharing of suffering, we had developed a special connection, and it was my privilege to have cared for them.
>
> My research journal, October 2000

> I had just returned from holiday and walked into the ward. The nurse said, "Oh! She's been waiting to see you. She is gasping, but I don't think she will

leave until she has seen you". Her body was so frail ... her eyes so sunken ... but her soul so restful. I held her hand and stroked her hair. After a while, I whispered, "It is okay now ... to go". Somehow, with my "permission", she left soon after. She was an elderly lady. Two weeks prior, I had facilitated the communication between her and her children to focus on those special times in her life, rather than her end of life.

My research journal, October 2000

There were also personal reflections on the beauty of palliative care:

Presence

"I know I have to leave soon, doctor, but could you just sit with me for a little while?" Immediately I sat down again by his side and held his hand. He held on to it tightly and so I put my other hand on top of his. He needed that comfort, that presence. "Doctor, I don't want to die ... "

Although I've known my patients for only a brief period of their lives, it was a privilege that they wanted to hold my hand. I was not their significant other, but they needed the presence and touch of another human being. It seemed as if any hand would do, anybody would do, as long as that somebody was willing and committed to be present. Probably they would prefer their loved ones, and it must increase their suffering when there are no significant others or their significant others are unwilling or unable to care ...

My research journal, October 2000

Listening

"I'm here to listen. I'm here to hold your hand. I'm here to wipe your tears ... my tears." He was tired but he still wanted to talk. He wanted me to stay with him for a little longer to listen to his suffering, to listen to his ambivalence. "It's all right to have a moment of silence. I'll wait for you to collect your thoughts. I'll wait for you to catch your breath. Take your time. I can hear you clearly. I may not understand fully how you feel, but I am here." After a while he said, "Now I've told you almost all of my innermost sorrows". I said, "Thank you for sharing your life. I'll remember you. When you're gone, I'll remember you ... "

Patients need to express their suffering and to be understood. Despite their weariness, they are very spontaneous in sharing their lived experience, even their innermost secrets ...

My research journal, November 2000

Connecting

"I was vulnerable but your warmth comforted me ... your sweet soft voice ... your silent presence. Yet I could feel the richness of your soul. You were just being present, not saying a word but waiting quietly and patiently. You surrounded me with your gentleness. It didn't matter if I couldn't put my sorrow into words. Somehow I knew you could sense my soul. Your touch's so comforting, like a mother's touch ... so serene and gentle ... soft and gracious ... like a lullaby singing into my ears, saying, 'Sweetheart, sleep and rest now'. Such unconditional love! Oh! Thank you! That's just what I needed. That's what we all need — that loving presence ... "

Patients need another human being to see them through their inevitable journey. They yearn to feel connected ... to know they still belong. As the loving presence of care-givers comforts them, their souls feel "touched". Despite the disintegration of the body and mind, the soul needs attention. Don't deny the soul!

My research journal, February 2001

Searching for Palliative Care

In caring for the dying, I could not ignore living. I was provoked to search more deeply into the meaning of suffering either through my patients, systematically through research, or internally within my inner self. As I searched deeper, I found healing — a sense of restoration to wholeness.

Through my most memorable patient

Having acknowledged my vulnerabilities, I began searching more deeply into the meaning of suffering. A significant part of my professional and personal growth included one particular patient, who had requested euthanasia. I had controlled his symptoms, so physically he was comfortable, but he had severe psycho-spiritual distress: fear of future suffering, a sense of burden, of worthlessness, helplessness, and hopelessness against a background of a previous suicidal attempt, multiple losses and unresolved grief. He felt he was lingering in a meaningless existence. His requests for euthanasia were persistent and seemed so rational that I felt the only way to relieve his suffering might be to heed his request. Thoughts of terminating his life as a compassionate act did cross my mind. Hastening his death would at least relieve my suffering of having to witness his emotional anguish every day. He had masked depression, which I had overlooked, and despite commencing him on anti-depressant therapy, I felt helpless but could only stand by him. The team felt burdened too, but we continued counselling, trying to ease his anguish. His family empathised with his reasons for wanting death and respected his decision if he were to commit suicide. Later, to my great relief, his anguish settled. A few days before he died, he asked to see me. As I sat down, he immediately took hold of my hands, smiling and saying,

> "Thank you! Thank you very much! You have been so helpful. I am so sorry
> … And you still look after me even when I've made life so difficult for you.
> I didn't really want to die … I was so very emotional … Thank you for putting
> up with me."

This vivid scene has never left me — that grateful look on his face and the genuineness of his hands. I thanked him for having the courage to share his vulnerabilities and for having trusted me. I realised I had done the right thing in not taking the easy way out. His words reassured me that euthanasia was not the answer to relieve suffering. A few days later, I began to grasp what "suffering" meant. His euthanasia requests signified the intensity and multi-dimensional nature of suffering. I wanted to thank him for being my best teacher. But when I reached the ward, I was too late to tell him or to say goodbye. He, however, affected how I subsequently practised palliative care. I began inquiring about suffering in every patient: "What's your suffering? Tell me how you are suffering most right at this moment". In many ways, this facilitated the doctor-patient rapport and conveyed the message that I was not just interested in physical symptoms but beyond.

Unknowingly, I had been grieving for this patient, but he had instilled in me a passion for two words: "suffering" and "euthanasia". Subsequently, I participated in a pilot study on reasons for requesting euthanasia.[2] This was followed by poster and oral presentations in Asia Pacific, European, and New York palliative care conferences to present his case history, our study findings, and the clinical mandate in managing euthanasia requests. One year later, I studied the meaning of the desire for euthanasia as part of a Master of Science (M.Sc.) course.[3] Two years later, I began advocating for the needs of terminally ill patients through teaching and paper publications.[4-6] I had no idea that this patient had been a major driving force behind my search to share, until four years after his death, right after I had finished teaching my medical students on the nature of suffering, using his case history as an illustration. Suddenly, I said to my colleague as we were leaving,

> "I've just realised that this teaching has been my way of grieving for this
> patient. I had to relive my memory of him month after month, year after
> year. Today, I no longer have to hold my tears as I teach. I can say goodbye
> to him now. And his suffering has not been in vain, for he has travelled with
> me from one conference to another, from one lecture to another. Isn't it
> ironic? In order to let go of grief, I have to relive it over and over again."

Through research

Euthanasia requests continued to bother me for some time, despite the reassurance I had from my most memorable patient. Although these requests were infrequent, I could still recall one patient saying, "Don't let me drag on like this; there is no meaning living like this". Another used to say, "If it is possible, you know what I mean, I would still want 'that' if you could do it". These voices hounded me and I pondered, "Am I a failure in being unable to relieve suffering? Is palliative care inadequate? Do all segments of society embrace the philosophy of palliative care to not hasten death? Is euthanasia really that bad an option? What are the dimensions of suffering contributing to the request for euthanasia? Are we lacking insight into the true meaning of these requests?"

The fundamental question was, "Why do patients desire euthanasia despite receiving palliative care?" This was what led me to undertake a M.Sc. research study to solve my clinical ethical dilemma in an evidence-based manner.[3] As my research question was sensitive and patients were considered vulnerable, I had to search for a humane methodology that would value the patients' subjective experiences and explore their meaning of desire for euthanasia in depth. Thus I chose a qualitative approach that emphasised how truth and meaning could be derived from daily experiences —"lived experience". So the patients' verbatim from study interviews were used as research data for exploration.

Qualitative approaches are complicated and diverse, and there are many philosophies that one can choose from to use as methodological frameworks. Initially, I considered phenomenology, but this approach focused mainly on description rather than interpretation of human experiences.[7,8] Finally I came across hermeneutics, which focused on interpretation as well as gaining deeper understanding into a phenomenon, and this philosophy fulfilled all my criteria for a humane, patient-centred, within-context, in-depth and interpretive methodology.[9–14]

Rather than discussing hermeneutics and my study findings, I elaborate on my research process. It promoted professional and personal self-development, as I learned to search in depth and breadth, not only about my patients but also about myself and the world around me. I searched in breadth, as the topic of euthanasia encompassed ethical, legal, medical, sociological, philosophical, religious, and cultural aspects, and the list was endless. The data collection was also multi-dimensional, as I explored a diversity of perspectives, primarily from patient interviews and medical literature. In addition, I paid attention to my personal reflections, daily experiences, and artistic sources. This process of data analysis required continual questioning, reflection, interpretation, and validation, during which I began an in-depth exploration of my own lived experience as well as those of my patients. Interpreting my inner self was an ongoing self-awareness workshop, as I began to search in a reflective and systematic manner.

I also began tuning in to the "taken for granted" world around me: people, conversations, daily routines, and artistic sources that surrounded me. An ordinary day became extra-ordinary. I listened carefully to dialogues, interpreting individual words and every sentence. I reflected on palliative care, and it generated more questions: "What is the essence of palliative care? How do we define care? Do we really care? Does society care? What is the soul? Is soul-care within the realm of medical practice?"

I began to see the phenomenon of meaning of desire for euthanasia hidden in my everydayness. For example, death, suffering, desire, care, and connectedness were evident themes in books, films and lyrics to songs. They generated provoking thoughts on human behaviour, societal attitudes, varying philosophies of life, and the meaning of existence. I became mindful and soulful, as if the research process had heightened my every perception and sensation. I also found myself regressing to a childlike state to being receptive, creative, imaginative, and de-conditioned from previously set boundaries. I began to value my intuition rather than relying entirely on logic. Overall, I could hear more clearly, think and feel more deeply. I summarised my research journey as follows:

> I read a book on phenomenological research.[15] Munhall crystallised my research experience beautifully — spontaneity of reflections, mindfulness, soulfulness, being wide awake to see phenomena everywhere, the creativity attached, the use of arts, the value of a research journal, and the frustrations with staying within boundaries. It is comforting to read that my "madness" has been documented!
>
> E-mail to my supervisor, April 2001

In effect, the research process refined my skills in care and communication. Hermeneutics promoted reflective practice. I was constantly questioning, renewing, and searching deeper. It also enhanced my ability to communicate as I learned to listen and interpret. I learned to connect with my patients by in-depth exploration in a compassionate way, so that I could understand their hidden agendas and thus respond to their genuine needs.

Hermeneutics also refined my art of caring. By appreciating the significance of contexts and subjective experiences, I was more capable of understanding their wishes in the light of their circumstances and personal values. Thus, caring became more authentic. As I began exploring the "taken for granted", I became more conscious of living. My daily encounters with patients were not ordinary but inspiring. Patients were teaching me about meaning: the essence of living and being human. The research process allowed me to search as a whole person. I appreciated the need for integrating personal experiences and patients' perspectives through research and clinical practice, our everydayness, and non-medical and medical literary sources in becoming a more holistic physician and rounded person (Diagram I).

Through reflective creative writing

> You can gain distance and perspective by writing down what you are going
> through. When I write my experiences, they seem to take a place outside of
> me on the paper. When I am reading about them, it is as if the events are
> happening to someone else, and I can look at that "someone else" more
> objectively.[16]

Morrie Schwartz

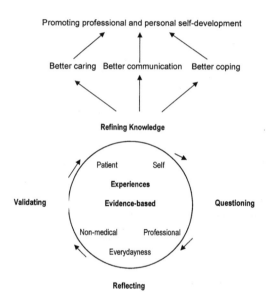

Diagram I. The process of self-development

Writing became a discipline for me, as the M.Sc. course required keeping
a research journal.[17] Writings recorded thoughts, feelings, and circumstances
that I would not have given a second thought to otherwise. Often, using
metaphors helped me to express meaning more clearly. Some thoughts were
abstract, and there seemed no limit to how the brain could create imageries
and inspirations to help reframe my mind. My writings became a mirror of
"me", a transcribed personal journey. As I reflected, I tried to make sense of
my brainstorms in a calm and constructive manner. Thus the process of
recording, reading, and reflecting provided a channel through which I could
find meaning — a way of connecting with my inner self, of gaining self-
awareness, and of reframing my mind. I have included a few excerpts from
my diary to illustrate the usefulness of reflective creative writings as I connected
with my ordinary daily experiences.

Reflections

Every day I drive from home to Bradbury and back again, approximately an hour in all. My reflections are spontaneous as I drive, especially with the accompaniment of music. I must have ruminated in my car for 2,000 hours, at least. Apart from being a dangerous driver and a daydreamer, the problem is that I cannot stop my car whenever "a wonderful thought" emerges and needs to be recorded. So I appreciate traffic jams, when I can snatch a moment to scribble! Driving past Tai Tam Reservoir is wonderful; it helps me to tune in to work and wind down as I return home ... During one dull morning, the stillness of the waters inspired me:

> The reservoir is like the brain. When the day is windy, there is no clear reflection. Although it may look dazzling in the sun, the waves stop you from seeing anything underneath. However, when the day is still or even dull, it reflects a clear, perfect mirror image of its surrounding scenery and what lies beneath ... Perhaps it is only through stillness and dark moments that we can reflect clearly and deeply. During sunny or stormy periods, life can seem too dazzling or overwhelming to give us meaning. But if we learn to be still, we can get a clearer and deeper reflection of our situations and of ourselves, so that we can find meaning and learn from our experiences, whatever the weather ...
>
> My diary, November 2000

Mindfulness

I attended a workshop on mindfulness, during which we were asked to talk with an object and see what it would say. This sounded ridiculous, but:

> I chose a picture in the hallway, next to the restrooms and lecture theatres. It had a lily blossom standing up in the muddy waters, surrounded by a few lily leaves, but nothing else. Nothing spoke, as I had expected. I was distracted by people rushing around me. And here I was, looking stupid, staring at and talking to a flower! It would have been justified if it were a painting from Florence, but this was just something "cheap". Then suddenly the blossom spoke!
>
> "No one ever takes notice of me. Am I not worth it? You're all rushing around but ignoring my existence. I've been waiting and waiting for someone to give me some attention and you're the first! Thank you."
>
> I felt sorry for this poor lily. It did look miserable, and I wanted to "touch" her to make a connection. This lily somehow represented my patients who have often been neglected. Then I looked around, and there was another picture — another single lily — but at least it had the company of a goldfish! What a strange experience! One participant had a dialogue with a mop, another with a withering weed ... We must be nuts after all!

If things that can't talk can manage to talk, how much easier it must be to connect with those who can actually talk … And if we stop talking, it'd be easier for the others to start talking. When we start connecting to interpret our surroundings, we will find meaning in our everydayness.

My diary, April 2001

Soulfulness

One day, I was flipping through *Architectural Digest* and a painting by Daniel F. Gerhartz titled "Her Favorite Place" caught my eye. It was a portrait of a lady standing alone in the forest, with her arms outstretched and her eyes shut. It looked like a dull winter day, and the trees were bare. For some reason, I cut it out, framed it, and put it on my desk. Then one evening, I wrote:

How could a place so dark and desolate be a favourite place for anyone? But it caught my eye and it didn't just catch my eye; it captivated my soul. I have yearned to be in a place like so. There seemed no sound and not a soul around … and yet she was not alone. She closed her eyes to enclose her soul. Gently with her outstretched arms, she placed her fine fingertips on a half-fallen trunk; the other hand was free to feel the air. She heard nothing except her soul, connected solely to her Creator. In her solitude, there lay an imagery of paradise, where no one could intrude. That was her space, her secret sanctuary. There she stood in perfect harmony. No one could appreciate the true beauty of such a place but only she could comprehend. And as she stilled herself to feel such wonder, it didn't matter what the reality was outside; all that mattered was her perceived reality inside … How I long to be in her place. "Could I be … and may I be that girl? Please take me to my favourite place!"

This painting depicted my desire for solitude and serenity. I found paradise as I searched deeper for soul and meaning. As I travelled deeper into my valley of vulnerabilities, I found myself in God's loving presence. I have ignored Him time after time, but He has found and never abandoned me. But I have been always so rushed that I could hardly afford a moment of that paradise. I must close my eyes, just one more time to feel my favourite place …

My diary, October 2001

Living nowadays requires multitasking and being at several places simultaneously to attend to everyone's demand of every kind. Thus, it becomes vitally important to find ways of being "me" without being conditioned by everything and everyone around me to be someone else. Connecting with artistic sources and creating tranquil imageries helps to still me into "being" rather than "doing" during the busyness of my day.

Being human

As I brought closure to my M.Sc. study, I wrote a dedication to my patients in my dissertation:

> In their vulnerability they showed me courage to search for soul and meaning ...
>
> And in their suffering they taught me compassion to stand by and walk with them ...
>
> In their dying they searched for serenity, for someone to hold and heal them ...
>
> And as I listened they became my greatest teachers on the meaning of suffering ...
>
> And in my search for knowledge they taught me wisdom, the meaning of being human ...
>
> My M.Sc. dissertation, [3] August 2001

I then pondered the meaning of being human:

> It is to have the mind of a man and the heart of a woman. It is to have the wisdom to realise our ignorance, our need to rely on God. It is not to assume that living everyday is ordinary but to continue processing our experiences consciously in finding inspiration and meaning. It is to know that we should not only trust our rationality but also train the other side of our brain to sense what doesn't make sense. It is to trust our intuition and be conscious of all our senses, to be ready to feel whatever there is to feel and express it in a way that's natural and appropriate. It is to learn to be loved and give love, not being afraid to love even though we know that inevitably love will hurt. It is to be compassionate and creative in our caring. It is to be spontaneous and sensitive in our serving. It is to be honest with ourselves in what we do or say and how we feel. It is to accept struggles in order to reach harmony. Struggling is part of living, and suffering a part of being human. As we learn to be better human beings by the grace of God, we try to make a difference and dream of a better world ...
>
> My diary, September 2001

Preaching Palliative Care

Teaching, as well as practising, researching, and writing about palliative care, has been a means of catharsis for me; it has allowed me to deal with grief and life more constructively. Experiential learning has also facilitated my process of professional and personal growth. What follows here is a seminar presentation I did on suffering and healing[18] in which years of palliative care have been crystallised into a thirty-minute presentation. This material contains the patients' perspectives on suffering from my M.Sc. study,[3] and my personal perspective as a professional and relative. It illustrates the process of meaning reconstruction and transcendence as the sufferer searches for healing. It is by no means a generalisation of the nature of suffering and palliative care.

The sufferer

Suffering does not involve patients alone but also relatives and health-care professionals. In order for palliative care to be effective, we need to attend to all three parties, as the suffering of each party can affect and exacerbate the suffering of others.[19] In order to facilitate healing, we need a "holding environment" — a sense of belonging with connectedness, care and respect. We also need continually to reflect and reframe our identity and reality. This presentation illustrates the nature of suffering from viewpoints of patients, the professional, and the relative, including their individual holding environment and healing process.

Firstly, let us consider the suffering of each party travelling along a curve, a journey from suffering to serenity (Diagram II). Whether we are dealing with the patient's suffering or our own suffering as a professional or relative, we need to connect with our patients, with ourselves, and with significant others. We need to understand in depth what is happening, to reflect on the situation, to surrender to aspects of our old self that might be hindering us from moving forward, and lastly to reframe a new reality or identity, a meaning that makes sense to us.

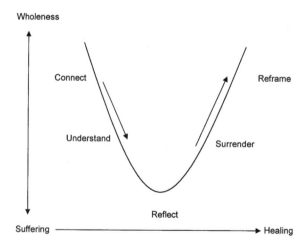

Diagram II. From suffering to serenity

Personhood

I also introduce the concept of personhood. Cassell refers to personhood as the experience of the whole person, which is not limited to the body, mind, and spirit but has many aspects.[20] Each of us has our own individual lived past, present, and perceived future; a personality and a set of values, hopes, secrets, desires, routines, roles, and rights within political and cultural contexts; and a sense of existence in relation to the world of objects, events, and relationships. So each being is unique, depending on the combination of all these aspects. Suffering must be understood in relation to one's personhood. Cassell defines suffering as "a state of severe distress associated with events that threaten the intactness of personhood". Anything perceived as a significant threat to any aspect of personhood can induce suffering. The nature of suffering will be unique, complex, and multi-dimensional for each person, depending on the meaning of the threat and which aspects of personhood are threatened.

Suffering of the patient

From my M.Sc. study on advanced cancer patients desiring euthanasia,[3] I conclude that suffering is multi-dimensional and can be classified according to the patient's personhood along a timeline of past, present, and future, rather than physical, psychosocial, and spiritual dimensions.

The patients' pasts are full of losses. They are no longer who they used to be, because of losses of roles and routines, mobility and independence, dreams and aspirations. Death is inevitable and an incurable illness means hopelessness. In the present, they perceive their suffering to be multi-dimensional. The suffering is confined not only to having cancer but also to their lived past, possibly with previous hardships, significant events, complicated social dynamics, and unresolved grief. Their suffering is also interrelated. They perceive suffering not only for themselves but also for their significant others. They feel a great sense of burden to others. Some anticipate their future with fear. As they have not experienced dying, they rely on what they have witnessed in hospitals or experienced personally as care-givers. Their future is also governed by what their doctors have told them. Therefore, unskilful communication can contribute to their suffering. They imagine their own dying trajectory with increasing suffering, dependency, burden and lack of care. They desire to be connected to their significant others and special surroundings in order to feel a sense of belonging. They want care and respect from their significant others. When these desires are unmet, they suffer.

An effective holding environment should encompass the presence of connectedness, care, and respect. Patients need a secure and comfortable place to suffer. This can be either their home in the presence of family, friends, and familiar surroundings, or a palliative care setting in which health-care professionals care with their hearts, hands, and minds. There are five steps in facilitating the patients' healing process:

(1) Establishing connectedness
   We need to establish a spiritual rapport with our patients by being present. Patients must feel that we are genuine, trustworthy, and that we respect them. We must really listen and trust our intuition to empathise.

(2) Understanding personhood
   We need to understand the various aspects of their individual personhood by listening to their stories, exploring their narratives in depth, and noting the metaphors they use in describing their suffering. We are not taking a medical history. Patients are talking according to their own agenda. As they tell their stories, we get a picture of their perceived reality, suffering, anticipated future, and hidden yearnings.

(3) Walking with patients in their suffering
   Once we get to know the depths of their suffering, we must show compassion. Not only do we acknowledge their suffering, we must also be committed and willing to actively walk with them in suffering. They need our assurance that we will not abandon them.

(4) Surrendering and setting realistic goals
   Apart from controlling the patients' symptoms and supporting their relatives, we need to help our patients let go of their old selves and explore meaning in their current situation. Although we cannot change their reality, we can reframe the perception of their reality and set realistic goals. We can help them let go of the physical, not to focus on what they no longer have but on what they still have and on psycho-spiritual aspects. We can gradually help them to let go of the need for control and independence. Paradoxically, it is when they surrender that they begin to feel in control. And when they begin to enjoy their dependency, they feel less of a burden.

(5) Empowering and restoring
   In the presence of a disintegrating body and an exhausted mind, we must empower their spiritual dimension. Even when they are most vulnerable, we can restore them to some sense of wholeness.

Suffering of the professional

Health-care professionals also suffer. Caring for dying patients invariably made me more aware of my own vulnerabilities. Many hidden wounds surfaced to my consciousness. I felt like a failure, as I could not control my patients' suffering. There was only so much I could do, but patients were expecting more from me. I was burdened emotionally, witnessing the impact of cancer on the physical, psychosocial, and spiritual wellbeing of my patients and their relatives. I held my tears as I listened to their stories. I, too, had separation grief. I struggled with ethical dilemmas in my clinical decision-making.

Like my patients, I needed a holding environment: I needed care, a sense of belonging, and respect from my colleagues at work and from my significant others at home. I needed to care for myself, to connect with myself, and respect my work. Self-awareness was the key to healing.

Reflecting

As I reflected, I became more aware of why I was behaving the way I was. "Why was I reacting or feeling that way?" "What are my needs?" "Was I treating my patient or myself?" As I explored my patients' personhood, I also searched my own personhood. This exploration of self revealed many hidden vulnerabilities, mistakes, fears, unresolved grief, significant events, and relationship problems. I realised I had to heal my own wounds before I could help others. My healing process was most intensive during my M.Sc. study. As the research process required a systematic analysis of the patients' subjective experiences, including their meaning of existence, values, and beliefs, I, too, began to reflect on the spiritual, existential, and philosophical aspects of my personhood. This reflective practice was somewhat painful but inspiring. It gave me the courage to work through my wounds and it brought me healing during the process.

Reframing

Over the years, I continually renewed my definition of care. Instead of being a professional, I became a student and my patients my teachers. I let go of the need for control. I realised I could not control life or death, however hard I tried. I let go of the need of having to "do" all the time. Rather, I learned to "be" with my patients, and even waste time with them. Instead of being rigid, I became flexible in negotiating care plans with my patients. Instead of being rational all the time, I also trusted my intuition. I surrendered to not having answers, as I realised that the more I learned, the more I did not know. As I was empowered during this healing process, I developed a passion to advocate. I did research because, like my patients, I also needed to search for soul and meaning. I taught so that my patients would not suffer in vain. Apart from evidence-based research and clinical experience, we must not ignore our creativity, intuition, virtues of compassion, empathy and patience, which are important tools for the art of healing.

Suffering of the relative

Relatives suffer, too, and I became a relative of a cancer patient several years ago. I could then truly empathise with a relative's suffering — the physical, social, and emotional burden in caring but not feeling confident in how to care; the empathic suffering in witnessing my loved one's suffering; the psychological reactions of grief, guilt, and regrets, coupled with fears of anticipatory loss; the dilemmas in decision-making and the burden of bearing the consequences if the decisions turned out to be wrong. It was a very testing time to practise palliative care for my family.

I needed my individualised holding environment. This came from my family but I had to remember that they were also grieving and needed their own holding environment. Colleagues and friends from both near and far, through prayers and e-mail, became a significant support network. I found ways to care for myself by getting inspiration through music and writing, finding space, and not neglecting my body.

Reflecting

After a brief period of denial, I connected with my reality and being. Again, I became aware of my behaviour, emotions, and grief, and how my relatives were reacting. "What am I doing?" "Why am I doing this?" "How am I feeling?" "Why are others saying things and behaving the way they are?"

I needed to understand my loved ones as well as myself. We had our individualised reality, perceptions, anticipations, and needs. I tried to empathise with the grief of my family. This required tolerance and patience, making sure that our anger and helplessness would not disrupt our cohesiveness. Again, I found reflecting invaluable. My media for reflections were literature and lyrics to songs: I found them comforting, as those words shared a common humanity that helped me feel less alone. I had to express my suffering; apart from sharing my grief with others, keeping a diary was my way of reliving and reflecting on what was happening. Every day was too overwhelming, and writing helped to bring meaning, structure, and a positive perspective to my chaos:

> I am consciously walking through grief, reflecting daily, and analysing myself and other people's behaviour, communication, emotions, and decision-making. There is so much to learn from life, but the hardest lesson is to provide palliative care for my loved one and so soon! But by holding on to and practising these principles of care, connectedness, and respect, it has somehow made our lives more bearable.

> E-mail to a friend, September 2002

A few months later, I wrote:

> I care for you from the alpha to the omega, whenever and wherever, living or dying ... Suffering is inevitable but not in vain ... Where there is love, there will be suffering. I'd rather have a world with suffering than a world without love.

My diary, December 2002

Reframing

From my reflections, I have surrendered to the brevity of life, as life is so fragile. I have surrendered to insecurities and uncertainties in life, as life is so unpredictable. Instead of striving for perfection, I accept my limitations. I try my best and appreciate our individual gifts in serving. Gradually, I learn to let go of parts of my old self and situations in order to feel whole again. I have reset my roles and priorities within my family and work, cherishing every moment with my loved ones. I want to hold them a little closer, a little tighter, and just a little longer. I have re-evaluated my values, learning to trust beyond human understanding.

I am grateful that I have been given the chance to care as a professional and a relative. I had to embrace death and suffering before I could learn how to care and live authentically. This sculpture depicts the beauty of palliative care (Diagram III). The vulnerable patient needs a holding environment. We, as care-givers, whether as a professional or a relative, need to grow those wings!

Diagram III. The beauty of palliative care

Practising Palliative Care as a Relative

"Do I practise what I preach?" Observing cancer in my family and participating in the caring process was painful but full of precious moments. I am grateful to my loved ones for having taught me these lessons of life. As I have already touched on the relative's suffering, I highlight some of my subjective experiences from my diary, taken chronologically from August to December 2002:

Death

Death is knocking at our door ... Numbness ... Disbelief ... Suddenly no day is ordinary anymore ... I can see ... I can hear ... I can feel and I have to write this all down ... Writing helps me to cope, to put my thoughts and feelings, my grief and tears, into words. It helps me to reflect and let it sink in gradually, to put it into perspective. Those memories are precious moments that I don't want to forget. I don't want to stop experiencing that loving presence of God.

Shock

The doctor held the photo in his hand. What he said I couldn't recall, but when I looked at that photo, an ugly looking malignant ulcer was staring at me. It was a picture of death! It meant death and nothing else. By evening, I was exhausted and overwhelmed. I wasn't aware of it at first until I realised I had ordered two main courses for dinner. I had no appetite and was in no mood to talk. I got home and stopped by my aunt's flat. She was the first person in the whole day to ask me how things were ... how I felt. I couldn't hold my emotions any longer; I burst into tears and cried uncontrollably. She hugged me until I gradually caught my breath. The children, who were usually hypnotised by Cartoon Network, ran up to hug and kiss me. I don't know whether they knew what had actually caused my outburst, but their instinct was to hold me. What a comfort they were to me!

Numbness

My mind is blank. Music has become noise and my love for work chores. Many a time I've left my purse, keys, and mobile phone at work when I went home. One time I got stranded between two tunnels, as I had no money to pay the toll and no mobile to call. It was embarrassing, but really, I was frantic. I drove dangerously too ... I don't seem to notice the number plates in front or the car behind me.

Hope

When she told me what treatment she could offer, I held my tears of "joy". Never mind about the prognosis, but the fact that something could be done gave me hope. I hadn't realised that treatment or just any treatment was so important in fostering hope ...

Decision-making

As all three of us in the family are doctors, we all differed in our opinions. But the professor replied that we were in no clear state of mind to decide. "The team decides!" This was hard to accept at first but he was absolutely right. We were emotional and clouded in our decision-making. Searching through medical literature was burdensome. Asking for second and third opinions was helpful, but what if each doctor recommended something different? What if my decision was wrong? Could I live with that? Ultimately, it depended on whether the patient trusted the doctors enough to make the decision.

Doctor communication

In the middle of the consultation, my relative said, "The most terrible thing is ... suffering". The doctor just ignored him or perhaps he didn't even hear. Where was his empathy?

This doctor was very different ... He came out of his room to greet us. After we sat down, he said, "I've been fully informed of your situation and I've reviewed your scans. But what is your primary concern?" What a wonderful way to communicate! He noted his concerns and listened to his losses. Then he discussed the pros and cons of each treatment option and gave his opinion. My relative later commented, "He is sensitive and very sensible. He doesn't take me as a case but as an individual".

Two junior doctors were doing their evening ward rounds. They did not introduce themselves but asked, "How are you?" As the patient was replying politely, he was interrupted, "Oh, we don't need to know that. We only want to know if you have any problems". So he answered their question but he was interrupted yet again, "Oh! We can't help you there because we deal only with specific problems that you may be having right this moment. " So he mentioned his insomnia and I asked them whether they could increase his dose of Ativan. One answered, "0.5 mg is already a very high dose. Piriton is better". Why did they come? It seemed as if all they wanted to do were to walk out again. Even my hairdresser could be more specific and sensitive in communicating!

Holding environment

I introduced to the children the different names of hospitals: Queen Mary Hospital, Princess Margaret. When I got to "Prince" immediately they shouted, "Prince of Egypt Hospital!" Don't they just cheer you up!

E-mail from my colleague: ... I am aware of the sense of shock and distress. Some days are so much worse than others. Large brick walls seem to suddenly appear for you to crash into ... Primarily, be a relative rather than a practitioner. Don't analyse too much; the bruising rawness of this is a totally different experience that is best put in perspective later ... ... It may sound perverse, but going with the flow of the hurt and rawness somehow allows for coping and easier sharing of feelings.

Understanding

I am so proud of him. He has such inner peace. This illness has brought us closer together. It gave us the opportunity to discuss something more philosophical, which we wouldn't have discussed otherwise. He got to know me better, too.

Transcendence

My mind has been so burdened that I wanted a burr hole, as those headaches just refused to leave me. It's been so clouded that music only resembled noise ... until last night, when I could feel those lyrics again:

When I am down and oh my soul so weary
When troubles come and my heart burdened be
Then, I am still and wait here in the silence
Until you come and sit awhile with me
You raise me up so I can stand on mountains
You raise me up to walk on stormy seas
I am strong when I am on your shoulders
You raise me up to more than I can be ...

From *You Raise Me Up*

By Brendan Graham; Music by Secret Garden 2002

It was only when I was lost that I could really see. Only when I was still that I could hear more clearly. And it was only when I was helpless and in deep despair that I could feel a precious kind of love. So suddenly, my earthly concerns no longer concerned me. My journey has become so much clearer now; it's prayer, family, and faith. So suddenly, my resentment and prejudice are gone but have been transformed into kisses and forgiveness. I'm now so conscious of those who surround me — many who have raised me up, many who have comforted me, and many who have loved and cared for me in their special ways. Thank you for raising me up to more than I can be. Thank you for bringing out the best in me. I pray we will all have another soul to raise us up in times of trouble. And I pray we will continue to sustain that gift of patience and presence, to sit awhile with others. When nothing seems humanly possible and life is out of our control, in my silence, God came and sat awhile with me. In my exhaustion, He strengthened and surrounded me. With His loving presence He raised me up. I see God's blessings and miracles amid my sorrows. I feel love amid my suffering. Though death's not quite round the corner yet, I wonder whether I've already sensed a glimpse of His eternity.

Reflecting

He asked me, "Why do you think there is suffering?" I thought for a moment. "It's because where there is love, there will be suffering. You cannot prove love scientifically, but it is evident by the intensity of hurt and sorrow one feels in his or her grieving. So suffering is inevitable."

Anticipatory grief

Usually he prints me a computer generated birthday card every year but this year he was too tired and said, "I'll make it up to you next year". We had a big and long hug. As he went to bed, I asked myself, "Is there going to be a next year?" Tears ran down my face and I felt so alone ...

Caring for others and self

I've been juggling between work and family ... I've been a professional and relative simultaneously — explaining, reassuring, advocating, comforting, "doing" and "being". You name it, I've done it. But everyone is so different and I am constantly switching from one mode to another, accommodating the needs of my patients at home and the worries of my relatives ... I thought I was coping all right, pampering myself in every way, but I am a bit burned out ... picking up, hopefully.

Reframing

We cannot extend or control time ... I have found that, when patients try to buy time, there is a cost. They get extra time but at the expense of extra suffering with no guarantee for its quality ... So we should take life as it is. If we ask for more, it comes with a cost and we have to suffer for it. But if we just accept life with all its suffering, there are blessings in our surrendering.

What is human worth? Just watch her ... Haven't you seen the way she touches his face? Haven't you heard the way she talks to him? There's not a careless word but only her healing touch. Can't you sense her care and connectedness, always holding and being with him, so selfless and gentle? She never abandons. There is no doubt he is loved and is worthy ... Human worth is how much you care when you can still do and how much you are cared for when you can no longer do. Witnessing her care answered my questions regarding futility, utility, and dignity. His living is worth every penny ... every moment ...

Palliative care and research have made me so self-aware ... When there is rain, I have been trained to search for the rainbow behind every dark cloud ...

Living Palliative Care as a Patient

To truly experience palliative care is to live it personally. I was recently diagnosed with cancer. Surprisingly, I have reacted to this bad news with calmness; the main reason is that I have a wonderful gift of faith from God. Crises over the years have forced me into deeper and deeper existential quests. I have come to trust beyond my own strength and human understanding. In addition, resources I have gathered as a palliative care physician, researcher and relative have helped to contribute to my sense of serenity.

I am sure you will cope well. After all, it is your specialist training that will help you through to the road of recovery.

A note from my sister, November 2003

Again, I share excerpts of my diary which I wrote during the first few months of my cancer journey. I have applied a similar framework to the one I used for my presentation on suffering and healing: from connecting, reflecting, and reframing before reaching transcendence. I have also included themes relating to my psychological reactions and communication.

Psychological reactions

Shock

I appeared calm but really I was numb. The body seemed more vulnerable than the soul. Spiritually, I might be coping but my body wasn't; it ended up with cells that went out of control. I looked calm but my blood pressure was up, my heart was pounding, my muscles were tense and my teeth chattering ...

Anticipatory grief

Suddenly, I was overwhelmed with grief ... It wasn't so much about my eventual mortality but what gave me most pain was the thought of separation. It felt as if everyone was dying and I was the only one being left behind. As a relative, I would have to grieve for the loss of only one loved one. But as a patient, I would have to grieve for all the ones I love — a much heavier loss and pain ... This brought tears to my eyes ...

Bargaining

Today has been a day of confusion and doubt. Does God want me to experience cancer in order to be a witness and then die? I'm ready to endure any physical trauma; I think I can cope, having experienced that excruciating fracture. But then to die as well! "But You just told me to focus on the children? Samuel and Katherine can't just grow up overnight and be thankful to You for a dead mother. I am willing to go through anything but please spare my life!"

Fears

As I woke up from the operation, I trembled and kept muttering, "I don't want to die! I don't want to die!" I overheard the surgeon saying in my semiconscious state that the cancer has spread ... I cried in fear and then I felt an angel; it was as if she were wiping my tears with her feathers. "No, you are not going to die." My lips, mouth, and throat were so dry. She gave me teaspoons of water, a bit at a time, and wetted my lips with cotton wool soaked in water. She caressed me gently, calming my nerves. I was in pain; I felt so stiff in my bottom and mummified with dressings over me. She turned me gently to relieve my pain and I responded, "Wow! Where did you learn to turn like this?" This angel was a he, my husband! Then I fell asleep, thinking how painful this must have been for him, too.

The fear of abandonment

I don't quite understand why but I'll go through whatever there is to go through ... but how about my significant others? Can they cope? Are You looking after them too? I dread the moment when they become too overwhelmed and abandon me, not because they are heartless but because they are heartbroken. Loving would then be too painful. When my time comes, let it be gentle so that they feel Your love and not hate You instead.

Tears

It's okay to be tearful, as emotions are so normal and often we don't know exactly what we are crying about. Emotions speak for us. It's not weakness either, but if we do feel weak, it just shows that we cannot rely on our own strength but God's. Crying is like a hug or a kiss — they are actions that convey emotions words cannot express. So if we know how to hug and kiss but not cry, we'd better start practising now!

Of all the psychological reactions to loss, I found denial necessary but depression unnecessary. I knew I must be honest with my true feelings and not suppress my low mood. But after acknowledging those negative feelings, I tried my best to reframe my mind with positive thoughts:

Acceptance

I seemed to have leapt to the stage of acceptance about my diagnosis of cancer. Perhaps the gift of faith has allowed me to believe that my cancer has a purpose for the good of all and therefore I have had no need to doubt the number of my days, as long as each day is purposeful. Or perhaps my denial has helped me to believe that all will be well again and there is no need to doubt my mortality ... yet!

Whatever the meaning of my cancer or however hard I tried to control my responses to my reactions to having cancer, fear was the worst emotion of all, which originated from doubts and uncertainties. When I ruminated on my doubts, my fears escalated uncontrollably:

I felt another lump. Is it scar tissue or tumour? After a day or two, I realised it was ridiculous to ask myself the same question, "Is it recurrence or progression of disease?" Other negative thoughts started pouring into my pool of anxiety and restlessness. Whether it was recurrence or for reassurance, I needed to know and act sensibly ... It seems that the fear is worse than the cancer itself. It's a horrible feeling. But having that gift of faith has helped to remove that fear. I must learn to hold on to that faith and let go of that fear!

My holding environment

Creating my individualised oasis enabled me to feel secure and serene. One thing I have noticed about Chinese patients is that they have been so used to "doing" that they find it intolerable just "being". Therefore I decided that I must find ways to "indulge" myself when I could no longer "do". This premature cultivation of learning to "be" was not too premature after all!

Resources

Morrie wrote, "All the works you have actively done on yourself — all the experiences you have had in your life — can be used to maintain your composure. Draw on them". [16] I think I have gained many resources. Practising, researching and teaching palliative care has helped me to live with my cancer.

Apart from palliative care, I gathered resources and recreations to prepare myself to become a human "being" rather than a human "doing" — writing for my hands; books, films, and nature for my eyes; music for my ears; imagery and memories for my mind; and a belief system for my soul. Imagery was useful, for it took me to another space and time without feeling disorientated. On the contrary, I felt very self-aware with mindfulness and soulfulness; I would call this "therapeutic daydreaming". I felt content and in control, even though there did not seem to be much that I could do.

I was specific to others about how I would like to be cared for. Otherwise, I would have got into the situation where my loved ones thought they were doing their very best for me but in fact were burdening me as well as themselves unnecessarily. For example, I preferred solitude, not surveillance. I detested those who were over-reactive or who disrespected my choices, telling me what I should do and disabling me. But there were others who knew exactly what I needed, when and how, even without my asking. They did not have to be physically present but were empathic and would respond willingly in a split second to my needs. For the former group, it was my responsibility to make my specific needs understood. For the latter, I appreciated their responsiveness and understanding. A few supportive care-givers are more than enough, and I have been blessed with many.

My angels

Many are rushing around just for me. Many are praying for me. There is an orchestra of angels making heaven on earth for me. I never knew there could be such bliss. It's not a glimpse but more than a moment!

Coping with cancer

Practising and researching palliative care has taught me to think reflectively and to learn experientially that I do not know how else to deal with my illness except to explore, interpret, and find meaning. My coping method is individualised, but you may find it helpful:

(1) Connecting and understanding

I connected with my reality according to my own pace. Denial and distancing helped so that I could deal with a bit of bad news at a time. I disliked receiving frequent telephone calls. It was as if I had to report my illness, symptoms, and progress repeatedly. This repetition reminded me of my reality, which I often tried to ignore until I felt more ready to face the whole truth. But having said that, making a connection with my reality was important; otherwise, I could not move forward. I have juggled between connecting and distancing/denying in order to maintain a sense of harmony. I connected not only with my own behaviour, feelings, thoughts, and deeper concerns; I needed to connect with others.

E-mail to Bradbury Hospice

I know that everyone has been stressed and I must congratulate you all for being so persevering and selfless. And thank you for looking after Bradbury while I've been away. I've been looking forward to returning to work ... But as you know, life is unpredictable, fragile, and brief. And bad news doesn't happen to our patients only ... I have some bad news too. I am awful when it comes to breaking bad news to colleagues, as I assume that you are all used to it and I forget that my most entrusted colleague is only human! Initially, I asked her to break this news on my behalf, but it was insensitive and cruel of me to think that she could convey this message without feelings and without support. I will tell you myself ...

Bradbury is like a big family. Entering into this family and over the years, I have learned about the essence of life — how to connect, care, and respect. I have learned to appreciate the brevity of life but also to live life lightly ... Bradbury also has had this magic of turning human beings into angels (and if you look behind you, you'll find you all have wings). We pluck our feathers to patch up wounds of sufferers and for one another. Though Bradbury is so full of death, I have found that only by accepting death could we truly live.

I have experienced suffering as a professional caring for the dying, suffering as a relative, and today, suffering as a patient. Recently I noted a lump ... Everything has been done and will be done so quickly that I could easily go through the stage of denial and say to myself that I never had a tumour! But I feel calm at the moment (I'll tell you when I don't), for I knew for certain that someday I'd get something affecting some part of my body. Years of palliative care have prepared me emotionally. Somehow, God has also prepared me; this cancer has hit me only after I rested and felt closer to Him.

I have learned not to run away from crises when they hit me but to face them and fight them so that I won't regret anything. These are the trials and tests for being in the world, the burdens everyone must carry. If I run, I am avoiding life itself. But where did I learn this? Bradbury, I think … Here within Bradbury lie virtues: patience, kindness, gentleness, perseverance, understanding, endurance, selflessness, and compassion. And where do I see these qualities? In you, and you, and every one of you! Do not underestimate the inner strength you have, despite your apparent vulnerabilities; realise and use these gifts for yourselves and to support others. Do not neglect yourself and stay strong … I'll be back!

I must mention my daughter, Katherine. As we connected, she taught me how to communicate. One night at 11:00 p.m., she came to my bedroom:

Katherine: Mummy, I don't want to sleep alone. I am afraid...

Mummy: Why? What is there to fear?

Katherine: I don't want to be alone. I don't want you to wear a mask. I don't want you to be ill. I want you to get better...

Mummy: Well, we'll see. Some cancer patients can live up to twenty years or more.

Katherine: I don't want you to live just three years … Can we have three million years?

Mummy: Well, I think we'll both be in heaven by then. I'll be singing and you'll be playing the piano or violin.

Katherine: Mummy, you're mine. I came from you. Daddy didn't come from you and so you are mine. But we can divide you. I'll have the top half and daddy will have the bottom half because I want to cuddle you. Mummy, you are good on the outside, good on the inside and so you are a good person. Mummy, don't leave me...

Mummy: [Cuddle, cuddle, hugs and kisses]...I won't leave you.

Katherine: I will try not to cough tonight.

Mummy: We will ask God how we should use the time we have. The only way to be together forever is to know God so that we will get to heaven. Otherwise, we can't meet again. I don't know when my time to leave is...

Katherine: I will not go out to dinner tomorrow. I want to be with you.

In the quietness of the night, a little girl could communicate her fear, realising the brevity of life, and could express her separation and anticipatory grief spontaneously, simply, clearly, and openly. We should learn to communicate like children. Her conversation moved quickly from the overt to the covert, expressing her fears, desires, and hopes. She needed reassurance.

I do not know how good I was at giving it verbally, but non-verbally I tried my best. By morning, she had figured out the reason for my getting cancer. "Mummy, I know why I don't have cancer. It's because I love my broccoli and you don't!"

(2) Reflecting and expressing

It was important to reflect and ventilate. I unloaded my many thoughts and feelings into my diary and attempted to validate the truthfulness of every brain wave and emotion. Reflecting on my brainstorms enabled me to acknowledge their existence, discard any unnecessary negative thoughts, appreciate my strengths and resources, and reframe my mind positively, thus renewing my reality into something less overwhelming. Finding structure or meaning gave me a sense of control and direction.

Ruminating

It's been only three weeks since my diagnosis. I can't believe that things could happen so fast — cancer, surgery, chemotherapy … I am now lying very still and resting … and keeping very, very still … but my brain can't stop ruminating!

Why

Perhaps my lesson is that … though I had paid much attention to the mind and soul and had felt great, my body couldn't catch up with all the stress, and the burdens have accumulated into one little lump. I will be glad to be rid of my burdens when she performs the operation.

Decision-making

I decided not to seek further medical opinions or search for treatment options. I have left everything to my doctors. It's good that I can be relieved of the burdens of decision-making, which I had found to be extremely stressful. The paternalistic approach is appropriate when my doctors are trustworthy. Being too autonomous may not be good for the patient psychologically. It's better to trust that the doctor does know best and that he or she would act in the patient's best interest, and mine does. I prefer to be a compliant patient and this would eliminate pressure on the doctor and any dilemmas for me …

Writing has been a means through which I could express myself spontaneously on anything rational or abstract, real or imaginary, appropriate or absurd, without interruption but according to my own pace and agenda. I have found music particularly useful in facilitating my process of reflection and expression. Different kinds of music parallel many themes of human experiences and emotions. Some revive the body, some uplift the mood, and others sooth the soul. Instrumentals help me to search for meaning, whereas lyrics give meaning and structure to my experiences. Music helps either to complement or counteract my thoughts, feelings, and imageries into creating a more positive frame of mind. In that way, I could formalise my "mess" into meaning. With the accompaniment of music, I wrote this e-mail to my colleagues about compassion burnout and self-care, using angels as a metaphor for palliative care care-givers:

Learning to Receive

Once there was an angel ... whomever she met she loved, wanting to still every storm. But she was unaware of how weary she'd become, collecting all those burdens on her wings. She was falling and her wings were failing. She knew it hurt to love and it's strenuous to care, but her heart couldn't help loving and her soul couldn't stop caring. So although she'd fallen, she continued her caring. "If I can't fly, I'll kneel and pray instead!" But finally, she became so weary that she could only be still. But in her stillness, she made this wonderful discovery: "Burdens have wings, too, and they can fly!" So in her stillness and uselessness, she unloaded her cares to God and allowed Him to care for her. And she gave Him her burdens in exchange for His blessings. So, while she learned to receive and revive those wings, she whispered, "I'll do better next time, now that I've learned how to receive as well as give!"

(3) Surrendering and reframing

I held on to what was still left, let go of what I could no longer be, and searched for a new self. This process was vital for reaching acceptance and transcendence. I found myself constantly connecting, reflecting, acknowledging, expressing, surrendering, and reframing with every dark moment. This prevented me from digging deeper into a dark hole, dragging me into despair. From my illness journey, I found a sense of restoration and felt whole by working systematically through my suffering with cancer.

Lesson

My journey is to be disciplined, to rest and be absolutely still, to listen to my body, myself, and that little voice, to trust and pray, to count my blessings and praise, to wait for whatever dreams may come my way.

Bad days

... I take a day at a time. I try to forget my bad days but make the most out of my good days. Though there are days of hell, there are also moments of heaven. I try to be a person and not a patient, whenever I can.

New role

This new "job" of being a patient is very tough but perhaps it is a very comprehensive way of learning medicine — the journey of being a professional and a researcher, then a relative, and now a patient. I hope I will be a better doctor after this ... and a better person

New possibilities

My friend also has cancer. I said, "Stay positive! That's the only way to be!" She replied, "Yes, I haven't really thought about my prognosis and statistics for the moment". Then I said, "You never know what new opportunities may come your way".

Feeling whole

I feel connected, cared for and respected … I have love, hope and peace … Family, friends and faith surround me … I feel so loved and so alive! I feel whole. Thank you!

Living as a patient

My daughter has defined patient-centred care as "Mummy is now the big princess. Daddy, you are only the little prince!" She was clear about who should get total attention! Patients have a secondary gain from being ill. But being ill does not give us the right to be demanding, manipulative, and mad. The world cannot revolve solely around us. It should be care-centred and not cancer-centred, so that everyone is cared for and not consumed amid suffering. Everyone suffers: the patient, family, friends, and professionals. I don't want my cancer to consume or control my world and the life of others. Similarly, I don't want my emotions to overtake my wellbeing. We should try to give and receive care whether we are ill or well. The goal is to try, but not to pressurise ourselves, by channelling our emotions positively so that we behave sensitively, sensibly and selflessly. We should not, however, deny our feelings and genuine needs. It is a choice that we try our best to live every day in harmony with our body, mind and soul, and those around us.

Care and connectedness

Morrie Schwartz, a professor of sociology, said, "I believe that even though each person has an individual and unique self, the self means nothing outside the context of community or meaningful contact with other people". [16] We can think of ourselves as being independent or dependent, but more than often we are interdependent. We share and learn from each other. I got a card that said, "Our lives are bits and pieces of each other". And my mother-in-law says, "We are each other's keepers". So, whether we are ill or well, we need to stay connected, to care and be cared for.

Living in the moment

Am I happy with how I've spent my day today? If not, why not? How would I like to have spent it? Be realistic, though. Reflect but don't dwell in the past. Are there people I need to apologise to or to thank? Are there things I must do to make my world and myself happier? I shouldn't delay or deny myself that opportunity or I'll regret that it's too late … I need to search for meaning from everyday experiences. Meaning is everywhere if we look hard enough with mindfulness and soulfulness. If we learn to live today as if there is no tomorrow, we can't go too wrong!

Attitude to suffering

My teacher wrote me a note saying, "Travel well … I hope you have a good process with the therapy". Could anyone imagine that an illness journey with cancer could ever be "good"? Actually, mine has been good because I feel whole. It is our attitude to suffering rather than the suffering itself that determines our perception, reactions, and coping. I don't want to travel alone and I hope that those who choose to travel with me will see the positive side to this process, for I believe that suffering is never in vain. Suffering has allowed me to experience the most wonderful care and connectedness. It has shown me that true love really exists. We do not live to suffer but we suffer in order to learn to live.

Conclusion

> As a physician, I came to acknowledge the word "suffering" and wondered why it was never taught in medical school. As a researcher, I understood the relevance of personhood to the multi-dimensional and complex nature of suffering. As a relative, I questioned why suffering was ever necessary. But I concluded that suffering was inevitable but not in vain. As a patient, I validated that suffering was not meaningless but could enable the sufferer to edify and comfort others with greater empathy and sensitivity.
>
> My diary, August 2004

Having undertaken a rather unorthodox medical career ladder as a physician, a researcher, then a relative and finally a cancer patient, I have a personal perspective of how suffering should be managed and how palliative care should be taught and practised. I summarise some points from my professional journey that I have treasured. These principles can be integrated into the palliative care curriculum for different disciplines, specialties, settings, and levels of medical education:

Principles of suffering and care to be integrated into the palliative care curriculum

1. To understand the patients' personhood rather than adhere to the boundaries of physical, social, psychological, and spiritual assessment
2. To understand the nature and complexity of suffering in relation to the patient's personhood
3. To focus on the principles of connectedness, care, and respect
4. To appreciate the value of narratives and subjective experiences in history taking
5. To explore the patients' inner world in depth and elicit their individualised holding environment
6. To restore patients to a sense of wholeness through transcendence rather than attempt to "control" suffering with methodical medical interventions

7. To enhance the art of palliative care through medical humanities such as art, music, philosophy, and non-medical literary sources
8. To enhance self-awareness and promote professional self-development through reflective practice, experiential learning, and creative writing

Learning how to connect, care, and respect is the essence of palliative care. Palliative care emphasises effective communication, but only when a spiritual connectedness has been established with our patients can we begin to communicate in a genuine manner. Holistic care can be understood simply as paying attention to the physical, social, psychological, and spiritual aspects of our patients, but authentic care consists of understanding their personhood and lived experience. Without attending to their individualised personhood, we cannot grasp the meaning of their suffering. Without attending to their subjective experiences and hidden agendas, we cannot understand their inner world and genuine needs. By exploring our patients' genuine concerns in depth and providing adequate information, we can empower them to set realistic goals through shared decision-making. In this way, their autonomy will be truly respected.

Although death is inevitable for patients with incurable cancer, healing is possible. Despite progressive physical disintegration, orientating our focus on the existential aspects of the whole person in the presence of a supportive environment can help our patients regain a sense of wholeness. Healing has been defined as "a relational process involving movement towards an experience of integrity and wholeness, which may be facilitated by a care-giver's intervention but is dependent on an innate potential within the patient". [21] Thus, healing is a process, a journey, and an experience, whereby patients can transcend in the presence and comfort of others.

As health-care professionals, we also need to attend to our own personhood. Self-awareness is the key to professional and personal self-development; reflective practice, experiential learning, and creative writing are useful skills in promoting this process of refinement. We need to integrate non-medical artistic literary sources, our compassion and creativity, and personal as well as clinical experience into evidence-based medicine. This humanistic dimension enhances the art of medicine.

I remember returning to work after I had completed my treatments. I entered the palliative care ward, feeling vulnerable and perplexed. "Who am I? Am I a professional or am I a patient?" Then my inner voice whispered, "You are a person! You go to work as a whole person!" As I listened to my patients, for the first time I felt truly qualified to say to them, "I understand fully how you feel". My personal experiences have given me a deeper awareness of my patients' needs and of their relatives' empathic suffering. These experiences have enabled me to be more sensitive and realistic in my clinical ethical decision-making, not relying solely on professional judgement but ensuring that all the other perspectives have been given fair attention.

From my personal and professional journey, I have experienced death inside me; I have witnessed death around me, and now I have become aware of my own mortality. But my discovery is this: as we care for the dying or as we ourselves are dying, we can learn to live. Only when we embrace death, will we begin to truly live. Death, dying and bereavement teach us invaluable lessons of life. Do not deny death; learn from it and you will discover the essence of living and its meaning.

4

"Letting Go" and "Holding On": Grieving and Traditional Death Rituals in Hong Kong

Peter Ka Hing CHEUNG, Cecilia Lai Wai CHAN, Wai FU, Yawen LI and Grace Yee Kam Pau CHEUNG

Introduction

It is now generally agreed that coping with grief involves not only accepting the reality of death,[1] developing the ability to live without the deceased,[2] relinquishing old attachments to the deceased and the old assumptive world,[3] and withdrawing emotional energy from the deceased so that it can be reinvested in other people and other things.[1] Coping with grief also involves staying connected with the deceased[4] and developing a new relationship with him or her.[5]

This is the interactive perspective of grief work that guides our exploration of traditional Chinese death rituals and how they are practised in Hong Kong. Traditionally, when a parent dies, sons are supposed to refrain from cutting their hair for three years and are supposed to stay home to mourn. Widows are expected to stay single for the rest of their lives, to fulfil their spousal responsibilities to the deceased husband. Prolonged grief is encouraged as a sign of commitment and obligation to the family hierarchy.

Traditionally, several reference dates guide mourning practice. These practices varied over the centuries and across different social strata. Generally, chanting and/or religious services are conducted for the deceased on each of the seven seven-day periods of the first forty-nine days after the death. At the end of the forty-nine days, some families end their mourning. Others mark the end of mourning on the 100th day after the death of the family member. Sons and daughters who observe the full rigour of mourning for their deceased parent don't return to normal routines until after the third anniversary of the death.

In highly modernized Hong Kong, prolonged grieving and mourning are not possible, and very few people practise the three-year mourning rituals. More people abide by the practices in the first forty-nine days or simply do not continue the rituals after the burial service.

Hong Kong has a predominantly Chinese population, about ten percent of whom are Christian. The rest are Confucian, Buddhist, Daoist, atheist, or do not belong to any organized religion. If one goes to a funeral service any day of the year, the ritual most likely to be encountered is Daoist, the single most practised funeral ritual in Hong Kong. Each day, it is estimated that there are more than 100 Daoist funeral services conducted by Daoist masters in six funeral halls in Hong Kong.[6]

Burials in traditional Chinese communities are commonly held in the family graveyard. Wealthy families have a big graveyard and an ancestors hall where the family can gather at all major festivals and feasts. Family members traditionally gather around the ancestor's grave at least twice a year to pay their respects and to have a picnic, offering delicious food that the deceased person loved. Today, as land is becoming more precious, cremation is in turn becoming both more common and more affordable.

According to Colette Lai (funeral service consultant and trainer of funeral directors),[#] seventy-five to eighty percent of all funeral services in Hong Kong are Daoist. Fifteen percent are Buddhist, and the rest are distributed among other rituals practised by Teochiu, Hoklo (dialect groups in Guangdong Province), fisherfolk, Christians (both Catholic and Protestant), Japanese Shintoists, and a few other small groups. A small number of individuals have no religious service conducted for them after their death. The minimum number of religious professionals who take part in a Daoist service is six, including a musician. The minimum number for a Buddhist service is nine persons.

This paper focuses on the most commonly practised Daoist ritual. However, it must be pointed out that there is no "pure" Daoist ritual as such. After centuries of interaction with other practices, the Daoist ritual is itself an amalgam of Confucian, Buddhist, and Daoist beliefs and practices.[7,8] Lai says that, from experience, there are more similarities than differences between Daoist and Buddhist funeral rituals; they are of the same family (*fo dao yi jia* 佛道一家).

As a preliminary exploration, this paper attempts to answer three questions. First, in what ways do traditional Chinese death rituals facilitate the bereaved person's process of letting go of (separating from) and holding on to (continuing a relationship with) the deceased? Second, in what ways do traditional death rituals in Hong Kong facilitate the same process? Three, are there significant emerging developments in Hong Kong relating to this process? Vignettes of actual mourning experiences shared by the co-authors and parts of conversations taken from taped counselling sessions from a local

---

[#] Colette Lai, funeral service consultant and trainer of funeral directors, comes from a family that has been in the provision of funeral services in Hong Kong for at least three generations. Lai herself has been in the service more than twenty years. She was interviewed for this paper on 20 February 2005.

community bereavement service in Hong Kong have been incorporated in different parts of the paper, with the objectives of connecting conceptualizations of funeral rituals with actual mourning experiences, and tradition with current cultural practice.

Negative Associations with Death and Funerals

Familiarity with the traditional concepts around funerals and rituals can also help professionals facilitate bereaved clients in articulating their common experiences. Fifty-two clients of the Jessie and Thomas Tam Centre (JTTC) of the Society for the Promotion of Hospice Care (SPHC), which provides community bereavement counselling services to individuals and groups in Hong Kong, gave consent for our research team to analyse tapes from their clinical sessions. In these counselling sessions, clients were asked to describe what happened to their loved ones when they died, how their funerals proceeded, what form of burial they had, and what helped them cope with their grief.[9]

The bereaved persons usually described the death of the loved one in great detail. They described the experience of illness, the hospitalization, the last moments before death, their loved one's last words, and their physical condition before death. The bereaved persons felt better if they had a clear image of what would happen to their loved one after death. Uncertainty is typically anxiety provoking and, as most of the subjects did not practise a religion, their images of death tended to be more negative than positive.[10] The negative death images mostly originated from traditional folklore and Daoist stories.

Unlike those with a Judeo-Christian background, the Chinese typically link death to ghostly actions, to painful death, and to judgement in hell as punishment for any wrongful act they might have committed during their lifetime. There is also a strong tendency for the Chinese to relate death to more traditional concepts of reincarnation. Of the fifty-two bereaved subjects, more than half of them (twenty-eight) mentioned bad luck and fate in their family before the death of the loved one. More than a quarter of them (fifteen) mentioned karma, or causes and consequences in one's life and subsequent lives. These individuals were sad because their loved ones worked very hard in their lifetime and did not have opportunities to enjoy life before they died. For them, death and the causes of death (cancer, illness, accident, suicide) were connected to bad karma (fifteen), evil spirits (nine), and a predestined path in life according to their horoscope (eight), as well as bad *feng shui* (the environmental energies of wind, water, and fate) and sick energy (three).

As a result of having someone die in the family, five of the bereaved persons mentioned that their family would have bad luck for three years. Five also said the greatest agony in life was for them (elderly parents with white hair) to witness the death of their children. Bereaved persons who were widows or widowers mentioned the common saying that children who lost their fathers would be poor, and those who lost their mothers would have no one to love them (five). These bereaved persons used traditional beliefs to justify their self-pity. These descriptions explained their social isolation and prolonged grief.

As a way to consolidate the grief experience, half of the respondents described their involvement in planning the funeral as active (twenty-six). Many of them (sixteen) described the deceased persons as putting on good clothes and wearing good make-up. Because they looked peaceful and calm, their family members felt relieved.

Five described the funeral as a good occasion to review their own life and relationship with their deceased loved one. However, there were also conflicts and differences in opinion on how the funerals should be organized. Ten of the bereaved persons specifically described the disagreement among family members and relatives in the extended family, and nine of them felt bad about the tensions and conflicts.

As land is very expensive and burial sites are hard to find, most of the bereaved persons described the cremation process (seventeen). Twelve of them reported that the burial was according to the wishes of the deceased family member. Four specifically mentioned the burial in a graveyard, something very few people can afford nowadays, given that it can cost more than $US30,000 if the site is in Hong Kong. For this reason, some Hong Kong residents are buying small graveyard sites in mainland China for themselves when they die. Even that typically costs between US$10,000 to US$30,000.

Longevity is regarded as key to a good life. Most of the respondents felt sad that their loved ones did not have a long life. Nineteen of the respondents said their loved ones died too young. Today in Hong Kong, the life expectancy for men is eighty-one years and for women, eighty-four years. However, many families refuse to prepare for death, even when their loved ones are in their seventies and eighties. If they do not prepare for death, there will be regrets among family members due to the unfinished business that they will have to deal with after the death of their loved one.[11]

"Letting Go" and "Holding On" in Traditional Chinese Death Rituals

Over the centuries, the Chinese have developed an elaborate and well-defined system for mourning the dead, especially their parents.[12–14] It would be an enormous task indeed to go through all the stages and actions involved and to analyse their effect on the grieving process. Here, we call attention to three ideas that appear therapeutically significant, in the hope that a fuller treatment of the material will be made in the future. These three ideas include achieving separation from the deceased by active involvement in the examination and preparation of the body of the deceased, detachment from contamination but attachment to blessings and virtuous practice, and accomplishing separation from and continuity of the relationship to the deceased by actively pursuing the transformation of the deceased.

Personal Involvement Facilitates Separation

For Worden,[1] seeing the corpse with one's own eyes, whether at home or in the hospital, positively reinforces the knowledge that the death of the beloved is real and final. According to Confucian traditions,[13,15] the bereaved, normally the eldest son, confirms the death of the deceased by placing new silk in his or her nostril. When death is confirmed, he takes a coat previously worn by the deceased and goes out of the house or up to the roof and waves it in the direction of the ancestral home, calling out the name of the deceased. This act is meant to try to call the soul back. Only when this fails and death is reconfirmed by new silk in the nostril, and by examining the heartbeat and the pulse, are procedures for preparing the funeral formally begun.

It then falls upon a family member to assume the task of preparing the body of the deceased, including shaving the individual and cutting the fingernails and toenails. Generally, if the deceased is male, a male member of the family does this job, and if the deceased is female, a female family member performs it.

Three days after death, the body is dressed up and prepared for the funeral, again by a member of the family. This three-day interval is to avoid any false death. The body is typically placed in a coffin only on the fourth day.

For the bereaved, direct involvement in the examination and preparation of the body has a salutary effect of allowing the bereaved to "let go" of the beloved. It is a personal confirmation of the death of one's beloved. The act of giving such personal caring service for the last time also makes a lasting impression on the consciousness of the bereaved: from then on, the deceased will not be there to receive the same care.

Analysis of the videotapes of clinical interviews of the fifty-two bereaved clients of JTTC indicates that family members remember vividly how the deceased person looked at death. During the bereavement counselling sessions, about half of the respondents (twenty-four) described the facial expression of their deceased loved one. Ten described their loved ones as dying with a peaceful look, but fourteen described the facial expression as pained and agonized. One crucial component of a good death is that individuals die with their eyes closed. If they do not, significant unfinished business must be bothering them.

In order to proceed to a smooth reincarnation, the Chinese believe the deceased must be cleansed and properly clothed. As a population that suffered from starvation, having a full meal before death is also regarded as important, so that the deceased do not become hungry ghosts after their deaths. One-quarter of the respondents (thirteen) mentioned the importance of being present during the moment of death. Almost half of the respondents (twenty-five) described how family members, children, and grandchildren gathered around the sickbed during the moment of death. This is seen as a necessary component of a good death, in order for reincarnation to occur. The children who are not around the sickbed when the parents die are seen as "sinners" who fail to fulfil the filial obligations of facilitating their deceased loved one's progress into the afterlife.

Detachment from Deadly Contamination but Attachment to Beneficial Presence

Chinese death rituals have a way of encouraging separation between the living and the dead. For the Chinese, the dead and the living belong to two different worlds. From the moment the deceased is interred, the living and the dead tread different paths. Any direct contact between them is considered contaminating and polluting for both parties. That is why, on their way home from the burial, the living are advised not to turn their head back. It is believed it would be damaging to both the living and the dead, if the living were to see the traces left by the deceased as the person journeyed to the underworld. The living are also supposed to bathe after returning home from burial rituals, in order to cleanse themselves from anything having to do with death.[11]

Generally, the Chinese believe that the deceased assume a transformed, beneficial status only after they have completed purification and are formally installed as an ancestor or become immortal in heaven, with the power to intercede with the gods for the living.

However, not all connections with the dead before they are declared ancestors are considered polluting. For instance, dying a good death, a natural, painless death at old age, is considered a blessing (*fu* 福), often believed to be a result of a life of virtuous practice (*hou de ji fu* 厚德積福). Connections with those who die a good death in turn bring blessings to the living.

In some parts of China, there is a tradition of sharing the bowls or chopsticks of the deceased among family members, if the deceased was over the age of seventy. It means the longevity can now be shared through the things used while the person was alive.

Later, the tradition developed of allowing all the guests invited to the last dinner served by the family in the presence of the deceased to take a bowl or a pair of chopsticks home.[12] Such blessing and virtue are to be shared not with family members alone but with all relatives and friends. This practice relates to the belief in the continuing and beneficial presence of the deceased in the whole community, even before the deceased becomes an ancestor or immortal.

Belief and Participation in the Deceased's Transformation

This positive and self-redeeming aspect for the bereaved in the traditional Chinese farewell ritual is connected with beliefs in life after death and in the efficacy of religious services for the expiation of sins. Here, the living, through participation in religious services, assist the deceased in terminating their relationship with this world and their passage into the next. Spiritual guides offer prayers during the wake and at the funeral as well as burial services. Prayers are also offered every seventh day from the date of death, up to seven times seven, or forty-nine, days.[12]

The number "seven" originates from Buddhist practice.[16] According to Wan,[12] the Buddhists believe that, after the seven seven-day periods are over, the destiny of the reincarnation of the spirit is determined. By then, it is already decided which of the six paths the deceased will take in the next life; for instance, the path of a human being instead of that of an animal. Any additional prayers will not change that decision. But prayers said before the expiration of the forty-nine days might move the deceased to an understanding of dharma so that he or she will repent and so be allowed to take the path of a human being instead of an animal, for instance.

For the Daoists, the number seven is related to their belief that a human being has seven *bo-souls* 魄 (at death these earthly *bo-souls* return to the underworld, as distinguished from the heavenly *hun-souls* 魂 that return to heaven. For an explanation of *hun-souls* and *bo-souls* see Lai C.T.'s[6] following chapter of this book. Every seven days after a person dies, a *bo* leaves the body. After forty-nine days, all the *bo* will have left. During this period, it is crucial that family members make sure that certain prayers are said to help the deceased repent, accomplish purification, and reach immortality before all seven *bo* have dissipated from the body.[12]

The forty-ninth day is traditionally an important day of separation. On this day, called the day for "the breaking of seven", relatives and friends are invited to a ceremony. A religious team (including the master 道士 and musicians) sets up an altar and pray, and attention this time is given to the living. Prayers are said for the repentance of the living and the cleansing of the house. After the tune played to the melody of peace (太平樂) is over, there comes the high point of the termination of mourning: the bereaved persons burn their mourning clothes and change back into ordinary clothing, to mark an end to the mourning period.[12]

Some families have religious experts pray on the 100th day[15] after the death of the deceased, at the end of which the picture of the deceased is formally put up alongside the pictures of other ancestors. For these individuals, this marks the end of the mourning period. From then on, the deceased has reached a new stage and begins to relate to family members in a new way.

Whether people mourn for 49 days or 100 days, for one year or three years, this period provides a timeframe for the mourning process, with the belief in the possibility of the transformation of the deceased into an immortal providing hope to the living. Prayer services provide the means through which the bereaved can achieve both separation from and continuity of relationship with the deceased, after he or she has gained the status of an immortal.

Continuation of a Tradition

Contemporary Hong Kong is very different from the society of imperial China politically, socially, culturally, and religiously. Even causes of death today in Hong Kong are different from those about fifty years ago, when people were still struggling to survive after the Second World War. Today, along with improved living conditions and health facilities, a decline in the mortality rate, and an increase in life expectancy, fewer people die of war, natural disaster, and plague than from aging, environmental pollution, pressures from crowded living conditions, unemployment, poverty, and accidents, as well as from problematic lifestyles that include smoking, insufficient physical activity, over- or under-eating, over-consumption of alcohol, drug dependence, reckless driving, suicide, and insufficient sleep.[17] The world has indeed changed, but tradition continues, including the tradition of observing death rituals.

Connect in Order to Be Free

Today, the general practice in Hong Kong is not for the family members to get involved but for the medical doctor to examine, confirm, and declare the death of the deceased. Family members, however, continue a tradition of maintaining some kind of connection with the body, making it an important moment for recognizing the reality of death. Being deprived of the opportunity for viewing the body can indeed create problems for some family members.

A lady in her twenties from the Mainland who was married to a Hong Kong man is still struggling with this problem. Her husband hurt his back and came back to Hong Kong for treatment. One day, she spoke on the telephone with her husband and he told her everything was okay. The next day when she called, he had died. By the time her papers were processed and she had made her way to Hong Kong, a month had passed and all the funeral and burial services had been completed, organized and directed by her husband's siblings. She did not even have the opportunity to view his body after he died. Ten years after his death, she still believed that it was not her husband who had died, and she hoped to see him again some day. Seeing, and if possible touching, the body of the deceased are important moments of recognition of death, leading to separation.

There is a ritual in the Daoist service, generally conducted during the wake, called "rites of bathing and dressing".[6] This is a cleansing ceremony that begins the process of purification and restoration. The deceased is cleansed in the waters of the heavenly river, symbolically purchased from the deity of the river. During the ceremony, the eldest son is asked to take a towel made wet by the water, go into the cold room at the back of the hall where the body lies, and clean the face of his parent, while the rest of the descendants kneel in the hall outside This is the gesture of a last caring touch performed by a son to his parent. At the same time, it is probably also the only act that has him come so close to his parent after death. The effect can be very salutary, especially for the son performing it.

> Touch can indeed be healing to the person who touches. One recently bereaved lady in Hong Kong was very grateful that, during the wake, the funeral director allowed her to go into the cold room and take her father's hand when his body was properly dressed and positioned. Being able to hold the hand of her father for the last time and to spend some time talking with him meant a lot to her.
>
> However, one must also notice inherent problems in the authoritarian system that houses the traditional Chinese mourning practice, which, in its inflexible application, may lend itself to forced imposition. Sam, a fearful six-year-old boy, was forced, despite his vigorous crying and struggling, to come face to face with the corpse of his deceased elderly grandfather and to place a coin in his mouth. Forty years later, Sam was still suffering from this childhood trauma of touching the dead body of his grandfather.

There is another tradition still practised today. If the deceased is the wife, the husband is asked to take a flower or jewellery and place it behind her ear as a symbol of adding a last adornment to her beauty. If the deceased is the husband, the wife is asked to break a comb in front of the corpse as a symbol of their going their separate ways and of her freedom in choosing her future path in remarriage. This is done particularly when the wife is young. Of course, the wife can choose to stay a widow, but the practice is a symbol of the freedom she enjoys.

This ritual grew out of Chinese legend in which a loving husband is said to comb the hair of his wife every morning and evening in a gesture of intimacy, and the tradition is continued to this day in Hong Kong. From the JTTC tapes, widows and widowers are reported to have gone through similar experiences, often feeling emotionally ambiguous. Eight of the respondents mentioned this ritual and indicated they performed it with great reluctance. If they did not perform the ritual, they were afraid they could not remarry because spousal obligations had not officially ended. If they performed the ritual, they felt they had betrayed their marital commitment to the recently deceased spouse.

This ritual of having the bereaved directly perform the last act to or in front of the deceased, in the form of a caring service such as adding a last adornment or breaking a comb in front of the husband's corpse, or stuffing rice in the mouth, is inherently Confucian. This belief might be verbalized as, "Treat your loved ones who die as if they were still alive". While fostering recognition of death, they can also be profoundly connecting (between the bereaved and the deceased) and freeing (for the bereaved) for new life and/ or from traditional bondage.

Assist in Transformation, Say Goodbye, and Prepare for New Relationships

The essence of traditional Daoist ritual is preserved during the wake. It involves beliefs in the connection between this life and the next and an exchange between the living and the dead, as well as religious services performed by the living for the dead.

"Attack on hell"[6] is normally the most dramatic and moving scene of the Daoist service during the wake. Here, the eldest son of the deceased is asked to carry in one hand a tablet on which is written the name of the deceased, and in the other hand a banner to lead the way for the spirit of the deceased. The eldest son follows the religious expert as he makes his rounds and as he uses his sword to break, one by one, the nine gates of hell represented by nine pieces of clay. Often the eldest son is followed in line by the other descendants, in the order of proximity of their relationship to the deceased, as they accompany the deceased in the descent into the underworld. Then the religious expert takes the tablet and, in a dramatic move, with the tablet in his hand, jumps over a pool of fire. Symbolically, the spirit of the deceased is now purified and freed from the torments of hell.

This is one of the few rituals in which all those who are present to mourn the death are given an opportunity to participate. This is usually done to the clang of cymbals or other musical accompaniment and is perceived to be the most critical ritual in transforming the deceased into an ancestor and an immortal. As Hill[18] aptly puts it: "The soul cannot be left among the living, and it is incumbent upon the descendants to see that the soul is assisted through the underworld. Only then can the soul make its way to heaven or be reborn".

The next ceremony worth noting in this respect is "untying the knots".[6] This is to symbolically disentangle the deceased from any knot or debt tied up in worldly relationships. The religious expert puts together forty-nine coins and forty-nine buttons and then separates them, symbolizing the deceased person's extrication from all incurred hatred and vengeance. No longer entangled with people and things of this world, the spirit of the deceased is now free to move on to heavenly bliss.

The ceremony most symbolic of saying farewell is called "crossing the bridge".[6] Here, the eldest son carries the tablet and the banner. He follows the religious expert and crosses the bridge of gold, silver, and helplessness. Symbolically, this is where the spirit of the deceased departs from this world and from the loved ones. This is where the journey to heaven begins. Having crossed the river, the spirit does not return.

These rituals are indeed charged with meaning, and they contain all the major ingredients of a traditional religious service that deals with complex relational issues with the deceased. They reflect a fundamental belief in life after death, and the communion of the human spirit with heavenly gods and immortals. The rituals also offer family members, especially the eldest son, direct participation in the process. He experientially "witnesses" the release of the deceased's spirit from the bondage of hell, its being assisted to repentance and dissolution from all past entanglements with this world, its passage over the bridge, and finally its being taken to heaven. The well-being of the deceased is ensured, and it is determined that the spirit of the deceased has vanished from this world. It will not come back to haunt the family but will ascend to heaven and intercede for the survivors in front of gods and other immortals. Symbolically, in one religious service, both transformation and separation are accomplished, and a new relationship with the deceased is made possible.

Again from the JTTC tapes, half of the respondents (twenty-six) described the attendance at the funeral, and of them, nineteen felt that attending the funeral was a positive experience for them. Thirteen respondents described the ritual of burning paper money and other offerings in detail. Eight expressed being consoled in participating in rituals that help the deceased progress to the land of eternal happiness.

Confirmation of Death: Personal and Social Dimensions

The visit of relatives and friends to pay their last respects to the deceased is also a continuation of tradition. In Hong Kong today, this normally takes place in a rented hall in a funeral parlour, either the day before the funeral or on the same day as the funeral but before it begins. Customarily, one is allowed to pay respects to the deceased by going to the cold room at the back of the hall where the corpse lies. One can stand outside the glass window and observe a moment of silence. There are often seats in the hall for friends to sit for some time, to keep company with the deceased and with the family.

Unlike some places in China where people seldom talk about the dead, in order to avoid the impression that they have those kinds of preoccupation or knowledge, given the proximity of the corpse,[18] here in Hong Kong, this is not a taboo subject. Family members tend to offer information to close friends and relatives relating to the condition of the deceased before and at the moment of death.

This behaviour of talking "about" the deceased and explaining to relatives and friends the circumstances and causes of death takes the act of confirming the death of the deceased from a personal level to one of social discourse. This knowledge concerning the death is now held not just by the bereaved alone but by a community of relatives and friends.

In one clinical session from the JTTC tapes, many of the fifty-two bereaved persons brought up what had happened in the funeral, including the type of funeral, and the completion and separation ceremonies. The majority of them had traditional funerals (eighteen), whereas fewer than one-tenth had Catholic or Protestant funerals in churches (seven). The overwhelming majority of those who had a religious funeral reported that the funeral rituals were helpful to them in their bereavement process. Seventeen out of eighteen had a traditional ritual with chanting by monks; five out of seven had a Christian funeral. They felt they were doing something "useful" for their deceased loved one through performing the necessary rituals, or what they considered to be "doing the right thing".

The Hero's Shedding of Mourning Clothes

In Hong Kong, according to Colette Lai, the shedding of mourning clothes is usually carried out at the graveyard immediately after the burial. This is called "the hero's shedding of mourning clothes". The idea is clear: from now on, there will be no more mourning. Previous to this, at the graveyard, family members are asked to cross over a pool of fire and to wash their hands in water immersed with pomelo leaves. This is to keep away anything ghostly and deadly that might come their way.

These rituals of thorough cleansing and the burning of clothes might have developed from traditional wisdom relating to control of infectious diseases. After this is over, some families immediately invite the religious experts home, to "warm" their house, to drive away unwelcome spirits, and to prepare for the deceased's ascending to the rank of ancestors.

For this last ritual, a colour picture of the deceased in ceramic is often used, instead of the black and white photograph for the funeral. As there is no more mourning, this is not part of the funerary service. This is called "good" service.

After the burial, all participants who came to pay their respects to the deceased are invited to a longevity meal, which usually takes place at a Chinese restaurant. Normally, a seven-course menu of simple food is prepared for the funeral party. The Cantonese name for the longevity banquet is *jie wei jiu* 解穢酒, meaning "wine that washes away the unclean". This is also a symbolic way of confirming the definite departure of the dead and the end of mourning. It is a final farewell to the deceased and a return to a life of normalcy.

Hong Kong's version of "the hero's shedding of mourning clothes" and having the whole mourning process end at burial is executed in typical Hong Kong style, with speed, precision, and efficiency. Whether and how much it facilitates or hinders the grieving process is a question to be discussed.

Mementos

The practice in some parts of China of distributing the utensils previously used by the deceased to the family or to relatives and friends is not common in Hong Kong. In fact, the Cantonese are especially concerned about the polluting powers of the dead and the bad air that contaminates all who come under its influence.[6] People give or throw away practically everything (except money, property and jewellery, of course) that belonged to the deceased, including clothing and utensils, and sometimes even the bed the deceased used to sleep on.

There is a certain fear of being exposed to or connected to the dead. That is why some people are reluctant to attend the funeral service even of close relatives.[6] Many turn their backs on the coffin whenever it is moved, afraid that the jostling of the corpse might release its ghostly soul to cause them misfortune. This applies to the Chinese in Chiang Mai, Thailand,[15] as well as to people in Hong Kong.

However, not everything connected with the dead is shunned. Taking home a photograph of the deceased and having it placed prominently in the living room is probably the most significant and conspicuous way of keeping alive the memory of the deceased, although this sometimes may pose other problems (discussed in the next section).

Funeral directors are also accustomed to giving, in a red envelope, the knobs of the coffin nails to the eldest son in the family at the end of the burial service. This custom of receiving the knobs of coffin nails is called *jie shou tou* 接壽頭, or "receiving the heads of longevity". It is believed that the older the deceased, the more these knobs are considered auspicious in bringing blessings to the descendants. Generally, people keep them close to the ancestral tablets at home.

Colette Lai told us what she does with the silk banners left by family members and relatives who use them to decorate the funeral hall and to express their sentiments of loss of the deceased. After the funeral service is over, Lai collects and gives them to elderly persons who have no money. This shows that, although such items are traditionally meant to be used by the family after the rituals are over and are in fact considered auspicious, especially if the deceased is an elderly person, many families simply leave them behind.

Apart from the photograph and the "longevity knobs," we have not found other parts in the traditional death rituals practised in Hong Kong that encourage a continuity of relationship between the bereaved and the deceased. This is obviously an area worthy of further study.

Emerging Developments

It seems that traditional funeral services currently practised in Hong Kong are not directed towards dealing with psychological matters relating to grief and loss. Traditionally, there was a process, and "letting go" was handled in stages. When the process ended, from between seven weeks to three years, most of the major concerns involved had already been dealt with. Now, everything is simplified and shortened. The global market economy provides little room for grieving, and people are expected to return to normal working life within a week, or at most two.

Colette Lai admitted that a lot of counselling needs to be done outside the rituals. She herself has been involved in some counselling sessions. This indicates that, in order to meet their emotional needs, people are resorting to means outside of rituals.

What major problems do people encounter with funeral rituals and the modern process of mourning? What experiences do people have? What can we learn from their experiences? Can some of their experiences be processed and incorporated into the funeral rituals, making them more sensitive and responsive to the needs of people today?

We are certain that many innovations are taking place within and outside of the profession. Here, we highlight a few of those that we know of, hoping this introduction will be followed up by broader and more in-depth studies:

The Unspoken Meeting before the Final Departure

A man lost his wife after twenty years of marriage and grieved for more than fifteen years thereafter. During all that time, he kept her ashes by his bedside and allowed no one, including his children, to talk about her in his presence. His inability to deal adequately with letting go and to maintain a healthy bond with his deceased wife also deprived the children of the continuing presence of their mother.

There are, however, people who creatively adapt traditional rituals to enable remembrance of and intimacy with the departed beloved. Bereavement counsellors at JTTC helped children reconstruct family photos by cutting and pasting or by using computer software. Writing letters, letting go of balloons, and sending messages through fish and birds are also intimate and socially acceptable ways to enable continuous communication.

There is a traditional belief that the spirit of the dead comes home to the family on specific days after death occurred, and family members traditionally prepare for this return.[19] According to Lai, experts can calculate, after a person is dead, the date and time the spirit will return home to see the family for the last time. On that day, family members traditionally prepare three cups of tea, three bowls of rice, three cups of wine, a plate of vegetarian food, sweets, and any special dish the deceased person liked. Then, they just stay home. The idea is to make the spirit feel comfortable in the knowledge that everyone in the family is conducting life normally and happily.

After her own mother-in-law died, Lai arranged for the whole family to be present. They played mah-jong and had a meal together. This was what her mother-in-law enjoyed most when she was alive, and this was what they prepared for her on the day of her return, to give her warmth and a sense of comfort in the knowledge that they were all living well, so that she could depart to the next world with little or no worry.

The mother of Grace Cheung, co-author, died some years ago.* She shared fond memories of how her father, a native of Ning Bo 寧波, gathered all the children together on the first three seventh days after his wife's death. He chatted with his children about events relating to the deceased, how he met her, how they got married, and interesting episodes between them. It was an effort to give to the returning spirit a sense of her being fondly remembered by her family, gathering in unity and harmony under the leadership of the father. It was also an expression of a desire for continuing communication with the deceased, as well as an attempt to appease her spirit, so that she could now go in peace, with no more worries.

In both cases, there was a great deal of intimacy as the family gathered together for the sake of the deceased. In both cases, there was also an unspoken but intimate contact between the deceased and the rest of the family. Moreover, this deeply felt, unspoken meeting was understood to be the final one between the returning spirit and the other members of the family. The connection experienced was not a "holding on" to someone about to depart. It was a connection in preparation for "letting go".

---

* Grace Cheung is one of the authors of this chapter. Many of the clinical case illustrations cited in this paper are stories from her clients and workshop participants.

Happy Memories Bind Joyful Relationships

A Chinese custom keeps the black and white photo of the deceased used for the funeral service in the home after the burial service as a manifestation of mournful remembrance.

Hill[18] reported an elaborate practice still prevalent among some wealthy Chinese families in Chiang Mai, Thailand. The portrait of the family's most recently deceased linear ancestor and/or his wife is hung at home for the first forty-nine days after death. Offerings are made to the deceased on an altar in front of the portrait every seventh day. During this time, portraits of other ancestors are covered in red paper, to protect them from the bad luck of the most recent death. Then, for three years, offerings to the recently deceased are made on the first and the fifteenth days of each month. At the end of the three years, the portrait of the recently deceased person is hung with other ancestral portraits and, with the others, is given an offering on the death anniversary.

In Hong Kong, for most families, mourning ritually stops after the burial. However, people do arrange to have a photo of the recently deceased prominently displayed in their home. This shows, to the deceased as well as to visiting relatives and friends, that the deceased is remembered and still occupies an important position in the family. However, some survivors, especially young ones, report having uneasy feelings and sometimes even fear that they have to face such pictures, especially when at home alone.

Quietly and without much fanfare, funeral directors are introducing some changes in cultural practices regarding the handling of the funeral photo. In Lai's description, the picture used for funerary services is usually black and white, not finely touched up, and is often just mounted in a black frame. When asked, funeral consultants often advise that this be burned immediately after the burial service. Then, if they want, families can keep a colour picture of the deceased. To those who want to take the black and white photo home, they advise that the frame be changed from black to one of a brighter colour. They also recommend that they use red paper to wrap the photo and keep it home for a period of not more than 100 days (or any auspicious number of days, such as 68, 78, or 88) before putting it up alongside the photos of other ancestors. This is an interesting example of how funeral directors can intervene in effective and beneficial ways in mourning practices and facilitate psychological healing, not through grand theoretical formulations but in living cultural practice and in people's emotionally most vulnerable moments.

Twenty-five years ago, when her mother was sixty, co-author Cecilia Chan asked a friend to take pictures of her mother. One very beautiful colour picture was made into fibreglass to be used for her mother's funeral hall. Her mother had also appeared on television twice to talk about death and the funeral she desired. Her in-laws also made colour pictures for their own funeral hall.

Similar changes are taking place through family counsellors. Grace shared the story of a forty-year-old lady who had three members of her family die within a period of three months. She had three black and white photographs lined up on the central wall of her living room, all honoured by burning candles. The sight was gloomy, and home was not a place this lady wanted to be. Facing those pictures by herself every evening after work was something she wanted to avoid. Grace asked if she would like to put up colour pictures to remind herself of the presence of these three beloved persons in her life. The lady said yes. Eventually, she put away all the black and white photographs and had them replaced with colour ones, picturing the deceased (and the lady herself, in some of the pictures) in ordinary situations, including birthdays and trips. For her, remembrance began to take on colour.

We checked with Colette Lai to see if there was any cultural taboo associated with such circumstances regarding the use of colour pictures and figuring both the deceased and the living in the same picture. She said she was not aware of any. Speaking from her experience, she agreed that this was a good practice.

"Memory binds family and communities together."[21] A small change can bring about important shifts in feeling and in cultural attitudes. Pictures that bring back happy memories can foster intimate relationships. Such pictures are far preferable to those that bring an aura of coldness, austerity, and fear.

Saying Goodbye Lovingly Makes a Long-term Difference

Many see their loved one for the last time before he or she dies and do not know what to say, when in such moments it seems so much needs to be said. Often, individuals feel compelled to say something against their knowledge and reason, like, "Don't worry, you will get well soon," or "No, you are not going to die. You want to see your grandson who will be born by the end of this year, right?"

Here we want to share Ka Hing's experience before his mother died several years ago, at the age of eighty-six. All her sons and daughters, except one, managed to be at her side before she died, and every one was able to talk to her, each in his or her own way. The one who could not make it to Canada, where she was hospitalized, communicated with her by telephone. Four words were common to all: "Thank you" and "I'm sorry". "Thank you" for the love received from her, and "I'm sorry" for anything hurtful that was done to her. This was not a task easily accomplished, because "Thank you" and "I'm sorry" were not often used in this family. Saying those magic farewell words to their mother at her deathbed was the greatest gift Ka Hing and his siblings were able to give to her, and to themselves.

Saying goodbye lovingly can be done in many more ways, and does not have to be done only at the deathbed. There is now among the people of Hong Kong a greater consciousness that it might be better to treat elderly people kindly while they are still alive than to give them a big funeral after they die. Today, people are more ready to do more for elderly people, such as going on vacation with them, being concerned about their habits relating to smoking, exercise, and diet, and saying "Thank you" and "I'm sorry" on their own terms, while these people are still around. This is the best gift they can give to the elderly people and to themselves, before they say a final goodbye. This is also a way to create many happy memories for a future when the elderly beloved person will no longer be physically present.

Death Rituals for the Living

Today we attend the funerals of our loved ones. Someday, other loved ones will attend our funeral. Very few people ever think of preparing their own funerals. For those who do, it can be the most transformative experience they ever have.

Grace shared with us some of her experiences in the workshops that she conducts on life and death. In one session, participants took turns lying inside a makeshift coffin while the others talked to them as if they were dead. One participant, Miss Yang, searched her memory trying to identify the things she did and said and the kind of impressions she might have left on others during the workshop. Then, as people began to talk, she was deeply moved and she wanted to thank them. As she was supposed to be dead and wasn't allowed to say anything, she felt a strong sense of regret. "There is so much I want to do and say," she said to herself, "but now, all is too late...When I 'come back' to life, I know what I want to do. I want to be more expressive of my appreciation for and concern of others, while I and others are still alive."

Another participant, Ms Lee, also wrote about her discovery: "When I composed my own epitaph, I constantly asked myself what it is that really matters when one comes to the terminal point of life. I think I will not try to pursue hitherto unfulfilled expectations. I will identify my needs and reset priorities for my life. Death is no longer to be feared. What is to be feared is to live as if I were already dead. Not knowing what I live for makes me fear all the more".

Our lives are often taken up by trivial earthly concerns. We are not present even to ourselves. "How can I touch you if you are not there?" asks Luce Irigaray, French feminist and philosopher.[21] Preparing our own funeral can facilitate the process of our becoming present, for ourselves as well as for others, and especially for the dying.

Discussion

Based on the pieces we have selected for presentation and discussion, we have the following concluding comments:

1. Saying goodbye with a caring touch is critically important. One of the most powerful traditional farewell rituals is the use of face-to-face, hand-to-body contact to examine the body of the deceased and to call for a return of the soul to the deceased. In Hong Kong, one is not expected to follow this tradition, but thanks to religious people, this final symbolic act of caring, which has also proved to be effective in preparing for the termination of a relationship while staying intimately connected, is still somewhat preserved in our rituals today.

   However, to be meaningful, touch has to be executed voluntarily, with adequate knowledge and awareness. Given certain prevailing excessive practices, our question is this: are there ways of providing a final ritual of caring to the deceased at different degrees of closeness, taking into consideration the emotional and cognitive associations that people generally have towards corpses?

2. Separation from, transformation of, and continuity of the relationship with the deceased are vital. The traditional Chinese death ritual emphasizes separation, but a separation that heralds a relationship with the deceased at a new level. Before the spirit of the deceased is immortalized or reincarnated, it is considered to belong to the world of the dead and is regarded with more fear and apprehension than with a sense of intimacy. There is a certain separation between the two worlds, in the sense that one world must not be contaminated by the other. When, however, the spirit is immortalized, when mourning is over and the time has come for "good service", connection is encouraged. That is why, although the death rituals themselves do not preclude continuity, there is little or no activity during the funeral services that directly and positively encourage a continuity of relationship between the bereaved and the deceased. Transformation has to happen in the state of being of the deceased, before connection is pursued. Unfortunately, this process of transformation is presented in a predominantly religious language that few people fully understand. This brings us to the next point.

3. It is unfortunate that the religious funeral service as practised is couched in the language of the Daoist religion and is alien to most twenty-first century cosmopolitan Hong Kong people. Furthermore, it is generally not explained before or during the service. Anthropologists like Hill,[18] who have attended traditional Chinese funeral services and asked participants and hosts to explain to them the meaning of those rituals, often get a typical answer: "I don't know. This is what we've always done".

People generally have a vague idea about the actions performed during the funerary rituals, but they usually cannot follow the prayers. For many, there is little understanding and maybe little desire to know more. As a result, a hitherto meaningful and enriching cultural and religious tradition that used to contribute to the mourning process seems to have become the best kept secret guarded by religious experts. The transformative power of the ritual is imprisoned within the system of religious symbols, unable to reach the family and relatives who are powerless and absorbed in grief. Our question is: has the problem to do with people themselves, who are so overwhelmed by materialistic concerns as to allow no room at all for matters relating to death and life? Or, are they put off and kept away from the mystery of death and life by the language and aura maintained by the funeral industry and the religious experts? Or, do they simply dismiss the whole ritual as a show or as superstition and in effect discard what is good about the ritual?

4. Simplify, but keep the process aspect of tradition. Traditional Chinese death rituals fully recognize that mourning is a process that takes time. In practice, the minimum period of mourning is forty-nine days, but the norm is three years for mourning the death of a parent. (Throughout most of Chinese imperial history, the state expected strict observance of the three-year mourning period from ministers and senior officials more than from commoners.[23]

   Here we are not defending or trying to revive the traditional system. Our focus is on the *process*. In Hong Kong, the increasingly popular phenomenon of "the hero shedding mourning clothes" immediately after burial allows little room for the process of grieving. The pre- and post-burial ritual is so simplified and shortened that mourning rituals are over in one or two weeks, before individuals are even fully aware of the event and its significance. Our question is: to what extent does the premature termination of mourning on the level of rituals affect the psychological process that is just about to begin? What do people do when they find themselves continued to be gripped by serious emotional matters relating to the death event after attending all the mourning rituals and services, including the "good service"? Do the bereaved feel socially unaccepted, when mourning is ritually and formally pronounced passé, if they continue to be in a mournful mood and to act sad? Is their grief disenfranchised? These are questions worth exploring.

5. Can we create a more responsive industry? In Japan, as reviewed by Rupp,[24] as a response to the market, the funeral industry came up with innovative programmes, one of which was to assist host families in constructing eulogies to beautify the deceased's life; to honour the contributions; to

appreciate the person's kindness, generosity, and social achievements; and to learn from his or her good deeds.

The industry also introduced a new service, the ritualized bathing of the deceased. Bathing the corpse was traditionally an act of purification. The new ceremony emphasizes bathing as an ordinary, relaxing activity that the deceased is now offered the last opportunity to enjoy, in the presence of the family. This innovation and sensitivity to the needs of the clientele seem to be markedly in contrast to what is mechanically being practised here in Hong Kong.

An interesting observation is that more and more young people are now joining the industry in Hong Kong as funeral directors and musicians. This may have to do with rising unemployment rates in recent years, but our question is: how can the funeral industry train its workforce to raise its standard of service and respond to the needs of its clientele? Will dialogue and innovation happen only when they are critically challenged, either by innovative newcomers to the industry who in time create a big enough influence, or by the public who become so generally disenchanted by their practice that they begin en masse to look for alternatives?

6. The strong impetus on the part of the bereaved to arrange for religious services to be conducted for the ultimate objective of immortalizing or reincarnating the spirit of the deceased is not well understood today. This idea can probably be traced to the Confucian idea of filial piety and/or to the belief in the ideas of cross-generation retribution and of exchange between the dead and the living.

For the Chinese, the sins of ancestors not expiated can have damaging consequences for their descendants in this world. Also, for the Chinese, happiness is perceived collectively. The destinies of family members merge, and the union is not disrupted by death. The liberation and happiness of the deceased becomes the liberation and happiness of the bereaved. Consequently, the intense involvement of the bereaved in the immortalization or reincarnation of the deceased benefits not only the deceased in the underworld or in the next world but also all of his or her descendants living in this world.

Our problem is this: traditional rituals persist, but the world and people's ideas have changed. Traditional contexts of action have been evacuated[25] or disembedded.[26] If the active concern of the bereaved for the well-being of the deceased is so much grounded in the idea of exchange between the living and the dead, how can this be made intelligible and acceptable to Hong Kong people who do not share such a traditional worldview? This, we consider, is an even more fundamental question than those raised above.

7.   There is something in traditional Chinese death rituals that contributes to the process of "letting go" and "holding on". Our question is: has this tradition become a relic? Is there a possibility of transformation for it to become a living heritage? If so, where is the locus of transformation?

Given a tradition that is today to a substantial degree oversimplified, dis-embedded, misunderstood, and unresponsive, where do we look for the transformation that is needed on the part of the bereaved to move from abandoning a worldly relationship to developing a new relationship between two parties in two different worlds?

For us, the answer lies in people's practices, especially those by conscientious and innovative individuals, families, religious persons, professionals, entrepreneurs, and communities. These practices must seek to discover new ways of saying goodbye, of connecting not only to separate but also to prepare for a new kind of connection: creating happy memories for the future rather than merely remembering happy memories from the past.

The answer also lies in practices of remembrance that transform occasions of anxiety and fear, which bring absence and consequently separation, into occasions of unspoken encounters filled with joy, intimacy, and colour.

The answer also lies in the practices of people who make life present by anticipating death, thereby making death an occasion for life, and separation an occasion for connection. It is in such practices that we find a connection between "letting go" and "holding on", between separation and continuity of relationship. It is also in such practices that transformation takes place.

5

Making Peace with the Unknown: A Reflection on Daoist Funerary Liturgy

Chi Tim LAI

Introduction

Daoism, or *daojiao* 道教 remains a central part of the daily life of the Chinese people in Hong Kong. The term "Daoism" has different connotations and content for scholars as well as believers in Daoism, including aspects relating to philosophical mysticism, mythology, immortals, nourishing life, meditation, and liturgies.[1] Daoism, in this chapter, is seen as a religious and liturgical institution profoundly rooted in the social life of local Chinese communities.

From Ming Dynasty (1368–1644) times on, Daoism comprised two main schools: that of the Orthodox Unity (*Zhengyi* 正一), passed on hereditarily since the end of Han Dynasty in the second century A.D.; and that of the School of Total Perfection (*Quanzhen* 全真). The latter school practised inner alchemy and was based on the Buddhist model in monastic communities.[2] The Zhengyi School fostered local communities and temple organizations and provided them with their liturgical framework and ritual specialists.[3]

It has always been thought that the ultimate Daoist principle is nourishing life (*yangsheng* 養生). Given the instance of the *Scripture of Great Peace* (*Taiping jing* 太平經), one of the most important Daoist texts of the Eastern Han Dynasty (25–220 A.D.), Daoism understands the Dao as pertaining to life but not death.[4] The scripture maintains that the fundamental belief in the Dao is its imperative in directing people towards life, i.e., nourishing, prolonging, and protecting the lives of all beings and all things in their natural course of development. Not surprisingly, Daoism claims, "A dead prince is not worth a live rat". Daoism can therefore be considered as a religion greatly concerned with life (*guisheng* 貴生). It is dedicated to the cultivation and prolongation of the human body and to becoming *xian*-transcendent (仙). In imperial China, Daoist masters were often connected with the practice of cultivation of life with a quest for a prolongation of physical life (*zhuiqui changsheng* 追求長生), understood as the perfection of the human body (*busi* 不死). So, some scholars of Daoism hold the view that the very heart of Daoist thought lies in its unique teaching on the fundamental role of the human body.[5]

Nevertheless, not simply pursuing long life and *xian*-transcendence, but mourning and care of the dead have long played a dominant role in Daoism. The emphasis on the salvation of the dead in the netherworld remains a central concern in Daoist funerary services. The most important part of the Daoist funerary services is the "Retreat" (*zhai* 齋), through which the living seek to accumulate "merit" (*gongde* 功德) for the benefit of the dead, by recitation from the sacred scriptures (*songjing* 誦經) and penitential litanies (*baichan* 拜懺). This is why funerary rituals today are generally called "rituals of merit" (*gongde fashi* 功德法事). In this chapter, I examine the psycho-religious meaning of Daoist funerary services. I ask what the role of the service is in alleviating the grief and bereavement of mourners.

The Problems of Death and the Identity of the Dead

The unfortunate likelihood of loss of life ensures that every generation bears the burden of losing many known and unknown lives before their time. Not only do we encounter timely deaths, but in this day and age we seem endlessly bombarded with reminders of untimely deaths. The parade of casualties from fire, flood, typhoon, tsunami, traffic accidents, earthquakes, war, and ethnic conflicts all leave us shocked with the immediate question about the meaning of life and death.

Fatalities make us realize that the moment of separation has arrived. The experience of loss of life and commemoration of the deceased not only call for mourning the dead but also force us to think about the "unknown", such as the identity of the dead and the relationship between the living and the dead.

Needless to say, knowing the "unknown" is culturally and religiously bound in different traditions. There is no absolute or universal truth about the meaning of life and death that can be accepted by all people in all ages. Given this understanding, the human need to make the unknown knowable is a common urge to know the identity of the dead, to re-establish the relationship between the living and the dead, and to enable one to live with thoughts of death, including the death of others and of our own death.

Yu Ying-shih (余英時), in his essay "O Soul, Come Back!" explicates a system of ancient Chinese beliefs concerning the human souls, *hun* 魂 and *bo* 魄, as well as their survival after death.[6] According to Yu, the fundamental belief of the Han Chinese in an afterlife includes: 1) When the *hun*-soul separates from the *bo*-soul and leaves the human body, life comes to an end,[6-8] and 2) At death, the heavenly *hun*-soul immediately returns to heaven and the earthly *bo*-soul returns to earth or the so-called underworld below. Based upon this Chinese conception of human souls, Yu shows that the burial objects of silk paintings, for example, which were found well preserved in the tombs at Ma-wang-dui, either functioned to summon the departed *hun*-soul of the dead or depicted the *hun*-soul's journey to Heaven. There is a different view. Wu[9] argues against Yu Ying-shih's view by stipulating that the ritual of the "summons of the soul" 招魂 functioned as a "final [healing] effort of the living to revive the life of a family member who had just ceased to breathe and seemed to be dead". Seidel[10] studied Han funeral texts but found that "[T]he souls do not separate at death but *hun* and *bo* together descend into the mountain netherworld. We are far from the literati theories about the spirit soul 魂 soaring up into space while the vitality 魄 lingering with the corpse descends into the tomb".

In addition to the above soul-concepts of *hun* and *po*, *gui* 鬼 is the Chinese character that is applied to devise the identity of the dead. For instance, the *Book of Rites* (Liji 禮記) has explicitly explained the origin of *gui*, saying, "When a person dies, he/she is called a *gui*" (*rensi weigui* 人死為鬼).[11] Although other spirits of 100 beings (*baiwu zhijing* 百物之精) could also be called *gui*, *gui*-ghost, in the *Book of Rites*, specifically refers to human ghost (*rengui* 人鬼).

Chinese people believe that death does not end the relationship between the living and the dead. This is partly due to the Chinese belief that "repayment" (*baoying* 報應) does not end with the death. Also, Chinese people widely believe that the ghost of the dead in the netherworld would influence, or even intervene in, the fate and fortune of the living.[7,12] The ghosts of the departed would inflict much misfortune and suffering upon living family members. This is especially true if the deceased's misdeeds and troubles during life could not be successfully eliminated from the punishment determined by the celestial gods.

One of the common misfortunes presumably inflicted upon the living by the ghosts of the dead when indicted in the netherworld is the suffering of the living from a terrifying array of diseases and epidemics.[13] The sickness caused and transmitted by the corpse (*shizhu* 尸注), the [evil] spirits (*jingzhu* 精注), or the demons (*guizhu* 鬼注) is interpreted as the return and activities of those troubled ghosts of the dead.[14] Relating to this belief, the *Taiping jing* says, "When the demon of the corpse is furnishing (*shuigui daxing* 尸鬼大興), it brings diseases and harm to the human, and inflicts many strange or calamitous phenomena (*zaibian guaiyi* 災變怪異)."[15] The avenging spirits of the dead (*ligui* 厲鬼) might also have the supernatural power to haunt the living. *Gunhui* 孤魂, desolate souls, who, due to the circumstances of their demise, are not cared for, deprived of offering, and are thus forgotten, go "hungry" and perhaps create problems for the living.

The above religious belief of the transmission of the evils of the dead to the living is in line with Daoism.[16] The *Taiping jing* uses the term the "inheritance of sins" *chengfu* 承負, which continues and grows over generations. Accordingly, the doctrine of *chengfu* is defined as follows:

Cheng 承 refers to "before" and *fu* 負 to "after." *Cheng* means that the ancestors originally acted in accordance with the will of heaven, and then slowly lost it; after a long time had elapsed, [their mistakes] had amassed and those of today living afterwards, then through no guilt of their own succeed to [the formers'] mistakes (*guo* 過) and culpability (*zhe* 謫) and so continuously suffer from the catastrophes engendered by them. Therefore, that which is before is *cheng* and that which is afterwards is *fu*. *Fu* means that the various catastrophes do not go back to the government of the one man but to a successive lack of balance. Those who live before put a burden on the back of those who come later. This is why it is called *fu*. *Fu* means that the ancestor puts a burden on the descendent.[15]

In this regard, the doctrine of *chengfu* is used to account for the connection of the misery, suffering and calamities received by the current generation with the evil deeds committed by the ancestors, who put the burden on the backs of their descendants.[17–19] The origin of *chengfu* primarily links with intra-family transmission.[a] Given the communal aspects of the inheritance of troubles, *chengfu* as an explanation of reception and transmission of sins of the past not simply morally lays all the blame at the feet of previous generations, but more importantly, it reminds the listeners of their individual responsibility that "individual behaviour will increase the burden of misery transmitted to the latter generations [as well as to the previous generation]".[19]

Daoist Death Liturgy of Eliminating the Sins of the Dead

How does Daoism, or especially Daoist ritual tradition, provide the means for making peace with the spirits of the dead?

First of all, there is no doubt that Daoism is very concerned about the fate and salvation of the spirits of the dead, whether they have an untimely death or not. The matter of death threatens the equilibrium of human inner psychology and social relationship. But, the Confucian notion that says "caring for the dead is similar to caring for the living" (*shisi ru shisheng* 事死如事生) does not help to combat the anxiety over the "unknown" accompanied with the above beliefs relating to the spirits of the dead in the netherworld. For the Confucians, "the post-mortem locale of the dead" remains obscure. Confucian ideology elaborates no specific notion of a netherworld (*yinjian* 陰間). It does not enunciate any idea that, in caring for the dead, one might be expiating his or her own sins.[20]

---

[a] "The children will receive and transmit (何過承負) the misdeeds of their parents in excess and will sometimes be called children of thieves and of robbers or meet with their own ruin".[15] (Wang M. Taiping jing heijao.Beijing: Chunghua Shuchu, 1960: 251).

In contrast, Daoism is an indigenous Chinese religion that adds imaginative and liturgical strategies in articulating the value of exchange with the dead. Unlike the naturalistic philosophy of Zhuangzi (Chuang-tzu) (莊子), Daoism does not end with any speculative or philosophical thought that simply presumes death as another natural end of the human lifecycle. For instance, Zhuangzi says, "Death and life are destined; that they have the constancy of morning and evening is of Heaven. Everything in which man cannot intervene belongs to the identities of things".[21] In contrast to Zhuangzi, Daoism adds death rituals to summon the dead soul, to deliver it from suffering in the underworld and transform it to a renewal of life.

The Daoist death ritual is performed on behalf of the spirits of the dead. So, it is supposed to represent and visualize the "passage" of the dead from the dark prison of the underworld to the world of the blessed, called *shenxian* (神仙). Moreover, Daoism adds the presumption that, through death rituals, the dead (and, of course, the living) can accumulate merit by recitation of the sacred scriptures and penitential litanies. Daoism provides the death liturgy as a means for the family members to help the dead person to repay long-lasting debts and expiate the sins of the dead. To aid this effort in funeral services, Daoist masters (*daoshi* 道士) are needed. They are trained intermediaries between the heavenly world and the underworld.[5]

Contemporary Daoist Funerary Services in Funeral Halls in Hong Kong

In contemporary Hong Kong, Daoist liturgy constitutes an essential part of the family funeral service. It is estimated that more than fifty funeral services are liturgically conducted in the *Zhengyi* Daoist manner by *nahm mouh* Daoist masters（喃嘸道士）in six funeral halls (殯儀館), Daoist halls (道院), or Daoist temples (道觀) throughout the city. In the past, the Daoist funerary services might last up to several consecutive days and nights. As a result of the great extent of urbanization and secularization in Hong Kong over the past few decades of the twentieth century, many Daoist funeral services now last only half a day.[22]

The most important parts of the *Zhengyi* Daoist funerary services include: (1) Invocation of Daoist gods (*qingsheng* 請聖), (2) Scripture recitation (*songjing* 誦經), (3) Recitation of litanies (*baichan* 拜懺), (4) Attack on hell (*poyu* 破獄), (5) Rites of bathing and dressing (*muyu gengyi* 沐浴更衣), (6) Crossing the bridge (*guoqiao* 過橋), (7) Untying the knots (*jiejie* 解結), and (8) Universal deliverance of hungry ghosts (*pudu gunhui* 普度孤魂).

In contemporary Daoist funerary services, the rite of "attack on hell" is particularly well elaborated and seems to be the focus of the ritual. It represents the deceased soul's deliverance from the dark prisons of the underworld. The "rites of bathing and dressing" indicate the reappearance of the soul in the world of light. Subsequently, the "rite of crossing the bridge" helps the deceased to cross the bridge separating the world of the dead from the universe of happiness and rebirth. On the departure of the deceased from the dark prison of the underworld, he or she receives a pass for the world of the blessed. The goal of the Daoist funerary services is that the family has a new ancestor who remains mourned and unforgotten, with proper offerings.

Making Meaning for the Living

Death is an apparent threat to the equilibrium of social relationships, which calls for reconciliation. Indeed, how we come to accept or deny that loss of life is shaped in large part by how we think about life and death. And how any family mourns and commemorates the deceased reflects the way it strives to achieve a sense of reconciliation.[23] The death ritual is certainly important to help us to acknowledge, mourn, and accept death. Funerary occasions of every religious liturgy, of course, can allow for expression of bereavement that might otherwise be suppressed. But, it is also true that not all funerary services like Daoism are performed on behalf of the spirits of the dead and provide means to re-establish the relationship between the living and the dead.

Given the potential anxiety over the dead, the need to make the unknown knowable is the urge to dispel the "terror" of irreversible separation between the living and the dead. Mourners want to know "Where are you, you who perished forever?" What this inquiry seems to convey is an unbearable pain in not being able to make the unknown knowable, to determine the identity and the destiny of the dead. To meet the questions of the dead at issue here with silence is to deny our bond already established between the deceased and us.

Beyond memory and the expression of grief, the Daoist death ritual remarkably provides the means for making reconciliation and peace with the dead known as *gui*, or our "ancestors". It is the effort of the Daoist funerary service to establish family ties with the deceased, now known and honoured as our "ancestors".

For the living, the performance of the Daoist death ritual is also a vision of the transcendent world, including the underworld and the immortal world. Through songs and chants, our eyes are exposed to a vision that enables us to live with our thoughts of death and, in commemorating the dead, we are reminded of our mortality.[23] What we perhaps find easier to bear is the thought that we will be commemorated in a similar way so that we will not be easily forgotten.

6

Death from the Buddhist View:
Knowing the Unknown

JING YIN

Our lifespan is controlled by our biological clocks, which continually tick away. When they run down, there is little we can do to gain extra time. We must be prepared for the natural process of death. Death is inevitable. Many people believe death brings an end to everything. But, according to Buddhism, our life does not begin only at the moment of birth, and death does not imply the end of life: it is the beginning of another life. By doing good deeds in this life, a better future life can follow. This is the basic concept of Buddhist theory on rebirth, which guarantees that death is not final.

Because life after death is beyond our direct experience, it is a phenomenon that is difficult to prove scientifically. It is the unknown. And knowing the unknown is a challenging task. Does life after death really exist? This question has intrigued the minds of people from all religions, throughout the ages.

This paper attempts to explore the possibility of life after death from the perspective of Buddhists. It addresses the following questions. Because Buddhism totally rejects an everlasting and permanent soul, who, then, is migrating from one life to another? How does the cycle of life and death occur? How long does rebirth take place? Who can merit being transferred to a departed being? How can a person live meaningfully and die peacefully?

Life after Death: Possible or Impossible?

The strongest argument against life after death comes from the scientific or atheistic view. People cannot see any mental life after the brain dies. Even when the brain is alive, a blow to the head may impair thinking. Consciousness seems to be related to matter, just as the light of a candle is to the candle: once the fuel is spent, the light will go out. The body and its nervous system seem like the fuel, or the cause, and immaterial activity, consciousness, seems like the effect. Therefore, those who take the scientific or atheistic view believe that death means the complete dissolution of a being without any after-effects.

However, according to the law of energy conservation, which is a fundamental concept of physics, and the conservation of mass and the conservation of momentum, the amount of energy remains constant within some domain, and energy is neither created nor destroyed. Energy can be converted from one form to another (e.g., potential energy can be converted to kinetic energy), but the total energy within the domain remains fixed.[1]

Similarly, according to the principle of dependent origination, which is the central teaching of the Buddha, all things arise from causes and conditions. In other words, everything in this world is a component thing or conditioned thing.[a] For example, a sprout that rises from a seed is dependent on soil, moisture, air and sunlight for its growth. If any of these conditions is missing, the sprout will not be able to grow. Similarly, the flame of an oil lamp depends on the wick and the oil. When either the wick is burnt through or the last drop of oil is used, the flame will die.

In the same way, life arises from causes and conditions. All living beings consist of physical and mental elements. The law of energy conservation implies both physical and mental energy of human life cannot disappear without cause, but they can manifest themselves simultaneously. After death, the physical body will return to nature, just as the fallen leaf will gradually decay and return to nature to be eventually absorbed by other plants. As well, the mental energies of the dead person do not terminate with the nonfunctioning of the body but continue to manifest themselves in another form, thus producing re-existence. This is called rebirth or re-becoming in Buddhism rather than "reincarnation", because there is no permanent entity or soul that is reincarnated or moving from one life to the next.

Although life after death cannot be proved scientifically, this does not mean that certain things unknown to us, or beyond our current knowledge, do not exist. Someone who has no scientific knowledge may have doubts about the existence of black holes or subatomic particles. But, anyone with a sound scientific background will have no doubt about the existence of these phenomena. Similarly, those with a personal experience of deep concentration will have no doubt about life after death. Some people who meditate and who have acquired the power of concentration have been able to recall their previous lives in great detail. The Buddha and his prominent disciples in many countries and at different times were able to prove the existence of past lives. On the night of his Enlightenment, the Buddha developed the ability to see his past lives. He also saw sentient beings dying in one state of existence and being reborn in another, according to their previous actions. It was from his

---

a. "諸法從緣起，如來説是因，彼法因緣盡，是大沙門説。" 大智度論 (The Mahaprajnaparamita-sastra) In: Takakusi J, Watanabe K. *et al.*, editors. 大正新修大藏經 [Taisho Edition of the Chinese Buddhist Tripiaka], 100 vols. Tokyo: Daizo Shuppansha, Inc. 1924–34; 25.136c.

personal experience that the Buddha taught his followers about the truth of rebirth.

Karma:[b] The Key Determining Factor for One's Rebirth

According to the theory of causality in Buddhism, nothing arises without causes or conditions and nothing arises from a single condition. In other words, if anything happens, it must be due to complex conditions or several causes. A "cause" is like a seed planted in the ground, whereas the "effect" is the fruit that it bears. So, what is the seed that is causing rebirth and shaping the destiny of beings? The answer is karma — volitional actions that become manifest as wholesome or unwholesome thoughts, speech or actions. For instance, when a girl sees a piece of cake, her reactions might be different (see the table below). She might dislike it if it has made her fat. Alternatively, she might want more if she has a good memory of the taste. In this way, people commit certain acts to obtain the things they crave, and they soon become used to acting in the same way. This can be applied to both wholesome and unwholesome actions. For example, if some people find they can obtain what they want by dishonest means on one occasion, they may be tempted to repeat the method on future occasions. Eventually, for them, dishonesty becomes a habit. However, others may find that they can succeed by hard work. As a result, they are encouraged to work hard on each task, and hard work becomes a habit for them. In the same way, other habits are formed and become part of the personality. When people encounter a new situation, they will respond to it in their accustomed way, thereby reinforcing their habits.

Table 1: Different reactions of our mind to the same object

An objective thing or event	Recognition and Perception	Sensations and feelings	Volition	Actions
Cake	It is a cake. It tastes good.	Happiness	I want it	Go get it.
Cake	It is a cake. It makes me fat.	Distress	I don't like it	Get rid of it.

[b.] The standard definition of karma is: "Volition *(cetan·),* o monks, is what I call action *(cetan·ham bhikkhave kammam vad·mi),* for through volition one performs the action by body, speech or mind. There is karma (action), O monks, that ripens in hell.... Karma that ripens in the animal world. Karma that ripens in the world of men.... Karma that ripens in the heavenly world." Morris R and Hardy E, editors. *Anguttaranikaya,* vols. VI. London: PTS; 1900, 63. Thus karma is nothing but volition, intention, what is deliberately done.

Once an action is performed, it will leave behind potentialities in the form of karmic force for something to be materialized in the future. In Buddhism, this potentiality is called seed (*biija*),[c] using the allegory of the biological seed, which indicates the stored elements waiting for the right conditions to germinate into a manifestation. According to the Yogacara School, seeds are stored in the eighth-consciousness,[d] which is very subtle and most often referred to as the sub-consciousness in Western psychology. Each of seed is one potentiality of mental and physical constructs. When the conditions are ripe, the seeds give rise to continued existence, which has a direct relationship to prior cause and conditions. Depending on the nature of the deeds, (whether they are good or bad), the ripened seeds will produce a fruit of retribution of the same nature. These effects would become the major forces for individuals to be perpetually reborn.[e] In *Angutara Nikaya*, the Buddha analyses the time for manifestation of seeds (karmic force) in three ways:

1. Karma ripening in this lifetime (*dittha-dhamma-vedan"ya kamma*)
2. Karma ripening in the next birth (*upapajja-vedan"ya-kamma*)
3. Karma ripening in later births (*apar-pariya-vedan"ya-kamma*).[2]

---

[c] Seed (*bija*) is the term that originally refers to the seeds of plants but is used in Buddhism in a metaphorical sense. (1) First, in a religion that relies so much on "cause and effect" theory, seeds are a metaphor for the causes 因 of things but especially as causes of the afflictions. (*The discourse on the stages of concentration practice* 瑜伽論, T30.364a) (2) The potentiality for something to be produced (T29.22c). (3) In the Yogacara School 瑜伽行派, the "seeds" are one phase of the latent potentialities of all mental and physical elemental constructs that are stored in the ,*laya* consciousness 阿賴耶識. Coming into existence as the result of present activities and conditions, the seeds result in new potentialities, giving rise to continued existence, which has a direct relationship to prior causes and conditions (成唯識論 (*Discourse on the theory of consciousness-only*). In: Takakusi J., Watanabe *et al.*, editors. 大正新修大藏經 [Taisho Edition of the Chinese Buddhist Tripiaka], 100 vols. Tokyo: Daizo Shuppansha, Inc. 1924–34; 31.8).

[d] Sentient beings possess eight distinct layers of consciousness that are a complex interaction of eight mental functions. They are: 1. eye-consciousness, 2. ear-consciousness, 3. nose-consciousness, 4. tongue-consciousness, 5. body-consciousness, 6. mind-consciousness (意識), 7. *Manas*-consciousness, and 8. *Alaya*-consciousness. The first five are mental faculties, or senses, which react to the external phenomena through the five organs. The sixth consciousness, like the CPU of a computer, can rapidly process information obtained from the first five consciousnesses and immediately perform three kinds of function of recognition and differentiation, based on past experience. The seventh consciousness, called *Manas* in Sanskrit, is the centre of egotism for each individual. As the result of "self-centeredness", all selfish thoughts, egotistic opinion, arrogance, self-love, etc. arise. Upon the actions taken by the first seven consciousnesses, the eighth consciousness (*Alaya* consciousness) is known as the base consciousness, store consciousness, or seed consciousness. It produces a result when the conditions are ripe.

[e] "此是能引諸界趣生善不善異熟果故。" 唯識三十論要釋 (*Brief commentary on thirty verses on Vijnapti-matra Treatise*) In: Takakusi J., Watanabe *et al.*, editors. 大正新修大藏經 [Taisho Edition of the Chinese Buddhist Tripiaka], 100 vols. Tokyo: Daizo Shuppansha, Inc. 1924–34; 85.964b.

The effect of an action taken in this life can be experienced within this lifetime. This is called "short-term karma" (i.e., karma ripening during the lifetime). For example, if a student refuses to study hard now, the examination result will be affected at the end of the semester. Unless this bad habit is broken, the student will experience suffering in this life. In contrast, studying hard now will result in the student passing the examination with good results at the end of the semester. In the same vein, those who hurt others will be hurt themselves. If one helps others, that person will be helped. These are the so-called effects of short-term karma.

Karma (volitional action) is like a seed. Seeds ripen only if they meet the right conditions. But if they do not meet the right conditions in this life, they remain as seeds which will then bear fruit in future lives (i.e., karma ripening in the next birth and karma ripening in later births), whenever and wherever there is an opportunity. Following the same logic, acts performed in past lives may produce effects in this life, due to the effects of long-term karma.

Obviously, effects that will arise in future lives are not visible to people unless they have developed the capacity and wisdom to see into the future. But, these effects will occur. The Buddha and his prominent disciples were able to see the future effects of karma through their own extraordinary understanding.

From the above discussion, it can be seen that death is not the end of everything. At death, a mind with its habitual actions becomes the determining factor for one's rebirth, just as a seed grows into a sprout. So long as people act in their accustomed ways, their habitual actions leave behind potentialities of mental and physical constructs in the form of karmic force, which serves as the driving force for their rebirth.

How Does the Cycle of Life and Death Occur?

As stated, karma is the energy, or potentiality, that is left behind by our actions and thoughts. These actions and thoughts serve as determining factors for our rebirth. Due to our past karma, we are born as human beings in this life. The good and evil karma in this life and past lives will also affect our future lives. Our actions in this life are innumerable. Many of them gradually develop into habitual actions, both good and evil. What is the priority for particular seeds to determine our next life? According to Buddhism, the last thought during the last moment of this life is the determining factor for the next life. It can occur under the following three situations.[3,4]

Weighty karma (garuka-kamma)

Usually, we generate a lot of good or bad karma every day. When we are on the brink of death, this karma will appear before our eyes. So, at the moment of our death, it is most likely that the strongest good or evil thoughts will arise, which will determine our future life. For example, the memory of killing one's own father is unforgettable. Such a thought will always be in the mind of the son. At the moment of death, this evil deed (karmic action) will reappear. Similarly, a person who is very filial will see his or her own faithfulness and good deeds at the moment of the last breath. This can be seen in the context of a debtor. At the end of the year, creditors will chase the debtor for their loans, and the debtor will have to repay the creditors.

This explains why the evil will be reborn in hell, and the good will be born in heaven immediately after the end of their present life. In the Tibetan tradition, it is said that when enlightened people die, they can predict where they will be reborn. After death, the followers will find the reincarnated "vehicle" of those people, usually in children, and those children have memories of their past lives, which matches the details of the enlightened people who passed away. These children also have knowledge beyond their years. This explains how the Dalai Lama and Panchen Lama are chosen.

Therefore, in order to be better prepared for dying, Buddhism encourages followers to try to avoid bad deeds so they can be reborn in a better place.

Habitual karma (cinnaka- or bahula-kamma)

Many people can have karma that is neither extremely good nor extremely bad. In these circumstances, habitual actions may become the major influence on their fate. The Buddha gave an example: If a large tree is leaning to the east when being fallen, it will certainly fall towards the east. Similarly, once a bad habit has been formed, it is very difficult to break. It will occur at the time of dying and will strongly affect the person's next life.

Therefore, it is most important for people to understand the need to develop good character in advance. Hence, Buddhism aims to train its followers to tread the right path that will lead to a better rebirth. For instance, Buddhists are encouraged to form the daily habit of chanting the name of Amitabha Buddha, so that, even in case of accidental death, their last thoughts will, as if by reflex, focus on the Buddha.

Death-proximate karma (maran·sanna-kamma)

Some people have neither weighty karma nor habitual karma. During their last moments, they may suddenly think of something. This last thought, whether good or evil, will influence their next rebirth. The Buddhist instruction for this category of people is to encourage them to recall all the good things they have done during their lifetime and think only positive thoughts. Relying on the energy of these good thoughts, people may have a good rebirth.

In summary, one's state of mind at the moment of death does not only passively reflect, but can actively influence, what happens after death. It is, therefore, paramount to prepare well for that final moment. The following points are conducive to a good rebirth.

1. When death is imminent, it is helpful to invite a Buddhist monk to instruct the dying person to meditate on the process of dying (if the person has experience of meditation) and to recite the name of Amitabha Buddha with the intention of being reborn in a Pure Land. The monk can radiate love and compassion and wish the person freedom from suffering. The monk can give assurance that the person's family is well and that the person is free to go in peace. The dying person should also be advised to let go and think about meritorious deeds that he or she has done and be calm in the face of death.

2. Family and friends should come together to peacefully recite the name of Amitabha Buddha around the dying person. The blessing of Amitabha Buddha is not limited to welcoming sentient beings to his Pure Land. His blessing can also help the person to recover from an illness.

3. Relatives should avoid resuscitating a dying person. When the pulse and brain waves are gone, a physician pronounces the person dead. However, from the Buddhist point of view, that person is still dying. The consciousness is in the process of separating from the body. In this state, it is very painful if the process is disturbed by movement of the body or an abrupt change in the environment. Immediately following signs of physical death, Buddhists believe that it is best to keep the body in a peaceful state. They endeavour to obtain approval for the body to remain untouched for eight hours, preferably until it is cold.

4. Relatives should avoid crying or making unnecessary noise, or quarrelling and fighting over property or other worldly matters. It is believed this could affect the dying person's emotional state and cause suffering. It is helpful if the relatives remain calm and quiet.

5. The relatives may invite the Help Chant Group (a voluntary service group) to organize shifts so that a dying Buddhist will be accompanied by clear and continuous chanting of Amitabha throughout the dying process. In so doing, they not only invoke the blessing of the Buddha and provide support and serenity to the situation but also learn for themselves how to face death in tranquillity.

The Period Between Death and Rebirth

How long after death does rebirth take place? This has been a controversial question even among prominent Buddhist scholars. Generally speaking, there are two popular views.

In Theravada Buddhist countries like Sri Lanka and Thailand, it is believed that, when a person dies, rebirth will occur in the next moment. As the last moment of this life is an important factor in determining the condition for rebirth in the next life, the final moments of consciousness are described in some detail in Theravada Buddhist books. For instance, when past karmic deeds or such signs "settle" on the dying individual, then a vision of the future destiny occurs, such as the appearance of fire signifying hell, a mother's womb indicating rebirth in the human realm, or pleasant groves and divine palaces for a future in heavenly realm. Then comes a momentary "death awareness" (*cuticitta*) followed immediately by "rebirth linking consciousness" (*patisandhivinndna*) signifying the next life. The relationship between these two is said to be neither one of identity nor otherness; it is likened to an echo caused by previous events but not identical to them. Theravada Buddhism also emphasizes the mental state of a dying person should be in a state of no attachment and peace, the mind on impermanence, suffering and emptiness, which is an important factor in determining the condition for rebirth.

In Mahayana Buddhist countries like China and Japan, there is an "in-between stage" between death and the next life, wherein one is transformed into an entity called *Bardo* (中陰身). In pre-Buddhist Indian myths, *Bardo* is originally referred to as a semi-divine being associated with fertility and the god Soma. It is the size of a little baby.[f] Most people in this state have some perception, but their willpower is very limited for finding an appropriate womb to descend into. It is commonly believed that a *Bardo* has forty-nine days to accomplish this task. This conception gives rise to a variety of beliefs and practices designed to help the recently deceased to alter their destined rebirths.

As *Bardo* is crucial for a better rebirth in the next life, it is important for a dying person to properly handle the in-between stage after death and before the next rebirth (i.e., the *bardo* stage). In the Mahayana schools, the Tibetan tradition in particular has offered a detailed study of the dying and rebirth processes.

As Buddhists believe the intermediary spirit body (*Bardo*) may remain in a very brief time or up to forty-nine days before the new life begins, every seventh day after the death, monks are invited to perform rituals. This is based on the Buddhist teaching that the consciousness in the limbo state will pass through a dying process every seven days. Hence, it is time to offer spiritual help for transcendence or a good rebirth. Buddhist followers of the Pure Land School usually chant the name of Amitabha, or different Pure Land sutras, on their own every day during this period.

---

f. "懸命過幡轉讀尊經竟三七日, 中陰中身如小兒, 罪福未定應為修福。" 佛説灌頂經 (The Sutra of Consecration) In Takakusi J., Watanabe *et al.*, editors 大正新修大藏經 [Taisho Edition of the Chinese Buddhist Tripiaka], 100 vols. Tokyo: Daizo Shuppansha, Inc. 1924–34; 21. 529c.

Transfer of Merit: Spiritual Help for Dying People

Just as Western people have Halloween for ghosts and ghouls, so do the Chinese. They have a special holiday dedicated to fete the departed spirits of the underworld: the Hungry Ghosts Festival on the fifteenth day of the seventh lunar month. It is based on the Buddhist story of Moggallana and his mother. According to popular Chinese tradition, Moggallana discovered through his meditative powers that his mother had been reborn in one of the realms of misery. Distressed over the tormented state of his mother, he approached the Buddha for help. The Buddha then advised Moggallana to make offerings to monks. The merit of making such offerings will help to relieve the suffering not only of his mother but also of other sentient beings in the realms of misery. It is said that, as a result of Moggallana's offerings, his mother was quickly released from her unhappy state. Based on this story, the act of making offerings to relieve the suffering of departed relatives, as well as other sentient beings in the realm of misery, has become a popular communal observance in countries like China, Japan and Korea. This festival is still popularly practised in various parts of the world, particularly in Hong Kong.

The most important event during the festival is to conduct a memorial service to transfer merit to departed relatives or friends. According to Buddhism, the transfer of merit can be directed individually, collectively, or both ways simultaneously. This leads us to several related questions: What is the significance of transferring merit? How can we transmit merit to the deceased? How can we guarantee the action really benefits specific individuals we wish to remember at that time?

From the religious point of view, after our relatives have passed away, they may suffer in the three realms of evil: hell, hungry ghosts, and brute beasts. If we pay no attention to the deceased while enjoying our comfortable lives, our deceased relatives may engender resentment that may adversely affect us. The only way to relieve the suffering of the deceased is to hold memorial services for them. That is why virtually all religions hold some ceremony on behalf of the deceased for the benefit of both the living and the dead.

From an empirical point of view, people hope and pray that their deceased relatives and friends can find happiness. Therefore, they opt to offer memorial services for the benefit of the deceased.

From a moral point of view, we are obliged to our parents for what they have done in raising us and giving us a good education. We owe them a debt of gratitude. Buddhism teaches us three ways to repay our debts to our parents. First, we should provide them with food and clothing. Second, we should honour their wishes and obey them while they are alive. Finally, we should conduct a memorial service to help them after they pass away, to facilitate their rebirth in a better realm.

From a spiritual point of view, when Buddhists perform memorial services, they traditionally recite Buddhist scriptures and offer flowers and incense. However, a memorial service cannot benefit the deceased if it is performed only as a routine or a superficial ritual without devotion. Only when relatives and close friends gather to chant scriptures with devotion will the deceased be attracted to the memorial service. The amount of merit the deceased can receive will depend on his or her ability to perceive the religious messages sent in the ritual and to appreciate their meaning.[g] If the deceased fully understands the meaning of Buddha's teachings, such as impermanence, no attachment, compassion and loving-kindness, the mind can find peace and the person may be reborn in a better realm. This is the true meaning of transfer of merit: providing spiritual help for the dying and the deceased.

Karma and Rebirth: Moral Retribution

Although Buddhism believes in rebirth, this does not mean it believes in a soul. On the contrary, Buddhism totally denies an everlasting, unchanging substance called soul. Karma and rebirth is moral retribution. As we are, so we will be. We will be murderers or saints according to traces of thought within us. Just as the flame of an oil lamp depends on the wick and the oil for existence, so the occurrence of rebirth and suffering depend on mind and actions (karma). In other words, wholesome actions will produce happiness; unwholesome actions will produce suffering. Just as the Buddha said: "It may be well with the evil-doer as long as the evil ripens not. But when it does ripen, then the evil-doer sees (the painful results of) his evil deeds".[5]

In this way, Buddhism attempts to explain moral causation without reference to law and without referring to a lord, an outside agent or a god. Within the act itself, there is the potential to bring about both good and bad results, without referring to someone else for resolution. In this sense, the relationship between karma and rebirth is moral retribution in Buddhism.

Living Meaningfully, Dying Peacefully

A widow who could not accept the death of her only child went to the Buddha and asked him to give her the medicine that would restore her son to life. The Buddha smiled and told her that he would be able to cure her son if she

---

g. "其鬼聞法生歡喜心。" 大道心驅策法 [The Method to Arouse the Mind of Great Enlightenment] In Takakusi J., Watanabe *et al.*, editors. 大正新修大藏經 [Taisho Edition of the Chinese Buddhist Tripiaka], 100 vols. Tokyo: Daizo Shuppansha, Inc. 1924–34; 20.653c

could bring him mustard seeds from a house where death had never occurred. Carrying her dead child, the widow went from house to house, with the request for some mustard seeds. Everyone was willing to help, but she could not find a single house where death had never occurred. Then, she realized the message the Buddha was trying to convey to her: "Mine is not the only family that has faced death. Death comes to all beings; before their desires are satiated death takes them away". As soon as she realized this, her attitude changed; she was no longer attached to the dead body of her son.

Once we accept the fact that life is uncertain and death is certain, then our attitude towards life will be different. It is like two boys building their own sandcastles. The castles are so beautiful that the boys become jealous and end up fighting with each other. While they are fighting, a wave washes away their castles. When they realize that the objects over which they are fighting no longer exist, the boys become good friends once again, and happily return home, hand-in-hand. Similarly, people fight over money, power, fame and sensual pleasure. Once they become aware of impermanence, in particular death, they realize that in the end they will have to give up everything. In this case, they learn from death, which can help them reflect on their lives as a whole. If they can become detached from worldly things but still make the best use of them, they can learn from the dead to improve their lives and prepare for a peaceful ending and a better next life.

7

Autopsy in Chinese: A Forensic Pathologist's View

Philip Swan Lip BEH

Introduction

In 2003, 30,000 people died in Hong Kong. Out of these deaths, nearly 7,000 were reported to the Coroner by the doctors caring for the deceased persons prior to their death, or by the police, when the deaths occur outside a hospital. Table 1 shows details for the five-year period 1999–2003. Table 2 shows details of some of the types of unnatural death.[1]

Table 1
Deaths in Hong Kong
Annual figures for 1999–2003

	1999	2000	2001	2002	2003
Total deaths	33387	33907	33305	34316	36421
Reported deaths	7793	7852	7733	7890	9315
Autopsy done	4902	4685	4320	4487	4621
Death investigated	2567	2311	2374	2451	2678

Table 2
Types of Unnatural Death in Hong Kong
Annual Figures for 1999–2003

	1999	2000	2001	2002	2003
Accidental	626	490	404	494	473
Suicide	882	915	988	1025	1152
Homicide	75	68	52	66	62
Occupational	88	59	61	36	42
Vehicular	228	200	165	194	180

The death of a family member is in itself an emotionally difficult event and often gives rise to many religious, social and familial issues. When the deaths are reportable to the Coroner, more problems arise, such as the question of autopsy, the conflict among surviving family members on funeral arrangements, conflict between family members and the health-care provider on areas ranging from treatment and management of the patient, to reporting or certification of the death, to the cause of death itself, etc.

Invariably, family members find themselves "trapped" in a situation of conflict with health-care providers and the mandatory requirement to report the death to the Coroner. A reportable death has the implied requirement of an autopsy. Family members often express a sense of "being victims of blackmail". On occasions when the need or requirement for reporting was not strictly adhered to, family members may find themselves facing potential financial loss as a result of disputes over claims for the payment of insurance, etc.

Making decisions about death and death-related matters are always emotive, especially when family members are required to do so under the added stressful situation of a sudden, unexpected death. Yet, to date, we in Hong Kong do not have a structured process for helping the family members of a deceased person.

A pathologist is a person who has been trained in the Western organ-based system of medicine, in which diseases and death can be explained by changes in the structure and functions of body organs and tissues. On the basis of the pathologist's professional practice, it is therefore neither unexpected nor surprising that the "true" pathologist believes that all deaths should be properly understood, and the "gold standard" of this understanding is the careful post-mortem examination of a deceased person's body. There is a logical correlation with the clinical history of disease and treatment providing the ultimate answer to "the cause of death".

The Cause of Death

Volumes have been written about how to write a "cause of death". Even so, there will never be any standardized way, because the "cause of death" is, in a sense, a conclusion arrived at through various mental processes after consideration of available information. It may be shocking to the public to know, but it is readily accepted by most pathologists that, if the relevant information available in arriving at a "cause of death" changed either in reliability or in details, it is perfectly reasonable to re-evaluate and re-issue a "cause of death". Let me give an illustrative example.

> An elderly man is reported to have fallen and was found to be unconscious
> with a fractured skull. His death would usually be attributed to head injury

PART I	
Immediate Cause (Final) Disease or conditions resulting	a.
Sequentially list conditions, if any, leading to immediate casue. Enter **UNDERLYING** **CAUSE.** (Disease or injury that initiated events resulting in death)	b. *(Due to or as a consequence of)* c. *(Due to or as a consequence of)* d. *(Due to or as a consequence of)*
PART II Other significant conditions contributing to death but not resulting in the underlying cause of death given Part I.	

Figure 1. Stantardised format for writing a cause of death.

and listed as "1. Head Injury". Yet, if it was to be discovered that the person had a history of uncontrolled hypertension, and a CT (computerized tomography) scan of the brain had shown the presence of a large intra-cerebral haemorrhage, the cause of death should be changed to "1a. Intracerebral Haemorrhage, 1b. Hypertension".

There is, however, an international format of recording the "cause of death" which has been adopted by the World Health Organisation.[2] It prescribes recording the way to record the "cause of death". (See Figure 1.) Although this allows international comparisons, there are actually different versions. Most countries are still on ICD-9 (International Classification of Diseases Version 9), but others have moved to ICD-10. Such version changes must be understood if anyone is involved in comparing international statistics on disease and death.

The System of Death Registration in Hong Kong

The Registrar of Births and Deaths under the Registration of Persons Section of the Immigration Department has the sole responsibility of maintaining the death register. The registrar is the official issuer of the death certificate.

About seventy percent of deaths annually are routinely registered without any further investigation or query. A registered medical practitioner, usually in a public or private hospital, would have certified these deaths. These registered medical practitioners will then issue a medical certificate of the Cause of Death to the next-of-kin or person responsible for the funeral arrangements of the deceased. This medical certificate of the Cause of Death is brought to the Registrar of Births and Deaths, all relevant particulars are recorded and the official death certificate is then issued.

Annually, approximately thirty percent of deaths are reported to the Coroner. In Hong Kong, *The Coroners Ordinance*[3] stipulates, under Schedule 2, a list of twenty circumstances of death whereby the deaths must be reported to the Coroner. (See Figure 2.) Failure to report can attract a jail term as penalty. The onus of reporting is placed on registered medical practitioners and/or hospital administrators.

In all reportable deaths, the following process will be followed. A registered medical practitioner will inform the Coroner's Office of the brief facts of a death. The next-of-kin or responsible informant will be required to file a report with the Hong Kong Police, Miscellaneous Enquiry Unit. An interview will be arranged with a pathologist, usually within forty-eight hours of the death, to facilitate the following:

a. A formal identification of the deceased person
b. An interview with the pathologist to discuss the circumstances of the death and in particular to obtain as much information as possible on the deceased person's medical history
c. A discussion on the necessity for an autopsy
d. Instructions for disposal of the body, either burial or cremation.

When an autopsy or a detailed police investigation is required in a death, family members are still permitted to dispose of the body once autopsy needs are completed. There is rarely any undue delay to arrangements for a funeral, due to the requirements of the investigation into the death.

When a death has been reported, the Cause of Death will be decided by the pathologist but issued by the Coroner (a judicial officer). The registrar of births and death will register whatever information the Coroner supplies.

Death Investigation

When an autopsy has been performed and a death investigation deemed required, the Coroner relies on the resources of the Hong Kong Police Force to carry out the investigation. Frequently, this would include taking witness statements, commissioning expert reports, etc.

In the majority of cases, the Coroner will be able to conclude the case on his own, and a cause of death certificate is issued. In a small percentage of cases, about 100 each year, an inquest is held.

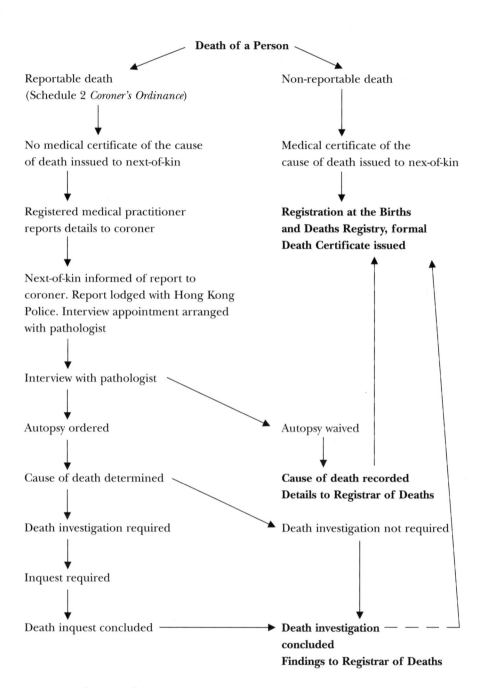

Figure 2. Schematic of death registration and death investigation in Hong Kong.

The inquest will call witnesses to present their evidence. Witnesses to the death can be questioned by all interested parties. Witnesses are, however, warned actively and prevented from any self-incriminatory evidence. The set aims of a Coroner's inquest are:

a. Determination of identity of the deceased person
b. Determination of the time and place of death
c. Determination of the medical cause of death
d. Determination of the manner of death.

The "manner of death" is a statement of whether the evidence allows a conclusion of death to be made. Such conclusions usually include death due to natural causes, death due to accident, death due to unlawful killing or death remains unascertained (recorded as an "open" verdict).

Interactions with Family Members of the Deceased

It is important to point out that the performance of an autopsy is not a common practice in Chinese communities. Historically, China has been credited with publishing the first comprehensive guide on death investigation, translated as the "washing away of wrongs". Careful scrutiny of this manuscript will reveal that, although it boldly talks about the examination of a dead body, it was extremely rare that the dead body was damaged or dissected. Insertion of silver needles into body cavities was about the most invasive method used.

This brings us to the first frequent cry of despair and anguish from family members of a deceased person interviewed in the course of the work of a forensic pathologist. This can manifest in the form of an angry outburst.

> "How dare you even suggest cutting up the body! You doctors have already caused him/her so much pain and misery and you have not been able to save him/her! Why do you want to cause more pain, by cutting up the body? What have we done to you?"

Or, it can manifest as distress:

> " No! No! No! Please do not cut up the body! We cannot bear the thought of him/her suffering anymore. We want to keep the body intact!"

Here lies the first myth about autopsies. Modern day post-mortem examinations, although quite thorough in coverage, leaves the external appearance of a body largely intact (with the exception of a long sutured wound on the front of the body, like that following surgery.

The explanation of this first fact about an autopsy has helped diffuse the distress and anguish of family members to an autopsy examination in the majority of encounters. It will, however, be insufficient to dissuade the angry outrage with the "How dare you!" outburst.

The next fact about an autopsy is that findings at an autopsy help doctors acquire new knowledge, understand their mistakes and may prevent future deaths. It may highlight patterns of death from a similar set of circumstances, thus allowing the search of preventive measures. This second reason for an autopsy will often win over a distressed but rational family member. It may satisfy the angry family member, too, as there is now a new focus of the anger: that of a potential mistake by the system or the health-care team. It sometimes is still not enough, because the angry family members will say, "My relative is dead. Whatever you find or do is not going to bring him/her back to life". There is no possible response but to agree wholeheartedly with the family member. This is not the time to be philosophical and talk about the concept of a "meaningful" death.

When all attempts at reasoning fail, in Hong Kong, where there is a comprehensive legal requirement and system of death investigation (discussed earlier), the pathologist will have no recourse but to fall back on the requirements of the law and the courts. Curiously, this seems to work. It may be a sign of how generally law-abiding the average person in Hong Kong is, or it may be a sign of how defeated the average person in Hong Kong is by the legal system that any potential "entanglement" with the legal system brings with it a sense of futility and defeat. A common remark indicating the latter sentiment would often be:

> "When you invoke the legal requirement, it is like using a big stone to squash a small crab. You leave us no choice!"

The spread of medical knowledge, the increased expectations on health care and treatment outcomes, coupled with the increasing inclination to initiate medical complaints and litigations have now introduced a completely different scenario. Here, the next-of-kin demands an autopsy and demands a death investigation. The family challenges the validity of any cause of death offered by doctors without supporting evidence from an autopsy examination. In some instances, these deaths do not really fall into the reportable deaths category, but the fact that the clinical decision on the cause of death is challenged means a situation of "unclear cause of death" is created, thus requiring reporting to the Coroner.

Interactions with a Pathologist

The young pathologist will find a lot of comfort in working within the "security" of legislation and the clarity of these legislations. Thought processes are simplistic and easy: does this death fall under the list of reportable deaths? If the answer is affirmative, proceed to an autopsy.

With experience, the inability to determine a cause of death even with an autopsy, the ability to predict the likely findings based on the history and circumstances of death creates a dilemma for the pathologist that challenges the simple decisions of the legal processes. Now, the pathologist knows that there are cases when the autopsy is not really required, as experience allows the accurate prediction of the likely cause of death. On other occasions, the pathologist is aware that the autopsy examination will not reveal any useful findings, because the death was due to abnormal functioning but not to abnormal structures in the body. (Abnormal structures can be seen; abnormal functions can at best be implied.) Increasingly, as a result of modern imaging capabilities, deaths due to injuries can be documented through a series of radiological methods, plain X-rays, CT scans, magnetic resonance imaging (MRI), etc.

Decisions on the need for an autopsy now are based on "Will I be able to find out what happened?" If yes, is this with or without the requirement of an autopsy? One will therefore observe that the "older" pathologist will be more sympathetic to the resistance of family members for an autopsy.

It would be philosophical to wonder if this may be driven by an awareness that, as a result of age, the chance that the pathologist may himself/herself be subject to an autopsy is increasing. Personally, I think not. I think it is more an acceptance that the pathologist and an autopsy are not always that important and critical to the end result of a case.

Dealing with Family and Friends

Family and friends will always seek advice and support for resistance to an autopsy request/requirement. Invariably, the request starts with " So-and-so has passed away and the body is in the mortuary. They say there may have to be an autopsy. Does there have to be an autopsy? We don't want to have an autopsy!" In circumstances like this, the pathologist is faced with the dilemma of applying his training and scientific, medico-legal approach or applying his natural instincts of a family member or friend. I can only say the pendulum swings according to the closeness of the ties and relationship. This is why pathologists the world over will refrain from working on a case involving someone they know, even casually. This system, which is generally accepted, avoids the challenge of impartiality in any subsequent report or opinions expressed about the death or the cause of death.

The Natural Instincts of Pathologists

Perhaps "natural instincts" is not the best term. Before a person becomes a medical doctor and then a pathologist, he or she is like everyone else in the community, growing up under the same sets of influences and subject to the same sets of beliefs. In my role as a medical teacher, I have organized autopsy teaching sessions for medical students. I have asked students to reflect on their perceptions of what they feel an autopsy will be like. Commonly, students speak of dark, cold smelly places. They worry about their own capacity to withstand the sight of such a procedure. They are all curious to know how the body will actually be dissected. The explosion of interest in the media of medical detective and forensic programmes has also fuelled the imagination of the young. These groups of students ooze enthusiasm about the opportunity to learn how to detect crime, how to find out the cause of death, etc.

The autopsy teaching session has engendered reflection on death and dying, and, in a small percentage of students, on the meaning of life. They reflect on the futility of suicide, the selflessness of a mother dying to save a child, the desperation and anger at the perpetrator of the homicide of an elderly victim.

Yet, many of these scientifically minded and trained medical students have expressed their definite wish of not having to be autopsied when they die. This, I submit, is that unseen but ever present element of mystery of death and the unknown after-death which is still widely prevalent in the Chinese culture, even in this modern age of technology and science. It transcends educational level and logic.

What Happens to the Body after Death

In Hong Kong, over ninety percent of bodies are now cremated. Burial will require disinterment of the remains after a maximum of seven years. The sense and need for perpetuity in death has all but disappeared because of practical circumstances. There is, however, a slight resurgence, noticed particularly in families who have strong connections to their ancestral village in mainland China. In these cases, the matter of burial is very important and prominent. Their resistance to an autopsy is also generally higher.

Finally, "we do not want the deceased to suffer again". Is this a cry of guilt for not providing better care during life? I do know that there is no pain in death. I do also believe that a meaningful death is better than a death wasted. "There is still much that the dead can teach the living, and we should never stop learning!"

Much of modern medicine as we know it is underpinned by the observations of changes to the body described at autopsies. Specifically, such examination of the dead gave rise to the field of anatomy and pathology. The importance of observing changes in the body that can be correlated to the complaints, symptoms and signs is still paramount, though in this the twenty-first century such observations are made through an increasing array of imaging machines such as ultrasound, CT-scans, MRIs and various endoscopic approaches. The increasing knowledge of the human genome is also leading to new tests that predict a person's susceptibility to disease even before the person is found to have the disease.

In this atmosphere of medical scientific and technological advances, it is easy to discard the need for the autopsy after death. It is common for doctors treating a patient to tell the pathologist, "We know the cause of death; we have a CT scan already". Yet, despite all these advances, approximately fifteen percent of deaths that are autopsied showed a major discrepancy between the "suspected cause of death" and the "actual cause of death". This discrepancy is classified as major, in that the condition was not suspected or the suspected diseased organ system was wrong.

Development of new imaging modalities, too, is reliant on a validation of the imaging with the actual condition as established by autopsy findings, sometimes referred to as the "gold standard". It is prudent to remember that, for all the advances in modern imaging technology, it is still an "image". An analogy would be that we would all be able to say that we saw a shadow of a human form, but few would be able to tell who that person is, if indeed it is a person and not a mannequin.

Modern medicine is extremely interventionist and many devices are introduced into the body. Despite stringent testing and design, these devices sometimes fail. Such dramatic failures may result in death, and it is the autopsy that helps us understand what happened and that leads to the discontinuation of the use of a particular device or a redesign to address flaws. Unexpected severity of side effects of very potent drugs has led to massive commercial losses for drug companies.

In this age of growing distrust among individuals, complaints and allegations of medical malpractice are ever increasing and Hong Kong is certainly not immune. The autopsy has helped substantiate some of these allegations, but equally important it has helped negate many of these allegations, too.

The Future

The number of autopsies performed worldwide is decreasing, and this trend is seen in Hong Kong. About ten years ago, the number of "hospital autopsies", i.e., autopsies performed with the consent of the family, was equal to those that were reported to the coroner. In recent years, this type of "hospital autopsy" is almost non-existent.

The medical curriculum worldwide has been reformed, and opportunities for anatomical dissection and autopsy teaching sessions in many medical schools are non-existent. Future doctors are therefore not exposed to such traditional sources of information and are unlikely to seek permission for autopsies.

New technologies are replacing the autopsy. In countries such as Switzerland and Japan, a full body post-mortem CT-scan is done in place of an autopsy. It is only a matter of time and cost until this spreads to more countries. It must be noted, however, that imaging does not provide tissue and cellular samples; the autopsy does. The autopsy is not just a gross examination of structures; it is also a microscopic examination of cells.

Ironically, the future of the autopsy is dependant on the economics of all health-related procedures. If a machine is deemed able to provide an acceptable result at a lower price than a proper dissection, the post-mortem dissection and examination will, in all likelihood, disappear.

A Personal Reflection

I grew up in an overseas Chinese community steeped in the practice of ancestral worship, Daoism, Confucianism and what I can only describe as Chinese Buddhism all mixed together.

I have attended and witnessed the elaborate funeral rites of family elders, in which proceedings lasted several days and nights. I distinctly remember wearing "mourning cloth" (a little piece of dark-coloured cloth) on my shirt for up to a year after the death of my paternal grandfather. I remember the visits to the grave during Ching Ming Festival, etc. These practices gradually became less and less elaborate with the death of grandmothers, uncles, and recently, of my father. Such changes, I believe, reflect the changing world we live in. The two decades since my grandfather's and my father's death have seen an increase in the pace of life and work in the community that we live in.

Although I can at one level understand the various "reasons" for the different aspects of these elaborate rituals, it does not sit well with my "Western style", education made even more so by my "medical education". I have told my children and siblings that "come my time, just cremate me and have a good party".

Despite this very personal decision, I have never had any difficulty respecting the beliefs and wishes of bereaved family members. The need for dealing with bereavement and the process of closure is rooted in the culture and beliefs of an individual, the immediate circle of family and friends and the society they live in.

Finally, recalling an entry I made in a publication during my medical school years, "Death is but a phase in life". Nearly thirty years down the road, I would only add, "Live a good life and let death be".

8

Death Metaphors in Chinese[a]

Wing Shan CHEUNG and Samuel HO

Introduction

As Feifel[1] remarked, one of humanity's most distinguishing characteristics is the capacity to grasp the concept of a "future and inevitable" death. The meanings of death and life are actually interdependent. Individuals' perceptions of death affect their priorities and life choices; whereas individuals' accomplishments, failures, changes and the cumulative effects of diverse experiences in life would also influence personal meanings of death.[2] Yet, only a limited number of research studies have focused on the personal meanings of death.

Among the studies concerned with meanings of death, many focus only on the developmental process for children to acquire the cognitive or physical concepts of death: the cessation of all bodily functions that is inevitable, irreversible, and universal for all human beings.[3–8] Kastenbaum[9] and Speece,[10] however, suggested that the personal meanings of death were not fully comprehended by these objective qualities, as they did not reflect belief systems with ideas about reincarnation and the afterlife. Their remark was supported by Holcomb et al.'s[11] finding that the views of "death as a continued existence in an afterlife" and "death as non-existence" were the two most common themes of death in the content analysis of the free-response narratives about personal meanings of death. Noppe and Noppe[12] also found that, from a developmental perspective, a general belief in continuation of the soul appeared to increase from late childhood to young adulthood. The noncorporeal beliefs and thematic meanings of death revealed have indicated the need for further exploration in the relation between personal meanings and reactions towards death-related matters.

[a.] The content of this chapter was presented at the The 10th Hong Kong International Cancer Congress (HKICC) Symposium: "Challenges in Life and Death Education" on 21 November 2003.

To understand the relation between the personal meaning of death and the attitudes towards death, Cicirelli[2] investigated three themes of death: seeing death as extinction, seeing death as the beginning of afterlife, and seeing death as marking a legacy of life achievement. He found that all the three themes are positively related to different subscale scores of the Leming Fear of Death Scale.[13] The presence of these themes only predicts a higher level of fear of death. We believe, however, that such themes of death revealed in Western participants may not be representative of Asian people, who tend to show a lower level of death anxiety in cross-cultural studies,[14, 15] whereas themes of death that can lead to greater acceptance of death or lower fear of death have not yet been well addressed.

Death in Chinese

Wilson and Ryan[16] observed that, culturally, Chinese people are more reluctant to talk about death for fear of associating with bad luck. "Death" is not a topic to be discussed openly. This "denial" tendency may give reasons for the lower conscious death anxiety observed. In conjunction with Kubler-Ross's[17] remark that cultures differ in their ways of explaining and giving meaning to death, we cannot simply impose Western death orientations onto Chinese people. Although individuals may hide their anxiety about death in general, it is more difficult to assess directly the personal meanings of and attitudes towards death.

In this aspect, McLennan and Stewart[18] suggested the use of images or metaphors of death to tap individuals' attitudes and anxiety towards death at an unconscious or preconscious level. The above proposition is indirectly supported by an early study in Hong Kong that cancer patients with a very high level of death anxiety tended to exhibit a lot of maladaptive fantasies about death which, in turn, may further increase their anxiety toward death.[19]

It was supported in Riley's study[20] that even people not preoccupied with thoughts of death carry about with them various images of death. Pollio and colleagues[21] also noted that images provide a way of describing and conceptualizing death constructs that cannot be expressed in verbal language. Therefore, in a previous study, Cheung and Ho[22] established thirty Chinese death metaphor statements on the basis of McLennan and Stewart's Revised Death Fantasy Scale (RDFS),[18] to examine the attitudes towards death of Chinese adolescents. Three of the ten highest scored items ("A separation from the loved one", "A thankful goodbye" and "People crying around my bed") are newly created items with an "interpersonal" focus.[23, 24] This is consistent with previous studies that Hong Kong Chinese are more concerned about the reactions of others in death-related matters,[25, 26] and we believe that "interpersonal relationship" maybe one of the major themes of death for Chinese people.

Death Metaphors

Subsequent to the above study, we conducted another study to collect data on the personal meanings of death among Chinese, through the images or metaphor of death. Furth[27] showed that drawing (or artwork) is indeed a valuable medium that allows individuals to express their ideas in an unfettered and uninhibited way. Therefore, we have collected multi-dimensional components of death metaphors in our study by using (1) descriptive death metaphor statements, (2) personal drawings of death, and (3) description of death with colours and adjectives, to understand the Chinese perceptions of death revealed in a more unconscious way. The thirty death metaphor items used in previous studies[22] were translated with back-translation and triangulation into Chinese. Participants were asked to rate each statement, on a five-point Likert scale (0 = not at all; 5 = quite well), the extent to which each metaphor describes their personal perception of death. Also, they were asked to draw a picture to describe their personal meaning of death (with written descriptions), and give a maximum of three adjectives and three colours about death. Templer's Death Anxiety Scale (DAS)[28] was used as the conventional death attitude construct, in which participants were asked to give true or false responses to fifteen questions, and a DAS score was calculated by summing the score of the fifteen items after reversion.

The questionnaires were administered to 217 participants (75 male and 142 female) from the University of Hong Kong. All participants were Chinese and were born and raised in Hong Kong. They ranged in age from eighteen to twenty-three years (X = 20.03, S.D. = 1.02). More than half of them (63. 1%) had experienced at least one life-threatening incident, and more than one-third (45.2%) had experienced bereavement in the previous five years. More than one-third of the participants (41.9%) hold religious beliefs.

This chapter describes some of our findings. We hope they will provide useful to people caring for the dead and dying, and as well as stimulate readers' thoughts about death — and life.

Descriptive Statement of Death

The mean scores of the ten highest scored death metaphor items and the ten lowest scored death metaphor items were calculated. They are shown with their correlations with the DAS score in Table 1.

Six out of the ten highest scored items were newly created items, whereas nine out of the ten lowest scored items were from the RDSF. The item "a separation from loved one" was again the highest scored item (refer to Table 1).

Table 1
Mean, Standard Deviation and Correlation of Death Metaphors Statements
for the Ten Highest and Ten Lowest Scored Items in Study One

Death Metaphor Items		Mean	(S.D.)	DAS
	Ranking			
10 Highest Scored Items				
A separation from loved one (10) #	1	4.24	(0.98)	−.06
A road to heaven (16) #	2	3.69	(1.17)	.35**
A gravestone with my photo (4) #	3	3.55	(1.21)	−.15*
People crying around my bed (6) #	4	3.41	(1.19)	−.05
A shining angel (22) #	5	3.13	(1.17)	.28**
A cold lonely journey (3)	6	3.04	(1.18)	−.23**
An empty grey space (24)	7	3.03	(1.26)	−.31**
A sweet sleep (21)	8	3.03	(1.24)	.29**
A black hole (23)	9	2.94	(1.28)	−.34**
A flat electrocardiogram (8) #	10	2.93	(1.29)	−.09
10 Lowest Scored Items	Ranking			
A devouring tiger (27)	30	1.82	(0.95)	-.07
A chrysalis becoming a butterfly(17) #	29	1.94	(1.09)	.17*
An ugly monster (20)	28	2.01	(1.08)	-.29**
A hammer blow (29)	27	2.02	(0.97)	-.08
A high stone wall (9)	26	2.04	(1.01)	-.08
A deserved holiday (5)	25	2.09	(1.16)	.32**
A comforting parent (15)	24	2.11	(1.12)	.42**
A family reunion (14)	23	2.24	(1.28)	.45**
A fall into fire (25)	22	2.30	(1.27)	-.26**
A great adventure (19)	21	2.32	(1.22)	.19**

Notes: (1) Item numbers are shown in parenthesis. (2) # = Self -developed items. Other items are adapted from the RDFS.[29]

Colours Describing Death

The most frequent colours describing death were "black" and "white", which was consistent with our daily experiences, as they are the major colours at funerals. "Blue" and "red" were the fourth and fifth largest group of colours, but some participants correlated these with sadness and blood in their descriptions of images of death. We noted one interesting thing: some participants used colours like "golden" or "bright light" to describe death, which may be explained by their personal religious beliefs that have a bright image of "death" or "life after death". The distribution of the colours describing death is shown in Table 2.

Table 2
The Distribution of Colours and Adjectives about Death (n = 217)

Colours about Death	Number	%
Black	143	53.6
White	61	22.8
Grey	30	11.2
Blue	11	4.1
Red	8	3
Bright or golden	6	2.2
Others	8	2.9
Total	267	100

Note. The total response (267) is larger than the sample size (n = 217) because participants were allowed to write up to three colours.

Adjectives and Drawings about Death

Both adjectives and drawings about death were analysed and categorized within the basic framework of Yang and Chen's[30] three categories: Biological Death Concepts, Psychological Death Concepts and the Metaphysical Concepts of Death, with modifications in the sublevels.

The largest category of adjectives describing death is the Psychological Death Concept that includes adjectives describing emotions towards death. Negative emotions (43.3%) was the largest sublevel, whereas fear and anxiety were the dominant emotions expressed in our participants. The second largest group of adjectives (natural law, 23.5%) concerned some definite characteristics of death (e.g., unavoidable, cannot escape, absolute), which reflects the "cognitive maturity" in understanding these basic characteristics of death. These adjectives were classified into biological death concepts. Besides presenting the understandings of these "basic" qualities of death, some participants used abstract items like empty, unknown, or mysterious (7.4%) to describe their views on death. These words were grouped as "mysterious or abstract" in the metaphysical concept of death category.

Interestingly, we found the third largest sublevel of adjectives (positive emotions, 13.7%) mainly presented positive attitudes towards death (e.g., peaceful, joyful, and relaxing). In contrast to the negative emotions of anxiety and avoidance, adjectives of "positive emotions" show the presence of another acceptance towards death. This positive acceptance may also be attributed to the participants' religious beliefs. As in independent sample *t*-tests, the difference of the probability of positive adjectives about death is significant (t = 2.311, p<.05) between participants with or without religious beliefs, although no significant difference was found in their conscious death anxiety. Some other adjectives like "god", "heaven", and "judgement" (6.6%) were also used to describe their understanding of death, which was grouped and labelled "religious symbols". The distribution of the adjectives about death is shown in Table 3.

Table 3
Categorization of Adjectives Describing Death (n = 217)

Categorization	Examples	N	%
Psychological Level		**337**	**57.0**
Negative Emotions	horrible, scary	256	43.3
Positive Emotions	relaxed, joyful	81	13.7
Biological Level		**139**	**23.5**
Natural Law	absolute, unavoidable	139	23.5
Metaphysical Level		**115**	**19.5**
Mysterious or Nothingness	empty, unknown	44	7.4
Religious Symbols	God, Heaven	39	6.6
Others	dark, clean	32	5.4
Total		**591**	**100**

Note. The total response (591) is larger than the sample size (n = 217) because participants were allowed to write as many as three adjectives.

Death Drawings

Compared with the adjectives used to describe death, the drawings about death were more focused in describing abstract ideas or concepts about death. We found that nearly two-thirds of the drawings show this kind of abstract thinking or query about death. We categorized these drawings into the metaphysical concepts of death (68.6%), and "mysterious", "nothingness", "journey" and "religious symbols" as the sublevels. Of these, drawings with religious elements like a cross or heaven was the largest group (religious symbols, 27.6%).

Although both positive (happiness) and negative (sorrow) emotions could be identified from some of the drawings, the percentage is lower (13.4%). Another interesting observation we found was the negative emotions shown in the drawings were usually concerned with the reactions of others significant to the deceased person. Most of these drawings showed the sorrow or grief of the people around the deceased person, which is consistent with our previous findings that Chinese people maybe more "interpersonally" focused.[22]

The biological concept of death (eighteen percent) consisted of drawings perceiving death as a physical state or something natural, in which participants describe death as an end to all physical activities. Categorization of the drawings about death is shown in Table 4.

Table 4
Categorization of Death Drawings (n = 217)

	N	%	Examples
Metaphysical Level	**149**	**68.6**	
Religious Symbols	60	27.6	
Mysterious	22	10.1	
Tunnel or Journey	24	11.1	
Nothingless	43	19.8	
Psychological Level	**29**	**13.4**	
Negative Emotions	19	8.8	
Positive Emotions	10	4.6	
Biological Level	**39**	**18**	
Natural Law	18	8.3	
State of Death	21	9.7	
Total	**217**	**100**	

Discussion

In this chapter, we have provided some systematic information about colours, adjectives, and personal images of death. Common themes of personal meaning of death were identified through the descriptive items of death metaphors, and the relationships between different personal perceptions of death and personal death anxieties were examined. The qualitative results indeed carry much stimulating information to explore (e.g., the meaning of using "black" and "white" to describe death, the representation of death as images of "natural law" etc.), but only the major results and applications are highlighted below.

Positive Orientation of Death

Interestingly, in our Hong Kong Chinese participants, positive orientations of death emerged in the colours, adjectives and the images of death. "Golden" and "bright" were used as colours to describe death. Adjectives carrying positive emotions like peaceful, joyful, and relaxing were presented as the third largest sub-group of adjectives (13.7%), and some participants drew smiling faces to represent their personal image of death. Although the previous literature has emphasized the negative attitudes towards death, the positive orientation revealed in both the words and drawings in our study have shown evidence for the need to further explore the aspects of death perceptions.

Religious beliefs were found to significantly affect participants' death orientation. One of the reasons may be that the systematic framework of life and death suggested in religions help the individuals to ease their fears of uncertainty or punishment after death. Answers were promised about the meaning of life and death, in which individuals can find direction in preparing for the present life and future death. In the present study, participants with religious beliefs were found to have a generally more positive orientation towards death and a higher probability of using positive adjectives to describe death ($t = 2.311$, $p < .05$).

Themes of "Journey" and "Mysterious or Abstract": Searching for Direction and Meaning in Adolescence

Leaving the stage of childhood, adolescents have just processed the increasing sophistication of reasoning power and begun to question their childhood ideas regarding religion, values, the future, relationships, and questions concerning death and dying. Most participants in the present study are adolescents or young adults, and they have the capacity to attain what Fowler[31] called "individuative-reflective" faith: they examine, evaluate, and restructure their beliefs and values. They are also undergoing the developmental process of intense searching for identity and struggling to establish the system of values in their world and the meaning of death, dying and living. Therefore, it was not surprising that the theme of "mysterious or abstract" emerged as the most common image in the personal drawings of death we collected (29.9%).

In comparison with "mysterious or abstract", the perception of death as a "journey" or "adventure" may reflect the search for direction and possibilities in life, in which adolescents are looking forward to guidance to integrate the past and the upcoming future.

In short, "mysterious or abstract" and "journey" are the themes of death that characterized the developmental uniqueness of adolescents/young adults, whereas their values and meaning of life and death are still at the stage of construction and are open for exploration with room for adjustment. The present results may also be another sign of the need for systematic education about life and death, to help adolescents in their search for the meaning of these concepts. As Noppe and Noppe[32] stated, "creating a meaning of death within the context of life may be the crucial achievement of adolescent development".

"Separation": The theme of death to be explored

Of the thirty descriptive metaphors on death that were used in both previous and present studies, "separation from a loved one" is the highest scored item. This result is consistent with previous studies that the tensions of "attachment, separation, identity and death of self" are uncovered in empirical research in adolescence/young adulthood. Davis *et al.*[33] noted that high school and college students who have higher self-esteem also experienced less death anxiety. Mikulincer *et al.*[34] found that individuals classified as secure in relation to attachment style experienced less fear of death than those classified as insecurely attached. As the development of one's identity is related to anxiety about death,[35] positive development of self-esteem and ego identity would be helpful for adolescents in coping with the stress in death-related issues like bereavement [36] and should be emphasized in the development of education about death.

When applying these observations in bereavement counselling, we can better understand the psychological processes involved in grieving with reference to separation and loss of the attachment figure.[37] Stroebe *et al.*[38] suggested that most adults would have a more mature developed identity and be more able to perceive that their core self remains intact even when important others die. But for adolescents, contemplation of death of significant others involves the threat of losing a self that *is*, as the self is intimately tied in with the decreased and is in an active process of creation. Therefore, Meshot and Leitner[39] observed that, when an adolescent grieves, the extent of identification with the deceased is significantly greater than what has been observed in adults. Helping adolescents to establish or reconstruct their personal identity would be a significant step for them to grow and get past the grieving process.

Conclusion

As medical technology has advanced in recent decades, we not only have a larger aging population but also more people wrestling with chronic, life-threatening illness and prolonged dying. Our personal meaning of death is also challenged by controversial ethical issues like abortion, euthanasia, suicide and capital punishment; and new societal diseases like HIV/AIDS, H5N1 and SARS. Further exploration of the personal meaning of death is valuable and enables us to have greater understanding of both others and of ourselves.

In this study, we explored death orientation of young adults with their use of colours, adjectives and drawings about death. The existence of a positive orientation to death was revealed, and this can be further investigated and compared among different cultures and religions. Four thematic factors of death orientation were also investigated with descriptive death metaphor items for assessment. These metaphors can help us explore the difference of death orientation among participants with or without religious beliefs. Using the death metaphor items in the clinical assessment of death orientation is a promising area to explore. Common themes of death observed in our adolescent participants were also highlighted with insights in death education and bereavement counselling.

We believe that the death orientations revealed are essential in understanding our personal meaning of death. Because of the narrow age range of the participants in the present study, groups of participants from early adolescence to young adulthood would be invited in future studies, to investigate and identify the specific death orientation in different developmental stages and their relation to their positive and negative attitudes to death. The descriptive death metaphor scale is also under further validation for the assessment of death orientation with data collected in Beijing. Our target is to develop a reliable quantitative assessment tool in death orientation studies for Chinese in the near future.

Acknowledgements

We would like to express our gratitude to the Centre on Behavioral Health, The University of Hong Kong, for funding part of this research project.

9

What Is Good Death: Bridging the Gap between Research and Intervention

Wallace Chi Ho CHAN, Heung Sang TSE
and Timothy Hang Yee CHAN

Introduction

Death is inevitable. But in view of this impossibility of further possibility, people still hope for "good death". Different cultures may construct different definitions of "good death", and Chinese culture is no exception. Our traditional Chinese philosophical and religious thought provides important cultural insights into the perception of death. Recent studies have tried to explore the meaning of "good death" in contemporary Chinese society.

Facing one's own death and the death of significant others are stressful and traumatic events that will shatter our fundamental assumptions and question the meaning of death.[1,2,3] Reconstruction of meaning[4] may be an important way to help terminally ill patients who are dying, and their bereaved families, if they can make sense of the "death" as "good".[5,6,7] Therefore, the meaning of "good death" in the Chinese context may have great implications for direct practice, such as intervention for terminally ill patients and bereaved families.

It is important for us to bridge the gap between research and practice for effective palliative and bereavement service.[8] To respond to this need, recent research findings concerning good death in Hong Kong are discussed in this paper, as a way to shed light on direct practice in the local context.[9]

What Is Good Death?

What good death is remains culturally laden and socially constructed.[10] Paradoxically, all cultures seem to conceptualize death into "good" and "bad".[5] The discussion of good death in Chinese culture, however, remains limited.[7]

Influence from Confucianism, Daoism and Buddhism

Chinese culture is predominantly influenced by Confucianism, Daoism and Buddhism,[6] all of which offer important insights into how the Chinese perceive death and in turn good death. Confucius answered his student's question about death: "While you do not know life, how can you know about death?" (in Lunyu, *Analects*[11]) Many have said that Confucius avoided facing death directly. However, others have said that what Confucius meant was that, if one handled things in life properly, the problem of death would be solved also.[12] This shows us that the way of inquiring into death as proposed by Confucianism is through life. Confucius proposed that ren (仁), a moral standard, was the rule of living. The nature of ren was "continuation" and "never ending". In this sense, if a person lived a life of ren, his or her mortality would be transcendent, and the spirit would be preserved. Spiritually, one transcended to "immortality".[13] In fact, Confucianism states that death is not horrible if one dies meaningfully. From this sense, a good death implies having lived a moral life and dying for the preservation of the virtues.

Daoism offers the Chinese another perspective on death. It emphasizes the importance of harmonizing with nature. Life and death seem to be the four seasons of nature. Death is viewed as natural and part of life. Thus, there is no inherent preference for life or death. One need not feel happy about life but need not grieve about death either. One would not be afraid of death, if one could fuse with nature and the universe, and in this way, transcend death. There would not be life and death, as one had already fused with the universe.[12, 13] In this sense, good death implies death that harmonizes with nature, and having an attitude of acceptance as result of this fusion.

Buddhism views life and death as major concerns.[14] The "Four Noble Truths", including "the existence of impermanence (suffering)" (dukkha), "the arising of suffering because of craving" (samudaya), "the cessation of suffering" (nirodha) and "the middle way or eightfold path" (magga), tells us that life is full of suffering, which is due to karma and samsara.[15] The way to cease suffering is through reaching of nirvana, by following the eightfold path. The inevitable death and the never-ending circle of life and death (reincarnation) is one of these sufferings. Influenced by the Buddhist belief in karma, ordinary people tend to view death as the outcome of misconduct.[6] Also, "looking through the suffering" becomes an appropriate way to transcend death.[16] Good death, from the Buddhist perspective, may imply a life full of good behaviour and virtues and may indicate the idea of "looking through" the physical life.

Good Death: Findings in the Chinese Context

(1) From the perspective of terminally ill patients

As well as a discussion based on these traditional beliefs, some empirical studies have been recently conducted to explore the views of Chinese on good death. Mak[17] interviewed thirty-three Chinese hospice patients, aged from thirty-four to eight-six, who had terminal cancer. He found seven important elements for good death: 1) being aware of dying (death awareness), 2) maintaining hope (hope), 3) being free from pain and suffering (comfort), 4) experiencing personal control (control), 5) maintaining social relationships (connectedness), 6) preparing to depart (preparation), and 7) accepting the timing of one's death (completion). Awareness of dying was found to be most important of the seven elements.[7] Accepting the timing of one's death is also essential, and the extent of acceptance was found to depend on whether the patients had completed their social roles, died at an old age, had religious beliefs and experienced meaningful lives with hope and control.[17]

Chao[18] also interviewed terminal cancer patients in Taiwan and analysed three important elements in constituting "good dying". They are " peace of body", "peace of mind" and "peace of thought". "Peace of body" refers to "minimizing the agony of physical symptoms, a short period of the dying process, cleanliness, neatness and integrity of the body, mobility". [19] "Peace of mind" indicates "yielding, non-attachment, not being lonely, settling all affairs, being in a preferred environment and enjoying nature.[11] Last, "peace of thought" means "getting through each day without thinking, having a meaningful life, an expectation that the suffering would end".[19]

(2) From the perspective of bereaved persons

Hsu, Kahn and Hsu[6] interviewed thirty-five Taiwanese widows. The authors stated that good death "connotes a combination of life accomplishments and death without suffering". Accomplishments, as defined by Confucianism, refers to the deceased husband who has fulfilled his familial responsibility, such as raising children to adulthood. Data also showed that it was not the physical age that predicted whether a person had good death but the accomplishment of familial responsibility. Older widows might better adjust to the loss, as the chance for their husbands to fulfil the family responsibility was greater. For example, their children might have grown up and married and have their own children.[6] Another aspect that was viewed as good death is "without suffering". Those who died unexpectedly due to accident or murder, and those who died after prolong physical struggle, were seen as not having good death, according to the cultural definition. It should be noted that old age was not found, in these recent studies, to be directly connected with good death, though traditionally old age is perceived to be good death and the funeral for an elderly person is called a "laughing funeral" (or a happy funeral that has nothing to be sad about).[20] However, old age does predict good death indirectly, because the person has a higher chance of fulfilling family roles and accepting the time of completion.

In Hong Kong, Chan[21] also interviewed fifteen bereaved Chinese older adults, who are between sixty-six and eighty-six years old. Time since spousal death when interviewed varied from 8.5 to 62 months. Data were analysed by grounded theory.[22] Five themes of good death were found: 1) little suffering before death, 2) presence of family members at the moment of death, 3) good family, 4) natural death, and 5) not being a burden to others.[12]

(3) From the perspective of the general public

Previous findings of good death mentioned above are mainly qualitative and involve only small numbers of either terminally ill patients or bereaved persons. It helps to explore the meanings of "good death", but the perception of good death among the general public remains unknown. As a result, a large-scale survey of "good death", which involved 738 Chinese adults, was conducted by the Society for the promotion of Hospice Care in Hong Kong in 2004.[22] An expert panel involving a bereavement counsellor and a medical social worker was set up. Based on a literature review and frontline experience, a questionnaire was then generated to explore to what extent, from 0 (totally disagree) to 10 (totally agree), the general public agreed to these definitions of good death. About 80% of the respondents are female, 30.4% of them aged below forty, 38.2% aged between forty and sixty-five, and 15.9% aged above sixty-five. Findings showed that "no physical suffering and torture" had the greatest mean score of 8.78, which indicated the greatest emphasis on this item by the general public. The second important criterion of good death is having "a painless death" (mean score 8.59), followed by the item, "not dependent on others" (mean score 7.93). By factor analysis, these three items actually form a "physical factor" of good death, which explained 14.3% of variance. "Psychosocial factors" which consisted of seven items, including "financial planning for the family", "fulfil last wishes", "reconcile with family", "no regrets", "fulfil family obligations", "pre-arrange funeral", and "psychologically prepared", explained 25.6% of variance. Except for no regrets, all these psychosocial items had a mean score above 7 out of 10. The general public was less concerned about post-mortem items. "Body not tampered with", "extravagant funeral", and "dying at home" got mean a score below 4.[23] Details of the individual mean score for each item is shown in Table 1.

Table 1 Level of agreement on good death items

Good death items	Mean score (1-10)
No physical torture 死前唔駛受病痛長時間折磨	8.78
A painless death 臨死之前能夠盡量減少身體上的痛楚	8.59
Not dependent on others 臨終前生活各方面都唔駛靠人幫	7.93
Reconcile with family 死前能夠同家人或親友和好	7.84
Financial planning for family 知道自己唔駛擔心家人以後生活	7.71
Finish family obligation 死前完成對家庭責任	7.66
Fulfill last wishes 死之前能夠完成埋未了心事	7.38
Pre-arrange funeral 能夠生前安排或決定點處理自己身後事	7.04
Psychologically prepared 心理上已預備好自己將會死去	7.01
No regrets 諗番自己一生，會覺得無咩遺憾	6.61
Body kept clean 身體能夠保持整齊清潔	6.39
Body not tampered 死後身體完整	3.63
Extravagant funeral 風光大葬	2.73
Dying at home 能夠係屋企死	2.72

Good Death and Good Bereavement

Achieving "good death" has become a great concern in palliative care for terminally ill patients, but the implications of good death for bereaved persons have not been thoroughly explored.

To fill this research gap, Carr[24] investigated the influence of "quality of death", such as the extent of having good death, on the adjustment of 210 bereaved older adults. Quality of death is defined as consisting of eight aspects, covering matters such as "acceptance of death", "presence of spouse at the moment of death", "extent of care-giving burden", "having a full life", "negligence of health-care providers" etc. The findings show that not all aspects of "good death" could predict better adjustment of bereaved older adults. However, being with the spouse at the moment of death seemed to protect bereaved older adults from intrusive thoughts during the first six months after loss. Positive spousal interaction during the last stage of the deceased spouse's life could predict lower levels of anger but also higher level of yearning. Painful death of spouse was correlated with higher anxiety level of bereaved older adults, and perceived negligence of health-care providers was found to elevate the anger of bereaved older adults. To our knowledge, this is the first systematic quantitative study focusing on "good death for the bereaved", but the validity of the findings may be questionable, as the eight components of good death defined in the study cannot be grouped as individual subscales by factor analysis.

In Hong Kong, Chan[9] also explored the influence of "good death" on bereaved older spouses from the qualitative findings. Results showed that "bad death" (versus good death), such as "unnatural death", "suffering in the dying process", and "spouse not present at the moment of death" had a negative effect on bereaved older adults, as conveyed in the narratives. "Hospital care and treatment" was found to play a vital role in determining the quality of death of the patients. For example, the negligence of doctors and nurses in the hospital was perceived to be responsible for creating additional suffering for dying spouses and delayed the timely presence of the spouse at the moment of death of the patient. Affected by this, negative consequences seemed to be reflected in the narratives of the bereaved older adults: 1) persistent anger and grievance, 2) increased sense of powerlessness, and 3) difficulty in accepting the loss. Chan[13] also stated that findings suggested that "good death" was not enough for "good bereavement". Instead, "good life" after spousal loss, such as the meaningful use of time, and perceiving contentment in volunteer work or in social activities, seemed to be crucial for "good bereavement". Chan[9] raised the question of how good the death is for the bereaved and proposed to pay more attention to "good life" as a proactive way of bereavement intervention.

Bridging the Gap: From Research Findings to Intervention

The research findings discussed above enhanced our understanding of "good death" and have great implications for the intervention. In fact, our frontline experience in working with terminally ill patients and bereaved persons has echoed these findings. In the following part, two cases are described to illustrate this.

Good Death: For Terminally Ill Patients

> Mr Lee was almost sixty years old when he was admitted to the hospital after suffering from terminal lung cancer. He was a successful ex-government official and spent most of his life working. One of his regrets was that he did not have a candlelight dinner with his wife on Valentine's Day. He said that he would not die peacefully if he could not take care of this unfinished business. However, he realized that he was so weak that he could not go out to have meal with his wife.
>
> To fulfil his wish, the whole hospice team helped him to prepare a candlelight "lunch" in the hospital. Volunteers prepared a bouquet of flowers for Mr Lee to present to his wife, and one of the hospice team members cooked Western food for them. Both Mr and Mrs Lee were delighted with this arrangement. Mr Lee died in the hospital peacefully, two weeks after this special celebration.

As suggested by the findings of Chan et al.[23], "finishing family obligations" and "fulfilling last wishes" are important psychosocial concerns in good death. For Mr Lee, "good death" may actually imply fulfilling his last wish, by being a "good husband" and celebrating Valentine's Day with wife with a candlelight meal. Though Mr Lee's original plan could not be fully realized, the hospice team tried their best to meet the needs of Mr Lee and provide the basis for him to experience good death. This also reminded us that working with terminally ill patients may not be just restricted to "counselling"; pragmatic as well as creative assistance may be equally important.

Good Death: For the Bereaved

Mr Cheung was fifty-seven years old. His wife was in her mid-forties. They had a daughter eighteen years old and a son of eight. Mr Cheung died of terminal lung cancer in hospital. The palliative team in the hospital ensured a painfree death for Mr Cheung and allowed Mrs Cheung to stay with him during his final days in hospital.

A medical social worker accompanied Mrs Cheung to the mortuary to see the body of Mr Cheung before he was transferred to the funeral parlour. The image of "good death" as perceived by Mrs Cheung was spoiled when the hospital worker mistakenly showed her another body to identify. Mrs Cheung was deeply frightened by this, and worse, she was overwhelmed by the horrible image of the anonymous body (that had a painful facial expression) she saw, and generalized this horrible, unpeaceful image to the death of her husband. This elevated Mrs Cheung's anxiety level and fear. When thinking of her spouse, Mrs Cheung was preoccupied with images of ghosts. For example, she was worried that Mr Cheung might become a horrible ghost.

A medical social worker provided grief counselling for Mrs Cheung. She was encouraged to reinforce the positive aspects of her spouse's death, or, in other words, the image of "good death". For example, she was reminded that Mr Cheung actually died without much pain, and she had tried her best to be with him during the last days. Mrs Cheung was allowed to vent her feelings, including the fears. Her fears were normalized by the medical social worker as one possible response in grieving, and her fear of fear was thus minimized. Gradually, Mrs Cheung's horrible image of bad death faded, and she started to appreciate the efforts and concern provided by the palliative team in hospital.

Research findings tell us that "minimizing pain and suffering" is important for good death, as perceived by both the dying patients and the bereaved persons. Mr Cheung's case suggests how crucial the perception of "good death" is for the adjustment of the bereaved spouse. However, this case also teaches us that promoting "good death" may not be the only contribution of a few hospital staff in the palliative care unit of the hospital. Instead, the whole process, from the care of terminally ill patients, to the handling of the dead body is equally important for enhancing the perception of "good death". Again, this case figuratively echoes the findings of Carr[24] and Chan[23] that the hospital plays a vital and crucial role in ensuring "good death" for both patients and bereaved family members.

Nam Long Hospital, which specialized in providing hospice care to cancer patients in Hong Kong, closed at the end of 2003. The good practice in ensuring "good death" for the bereaved remains an excellent model for us to learn from. For example, a "viewing room" was set up for family members to be with the dying patient or to see the dead body. This room was designed to be "family style", similar to a comfortable bedroom at home. Hospital staff in the mortuary would help to "handle" the dead body first, like combing the hair and cleaning the face, before arranging for family members to see the deceased in the viewing room. In this peaceful environment, bereaved family members could then recognize the dead body. Family members who could not arrive at the hospital in time now had a valuable chance to say good-bye to the deceased family member in a "non-hurried" manner, and this helped to minimize their guilt. This viewing room in Nam Long Hospital was recognized by the public as a way to promote "good death" for both patients and family members.

Conclusion: Further Reflections on Good Death

Research studies on "good death" have increased our awareness of what is important for both terminally ill patients and bereaved family members. Nevertheless, these findings should not be considered the "norm" for every individual, and those who cannot meet the criteria of "good death" as found in these studies should not be viewed as having "bad death". Walter[25] also indicated that some norms in the culture may constrain how one should grieve, thus causing "policing grief" which may not be adaptive.

One of the reflections of this challenge is to reject the dichotomous thinking of death into just "good" and "bad". Masson[26] indicated that the terminology of "good death" failed to reflect the complex process of death and dying. He suggested that the term "good-enough death" could better explain the situation, as it emphasized the realistic context and contingency. Instead of evaluating the death simply as "good" or "bad", helping professionals may facilitate bereaved persons' consideration of their specific contexts and appreciate the "good-enough death" under the circumstances.

Another reflection on "good death" is that, no matter how good the death, it is still a great loss for many bereaved persons. Thus, by no means can "good death" necessarily predict "good bereavement" in all situations. As Chan[9] proposed, both "good death" and "good life" are required for achieving "good bereavement". Ensuring a "good life" of bereaved persons, like reconstructing the meaning of life after loss[27] in a totally different world after the death of loved ones,[28] may better facilitate the bereaved in coping with their grief. Henderson and Hayslip[29] have shown that general adjustment in life can better predict the level of bereavement-related distress, whereas the reverse is not true. Thus, instead of just focusing on grief work, helping the bereaved persons to adjust to changes in daily life circumstances may be effective in bereavement intervention.

Moreover, intervention focusing on ensuring "good life" can be more proactive, and may match well the pragmatic orientation of bereaved persons.[21] For example, it will be of great importance if bereaved older adults can be helped to spend time more meaningfully, in order to face loneliness in old age after the death of a spouse.

There is room for further research on "good death", "good life" and "good bereavement". What are the long-term effects of "good death" on the adjustment of bereaved persons? Will "good death" predict the personal growth of bereaved persons? What is "good life" as perceived by bereaved persons in different age groups? What is "good bereavement" as perceived by bereaved persons? All these research findings will probably shed much more light on our intervention, and integrating this new knowledge into our practice will be the next step forward.

PART TWO

DYING

10

Impact of Palliative Care on the Quality of Life of the Dying

Michael Mau Kong SHAM, Kin Sang CHAN, Doris Man Wah TSE and Raymond See Kit LO

The Transition from Curative to Palliative Care

Palliative care has been developing in Hong Kong for more than twenty years, gaining wider coverage and more sophisticated service.[1] The modes of delivery include in-patient care, home care, out-patient care, day care and hospital consultative services, looking after cancer patients as well as patients in the advanced stage of other diseases such as HIV/AIDS.

Nonetheless, for any patient, the personal experience of the last journey is always an individual one. This is reflected by struggles that patients, family members and health-care workers face during the transition from curative to palliative care. The transition of the goals of care from curative to palliative care has a significant influence on how patients plan their remaining days. However, this means more than the cognitive realization of the patient's limited prognosis: it also means emotional acceptance. This is greatly affected by how patients and their families come to terms with the illness. The last journey in life is often characterized by deep psychological and spiritual struggles,[2] especially when the patient's condition begins to deteriorate. Patients, families and health-care workers repeatedly face ethical and practical dilemmas.[3] Should quality of life be sacrificed in order to prolong life? Should a treatment with a low response rate be considered futile?

A local qualitative study on advanced cancer patients who were receiving palliative care revealed that several factors affected the patient's decisions on limited treatment. They include prognostic factors; quality of life issues such as burden of illness; and existential concerns such as will to live, life values and death-related concerns.[4] Patients may present with quite polarized responses of "struggle for life" or "desire for hastened death". The therapeutic use of self becomes an art for palliative care workers to facilitate the transformation of these two extreme responses to a peaceful and dignified death.[5]

The transition to palliative care very much depends on the doctor's personal attitude towards death and dying. The attitude of the doctor towards palliative care is pivotal in guiding patients entering into the palliative phase. This involves an active paradigm shift[6] of the treatment goals of health-care workers, from the biomedical to the bio-psycho-spiritual model, from a disease-centred approach to person-centred care, and from prolongation of survival to enhancement of meaningfulness in the last journey.[1] It is important for the doctor to be aware that the transition may be a very painful step for the patient. A sense of abandonment may prevail and become a hurdle for transition. Doctors should have the sensitivity to continue guidance and understanding of a patient's fluctuation of acceptance during the journey. The development of palliative medicine in Hong Kong and a territory-wide referral system provide a platform for such a transition. The quality of palliative care provided is of paramount importance in facilitating the shift of the patient's goal of care from prolongation of life to quality of life.

Development of Palliative Care in Hong Kong

Although palliative care started in Hong Kong in 1982, by the late 1980s, there were only a few hospital-based palliative care units. Palliative care was operated solely by voluntary organizations until 1991, when the government started to fund a few nurses in a palliative care unit. As it gain acceptance by the public, palliative care gradually became a priority in the development of health-care services. In 1994, more palliative care units were established using government funding.

In the beginning, training in palliative care had to be obtained from overseas. As more hospitals became involved in palliative care, regular academic meetings were organized to facilitate knowledge and skill transfer among palliative care professionals. The Hospital Authority started to organized certificate courses in hospice nursing in 1995. In 1996, the University of Wales College of Medicine organized a diploma course in palliative medicine in Hong Kong. This course attracted a lot of doctors, as, instead of going overseas, they could receive training locally in palliative medicine. As more doctors and nurses became trained in palliative care, professional societies were established in 1997: the Hong Kong Society of Palliative Medicine for doctors, and the Hong Kong Hospice Nurses Association for nurses. These societies provide training and ensure the standard of palliative care in Hong Kong.

The specialty of palliative medicine was established in 1998 in Hong Kong. In 2003, there were eleven accredited trainers in six training units. As a result of the development of the specialty, a structured training programme was designed for doctors interested in this field. Entry requirement includes completion of three years of basic physician training and a pass in the intermediate examination. The programme consists of two years of training in a recognized palliative medicine training unit by accredited trainers, in addition to two years of training in general internal medicine. Symptom control is a very important core component. Intimately interwoven with symptom control are other aspects of palliative care, including the hospice philosophy, the concept of death and dying, communication skills, ethical principles, working with families, etc. Without a holistic health and palliative care perspective, a palliative care doctor might become a "symptomatologist", interested only in physical symptoms, instead of one who is addressing the distress and suffering of the patient as a whole person. (See Table 1.)

Table 1
Development of Palliative Care in Hong Kong

1982	Palliative Care Team was established at Our Lady of Maryknoll Hospital
1986	Palliative Care Team was established at Ruttonjee Sanatorium
1987	Hospice Units were established at Haven of Hope Hospital, Nam Long Hospital and United Christian Hospital
1988	Society for the Promotion of Hospice Care, a non-government organization, started Hospice Home Care Service
1991	Government started to fund hospice service (at Nam Long Hospital)
1992	Bradbury Hospice was established
1994	More hospice units were established, as hospice care became a priority area of the Government.
1995	Hospital Authority organized a certificate course in hospice nursing, reflecting Government acknowledgement of the importance of hospice care.
1996	The University of Wales College of Medicine conducted the Diploma in Palliative Medicine course in Hong Kong.
1997	The Hong Kong Society of Palliative Medicine and the Hong Kong Hospice Nurses' Association were established.
1998	The Specialty of Palliative Medicine was established in the Hong Kong College of Physicians.
1999	Hong Kong hosted the Asia Pacific Hospice Conference.
2004	The First Hongkong Macau Palliative Medicine Symposium was organized.

Quality of Life (QOL) of the Dying

Both the Royal College of Physicians and the World Health Organisation have stated that the goal of palliative care is the achievement of best quality of life (QOL) for patients and their families.[7,8] Palliative medicine specialists work hard to provide holistic care to the dying, to improve their quality of life. However, what do dying patients expect from health-care professionals, and how are dying patients suffering?

Although some patients entering a hospice may expect a cure or prolongation of life, most are more realistic and expect pain and symptom control. When patients are admitted to a hospice, they are often asked to identify their main concern, among the many symptoms and pains they have. In one study, the main concerns included pain, shortness of breath, abdominal distension, nausea and vomiting, constipation, weakness or paralysis, poor appetite, difficulty in swallowing, swollen limbs and cough. Some also reported psychosocial problems as their main concern.[9]

Although more than half of the patients reported pain as their main concern, the prevalence of pain is much higher. Up to ninety percent of the patients that were referred to a palliative care team had pain requiring treatment,[10] although other units reported lower incidences of pain, ranging from forty-four to fifty-six percent.[11,12] Pain is often associated with disturbed sleep and impairment of activities of daily living.[11]

Shortness of breath is another common symptom in terminally ill patients. In a study of patients who were short of breath even at rest, even talking and eating were affected in seventy percent of patients, in addition to impairment of other normal activities. Shortness of breath made the patients dependent on others and was associated with a fear of death. Patients who were short of breath at rest might feel satisfied only if they were able to move around.[13]

Although Chinese patients expect alleviation of pain and other symptoms, like patients elsewhere, eating (the ability to eat as well as enjoy food) is an important facet of QOL of patients in Hong Kong.[14] Some patients, short of breath at rest, wish that they could recover so that they could go out for dim sum.[13] Although the Chinese may be reserved in verbally expressing love, preparing and offering food is often a way to show care and concern to patients.[15]

The psychosocial problems of patients have been reported to include fear of suffering, loss of independence, fear of death, thoughts of suicide, loneliness, loss of social role, concern about their appearance or odour, loss of dignity, and feeling worthless and insecure. Because of the strong family ties in Chinese communities, it is not surprising that a lot of the psychosocial concerns reported concerned the family. These included guilt at being a burden to the family, worries about the future of the family, sadness about separation, feeling abandoned by the family, and communication and relationship problems within the family.[9,10] Fulfilling familial obligations is the most common last wish.[15]

Confucianism focuses on family relationships. Although Chinese patients are very concerned about the family, they emphasize the duty to the family rather than the right to be cared for by the children, even though filial piety is expected.[16] It is thus not surprising that Chinese patients feel they are a burden to the family[9] and have difficulty finding the meaning of existence when they are dying.[17]

"Face" is important in Chinese culture, which means being respected or feeling one is respected. Patients demand respect from family and friends, as well as from health-care workers. However, having control over life may not be as important in Chinese patients as it is for Western patients.[14] This may be again related to the emphasis on family interdependence in Chinese culture as well as the Daoist tendency to accept the course of nature.[15]

Indeed, Confucianism, Daoism and Buddhism are the three classical sets of belief in Chinese culture.[15] Despite the important influence of Daoism and Buddhism in Chinese culture, the majority of patients claim that they have no religion.[9] Nevertheless, existential well-being and spirituality have been shown to be important in contributing to the QOL of Chinese patients in Hong Kong, similar to Western patients.[14]

Impact of Palliative Care on QOL of Dying Patients in Hong Kong

Palliative care workers may not be able to control suffering, but symptoms can often be alleviated. In a patient satisfaction survey, the palliative care service was found to be satisfactory or very satisfactory to 100% of the patients and 95% of relatives, and helpful to 99% of patients and 93% of relatives.[10] With appropriate assessment and management, thirty percent of the episodes of shortness of breath at rest could be controlled.[13] Appetite could be improved with treatment in fifty-six percent of patients.[10] Pain could also be controlled in ninety-three percent of patients within a week, and seventy-six percent of patients with pain slept well in the first night after admission to a hospice.[12] In another study, patients gave pain relief a mean score of 3.49, a score of 1 being "not helpful" and 4 being "very helpful".[18]

Pain management in Hong Kong is complicated by difficulties in pain assessment and patients' misconceptions. A lot of cancer patients might consider pain unavoidable and would not want to distract the doctors from cancer treatment.[19] Others fear addiction and other adverse effects of painkillers.[20] They therefore might not even report it to doctors, thus making accurate pain assessment difficult. Although quantifying pain with a numerical rating scale or visual analogue scale may help with pain assessment, not all patients can express the intensity of pain according to the scales.[21] A multi-dimensional scale, however, has been developed for Chinese patients, total pain intensity being the dependent variable; psychosocial, emotional, pharmacological and functional dimensions the independent variables; and pain relief and meaning mediating variables.[22]

The choice of treatment often depends on a balance between benefit and burden. Terminally ill patients are often considered less likely to benefit from aggressive intervention because of their short life expectancy. However, they should not be deprived of these interventions when appropriate. For example, pleurodesis, though invasive, has been shown to be effective in the control of malignant pleural effusions.[10] Surgery should also be considered for patients with bowel obstruction.

Applying new indications or new routes of administration to old drugs can sometimes control difficult symptoms. For example, pain may be controlled with drugs originally marketed for epilepsy or depression. Morphine[9] and Fentanyl,[23] the mainstay of pain management, can also be used to alleviate shortness of breath. Methadone has been found to be useful in cancer pain, especially in those intolerant to morphine.[24] In addition to the oral route of administration, continuous subcutaneous infusion of drugs with a syringe driver is used in as many as forty-two percent of patients in the treatment of pain, shortness of breath, nausea and vomiting.[25] Although, as mentioned, surgery should be considered for patients with bowel obstruction, continuous subcutaneous infusion of anti-emetics and painkillers can often alleviate symptoms in those patients who are unfit for surgery.[9,25]

In addition to cancer patients, palliative care has been extended to patients with chronic obstructive lung disease (COPD) and HIV/AIDS.[26,27] In advanced COPD patients, the results of palliation of dyspnoea with opioids have been reported.[28]

The place one dies is often considered an important factor affecting the QOL. Dying at home is unusual in Hong Kong. However, recently there was a breakthrough in end-of-life care in a nursing home in Hong Kong. Supported by the home palliative care team, the residents could die in the familiar environment of the nursing home with symptoms reasonably controlled.[29]

Audits on Service Outcomes

From 1996 to 1998, an audit was carried out in 3,612 hospice patients on control of their pain, dyspnoea, nausea and vomiting. Results showed that the probability of controlling pain, dyspnoea, nausea and vomiting by day six of admission was 83.8% (95% CI 81.8–85.8), 75.1% (95% CI 72.1–78.2) and 83.9% (95% CI 80.1–87.6) respectively. In 1999, an audit on alleviation of constipation was carried out, showing that eighty percent of patients were relieved from constipation by day six of admission. In the year 2000, an audit on mouth care of 360 hospice patients showed that more than fifty-five percent had improvement in all of the audit items by day four of admission. Audit items included dry lips, cracked corners of the mouth, coated tongue, dry tongue, dry mouth and overall satisfaction with mouth care. All these programmes were coupled with the formulation and promulgation of guidelines to facilitate symptom control.

The audit has also moved beyond the physical domain to other aspects of care. In 2000, an audit using the Hospice Care Performance Inventory designed by Yeung, (see Appendix 1) a validated tool for evaluation of the hospice service, showed that, overall, patients were very satisfied with the care provided. The mean score of satisfaction for physical domain was 4.01, psychological domain 4.07, and social and spiritual domain 3.73, in which a score of 5 indicates the highest level of satisfaction and a score of 1 the lowest level.

In an audit on the communication of staff with 286 hospice patients in Hong Kong, the overall effectiveness of the communication in addressing the physical, emotional, social and spiritual distress of the patients had a mean score of 2.04 (1 = most effective, 5 = least effective) (SD 0.70). A similar audit on the effectiveness of communication with the relatives gave a mean score of 1.88 (SD 0.64).

Measurement of QOL in Palliative Care

The active, total, holistic care given by palliative care professionals is inherently no different from the widely accepted global constructs of QOL. Physical, psychological, social and spiritual aspects of care are the main domains to measure in a palliative-care-specific QOL scale. A study has been conducted on 467 patients with a QOL questionnaire[30], the validity, reliability and sensitivity of which was confirmed.[14, 17, 31-34] QOL as a concept could be perceived by our local palliative care patients. The main QOL domains — physical, psychological, social, and spiritual/existential — could be understood by local Chinese. Furthermore, the spiritual/existential construct was actually found to be the most important domain in predicting overall QOL. Fifty-eight patients on follow-up were able to complete the QOL questionnaire on an average of 5.6 days before they died, reflecting a very close approximation of a self-perceived quality of death. The recorded qualitative comments illustrated that many patients found such a structured assessment beneficial, in that it helped them to discuss sensitive issues that they previously found difficult to raise. Others reported that the QOL interview actually helped them recognize the source of their anguish and distress. The key to a successful QOL assessment necessitates an empathic, sensitive approach with patience, together with good interview and communication skills, which actually should be a required quality of palliative care professionals. Indeed, a well-conducted QOL interview could be therapeutic in itself. There was a case of a 24-year-old lady who refused to talk in depth to any of the staff, since admission into the palliative care unit. She clearly was in psychosocial distress but she was very much a private person, reluctant to share her inner feelings. It was only after the QOL interview that she began to establish rapport with staff. She recounted in retrospect that, during the interview, it was the identification and appreciation of her deep love for the piano that led her to open up and receive our support.

The differences between the local Chinese patients' QOL and those of the West are also interesting. Psychological domain scores were consistently well above average for local Chinese compared with scores in the West, after adjusting the scores to the original version. This may represent a genuine cultural difference, in which the Chinese are more accepting of the traditional belief to "let nature take its course". In contrast, the physical and existential domains of patients scored relatively poorly on admission. The following items had the poorest scores: worst physical symptom, eating, physical well-being, and personal existence. The low physical domain score may be partly that the scores were rated very close to death, reflecting that symptoms pre-death need to be recognized and treated even more promptly. The relatively lower score of the spiritual/existential domain again reflects that more attention needs to be paid to this aspect. These findings are very pertinent from the consideration of service delivery.

Sexuality/intimacy is a taboo subject, especially in the stage close to dying. However, sexuality/intimacy was proven to be an independent domain, albeit with the least significant variance among all domains. Nonetheless, it should not be ignored as irrelevant in our daily care of our patients. It has to be said, though, that patients' self-rated scores on this item were high, pointing to a degree of acceptance of their present state of personal intimacy with the spouse or partner. This may be true for the cohort of patients who were predominantly older. But remarkably enough, for those who could be discharged back into community, follow-up scores on the sexuality/intimacy item did register a significant improvement.

In addition to the evaluation of physical, psychological, social and spiritual symptoms, the extent of effectiveness of palliative care services in alleviating these symptoms could be revealed by measuring QOL. Comparison of QOL on admission with QOL two weeks pre-death showed that palliative care services were able to maintain the overall QOL right to the very end. As for those who were well enough to be discharged, repeat assessment on follow-up was able to show an improvement of their different domains of QOL. There was a significant improvement in the physical, psychological, and sexual domains as well as the overall QOL compared to what it was on admission.

The Last Weeks of Life

Even though death of the patients was reported to be peaceful in eighty-two percent of cases[10] it has also been reported that the QOL scores in the physical domain as well as the existential domain deteriorated within two weeks of death.[17] More than half of the patients still complained of pain in the last two weeks of life, and fatigue and shortness of breath were reported by forty-one percent and twenty-nine percent respectively.[17] In another study on advanced cancer patients during their last week of life,[35] the three most common symptoms were fatigue (94.4%), loss of appetite (87.6%) and cachexia (84. 3%). The prevalence of dyspnoea and pain were sixty-eight percent and forty-nine percent respectively. When asked to rate their symptom distress, patients regarded fatigue, cachexia and loss of appetite as most distressing, with a median distress score of 3 (scale of 0 to 4, 4 = most distressful), and persistently underrated by the physicians. Dyspnoea and pain were only associated with a median distress score of 1. The contribution of dyspnoea and pain to suffering in the last weeks of life requires further investigation. Nevertheless, the results alert us to that fact that, despite efforts and progress in symptom control, difficult symptoms at the end of life are still waiting to be addressed.

The Future

Throughout the past twenty years, palliative care has developed territory-wide, and patients are looked after both at home and in hospice units. The development of the specialty of palliative medicine and the establishment of professional societies serve to ensure the standard of palliative care in Hong Kong. There is, however, no room for complacency. As mentioned, patients still suffer from deterioration in physical well-being and difficulty in finding the meaning of existence. Moreover, the consultative service in general hospitals is not yet well developed. Patients living on outlying islands may not be able to receive optimal home care. Palliative care for patients suffering from diseases other than cancer is still inadequate. Many patients, even if they wish to die at home, may be forced by their sub-optimal home environment to die in hospitals. The transition from curative to palliative care being a painful step, patients in need of palliative care still may not be referred.

Hence, a lot of work still needs to be done. Further research on clinical management is required, especially in the alleviation of suffering in the last days. Further development of the palliative care service is necessary, to ensure seamless coverage of the home care service for patients living in every corner of the territory, provision of hospice consultative services to every patient in the general hospitals in need of palliative care, and extension of palliative care to patients with advanced diseases other than cancer. However well palliative care is developed, efforts have to be made to ensure that patients in need can receive it. Further community education on death and further training of health-care professionals will be necessary to develop the appropriate attitude towards death, to facilitate patients in their transition from curative to palliative care. It is hoped that, in future, every patient in need of palliative care, whether suffering from cancer or other advanced diseases, wherever the patient lives, can receive palliative care in the location he or she prefers.

Appendix 1.

Serial #:   Date:

Hospice Care Performance Inventory–Version 2 (HCPI-V2)

This questionnaire is designed to evaluate the effectiveness of hospice in-patient care in improving patients' quality of life.

Please choose the sets of description in (A) and (B) to answer the corresponding questions which best reflect your opinion on hospice care.

The following components of hospice care are expected to be able to improve cancer patients' quality of life. How important do you think they are in improving your quality of life?

(A) 1. Unimportant   2. Slightly important   3. Moderately important
     4. Significantly important   5. Very important

Please evaluate the standard of care you are receiving from the hospice care team during your stay in the hospice unit. How helpful do you find the hospice care team has been in providing the following items of care?

(B) 1. Not helpful   2. Slightly helpful   3. Moderately helpful
     4. Significantly helpful   5. Very helpful

Please circle the most appropriate description in (A) and (B)	(A) How important are the following items in improving your quality of life?					(B) How helpful do you find the hospice care team has been in providing the following items of care?				
	Unimportant	Slightly important	Moderately important	Significantly important	Very important	Not helpful	Slightly helpful	Moderately helpful	Significantly helpful	Very helpful
I. Physical comfort care 1. Helps to minimize your discomfort symptoms, e.g., pain, shortness of breath, constipation, nausea, oedema, dizziness, etc.	1	2	3	4	5	1	2	3	4	5
2. Helps you to have enough rest and sleep	1	2	3	4	5	1	2	3	4	5
3. Looks after your dietary preferences and needs	1	2	3	4	5	1	2	3	4	5
4. Provides you with a comfortable living environment, e.g., comfortable bed & chair, tidiness, suitable temperature & lighting, etc.	1	2	3	4	5	1	2	3	4	5
Total score in physical comfort care	IA ( )					IB ( )				

Please circle the most appropriate description in (A) and (B)	(A) How important are the following items in improving your quality of life?					(B) How helpful do you find the hospice care team has been in providing the following items of care?				
	Unimportant	Slightly important	Moderately important	Significantly important	Very important	Not helpful	Slightly helpful	Moderately helpful	Significantly helpful	Very helpful
II. Psychological care 5. Helps you to express your personal needs and feelings	1	2	3	4	5	1	2	3	4	5
6. Provides appropriate care and psychological support	1	2	3	4	5	1	2	3	4	5
7. Assures you have personal space	1	2	3	4	5	1	2	3	4	5
Total score for psychological care	IIA	(	)			IIB	(	)		
III. Social care, enhanced autonomy & independence 8. Helps you to organize personal or social resources to solve financial and practical problems	1	2	3	4	5	1	2	3	4	5
9. Helps you to participate in appropriate leisure activities	1	2	3	4	5	1	2	3	4	5
10. Encourages and facilitates companionship and visitation from family and friends	1	2	3	4	5	1	2	3	4	5
11. Provides adequate information to help you and your family to participate in the care and treatment plan	1	2	3	4	5	1	2	3	4	5
12. Respects your autonomy and choices	1	2	3	4	5	1	2	3	4	5
13. Helps to maximize your self-care abilities	1	2	3	4	5	1	2	3	4	5
Total score for social care, enhanced autonomy and independence	IIIA	(	)			IIIB	(	)		

Please circle the most appropriate description in (A) and (B)	(A) How important are the following items in improving your quality of life?					(B) How helpful do you find the hospice care team has been in providing the following items of care?				
	Unimportant	Slightly important	Moderately important	Significantly important	Very important	Not helpful	Slightly helpful	Moderately helpful	Significantly helpful	Very helpful
IV. Spiritual support 14. Respects your religious, personal beliefs and your views of life	1	2	3	4	5	1	2	3	4	5
15. Helps you to complete unfinished business	1	2	3	4	5	1	2	3	4	5
16. Helps you to have peace of mind	1	2	3	4	5	1	2	3	4	5
Total score for spiritual support	IVA ( )					IVB ( )				

V. Overall performance

17. Overall, how helpful is hospice care in improving your quality of life?
    - ❑ 1. Unhelpful
    - ❑ 2. Slightly helpful
    - ❑ 3. Moderately helpful
    - ❑ 4. Significantly helpful
    - ❑ 5. Very helpful

18. How satisfied are you with your quality of life in the past two days?
    - ❑ 1. Unsatisfied
    - ❑ 2. Slightly satisfied
    - ❑ 3. Moderately satisfied
    - ❑ 4. Significantly satisfied
    - ❑ 5. Very satisfied

Please review your answers to all the questions.
[Thank you.]

11

Dying: The Last Month

Raymond See Kit LO

The Dying Phase

Good comfort care for dying patients at the final stage of life is crucial, though of course palliative care does not begin only from the countdown of the patient's last month. Palliative care should commence right from the moment of the diagnosis of any incurable illness that is expected to deteriorate with inexorable progression. It is essential to ensure early integration of the palliative care component, with a smooth transition from an active curative intent to a palliative emphasis. Indeed, it has been recently advocated that palliative care should begin even at the pre-diagnostic phase, when cancer is suspected pending confirmation.[1] Regardless at which point of the disease trajectory palliative care is started, patients in the last month of life still face difficult problems and new concerns and need our utmost care and attention. As a patient enters the dying phase, worsening physical, psychological, social, and spiritual distress may be present and should be anticipated by health professionals and care-givers.

However, the dying phase may be abrupt and cannot always be predicted by staff and carers.[2] Sudden conditions e.g., haemorrhage into intracerebral metastases, massive pulmonary embolism, and acute bleeding from advanced head and neck tumours are only several problems among many that could lead to a rapid, unexpected decline of the patient. Further, diagnosing the dying phase can be more difficult than it appears to be. This is especially true in non-cancer conditions, when the progress of the disease is less easily predictable.[2] For example, in advanced heart failure or pulmonary diseases, reversible causes such as arrhythmia, anaemia or infection may be present and amenable to correction. Notwithstanding such difficulty and challenges, experienced clinicians can still be accurate in identifying those patients in the dying phase whose prognosis is going to be poor, despite optimal therapy.

Recognition of clinical deterioration of palliative care patients of the older age group especially requires skill and expertise.[3] Symptoms in elderly people are frequently non-specific and atypical. For example, life-threatening sepsis can present with just increasing confusion in an elderly person with a background of cognitive impairment. Symptoms of malignant hypercalcaemia are often non-specific and can be easily overlooked. Malignant cord compression may not be immediately obvious in an elderly patient already de-conditioned with leg weakness. Diagnosing the final deteriorating phase in the elderly patient necessitates even more caution and alertness.

Coming to Terms with the Dying Phase

In addition to the various clinical challenges, other barriers exist in decision-making in the diagnosis of the dying phase. Health-care professionals may be reluctant for various reasons.[2] Different team members may not always be in consensus about a patient's condition and prognosis. Some may find it difficult to let go, and continue to pursue futile interventions. Others may be concerned about ethical issues such as withholding and withdrawing treatment. There may also be some who are uncomfortable communicating with the patient and family on the matter of death and dying. These barriers may be especially difficult to overcome in an acute care setting, where intensive effort to search for a cure is the usual aim.

The same barriers would also be found in the close relatives of our dying patients. If not offered appropriate help and support, some relatives may also find it difficult to accept the dying phase and continue to insist on active though futile treatment. From the experience in my unit, this may be more so when the patient has a large family, when various family members may not have the same views, or if the family members have not been previously close to the patient but now have guilt and difficulty in accepting the situation, or if the family members are not adequately informed and some have incomplete or incorrect understanding of the clinical picture.

Failure to overcome these barriers will render the dying patient at risk of prolonged suffering and undignified death. It is regrettably often that too much has been too little in the care for the dying. The US Support Study has amply demonstrated this situation.[4] In the era of ever-advancing medical technology, the technical imperative becomes a burden for both staff and patients concerned, overusing invasive treatment at the inevitable end of life, which is not only futile but will merely prolong the distress and suffering.

It is vital, therefore, that the concept of good palliative care needs to be widely disseminated, in order that the best comfort care for the dying can be provided in whichever clinical setting, if necessary. Over the last few decades, the hospice development has greatly contributed to better care for the dying, both worldwide and locally in Hong Kong. Yet much work is still to be done in bridging the gap between hospice/palliative care units and other medical care settings, as well as translating the approach and philosophy to other patients who are dying from non-cancer conditions. More training opportunities in the field of palliative care need to be provided. Both undergraduate and postgraduate education on general palliative care is required, not just in medicine and nursing but also in allied health, social work and other related disciplines. In my palliative care unit, final-year medical students have the opportunity to rotate through to receive a tutorial, clerk a case to present in multidisciplinary case conference, and to be examined in vivas. Societal education on facing death and dying also should be promoted.

Symptom Assessment in the Dying Phase

Optimal control of each and every symptom is the fundamental aim in the care for the dying patient. Of the various dimensions of symptoms, physical symptoms especially need prompt control. It would be difficult to explore any psycho-spiritual issues in depth, when the physical symptoms are not yet resolved. It would be meaningless to begin a conversation on quality of life, for instance, when the patient is in agony and the basic requirement of pain relief is not even met.

Palliative care for patients is active rather than passive at every stage. Active care, as emphasized, does not imply futile investigations or interventions but refers to an intensive approach in rapid recognition and relief of symptoms. Knowledge of the prevalence and range of symptoms for our local patients is advantageous in offering prompt identification and treatment. The prevalence of physical symptoms of palliative care patients on presentation to my unit was surveyed, and the pattern was remarkably consistent. In a prospective study of symptom control in 133 consecutive palliative care patients,[5] as well as in a separate multi-centre study of quality of life in 462 patients,[6] the top three most prevalent symptoms on admission were pain, fatigue, and dyspnoea.

Palliative care patients frequently have more than one symptom, especially in elderly patients with multiple co-morbidities.[7] It is essential that palliative care professionals attend to every detail. It is important to focus not only on the most obvious symptom like pain or dyspnoea but also not to neglect other symptoms. Some symptoms are not immediately obvious and may easily be overlooked. For example, fatigue is an important symptom that affects quality of life. Despite being self-reported by patients consistently as the second most prevalent symptom, it may not have received full attention. Likewise, nausea is not as visible as vomiting is in alerting the staff. It is therefore worthwhile to have a systematic screening of symptoms on admission, so that any symptoms causing discomfort are caught. Such screening of symptoms is preferably conducted at regular intervals, including the terminal phase, in order to note changes or deterioration without undue delay. A support team assessment schedule is available for such use and has been shown to be practicable and beneficial in local settings.[5] The following symptoms are regularly monitored in my unit: pain, fatigue, dyspnoea, cough, anorexia, nausea, dysphagia, vomiting, constipation, diarrhoea, lymphoedema, ascites, dizziness, and insomnia. The Support Team Assessment Schedule is also most valuable for clinical audit purposes.

Principles of Symptom Control in the Dying Phase

Cancer may be incurable, but symptoms and complications arising from cancer can be imminently treatable, even at the very end of life. Symptoms may recur or worsen near the time of death, and every effort must be made to detect and alleviate such symptoms as soon as possible, so that the patient can have a peaceful death, and relatives attending the patient can be comforted. In the approach of symptoms in palliative care, three guiding principles should be followed. Firstly, health professionals must believe and take serious account of the symptoms that their dying patients report. It should be remembered that symptoms are inherently subjective multi-dimensional experiences. One person's agony is only another person's ache, and only the patients will best know the degree of distress the symptoms they are suffering from. The symptoms should not be disregarded or disbelieved just because an apparent physical cause cannot be found or the physical component is thought to be insignificant. It would be most disconcerting for the dying patients when the distress that they voice is not believed.

The second principle is that the underlying cause of symptoms should be identified, if possible, and treated, rather than just offering a blanket treatment. Pain should always be considered in its totality of physical, psychological, social and spiritual; and physical pain itself may have different components such as nociceptive, neuropathic, inflammatory and functional, each warranting different treatment rather than just a blind escalation of morphine dose. Likewise, dyspnoea can have up to a dozen different causes such as pneumonia, pleural effusion, lymphangitis carcinomatosis, superior venous cava obstruction, and so on. Like pain, the psychological components and consequences related to dyspnoea are equally significant and should not be neglected. Similarly, not all vomiting is due to morphine. There are many other causes to consider, e.g., constipation, hypercalcaemia, raised intra-cranial pressure and so on.

The third principle is of utmost importance, in that the benefit of whatever investigation, intervention or treatment planned for a patient should always be balanced with the potential burden, risks and harm, and should only be performed if there is a net benefit in the best interests of the patient. It would be absolutely against the philosophy of palliative medicine when the treatment for a symptom in the dying patient ends up introducing more suffering and distress. The same applies to the amount of information and discussion we deliver to our patients, bearing in mind any potential stress and burden that it may bring. There is not a clear-cut answer for each scenario, and the treatment decision must be carefully individualized. For example, would further blood transfusion be justified for the patient dying with end-stage leukaemia? Would the patient with recurrent encephalopathy from extensive multiple liver metastases benefit from further aggressive treatment? Should the elderly patient with brain metastases undergo whole brain radiotherapy?

Caring for Physical Suffering of the Dying

Full coverage of physical symptom control is beyond the remit of this chapter, though a few important and prevalent symptoms encountered during the last month of life are highlighted here. At the terminal phase, the most worrying physical symptom would still be any recurring or escalating pain, and judicious use of continuous subcutaneous delivery of morphine through syringe driver is most effective. Oral morphine may no longer be tolerated, as the patient is too weak to eat or swallow, and indeed the burden of taking several medications needs to be minimized. The subcutaneous syringe driver itself does not necessarily preclude the patient from ambulation and daily activities, though. In the past, my team has seen patients take successful home leave, a trip to the bank to complete unfinished business, the last opportunity to have dim sum at a family gathering etc., with the syringe driver *in situ*, after careful instructions to patients and carers were given. Patients and relatives need not associate the use of syringe driver with impending death either, as there have also been circumstances of the patient being weaned off the syringe driver when the source of pain was removed or controlled. Intravenous morphine infusion is an alternative, though it requires intravenous access that can be difficult, and the accompanying intravenous fluids may not always be well tolerated. Any accidental overdose of morphine would also be more dangerous with the intravenous route than with the subcutaneous route. However, there are contraindications to the subcutaneous route, as in gross oedema, skin infections and disorders, and bleeding tendencies.

The other symptom in the dying phase that should be promptly attended to is the sensation of dyspnoea. Uncontrolled dyspnoea, just like uncontrolled pain, will bring much fear, anxiety, and distress. Increments of oxygen and morphine, together with addition of anxiolytics such as midazolam can help greatly in controlling the shortness of breath in the terminal situation. As mentioned, dyspnoea in the dying phase may still have reversible causes that can be treated. Simple measures such as a fan or cool draught of air by themselves also can be soothing and should be tried. The psychological component should always be explored rather than ignored. I remember vividly a young single lady who was extremely breathless and clearly hyperventilating. She was previously in cosmetic sales and was very particular about her personal appearance. Her only close family member was her younger sister. She was beginning to be hysterical with breathlessness, though her lungs were clear without metastases. Despite reassurance, her hyperventilation continued. It was noted from the social and family history that the patient in fact placed trust only in this younger sister. The author made the unusual move of offering the stethoscope for the patient's younger sister to try and listen and to help reassure the patient. With that, the patient immediately stopped hyperventilating.

Another very worrying symptom is the intractable vomiting from progressive malignant bowel obstruction. The conventional treatment is "drip and suck", through insertion of nasogastric tube and intravenous fluids, or surgical means of bypass with gastrostomy and colostomy. The latter method is clearly not advisable in the terminal phase. The drip and suck approach is not preferred either, as the nasogastric tube itself is uncomfortable and poorly tolerated, often resulting in repeated attempts by confused patients to pull it out, leading to the undesirable use of restraints. Enough experience has now been accumulated in the use of the syringe driver with a cocktail of drugs including morphine to relieve the pain, antiemetics to reduce vomiting, anticholinergics to control the colic and intestinal secretion, plus or minus steroids to try to reduce peri-tumoural oedema and minimize the obstruction. This regimen can spare patients from the trauma of nasogastric tube insertion and is frequently effective enough for the patient to tolerate a small amount of liquid. A more dramatic response was seen in my unit, when patients could be completely weaned off the nasogastric tube with previous drainage of over a litre, and the symptoms of bowel obstruction adequately controlled with just subcutaneous drugs until the point of death.

At the dying moment, there might be what's called the death rattle, which refers to the upper bronchial secretions that the dying patient is no longer able to expectorate. Quite often, by this point, the patient is already unconscious and might not actually feel any of the resulting distress. However, the secretions are audible and can be disturbing to relatives or staff. If the secretions are copious, subcutaneous injection or infusion of anticholinergic drugs such as hyoscine hydrobromide or hyoscine butylbromide can often control the secretions, and repeated suction can be avoided.

Caring for Psycho-socio-spiritual Suffering of the Dying

It should be remembered that the complete extent of the psycho-socio-spiritual distress that our patients may undergo in the final phase of life can never be fully estimated and comprehended by our staff and carers. It should be with great humility that we counsel our patients and deliver our support and care. The background of each patient and family is different, and we should try to refrain from passing judgement on their actions and behaviour. In fact, it is often the opposite: caring for dying patients helps us to reflect on our own work and lives. The often-quoted phrase of learning from your patients can never be truer than in the terminal care setting. A well-delivered palliative care service successful in helping terminal patients to have a peaceful death is in itself most rewarding and satisfying. Professionals in the field are always appreciative of having this very worthwhile opportunity to serve.

The spectrum of psycho-socio-spiritual distress in the last month of life may be different from that encountered in the earlier phases of palliative care. Several commonly quoted conditions may become more problematic and deserve special mention. Fear of dying, if present, undoubtedly would be the biggest concern. Dying is actually a lonely journey. The patient may be in the middle of a hospice ward or acute general ward, surrounded by other patients and busy ward activities, but no one else apart from the dying patient alone is experiencing the journey. Not even another dying patient lying next to him or her in the same cubicle may share the same thoughts and emotions. The fear of dying can manifest in different degrees and intensities. I remember seeing a young patient holding on to the Bible and almost shaking with fear and requiring anxiolytics. Another patient afraid of dying triggered by shortness of breath became agitated and confused but reverted to a normal mental state after administration of a subcutaneous haloperidol infusion. Another situation was encountered of the patient becoming acutely breathless at 3:00 a.m. and yet subsequent workup revealed no organic cause of shortness of breath. It transpired that the patient was in the same room with another patient who had died with a sudden episode of visible bleeding from a head and neck tumour, in the small hours of the morning.

The fear of dying is not always present with every patient, though. In fact, results from local research on quality of life of dying patients show that many patients don't actually have a fear of dying as such.[8] In fact, they are only concerned with the physical symptoms before dying. One phrase often quoted by patients may illustrate this: "everything is planned by heaven; there is nothing we can do to alter this, or for us to worry about and fear". In the multi-centred study of quality of life using the McGill QOL-Hong Kong version, one questionnaire item also addressed this issue.[6] The item asked whether the patient had any fear of the future. The overall response in 462 patients on admission to palliative care unit was actually good at 8.5 out of 10, 10 being the best score. In a longitudinal follow-up in a subgroup of fifty-eight patients at a median of 5.6 days before their death, there was no increase of fear. The mean score on the fear of future item was maintained at 8.8, the same as that on admission. Clinical experience and feedback by colleagues do seem to suggest that the elderly group have fewer problems with the fear of death. The reason may be that elderly patients have already lived life to the full, or maybe they take the traditional Chinese view of "let nature take its course". Strong family support at the bedside, if available, would also help much to allay fear and anxiety, and it is necessary for in-patient units to allow flexible visiting hours even at times of strict infection control, as per the patients' needs. Religious beliefs may also help for some who believe in and find comfort from their religion. It should be a requirement for all palliative care units to have spiritual care workers as regular members of the team, to help address the patients' spiritual concerns. Chaplains and Buddhist volunteers are available in my unit for support, irrespective of a patient's religious background.

Another psycho-spiritual concern for patients is the matter of dignity. Dignity spans many aspects from adequate relief of pain and suffering, to care of basic needs such as toileting and bathing, to management of humiliating symptoms like disfiguring tumours, odorous wounds, fistulae, incontinence, total dependence, and further to empowerment, autonomy, respect and self-esteem. Invasive and futile treatment with multiple injections, tubes, catheters, or interventions would add further to indignity. The matter of dignity should not be neglected, especially in patients from lower educational, social or financial backgrounds, or minority racial or ethnic groups, who may be less outspoken of their needs. The older patients, cognitively impaired patients, and psychiatric patients are also less able to voice their concerns, and they need our full attention in this regard. I remember an elderly lady who repeatedly refused her relatives' persuasion to take her out on home leave. After further in-depth exploration, it was found out that this was mainly due to the patient's fear of incontinence and embarrassment, from the frequent bowel openings due to the increased laxatives that she was taking to prevent hepatic encephalopathy. This was easily solved after her laxatives were carefully adjusted, and the patient successfully went on home leave before she died. Dying with dignity itself indeed is very much a human need and right, and it is a duty of palliative care professionals to uphold this right as much as possible.

Apart from dignity and fear of dying, meaning and purpose of life is the other major component of spiritual/existential well-being in the last month of life. This notion of meaning or purpose of life may seem philosophical, yet local research has already proven that it is relevant and significant, belonging to the spiritual/existential domain that can be perceived by our local palliative care patients, including our elderly.[6] When faced with critical illnesses that are life threatening, existential issues become real concerns. This is true especially when the terminal phase is slow rather than sudden, and if the patient remains cognitively sound. The questions surrounding the meaning of life can be present and unrecognized yet give rise to distress. In the feedback from research assistants in conducting quality of life interviews with palliative care patients, many of the patients in fact said that only through the interviews did they realize for the first time that it was psycho-spiritual issues that had been bothering them. Some said the questionnaire and interview allowed them an opportunity to raise these concerns which otherwise they had difficulty broaching.

In the McGill QOL-Hong Kong version, the following questions relating to spiritual/existential issues were included: meaning and purpose of life, achieving life goals, whether life is worth living, and feeling generally good about oneself. In the longitudinal series of 462 palliative care patients, the average score of the existential domain was the second poorest, next only to physical domain. In the quality of life in the two weeks pre-death, the existential score of our patients was still average, scoring only six out of ten. The individual item on the meaning of existence scored the third lowest of all items at 5.4 out of 10.[9] More effort is needed in helping our patients face this concern when approaching the terminal phase. The difficulties in coming to terms with spiritual and existential issues may indeed become more pronounced as the patient draws closer and closer to death. When faced with impending death, not every patient can transcend the hardship and suffering and find a meaning that allows him or her to make sense of the helpless situation. Terminal patients experience a variety of existential concerns, ranging from not just meaning and purpose of existence, but also to a broad spectrum of aspects like burden on others, self-esteem, hope, relations, forgiveness, or reconciliation.

Our Chinese patients may, however, also have other interpretations of the meaning of life and suffering, as illustrated by the following two cases. An elderly patient with metastatic cancer of the prostate and cord compression was in severe spinal and neuropathic pain. He previously was involved in recruiting ladies into the prostitution business in the old Shek Tong Tsui district of Hong Kong. On admission, he was clearly in agonizing pain and yet strongly refused all analgesics. This was not out of any fear of drug side effects or any misconception about morphine. On further interview and questioning, it transpired that he believed in reincarnation and was scared of being punished in the next life for the previous sins that he knew he had committed. This became increasingly distressing for him, as he realized his life was coming to a close. He hoped that, by suffering in pain now, he would be forgiven and borne again into a good life. In fact, he said, "the more pain the better".

The following story reveals yet another interesting perspective of the meaning of life. A 75-year-old man was slowly dying from lung cancer. His symptoms of pain and dyspnoea were already well controlled. He was weak though mentally sound and had no fear of death. His family was supportive, and he was not lonely. There was no anxiety and depression, and he scored well on the Geriatric Depression Scale. He had no unfinished business. There was no worry of being a burden on his family. He was not pressurized for discharge. Yet he was quiet, withdrawn and seemed increasingly demoralized, until one day when I asked a medical student to visit and interview this gentleman. I especially warned the student to take care not to upset the patient during clerking. On the ward round the following morning, the patient appeared much brighter and cheerful and was more talkative. I thanked the student and thought the student must have had extraordinary counselling skills, though the student denied any. In fact, the patient thanked us for the opportunity to let medical students to learn from him, which made him rediscover a purpose of living in this terminal phase of life. He was still able to contribute, so that future doctors could help other patients suffering from his disease. In fact, he asked me to let more students visit him. He died peacefully two weeks later. Since then, I have encountered another patient with the same existential need and request.

There are other differences between the Chinese and Western patients, in their perceived quality of life in the dying phase. Of the various quality of life domains, the Chinese patients scored persistently better in the psychological domain. The average psychological domain score was high at 7.7 out of 10, in fact the highest of all domains. All items within the psychological domains had consistently good scores. This was notably different from the research findings in the West. Although this was not a formal study with direct comparison between the two cultures, the findings do suggest a potential difference. This might again be due to the traditional Chinese belief of letting nature takes its course and accepting fate. Plenty of statements and anecdotes from the patients during the quality of life interviews support this; for example "whatever will be will be", "take things as they come", "this is meant to be", "there is nothing to fear", "I'm not afraid of dying, but only the symptoms".

Further analysis of the different facets within the psychological domain helped identify the reasons for the observed differences. There were indeed markedly different perspectives between the Hong Kong Chinese patients and those in the West, in interpreting the individual psychosocial components. In the original questionnaire, there was an item asking whether the patient felt close to people, which the original Canadian population found hard to understand. In contrast, the Hong Kong Chinese had no problem in interpreting this item. Chinese patients interpret this to mean how much support they receive from others. This variation in interpretation might well be again attributable to the traditional, strong Chinese culture of the extended family and support network system. However, our local patients had difficulty in interpreting an item on life control. To be in control of one's life may perhaps be a Western concept, not equally perceived in a traditional Asián culture emphasizing the collective interdependence. Another feature that was found to have a positive contribution to the Hong Kong Chinese psychological well-being was the matter of "face". In Chinese, the word "face" refers to the respect the patient received or perceived to have received. The item on "face" was found to be relevant and confirmed to be a component of the psychological domain. The overall score on the item face was very good at 8.9, demonstrating a time-honoured Chinese custom of paying respect to those who are ill.

End-of-Life Concerns

In the last month of life, various treatment decisions will require careful deliberation of clinical and ethical matters. These need to be carefully considered so that the ultimate decisions are in the best interests of each patient as an individual. However, in Chinese culture, family consensus is also important and needs to be taken into active account. Decisions become especially difficult when there is no consensus between patient and family, or when the patient does not possess the mental capacity to make independent decisions. The mode of feeding and cardiopulmonary resuscitation are examples of such situations.

Eating and enjoyment from food is a very much a concern in Chinese culture, as evidenced by the Chinese saying, that "mortals treat eating with heavenly importance". The enjoyment of eating refers of course not just to the physical aspect but also to the social aspect of gathering with friends and family. It has already been demonstrated that eating is indeed an important facet of quality of life for our local Chinese patients. However, at the end of life, both eating and nutrition may be affected, causing patients and families much worry and anguish. Palliative care patients often suffer from anorexia and vomiting. They often also have altered taste function and further decrease of enjoyment from food.[10] They may also suffer from various causes of dysphagia, requiring a change to less desirable modified diet or to a non-oral mode of feeding.

Difficulties arise when the patient and the family may not opt for the same treatment decision, when it comes to problems with eating and nutrition. A 78-year-old ex-police officer with cancer of the pyriform fossa had difficulty swallowing and needed tube feeding. He refused tube feeding and repeatedly pulled out the nasogastric tube, with wild temper tantrums. He was known to be an alcoholic and was labelled as having dementia prior to admission. On arrival in the palliative care unit, team members were deliberating whether he would need restraints for tube feeding. Family members were very concerned and insisted the patient have a feeding tube, with restraints if necessary, to maintain nutrition for subsequent radiotherapy. On further interviewing the patient, it was found he was alert and orientated. Although he did have aggressive episodes, he was not found to be demented. We found his mental state examination score was good at 21/30. On discussing the pros and cons of tube feeding, and the risk of aspiration pneumonia and death, he opted for thickened fluid and puree diet, accepting the risk with oral feeding even with this altered diet regime. He also opted for comfort care rather than pursuing radiotherapy. The family were initially disappointed with his decision and pressurized staff not to comply. Nonetheless, the team respected the patient's wishes. The patient went on to tolerate the altered diet well and remained peaceful and settled in the ward, with reasonable quality of life up to the moment of writing this chapter.

Another story illustrates the complexity of the feeding problem in palliative care. A palliative care patient with disseminated carcinomatosis was unconscious and had progressive brain metastases. He was clearly dying and not fit for oral or tube feeding. His children also agreed, though his elderly wife was reluctant to accept the situation. She held the traditional belief that her husband should not die hungry. She had been found to be secretly feeding her unconscious husband with homemade food on several occasions, despite being counselled and advised against doing this by the nurses. Unfortunately, the elderly wife could not let go, resulting in a tragic incident when the patient sustained cardiopulmonary arrest possibly from aspiration, during another feeding episode by his wife. The wife witnessed the arrest and had tremendous guilt and bereavement problems afterwards.

Nutrition and hydration are important concerns for patients and relatives in the last month of life. In advanced malignancy, cachexia and anorexia frequently prevent the maintenance of an adequate nutritional state. It should be remembered that artificial means of nutrition and hydration, such as non-oral feeding and intravenous or subcutaneous hydration, are considered medical interventions, which patients have the right to refuse. However, caution should be taken to ensure that patients possess normal mental capacity and be fully informed of the pros and cons of such intervention, and that decisions are not made under any influence of depression. The decision is often difficult when the patient is not mentally fit. Another story of a palliative care patient illustrates this. She was an elderly female with lung cancer, who became more and more withdrawn and depressed after developing cord compression. She could not accept this disability and refused to eat and drink, becoming progressively weak and drowsy. Although the cancer was definitely progressing, it was also felt that the deterioration was partly due to a state of depressive stupor that could be imminently treatable. After discussing the problem with relatives, it was agreed to start a trial of nasogastric tube feeding together with antidepressant drugs. The patient subsequently made a good response, becoming more alert and in a better mood. She resumed oral feeding and started mobilizing with a wheelchair. She was discharged home to her husband, with a reasonable quality of life for six more months before she passed away.

Cardiopulmonary resuscitation at the end of life is another challenging problem. In most circumstances, cardiopulmonary resuscitation is futile for patients who are at the terminal phase, dying from an irreversible cause. The process of cardiopulmonary resuscitation involves external cardiac massage, intubation, ventilation, and defibrillation, which will only add pain and suffering and prolong the dying process. In some traditional hospice units, patients are already screened and informed prior to admission that cardiopulmonary resuscitation is not available. In other palliative care units, the policy is such that no cardiopulmonary resuscitation will be performed. In other settings, like in acute palliative care units or palliative care beds in acute hospitals, which receive patients at different stages of palliative care, the question may be discussed with patients and relatives. The purpose is so patients can be offered an option in advanced care planning, in choosing not to undergo a futile procedure.

My team has come across some patients and relatives who actually initiate the discussion on admission and voice their wish not to have the patient resuscitated. Some others find the discussion useful, which can enable them to have a more in-depth discussion on prognosis with staff and reflection on spiritual issues of death and dying. A local study on discussion of cardiopulmonary resuscitation in 200 palliative care patients showed that such discussion on advanced care planning was well accepted and most patients would choose the option of not being resuscitated.[11] This actually helped dispel the myth that a discussion on death and dying was an absolute taboo subject in Chinese. The discussion on these issues will of course need to be sensitive. Although health-care professionals are not under any obligation to perform futile treatment that is not in the patients' best interests, the patients' wishes should be respected, regardless of the final decision.

Meeting the Needs of Patients and Families in the Last Month of Life

Palliative care services in Hong Kong endeavour to continuously improve in order to meet the needs of our patients and families in the last stage of illness. Each palliative care unit has made every effort to provide the best services possible, within the restraints of its resources. The palliative care ward environment is one example. For instance, early after the establishment of the palliative care unit in 1995, Shatin Hospital embarked on continuous quality improvement to explore what the patients and team perceive as inadequacies in the ward facilities, with an aim for creating a less institutionalized and regimented environment with better atmosphere and privacy.[12] Patients at the end of life need their own privacy both in space and time. Quiet talk behind the curtain is only an illusion and will only interest strangers in listening to the conversation. In this project, a suitable environment conducive to discussing innermost feelings and for counselling was confirmed by patients themselves as a definite need rather than a luxury. The project resulted in successful allotment of resources to furnish a quiet room and overnight stay facility for our patients.

Another obvious and important patient need is the adequate training of palliative care staff and volunteers. For instance, during the early days of establishing a palliative care unit, Shatin Hospital ran continuous quality improvement programmes to promote staff and volunteer training.[13] All staff and volunteers were surveyed to elicit their day-to-day difficulties in delivering palliative care and its philosophy, and priorities of training they wished to receive. Medical knowledge about cancer, the art of establishing rapport with patients who refused communication, understanding the complex psycho-spiritual state of mind of dying patients, and assisting carers in looking after terminal patients at home were identified as top concerns at that time.[13] The programme was found to be helpful in identifying staff training needs, which should be reviewed periodically.

Another aspect of the need of palliative care patients is in community care, for which the effectiveness of our palliative day and home care requires evaluation. The performance of the day care services in Shatin Hospital were reviewed soon after establishment in 1997.[14] The day care service was found to be able to facilitate in-patient discharges with an increase in monthly discharge rates by thirty-three percent. It also reduced in-patient length of stay by an average of six days. More importantly, there was a lower percentage of day/home care patients requiring emergency admission, compared to those discharged without day/home care. The day care unit in Shatin Hospital provides symptom monitoring, continuing rehabilitation, nursing support and counselling as well as peer group support and festive activities by volunteers. By providing day and home care, we can help our palliative care patients to live in the community as much and as long as possible, even within the last month of life. Various alternative treatment modalities such as aromatherapy and tai chi have also been offered and their effectiveness investigated.[15,16] In a cross-over trial of twenty palliative care patients, quantitative and qualitative outcome measurements revealed that the effect of aromatherapy was not universal and should be individualized according to symptoms and preferences. The form of aromatherapy used in the study, a scented neck wrap, was found to be useful, especially in patients with head and neck symptoms. The benefit of tai chi was also found in palliative care patients, with statistically significant improvement in outcome parameters of functional reach, timed up and go, Berg's balance score and handicap score. The study was, however, not of a randomized controlled design, and more studies are needed to confirm its full efficacy in the palliative care setting.

Centrally, the Quality Assurance Subcommittee of the Hong Kong Hospital Authority Central Co-ordinating Committee on Palliative Care has, over the years, developed various programmes to uphold and improve standards in meeting patients' needs. As mentioned, symptom control is of paramount importance, and guidelines on pain control, dyspnoea, nausea and vomiting, constipation, and mouth care have been established and disseminated.[17] Another important aspect of patients' needs and service standard is in communication. In caring for terminally ill patients and their relatives, appropriate, empathic and quality communication is essential. The QA subcommittee coordinated a territory-wide survey on 286 palliative care patients and 340 relatives on their satisfaction and needs and for improvement in three aspects of communication: quality, content and effectiveness.[18] The overall satisfaction was reassuringly good, and effectiveness of staff communication was demonstrated to have improved the patients' physical, psychological, social and spiritual well-being. The room for improvement in communication is in information on social resources, explanation of drug use/ side effects, and resources for spiritual support.

A new series of audits using the Trent Palliative Care Audit Schedule is ongoing, to further identify the needs of our palliative care patients and services in different aspects. The Trent audit is a recognized international audit schedule, with audit packages ranging from management, patients' and carers' self-feedback to bereavement.[19] A management audit has been completed, and audits on patients' feedback will take place. It is hoped that, as a result of the Trent audit, the palliative care services in Hong Kong can be further improved to better meet the needs of our patients and their families, especially in the last month of the patient's illness.

Quality of Death and Dying

Quality of life is the ultimate aim of palliative care professionals in caring for patients and families. Yet quality of death and dying is perhaps an even more important final outcome of the continuum of care, though it is more difficult to quantify and qualify. Proxy assessment by interviewing relatives on their perception of the patient's death can be attempted but is unlikely to be an accurate representation of the patient's own experience. Moreover, the relatives would be in bereavement, making the proxy assessment more difficult and subject to other influences.

The self-assessment of patients' quality of life at the final phase will be the only best approximation of patients' perceived quality of death and dying. Of a large longitudinal cohort of palliative care patients, a subgroup of fifty-eight patients were able to have their quality of life assessed within two weeks of death.[9] These quality of life assessments were made at a mean duration of 5.6 days pre-death, very close to the quality of their death and dying. The mean quality of life score was satisfactory at 7 out of 10, though the single item overall score was less satisfactory at 5.6 out of 10. The weakest scores were in the physical and existential domain (at 5.9 and 6.0 out of 10 respectively).

The determinants of what would constitute a better quality of life of our dying patients have also been investigated. Multiple regression analysis has identified that age, family support, financial sufficiency and staff support are independent predictors of good quality of life in 389 palliative care patients.[20] In lay terms, if a patient has already lived life to a good age, accompanied by caring and supportive family members, with no major worries about the financial situation, and is receiving good professional care, then the quality of death and dying might not be too poor.

In fact, many patients have stated that their last period of life was in fact the best part of their life. One male patient, despite having been admitted to the palliative care ward with terminal lung cancer, was threatened with divorce by his wife. His wife would humiliate him in the ward and allegedly had slapped him on the face in public on several occasions. The patient's relationship with his only 16-year-old son was only fair. His son seldom communicated with him. Although the patient was physically fit to go for a short period of home leave, his wife was reluctant and he could not face the poor family relationship at home either. After family therapy and tireless input from various colleagues, the patient's wife reconciled with him. The patient was also on better speaking terms with his son, who later was also successfully promoted to form six of his school. The patient subsequently went on home leave, and on returning sometime later said he just had had the best moments of his life and had no regrets. He subsequently had a peaceful death.

The story of another patient also illustrates the precious moments of the last stage of life. The patient was a 16-year-old student in what was then a band-one school. He had good academic results and was a member of his school basketball team. He unfortunately developed hepatocellular carcinoma, which was complicated with cord compression. On arrival in the palliative care unit, he was incontinent and had bedsores. He was in tremendous pain, not responding to very high doses of morphine. He was withdrawn and not forthcoming in discussing with team members any of his problems. His parents divorced when the patient was young, and his mother had been on very hostile terms with his father. Indeed, his mother had given clear instructions to the staff not to allow his father to visit the patient in hospital; otherwise, she would make a formal complaint. After spending much time gaining the patient's trust and rapport, the patient began to confide in us that he very much longed to see his father. He said that he had one only father, no matter how irresponsible that father had been, and he hoped that his parents could one day reconcile. The patient's mother was made aware of his wish, and she did at the end allow her ex-husband to visit the patient. The team helped the patient to make a videotape, expressing his emotions and final words to his parents. His father was not very good with words, though had also written short letters to his son revealing his sorrow and guilt. The mother's heart gradually softened and she began to forgive the patient's father. The patient was much relieved after seeing his parents' relationship improve. In fact, his morphine requirement dramatically dropped from a previous high dose of over 200 mg of morphine per day on admission to only 20 mg every four hours, demonstrating that the previous immense pain he suffered was indeed a total pain with a significant psycho-spiritual component. The patient subsequently died, expressing to the team his thanks that the final period of life was the best, of being able to know his father better and finally seeing his parents at least back on speaking terms.

Care for the Dying: The Future

Death and dying is an inevitable event all of us would face. Comfort care for the dying should be seen as a necessity rather than a luxury in modern health care. The responsibility lies not just on the palliative care staff but on all health-care professionals involved in the care of any incurable illnesses. More work and research on this previously overlooked component of health-care service has yet to be undertaken. With the concerted effort by all professionals, in partnership with our patients and their relatives, quality care for the dying will be and can be enhanced. The world will be a better world, when all human beings can have the assurance that we will be well looked after, when our cherished lives come to an end.

12

Euthanasia and Forgoing Life-sustaining Treatment in the Chinese Context

Chun Yan TSE and Samantha Mei Che PANG

Introduction

Euthanasia is derived from the Greek *euthanatos*, which means a good or peaceful death.[1] There have been many definitions of the term, and many forms of euthanasia have been described, including active euthanasia, passive euthanasia, voluntary euthanasia, non-voluntary euthanasia and involuntary euthanasia. When used without qualification, the term *euthanasia* usually signifies "voluntary active euthanasia".[2] Euthanasia is illegal in most parts of the world, except in the Netherlands and Belgium, where euthanasia was legalized in April and May 2002 respectively. Physician-assisted suicide is similarly illegal in most parts of the world, though it was legalized (but not euthanasia) in the US state of Oregon in 1997.

Forgoing futile life-sustaining treatment in the terminally ill, however, is a widely accepted practice in medically advanced countries. As a result of advances in medical technology to prolong life, there are situations when further life-sustaining treatment only prolongs the dying process and becomes a burden on the patient. A decision needs to be made on whether to forgoing such life-sustaining treatment that is not in the best interests of the patient. Such a decision is not easy and involves medical, psychosocial and ethical considerations. Professional bodies in many medically advanced countries like the US, the UK, and Canada, while opposing euthanasia, support the forgoing of life-sustaining treatment that is not in the best interests of the patient. Detailed guidelines have been published on this.[3–5] Recently, the Hospital Authority of Hong Kong has also issued a set of guidelines on the subject.[6]

There is still controversy surrounding the above two issues. Public opinion differs widely on whether euthanasia should be legalized or not. What constitutes futile treatment and thus can be forgone, and what constitutes a proper decision-making process is also hotly debated. The controversy is often compounded by the different interpretations of the terms used. In biomedical ethics literature and in public debates, the term "passive euthanasia" is sometimes used to describe forging life-sustaining treatment. However, the use of this term is often considered inappropriate in the medical and legal fields, because forgoing life-sustaining treatment is considered different from euthanasia. The House of Lords Select Committee on Medical Ethics stated that the term is "misleading".[7] The Hospital Authority of Hong Kong listed in an appendix of its guidelines why the term should not be used (Appendix 1). The Hospital Authority Guidelines concluded that avoidance of this misleading term would facilitate public discussion on the topic and discussion with the patients and their family in individual cases.

This chapter contains two parts. The first part examines the controversies regarding the legalization of euthanasia in China. Drawing on traditional Chinese thoughts on death and dying, the authors argue that the confusion in terms and concepts should be disentangled and palliative care should be promoted, before the debate on euthanasia in China can continue in a healthier way. The second part of this chapter then examines how a decision on forgoing life-sustaining treatment could be made in the Chinese context, taking into account the traditional practice of family determination, and discusses how the process-based approach of the guidelines of the Hospital Authority of Hong Kong addressed the issue.

Euthanasia or Not?

Discussion on euthanasia in China

Since 1979, when a conference on the philosophy of medicine, held in Guangzhou, first discussed euthanasia in China, there has been much attention on the subject, both in public debates and among medical ethics academics in China.[8] Proposals to draft a law on euthanasia were brought to China's National People's Congress.[9–10] Qiu Ren-Zong, a prominent ethicist in China, said that "there seems to be common assent" that euthanasia may be considered for "the comatose, the terminally ill, seriously defective newborns, and very low birthweight infants".[8] He described strong public support for legalizing euthanasia for these groups of patients. This is a disturbing description and goes beyond the law in the Netherlands and Belgium, where only voluntary euthanasia is legalized, and "euthanasia" for the comatose, newborns and infants is not legal. If the Chinese government follows this opinion, China might end up as the first country in Asia to legalize euthanasia and the first country in the world to legalize involuntary euthanasia. The thought of this is of great concern to the majority of health-care professionals, especially to the majority of palliative care workers, who are against euthanasia.

Problems in terminology

Euthanasia is not a traditional concept in Chinese. The term 安樂死, *anlesi*, having the literal meaning of "peaceful death", is the widely accepted Chinese translation for euthanasia. However, the use of the term euthanasia in the Chinese community is loose. It may mean euthanasia in the standard sense, or it may mean forgoing life-sustaining treatment.[8-9] The Chinese term *anlesi* is used even more loosely. Besides euthanasia in the standard sense or forgoing life-sustaining treatment, it may be used to describe the state of the dying process or even palliative or hospice care.[11]

Such a loose usage of the term would lead to difficulties in academic discussion and in doing research studies. Public opinion in support of euthanasia may actually include support for forgoing life-sustaining treatment and support for palliative care.

This confusion is totally unnecessary.

Firstly, though *anlesi* literally means peaceful death, the term can be reserved as a "proper noun" for euthanasia. Other phrases in the Chinese language could be chosen to describe a peaceful dying process, e.g., 安詳死亡.

Secondly, quite a number of Chinese terms are used to describe palliative or hospice care, e.g., 紓緩治療、善終服務、寧養服務、臨終關懷. Though a more standardized term is preferred, the abundance of available terms shows that there is no need to use the term *anlesi* to describe palliative or hospice care.

Thirdly, there appear to be no specific cultural reasons why euthanasia could not be discussed separately from forgoing life-sustaining treatment in the Chinese. This is elaborated in the following sub-section.

Views from traditional Chinese philosophy

Daoist philosophy accepts death as a process of nature. The following famous passage from 莊子, Zhuang Zi (Chuang-tzu), clearly illustrates this:

> (Responding to the question why he was singing and beating upon a basin when his wife died) Chuang-tzu said, "If, however, we examine this question of beginnings, originally there was no birth. Not only there was no birth but originally there was no body ... This breath changed and body came into existence. This body then changed and birth occurred. Today another change has occurred, and she has reached death. It is analogous to the progression of the four seasons ... This person, my wife, is resting peacefully in the largest of abodes, but if I were to mourn her with a lot of sobbing, I should feel that I did not understand Fate. That is why I desist."[12]

It would seem that this view of death as a natural process would oppose using artificial means to prolong the dying process and oppose euthanasia as an active process to end the patient's life.[13]

Confucian philosophy would support altruistic suicide or "allowing oneself to be killed for virtuous reasons" (殺身成仁，捨生取義). However, the reasons for euthanasia can hardly be considered virtuous.[14]

Thus, forgoing futile life-sustaining treatment finds resonance in traditional Chinese philosophy, but euthanasia does not. One may argue that the contemporary Chinese culture is shaped by many factors besides traditional Chinese philosophy and that contemporary Chinese culture may support euthanasia despite the traditional view.[15] However, the different lines of thinking in traditional Chinese philosophy at least demonstrate that, culturally, euthanasia could be discussed separately from forgoing life-sustaining treatment.

Palliative care as the preferred option

Besides the confusion in terminology, a problem with public opinion surveys is the lack of understanding about palliative care by the general public, because palliative care is not widely practised in China.[16–17] Without a proper understanding of palliative care, given the dilemma of either uncontrolled suffering or euthanasia, respondents in public surveys may choose euthanasia.[18] However, good palliative care could relieve the pain and suffering of most terminally ill patients. Palliative care respects death as a natural process,[19] and artificial prolongation of the dying process is not advocated. This finds resonance in traditional Chinese philosophy. If the public understands the nature of palliative care, and palliative care is provided as a choice along with forgoing futile life-sustaining treatment, public opinion may be very different.

Resources as a major reason for advocating euthanasia in China

In Western countries, besides the relief of suffering, respecting a person's autonomy is a major reason for advocating euthanasia.[20] In China, however, a drain on resources in treating terminally ill patients, patients in a vegetative state,[18,21] or defective newborns[22] is a major reason for advocating euthanasia. It has even been argued that choosing euthanasia to relieve the financial burden on the family or society should be considered a virtuous act.[23] Financial constraints in providing expensive medical treatment is a fact of life not only in China but in many parts of the world. Discussion of the difficult principles of resource allocation involves ethical, social, economic, and political factors.

However, to use euthanasia to solve the problem of resource allocation would be dangerous. One can easily go down the slippery slope towards coercing elderly people, those with disabilities, and people who are socially disadvantaged to choose euthanasia.

The problems of financial constraints should be addressed separately from euthanasia. Futile life-sustaining treatment with no benefits to the patients should be withheld or withdrawn, primarily for the principle of non-maleficence, whereas sparing resources is a secondary though important gain. Expensive medical treatment with marginal benefits to patients should be given lower priority, and institutional guidelines should be drawn up for frontline staff to follow. However, comfort care and symptom control, as well as life-sustaining treatment with clear benefits, should be provided. If there are still financial difficulties in managing these more essential treatments, reforms in the health-care system may be required rather than resorting to euthanasia.

Future debates

If one examines more critically the discussion on euthanasia in China, there should be less worry about the possibility of legalizing voluntary or involuntary euthanasia there. The discussion arose mainly because of the concern for suffering during the dying process in modern medical practice. Such suffering should be alleviated by good palliative care and by establishing guidelines on forgoing futile life-sustaining treatment. Effort should be made to promote palliative care in China, among the public, professional health-care workers, and government officials. Academics and the media should be encouraged to separate the discussion on euthanasia from the discussion on forgoing life-sustaining treatment and the discussion on resource allocation. Being better informed and having clearer terminology, the Chinese people would be in a better position to debate and decide whether to legalize euthanasia or not.

Deciding to Forgo Life-sustaining Treatment in the Terminally Ill

The need for guidelines drafted in the local legal and cultural context

It is generally agreed that life-sustaining treatment can be withheld or withdrawn if it is the wish of a competent and properly informed patient[24] or if the treatment is against the best interests of the patient.[4] However, the consideration of best interests is often value laden, and the decision process is complex. The laws governing such decisions are also different in different places. It is thus important to have local guidelines on forgoing life-sustaining treatment, taking into account the local legal and cultural context, so that health-care professionals, the patient and the family know how to approach this complex issue. For Chinese people, the family traditionally plays a very important role in decision-making for sick family members.[25] A set of guidelines that suits the Chinese must consider the role of the family in the decision-making process.

Role of the family for a mentally competent patient

For a mentally competent patient to make a decision regarding life-sustaining treatment, the patient needs to be properly informed of the medical condition first. However, in some countries, including China, it is common for the patient's family members to want to withhold information about the diagnosis or prognosis from a terminally ill patient and to make the decision on behalf of the patient.[25-27] For the Chinese, the concept of "family autonomy" is considered justification of this practice.[28] The Chinese "self" is a relational one, [29] and it is important that family members be involved in decision-making that affects the harmonious relationship among them. However, family involvement in decision-making can be divided into three levels.[30] Firstly, the family decides together with the patient. Secondly, the patient asks the family to decide on his or her behalf. Thirdly, the family decides without involving the patient. It is only the third level of family determination that excludes the patient involuntarily. Such a strong paternalistic approach overriding the patient's autonomy needs further justification by showing that the disclosure of the information brings much harm to the patient.

Chun Yan Tse[30] discussed this from the perspectives of traditional Chinese philosophy, sociological studies and traditional Chinese medicine (Appendix 2) and concluded that the psychosocial and spiritual burden for the Chinese on facing death may not be necessarily worse than that for Western people. This is in line with a qualitative study by Samantha Pang [31] which showed that terminally ill Chinese patients facing a decision to forgo life-sustaining treatment were able to discuss death issues openly and accepted death as a natural process (some examples are given in Appendix 3). Tse *et al.* concluded that there might be little justification for doctors to collude with Chinese families. Telling the truth should depend on what the patient wants to know and is prepared to know and not on what the family wants to disclose. However, the disclosure process should be tactful, taking into account the "death as taboo" concern and the "family determination" matter.

Thus, a mentally competent patient should be given the appropriate information to decide whether to forgo certain life-sustaining treatment. The family is best involved in the decision-making process, providing psychological support to the patient, and reaching a consensus with the patient.

The above discussion does not mean that all technically possible treatment options must be discussed in full with a mentally competent patient. Sometimes, there is abundant and clear objective evidence that a life-sustaining treatment is of no benefit to the patient at all. Such a treatment is not really a viable option to be presented to the patient to decide whether to accept the treatment or not, because the obvious answer to the question is "no". Even if the patient says "yes", the health-care team would not want to proceed, because of the lack of benefits. In such situations, discussion on this non-viable option with the patient may only add psychological and spiritual stress on him or her. The management of such situations should again be tactful and depend on how much the patient wants to know and is prepared to know.

Role of the family in a mentally incompetent patient

When a patient is mentally incompetent, the approach towards the role of the family differs in different countries. In the US, the family acts as the surrogate decision-maker, using the principle of substituted judgement, and the medical team would accept the decision in the majority of cases.[3] In the UK, the family has no legal authority to make such decisions,[4] and the doctor in charge makes the final decision based on the best interests of the patient. For the Chinese, the family traditionally has an important role in decision-making for the patient. When the Hospital Authority of Hong Kong drafted the guidelines on life-sustaining treatment, there was a dilemma on what model to follow. In Hong Kong, the family has no legal authority to make such decisions.[32] If Hong Kong follows the UK model, the family would be a third party providing information to the health-care team to make the decision. The family would feel alienated and as if they were not fulfilling their moral duties. Also, as the interpretation of values and wishes of the patient is contextual, without direct participation of the family in the decision-making process, the decision may not be the most appropriate. However, if the US model is followed and the family is the dominant decision-maker, there would be concern that the decision might not be objective, because of the strong emotional ties between the patient and the family. The family members may have difficulty accepting the terminal nature of the illness, and they may misinterpret that and think that, to show filial piety, they should not forego life-sustaining treatment for their ill parents.[25] Regarding substituted judgement, the common practice for the Chinese to consider the benefits to other family members would make the approach difficult,[32] as a decision to benefit other family members may be at the expense of the benefits to the patient. Firstly, it is difficult for health-care workers to differentiate whether such a decision is what the family sees as the patient's wish or what the family members want to benefit themselves. Secondly, the family also has difficulty balancing the benefits to the family and the benefits to the patient. Judging from the view of the patient, the benefits to the family may have a higher priority, but this would contradict the family's moral duty to provide the best care to the patient.

To overcome this, the Hospital Authority of Hong Kong adopted in the guidelines a consensus-building approach based on the best interests principle.[6] Though legally, in Hong Kong, the doctor in charge is finally responsible, a shared decision process with the family is emphasized, neither side dominating. Using the best interests principle, priority would be given to the benefits to the patient instead of the benefits to the family. If consensus could not be reached between the health-care team and the family, there should be repeated communication to clarify incorrect information and unrealistic expectation. If this still fails, the case could be brought to the ethics committee or in extreme cases, to the court.

Details of the above discussion on the role of the family in the mentally incompetent patients are in a paper by Chun Yan Tse and Julia Tao.[32] In the paper, Julia Tao also pointed out the ritualistic aspect of the process-based approach. From the ritualistic perspective, the Hong Kong shared decision-making model "is deep and significant in the way it affirms solidarity, trust, respect and connectedness while offering opportunities for the concerned parties to seek harmonious relations with the fundamental realities of their lives".

It is hoped that the process-based approach of the guidelines of the Hospital Authority of Hong Kong constitutes a sensitively balanced approach amid the legal, ethical and cultural factors in Hong Kong and may act as a useful reference for the development of national guidelines in China.

Conclusion

As a result of the institutionalization and medicalization of death, death has lost its "tameness" [33] and became fearful. Requests for euthanasia arise partly because of such fear. While the debate on euthanasia in China continues, it is hoped that professional bodies in mainland China will develop a set of guidelines on forgoing life-sustaining treatment that would suit the national context. Coupled with development of palliative care in China, the plight and suffering of dying patients and their family would then be eased, and the widespread request for euthanasia would no longer be necessary. The dying process would resume its meaning as a natural process, as what it has always been. Death is sad but would no longer be frightening. When a loved one dies, we may not like to sing and beat a basin as Zhuang Zi did, but it would be comforting when the death of our loved one is natural and peaceful.

Acknowledgement

The section on "Deciding to forgoing life-sustaining treatment in the terminally ill" is based on a paper by Chun Yan Tse (with Chong A and Fok SY), "Breaking bad news: a Chinese perspective" (*Palliative Medicine* 2003; 17: 339–43) and the paper by Chun Yan Tse (with Tao J), "Strategic ambiguities in the process of consent: role of the family in decisions to forgo life-sustaining treatment for incompetent elderly patients" (*Journal of Medicine and Philosophy* 2004; 29 (2): 207–23). The same section was presented by Samantha Pang in the fourth International Conference of Bioethics in Taipei in June 2004.

Appendix 1
Reasons Why the Term "Passive Euthanasia"
Should Not Be Used*

(Appendix 2 of the Guidelines on Life-sustaining Treatment in the Terminally Ill, Hospital Authority of Hong Kong)

Although the term "passive euthanasia" is used by some people to mean "withholding or withdrawing life sustaining treatment", the term is not used in medically advanced countries when the subject is officially discussed. Notable examples include "Deciding to Forego Life-Sustaining Treatment" (A report on the ethical, medical, and legal issues in treatment decisions) published by the President's Commission for the Study of Ethical Problems in Medicine and Biomedical and Behavioral Research of the US (1983), and the Report of the House of Lords Select Committee on Medical Ethics of the UK (1994). The term is also not used in the professional guidelines on the subject in various medically advanced countries. Similarly, the Hospital Authority does not support the use of the term "passive euthanasia" because of the misleading connotations that may entail:

(a) "Withholding or withdrawing life sustaining treatment", if done under appropriate circumstances, is ethically and legally acceptable. This is ethically and legally different from "euthanasia" as defined in the Medical Council Code as "direct intentional killing of a person as part of the medical care being offered". The latter, which some people call "active euthanasia", is illegal around the world except in Holland. To use the term "passive euthanasia" to describe the appropriate withholding or withdrawal of life sustaining treatment may give people the wrong impression that such a decision is ethically and legally similar to "active euthanasia".

(b) "Withholding or withdrawing life-sustaining treatment" includes widely different situations, ranging from withholding cardiopulmonary resuscitation in a terminally ill malignancy patient, to withdrawing artificial nutrition in a patient in a persistent vegetative state. The former is non-controversial but the latter is very controversial. If the term "passive euthanasia" is used, people may relate all discussions about "withholding or withdrawing life sustaining treatment" to the controversial situation like the latter one.

(c) The term "passive euthanasia" may contain the meaning of "an intention to kill". We support withholding or withdrawing futile treatment that only prolongs the dying process, but we do not support an intention to kill.

Avoiding the misleading term "passive euthanasia" but using the more neutral term "withholding or withdrawing life sustaining treatment" would thus facilitate public discussion on the topic. This would also facilitate discussion with the patients and families in individual cases when such discussion is required.

---

* Source: Hospital Authority of Hong Kong. HA *Guidelines on Life-Sustaining Treatment in the Terminally Ill*. Hong Kong, 2002.

Appendix 2
Quotes from Traditional Chinese Medicine Literature on Truth Telling and on Facing Death*

From "Introduction to Medicine", by Li Chan, Ming Dynasty:
After the diagnosis, one must tell the truth to the patient.

醫學入門 明 李梴
既診後，對病家言必以實

From "Introduction to Medicine", by Li Chan, Ming Dynasty:
If one uses a single word as our contract with the patient, it should be "no deceit" ... one does not tell the truth after diagnosis, it is deceit ... .

醫學入門 明 李梴
或問 一言為約，曰：不欺而已矣。…
診脈而不以實告者，欺也。…

From "Recovery from Illnesses" by Gong Ting Xian, Ming Dynasty:
... Fourth, you should identify the underlying pathology, and be bold enough to talk about life and death.

萬病回春 明 龔廷賢
… 四識病原，生死敢言

From "Miscellaneous Writings of a Doctor" by Wang Lun, Ming Dynasty:
Previous people said: "If you are ill, you should write the word death with your fingers on your chest. Then your worries will be gone and your heart will attain peace. This is better than medication". This is really an excellent therapy.

明醫雜著 明 王綸
昔人有云：我但臥病，即於胸前不時手寫死字，則百般思慮俱息，此心便得安靜，勝於服藥。此真無上妙方也。

* Source: Tse CY, Chong A, and Fok SY. Breaking bad news: a Chinese perspective. *Pall Med* 2003; 17: 339–43.

Appendix 3
Forgoing Life-Sustaining Treatment: Patient Perspective*

Theme	Verbatim Statements from Patients
Prognostic Awareness	
	I know my illness cannot be cured. Even though my life can be saved, my general condition will not improve.
	The doctor has told me about my condition. There is no cure. Sooner or later I am going to die. I do not want to go through such an unpleasant experience before I die.
	I have been sick for so many years; there is no hope of a cure. I do not want to do anything; just let nature takes its course.
	I am already so old, ventilation support will not help; everything is going to vanish anyway.
Burdens of Illness	
Treatment Burdens	I do not want to lie in bed unconscious, full of tubes. To live in this way is meaningless.
	I need frequent hospitalization. I have experienced so much suffering, going in and out of hospital.
	To rely on medicines and machines to prolong life is meaningless.
	I am now having non-invasive positive pressure ventilation, which is already unpleasant. I do not want endotracheal mechanical ventilation, which will be even more unpleasant.
	I am afraid of intubation. Last time, I saw a patient die after intubation. He never regained consciousness after being hooked onto the machine.
	Intubation is unpleasant, and breathlessness is unpleasant. Both are suffering to me. I let the doctor to make the decision for me.
Symptom Burdens	I have many illnesses, am often breathless, have problems in eating and excretion.
	I have constant leg pain so that I need others to help me even to go to the bathroom.
	I feel that I am living in a prison, totally restricted in activities.
Care Burdens	I feel that I am a burden to others; why not return to the heavenly god earlier?
	I feel that I am a burden to my family and to society. I do not want to waste public resources.

Existential Concerns	
The Will to Live	Last time, I was so breathless and distressed that I was frightened to death. I am grateful to the nurse who comforted me and helped me with better positioning and adjustment of oxygen devices. I feel these days are a bonus to me.
	I survived the last episode. It must be due to luck. I do not know whether I can be so lucky next time.
	Last time the physician advised me to have intubation. I refused, and I survived. He said that I am lucky; I know I am gaining time.
Life Values	I am already so old. I have enough years of life.
	I am at peace with myself because I did nothing purposely to harm others and I did not owe anybody anything that I did not return in my life.
	I have raised my family, and I have fulfilled my life responsibilities. I have no more worries.
	Other than anticipating my son's visit, I do not have any desire for life.
	I do not have money or close relatives; I have nothing to worry about if I die.
Death & Dying Concerns	Who is not afraid of death? It is quite normal to have fear. But can we prevent this from happening?
	To live or to die is the heaven's will; my concern is to remain clean and tidy when I die.
	Everyone has to die once. There is a time to be born and a time to die.
	I am already so old. I am not afraid of death. I only want to die in peace, without causing more trouble.

* Source: Pang MCS, Tse CY, Chan KS, Chung BPM, Leung AKA, Leung EMF, et al. An empirical analysis of the decision-making of limiting life-sustaining treatment for patients with advanced chronic obstructive pulmonary disease in Hong Kong China. *Journal of Critical Care* 2004; 19(3): 135–44.

13

Community Palliative Care in Hong Kong

Faith Chun Fong LIU

Palliative Care in Hong Kong

The purpose of palliative care is to enhance the quality and meaning of life and death for both terminal patients (those with cancer or non-cancer disease) and their family members and in their bereavement period. As a modern health-care specialty, palliative care has rapidly developed in the last decade in Hong Kong. The Co-ordinating Committee (Hospice) of Hospital Authority (HA) of the Hong Kong SAR Government defines hospice/palliative care as[1] "the care of the patients & their families with active progressive advanced disease and a limited prognosis for whom the focus of care is the quality of life".

The terms "hospice" and "palliative", with respect to service and care, are used interchangeably in this chapter.

Community palliative care was established as a health care policy by the HA, in order to provide continuous and holistic care for discharged terminally ill patients and their family members. The development of community service aims to improve access across the population and improve the standard of care at sites for those living with advanced disease. This is seen as an economic necessity.[2,3] There is also a strong perception that the provision of palliative care should be carried out at home and enable the patient to be cared for in the environment of choice.[4] The British Government White Paper - 'Caring for People',[5] views community care in the following way:

> Community care means providing the right level of intervention and support to enable people to achieve maximum independence and control over their own lives. For this aim to become a reality, the development of a wide range of services provided in a variety of ways is essential.

Model of Community Palliative Care

In Hong Kong, community palliative care, operated as cluster-based, is provided by either the Palliative Home Care Service or the Community Nursing Service. Both programmes facilitate transition from hospital to home, encompass the care of the patient and family and target symptom management.

Palliative Home Care Service

The main workers in the service are palliative home-care nurses who are trained and experienced in hospice care, supported by a multidisciplinary team designated solely to take care of terminally ill patients in the community. The multidisciplinary experts, e.g., palliative physician, clinical nurse specialist, social worker, clinical psychologist, physiotherapist, occupational therapist and pastoral worker, are also accessible for consultation and home visits as needed. The service is supported by palliative in-patient units. Self-referral is accepted to facilitate the accessibility of the service.

Community Nursing Service

Another service model is provided by community nurses in a general hospital. The nurses are often trained in hospice care but are not necessarily clinically specialized in taking care of terminally ill patients. Support from other disciplines is relatively minimal.

Evaluation of these models

No local research has yet been conducted to investigate the cost-effectiveness and efficiency of community palliative models. According to the literature review[6] in examining the effect of specialist models of palliative care on consumer satisfaction, opinion and preference over the past twenty years and eighty-three relevant papers were identified. Research findings consistently indicate that patients and care-givers are more satisfied with specialist palliative care than with general care,[7] and the care- receivers of cancer perceive quality of services from specialists as better than generic services.[8]

Service development

A model of outreaching consultative service has been developed recently, in which palliative home-care nurses and physicians provide palliative care jointly with other specialties. The service aims to ensure provision of palliative care to patients not necessitating palliative in-patient care, facilitate smooth transition from curative to palliative care, improve collaboration between hospice units and clinical departments of cluster hospitals, and reduce barriers to palliative care referral. The outreaching team continues to follow up on discharged patients at home. A pilot survey revealed that patients were satisfied with the programme.[9]

Taking Care of Terminal Patients at Home

Caring for terminally ill patients at home is a trend. However, the shift from institutionalization to a family care system may cause disruption to the patients and the care-givers,[10] especially those who may not be prepared to assume caring responsibilities.[11] Care-givers here are family members and friends who provide care in the home setting and are unpaid.

Needs of patients while at home

Studies showed that discharged terminally ill cancer patients professed to have a strong family or social network and in general were living in good environmental and social conditions.[12,13] The psychological aspects and the physical symptoms, however, caused the most concern to patients and families. [13] Patients commonly expressed fear of overloading the family. [13,14]

Needs of care-givers

A local study[15] found that care-givers experienced of some difficulties. Half reported moderate or high levels of difficulty in "bonding with the care-receiver", "emotional reaction to caring", "physical demands of caring" and "restricted social life". The literature reveals that poor quality of patient care, lack of communication support to families and limited internal family resources can prevent family members from staying healthy or attaining a healthy balance through the journey of the illness. [16]

Care-giving demands include:

1. Physical demands

Taking care of terminally ill patients at home requires a twenty-four-hour commitment, additional responsibilities that compete for time, energy, and attention in the family members' own daily lives.[17,18] In addition to accompanying the patients to follow-up medical visits and treatments, care-givers often go with patients for Chinese herbalist consultations. It means that care-givers also have to prepare the herbal medicine, usually cooked as soup, which takes significant amounts of time. Moreover, care-givers often feel out of control, as the patients for whom they are caring are unappreciative, demanding and manipulative.[19] These demands often cause physical problems for the care-givers.[11, 20]

2. Emotional demands

Taking care of a loved one, especially at the terminal stage, often evokes emotions.[21] Feelings of helplessness, loneliness, confusion, depression, guilt, resentment and anger are commonly found in the care-givers.[11,12] Studies have confirmed that care-givers experience more psychological symptoms than physical symptoms.[20]

3. Financial demands

Economic hardship is induced by the added financial strain of buying medical necessities and aids.[22] A study by Mok *et al.*[11] reported that forty-percent of care-givers lost income and worried about their future financial situation.

Cultural concerns

The study by Mok *et al.*[23] demonstrated that cultural beliefs have a great influence on care-givers when taking care of terminal patients at home. Firstly, in Confucian thought, the role of the self is not to express and manifest itself but to develop the internal moral self. It has always been expressed as conquering selfishness to restore ritual propriety. The cultural concept of *yi* (義) (rightness and responsibility) — a major component of Confucianism to sustain bonding between people, family and country, and filial duty — is salient. Although the care-givers feel tired and sad, they do not perceive care-giving as a burden. On the contrary, they believe that their care-giving is important for the patient, and therefore they are motivated to move beyond the immediate circumstances and experience meaning of their effort. Secondly, family care-givers often do not take the initiative to look for guidance and support from neighbours and friends. This may be influenced by the Chinese perception of different relationships. The care-givers do not want to give them trouble, because there is an expectation of moderate reciprocity and a conditional sense of independence.[23] Care-givers suffered, partly due to the diminishing kinship ties[24] and inadequate support from the nuclear family.[25] Studies [13,15,23] strongly support the findings [26,27] that health-care providers play an important role in helping care-givers manage the burdens and demands of care-giving.

Characteristics of care-givers

Chinese women are expected to take the role of wife and mother as their priority.[28] The main burden of care has been placed on women, even though they have to earn an income.[29] Loke[15] recruited twenty-six subjects taking care of terminal cancer patients in Hong Kong. Results showed that more than two-thirds of the care-givers were female; they ranged from 39 to 84 years of age, with a mean age of 63.5; and one-third of the care-givers were under the age of 59. All of the care-givers resided with the patients. Eighty percent of them had no formal education or had primary school education only. Two-thirds were retirees and were the spouse of the patients. Most of the care-givers suffered from chronic disease, e.g., heart disease, diabetic mellitus or arthritis. This finding reflects again that support for care-givers is necessary.

What Home Care Service Can Provide

Home-care nurses support patients and their family by visiting and phoning. The service is a holistic approach which can help the patients to maximize self-care abilities,[13] ease tension and strengthen the relationship between patient and family,[13] increase comfort and support the family of a dependent patient,[30] increase control to enhance coping[31] and help the patient die at home.[32] Hinton [32] demonstrated that care-givers' perception of help about home care service includes contact, explanation, support, physical treatment and practical nursing. Patients and their family members value health-care professionals' kindness, caring, reliability, support, ready response, and twenty-four-hour availability.

Wong *et al.*[13] conducted a study on exploring the problems of terminal patients and the contributions of nursing to both the patients and family members, from referral until death. Thirty-two subjects were recruited. The result of the study revealed that the need for physiological care to dying patients is less than the need for psychological care. The results[13] indicated that lower limb oedema, pain, ascites and dyspnoea are the main symptoms that showed significant statistical improvement over time. Interventions of supervision and education achieved statistical significance. The findings of the psychosocial problems of stress, fear, anger, anxiety, grief and spiritual distress showed significant improvement over time, whereas guilt did not. Another study of Loke *et al.*[15] demonstrated that twenty out of the twenty-one (95.2%) care-givers considered the support received from hospice home care nurses useful, especially in informational support (n=20, 95.2%), emotional support (n=20, 95.2%) and in skill training (n=16, 76.2%). Care-givers also indicated that home-care nurses provided more useful support than that received from family members and friends ($c^2=11.35$, p=0.003). This result is similar to

Lundh's findings.[33]

The results of the studies further support the necessity and contribution of palliative home care service to both the patients and the care-givers in the community.

What the Home-care Nurses Assess and Intervene

Palliative home-care nurses, as direct care providers and coordinators of appropriate professionals and resources for meeting the complex needs of the individuals and their families, need a framework in their clinical practice. A framework of assessment and intervention is used in the author's clinical practice setting as follows:

1.	General condition	8.	Bladder & bowel functions
2.	Symptom management	9.	Sleep pattern
3.	Self-care ability	10.	Psychological aspect
4.	Nutrition	11.	Social aspect
5.	Medication	12.	Spiritual aspect
6.	Home & community adjustment	13.	Family care
7.	Skin condition	14.	Bereavement care

Patients Who Die at Home

Staying at home allows terminally ill patients to have greater control over their environment, more autonomy and privacy, and a sense of normality.[34] For Chinese people, dying at home has special cultural meaning to them and their families.[35] When death occurs at home, the spirit of the dead can reunite with the forebears, and thus "the fallen leaves can return to their roots". Dying at home means the spirit of the dead has a place to rest and he or she will not be a *koo'un' ia' kui* (wandering spirit 孤魂野鬼), a solitary soul with no one to depend on.[35]

Dying at home is not common in Hong Kong. Of the 1,300 patients under the care of the author's clinical worksite in 1999–2003, only six patients died at home. Complex factors include medical reasons,[36] uncontrolled pain and symptoms in the dying process,[37,38] anxiety of the patient and family,[39] no access by the family to the services, and inadequate support in the community.[40]

Contributing factors for these patients to be cared for at home until death are as follows. [41] The availability of the carers is a determinant that includes patient access to a support network; carers are female, young, educated, available twenty-four hours and have good support from other family members. Additionally, patients have a good relationship with family members, live with them in a relatively spacious accommodation and have satisfactory stable financial status. The second determinant is that the patients are cared for by competent experts with knowledge, skill, experience and confidence in terminal care, and who are prepared to visit regularly and are available when needed.

A Case Study

The story of Calvin may portray the unique experiences of a Chinese family in facing the death of a young adult. Calvin, thirty years old, suffered from terminal carcinoma of the liver. He was referred to home-care service for symptom management. Except for minor discomfort of ascitis and lower limb oedema, he managed well at home. The nurse suggested demonstrating leg massage to his mother. During the procedure, he expressed the wish for his mother to become a Christian. The nurse responded that if his mother hadn't handled her anger towards God, she couldn't accept God. His mother cried and Calvin didn't say anything.

When Calvin wasn't present, his mother told the nurse that she was disappointed with Calvin, because he did not fulfil his responsibility as a son. To be a good son in a Chinese family, he was supposed to take up the main responsibility for the family, especially in decision-making and financial support. However, he failed to do this, and his detachment from the family made her feel angry. She further explained that, at the time of Calvin's illness, her mother was diagnosed with cancer too. In order not to upset her mother, the family decided not to tell her about Calvin's illness. The whole family, therefore, bore the blame of not being filial, because they did not visit Calvin's grandmother. Overwhelmed with emotions and blame, Calvin's mother could not effectively cope and even thought of committing suicide. Having someone to listen to her, she found relief. The nurse asked for permission to talk to Calvin to settle the problems between them. She agreed, on the condition the nurse could not disclose this conversation.

In the next visit, the nurse told Calvin that his mother blamed herself for failing as a mother and wife and asked his opinion. He didn't agree with that. The nurse invited Calvin to talk to his mother to relieve her of guilt. He said, "It will not be a problem after I pass away". The nurse challenged him: "Yes, it will not be a problem for you. But your mum will carry the guilt all her life". Calvin fell into deep thought. After a long silence, he told the nurse, "Okay, I'll talk to mum".

Calvin was excited to tell the nurse at the following visit that he had a long chat with his mother. Not only had they settled the misunderstanding but his mother accepted God also. Sharing his happiness, the nurse reminded him that, as the eldest son, he had a unique role in the family. He fully agreed. The reminder was made because neither Calvin nor his mother had mentioned

Calvin's father.

At the fourth and last visit, he told the nurse that he had a long chat with his father. He revealed that his father had had an affair a few years ago. The family felt ashamed and kept the secret from others, including their extended family. That was really a very difficult time for them. As the eldest son in the family, Calvin implored his father take care of his mother and the family after his death. His father promised.

Calvin's story shows that the physical symptoms were relatively less severe, and the most challenging problem was related to the relationship among family members. Frustration, disappointment and anger demonstrated that the family needed to take care of unfinished business. Calvin's story may show that Chinese culture and values still play an important role, even though people in Hong Kong are influenced by Western culture.

1. In Chinese culture, the most painful event in life for the elderly is to view the death of a younger one. Moreover, a younger one should not add any burden on the elderly. That is why Calvin's mother kept the truth of Calvin's illness from her mother.

2. The loss of a son in a Chinese family is more painful than the loss of a daughter. A son is supposed to continue the family line. Moreover, a son, especially the eldest, is expected to be responsible for the affairs of the whole family, including, financial, decision-making, handling conflicts, etc. Both the son and the parents, therefore, had difficulty facing this situation.

3. Some Chinese have a strong feeling that one should not expose family "shameful" affairs to others (家醜不出外傳), in order to protect the family. However, this caused stress for the family. Reluctance to seek help may be a common pattern in Chinese culture. Therefore, health-care professionals need to build rapport and handle family concerns with care and sensitivity.

Cultural Information

According to the author's clinical experience, some cultural information is as follows:

Information	Reasons	Advice
Chinese may be reluctant to take morphine as an analgesic.	This is a reminder of the Opium War which may arouse complex feelings and fear of morphine addiction.	Explain the need for the treatment and clarify any misconceptions. Use alternatives if the patient strongly opposes taking the drug.

Information	Reasons	Advice
Chinese cancer patients often are not allowed to take chicken and beef but do eat pork.	Chinese believe that beef and chicken are toxic to the patient.	Respect the choice, explain and introduce the options.
Chinese are keen about having rice and they may not accept other nutritional products as alternatives.	Chinese believe that only rice can retain and restore strength.	Advise adding protein powder into congee or soup as a nutritional supplement.
It is not acceptable to disclose the diagnosis or the prognosis of the disease to the patient prior to discussing it with the family members.	As a family is more highly valued than an individual in Chinese culture, it is important to have consensus with the family members about the truth-telling. Discussing death and dying is taboo, and many Chinese believe that once the patient knows about the disease, he or she may lose the spirit to fight the disease or may commit suicide.	It is advisable to break the bad news to the family members first; then seek consensus to tell the truth to the patient, especially elderly people. Show empathy and explore what will happen if the patient asks about the illness and come to a consensus. Disclose the truth step by step and offer adequate support.
The eldest son is the key family member in a Chinese family; therefore, health-care professionals should gain his support.	The eldest son is highly respected in Chinese culture and is the one who inherits the family fortune. He is expected to shoulder the responsibility for the family.	It is essential to involve the eldest child, especially the son, in the process of decision-making regarding the illness.
Complementary therapies are commonly used, e.g., herbs, acupuncture.	Chinese seek Western medical advice first and then go for traditional Chinese treatment.	Advise the patient to look for side effects of the Chinese treatment, e.g., gastrointestinal bleeding. Remind the patient that the treatment fee should be affordable.

Information	Reasons	Advice
Some Chinese may practise superstitious rituals, e.g., patients drink water with the ashes from blessed incense brought from temple.	Traditional superstitious rituals were quite common when modern medicine was not well accepted. Some Chinese still believe these superstitions.	Respect the ritual, but remind the patient about the hygiene factor.
Family members are not allowed to touch the dead body or let tears fall on it.	Some Chinese believe that even after the patient has died, a form of *qi* is still flowing in the body. The *qi* of the dead can transfer to those touching the body and bring them bad health or bad luck.	The ritual should be respected and be sensibly handled. Nurses can act as a role model to touch the dead body, especially when some family members want to have a touch with the dead.
Some Chinese yell loudly at the dead body after death has been verified.	Chinese believe that the deceased will transform to an invisible spirit. If the deceased is not reminded to go home, he or she may get lost. If the dead person knows the way home, he or she can shelter the descendents and won't become a spirit with no place to go to.	Respect the ritual. Informing the family members to stay with the dying patient until the last breathe is important for the Chinese; otherwise, they will feel guilty.
The deceased will be put on some suits of clothes after death has been verified.	This is a gift to the deceased from the decedents that he/she can have enough clothes to change in the next world.	Advise that the clothes may get wet or dirty, so they can be put on by the funeral attendants later.
Most Chinese families do not allow elderly people to view the death of a younger one or attend the funeral. 'White-head should not say final farewell to the black-head' (白頭人不可送黑頭人)	It is believed that bad luck will come to the family. In fact, it is a a protection to elderly people from overwhelming sadness.	Health-care workers can observe the needs of elderly people. Support and accompany them to see the dead body if so desired.

Conclusion

This chapter focuses on introducing community palliative care in Hong Kong; for example, service delivery models, and problems of physical, psychosocial and financial strain on patients and care-givers when taking care of patients at home. Studies reveal, with evidence, that the service can meet the complex needs of the patients and care-givers and can support them in being where they prefer. Dying at home is not common in Hong Kong, though most Chinese want to die in their own bed. Factors to assist care-givers in taking care of terminal patients until death are discussed. Cultural advice about taking care of Chinese patients is also enumerated and explained.

14

The Role of Chinese Medicine in Cancer Palliative Care

Siu Man NG

A Modern Role for a Traditional Medicine

Despite rapid advancements in medical science, a number of complementary and alternative medicines (CAM), including Chinese medicine, remain popular. According to WHO[1] figures, seventy-five percent of people in a number of developed countries used CAM in 1997. In the US, it was estimated that the percentage of Americans using CAM increased from thirty-two to forty-two percent between 1990 and 1997.[2] The types of CAM include Chinese medicine, chiropractic, naturopathy, homeopathy, and Indian Ayurvedic medicine. A population-based survey in San Francisco indicated that seventy-two percent of women with breast cancer used at least one form of CAM.[3] Although most of them continued seeking conventional treatment, only half reported the use of CAM to their physicians.

In Hong Kong, Chinese medicine was not systematically developed until the handover of sovereignty from the British to the Chinese government in 1997. The Chinese Medicine Council of Hong Kong (CMCHK) was subsequently developed, and a statutory professional registration system was gradually implemented. According to CMCHK,[4] there were about 5,000 registered Chinese medicine practitioners (RCMP) as of January 2005. For a territory with a population of about 6.8 million, that means one RCMP per 1,400 people. As such, Chinese medicine is playing an important role in the health-care system of Hong Kong, especially at the primary-care level. As Hong Kong people perceive Chinese medicine "better at curing the root of the problem" , many of them will seek this treatment for conditions that cannot be dealt with well by Western medicine.[5] In the context of palliative care, many patients and their relatives are keen to have Chinese medicine treatment in addition to conventional treatment. To meet these strong wishes as well as to improve doctor-patient communication and cooperation, it is essential for health-care professionals to develop a better understanding of Chinese medicine in an open yet scientific manner.

What exactly might Chinese medicine contribute to modern palliative care? In the era of evidence-based medicine, clinical decisions have to be made based on knowledge of the efficacy of an intervention as well as its effect on the quality of life. Because existing evidence is mainly on the application of Chinese medicine in supportive cancer care, the focus of this chapter is correspondingly narrowed to this domain only.

The major roles of Chinese medicine in cancer supportive care are:[6-8]
1. As adjunctive cancer treatment
   a. Potentiating conventional chemo- and radiotherapies
   b. Reducing adverse effects of conventional treatment
2. As enhancement of total well-being
   a. Providing a sense of control and continuity of treatment when conventional treatments stop
   b. Reducing symptoms in the late-stage cancer
   c. Enhancing physical and mental health.

This chapter first gives a brief account of the unique theoretical framework of Chinese medicine. It then considers in detail the possible roles of Chinese medicine in cancer palliative care.

Core Theoretical Characteristics of Chinese Medicine

The fundamental theoretical framework of Chinese medicine was established over 2,000 years ago. *The Inner Canon of Yellow Emperor,* written in the first century B.C., laid down the basic principles that have all along been guiding the development of Chinese medicine.[9] There are two core theories that characterize Chinese medicine:[10]
1. Holistic perspective (整體觀念)
2. Syndromatic diagnosis as the basis for treatment formulation (辨證論治).

Before going into these difficult concepts, it is necessary to give a brief account of the yin-yang theory and the five elements theory. Both are depicted in the ancient book *I Ching* (also known as the *Book of Changes,* written in the fifth century B.C.) and had great influence on the conceptualization of the original theories of Chinese medicine.

Yin-yang theory and five elements theory

The yin-yang theory and five elements theory propose a universal model to understand the pattern of change of all things in the world, from microscopic to celestial phenomena. Firstly, the theories propose that all things in the world can be classified by broad categorical systems: the yin-yang system or the five elements system. Secondly, there is a universal pattern of change and dynamic relationships in the broad categories. Thirdly, by applying the knowledge of the universal model, one can understand the pattern of change in the items being investigated; for example, the relationship among various organs inside the human body.

Yin and yang are opposites, a mutually facilitating but also mutually repressing pair. Yin is about substance, stillness, storage, darkness, softness, etc. Yang is about energy, movement, transporting, brightness, hardness, etc. Examples of such yin-yang pairs are earth and sky, night and day, moon and sun, winter and summer, women and men, etc. The yin-yang theory proposes a universal model depicting the pattern of relationship and change between a dyadic pair.

The five elements theory proposes classifying things into five broad categories: wood, fire, earth, metal, and water. There are two normal forces — the facilitating force and the repressing force — working on each other among the elements. Wood facilitates fire, fire facilitates earth, earth facilitates metal, metal facilitates water, and water facilitates wood. Likewise, wood represses earth, fire represses metal, earth represses water, metal represses wood, and water represses fire. The two forces working together maintain the dynamic equilibrium among the five elements, without any one becoming "hypo" or "hyper". Systemic balance is regarded as the healthy state.

Holistic perspective

Chinese medicine has a dynamic, systemic perspective in understanding the functioning of a person. Regarding the physical body, there are five yin organs (called the *zhang* 臟): liver, heart, spleen, lung, and kidney. Or, to be more exact, the "liver system", "heart system", "spleen system", "lung system", and "kidney system". Although Chinese medicine uses the same anatomical names as those in Western medicine, it actually refers to systems bigger than that. For example, the kidney system is more than a urinary organ. It is also concerned with the storage of vital energy, growth during childhood and adolescence, the reproductive function, strength of bones, and generation of marrow. Its health status can be seen indirectly by observing the hair. It is connected to the outside through the ears. In the mind/body connection, the kidney system is closely related to the emotion of fear.

Such grouping of additional physiological functions to the five *zhang* was made with reference to the clinical experience of physicians in ancient times, as well as the yin-yang theory and five elements theory. According to the yin-yang theory, the five *zhang* are yin. Correspondingly, there are five yang organ systems, called the *fu* (腑).They are the "gall bladder system", "small intestine system", "stomach system", "large intestine system", and "urinary bladder system". Therefore, the liver system and the gall bladder system are a yin-yang pair, the heart system and small intestine is another yin-yang pair, and so on. With reference to the yin-yang theory, some fundamental relationships between the two elements of a pair can be expected.

The five *zhang* and five *fu* actually correspond to the five elements: wood, fire, earth, metal and water. Therefore, there is also a pattern of relationships and changes among the five *zhang* and five *fu*. For example, wood represses earth. When the liver system has problem, it will likely lead to problems with the spleen system as well. Another example is to rectify a "hypo" spleen system, one approach can be "calming" the liver system.

To complicate the picture, emotions can also be classified according to the five elements theory. The five emotions — anger, joy, worry, sorrow, and fear — correspond to the five elements. Moreover, each is closely linked with the corresponding *zhang* and *fu*. This is the *zhang-fu*-emotion interconnectedness theory. The resulting interplay among these *zhang*, *fu* and emotions forms a highly dynamic network of mind/body subsystems.

The meridian theory is also highly relevant and important in understanding this dynamic network. The meridian network was discovered in ancient China through consolidating hundreds, or perhaps thousands, of years of clinical experience. There are twelve chief meridians, eight special meridians, and numerous smaller meridians going through and connecting the *zhang*, *fu*, and virtually the whole body into a holistic system. *Qi* and blood are circulating through the network through a sophisticated regulation mechanism.

In a nutshell, Chinese medicine takes a holistic perspective in understanding a person, consisting of a dynamic network of body and mind subsystems. According to the Inner Canon of Yellow Emperor, in the broadest sense, yin and yang in harmonious dynamic equilibrium is good health.[9] In other words, yin and yang out of balance is ill health. Adding in the *zhang*, *fu*, emotions, meridians, *qi* and blood components, etc., the assessment of the systemic balance or imbalance can be highly sophisticated.

Chinese medicine's holistic perspective actually goes beyond the body. It also concerns the relationship between the person and the environment — both the social and natural worlds. Heavily influenced by the teachings of Daoism, Chinese medicine advocates a simple life, few desires, respect for nature, and a harmonious relationship with nature. The internal and external systems are also interconnected and are in dynamic equilibrium. Upsetting the balance on one side can affect the other.

Syndromatic diagnosis as the basis for treatment formulation

The second core theory of Chinese medicine is that syndromatic diagnosis is the basis for formulating treatment.[11] In Chinese medicine, there are two levels of diagnosis: disease diagnosis and the syndromatic diagnosis. Disease diagnosis is conceptually the same as that in Western medicine, though the two systems have very different systems of disease classification. In Chinese medicine, disease classification is basically by symptoms. Therefore, treating the disease is virtually equivalent to treating or relieving the presenting symptoms.

Syndromatic diagnosis is unique in Chinese medicine. It is the diagnosis of the status of equilibrium among the subsystems. Chinese medicine strongly believes that restoring the equilibrium can help the organism heal itself. It is an orientation toward the facilitation of self-healing. Such intervention is regarded as fundamental and more important than targeting the disease directly.

Therefore, in Chinese medicine, neither the agents of disease nor the symptoms are the key targets of treatment. The primary target of treatment is the imbalance in the system, and therefore the treatment focuses on restoring the harmonious dynamic equilibrium among various body and mind subsystems. In clinical practice, this approach works well in many conditions of illness. It is the unique conceptual framework of Chinese medicine that ensures it a role in the modern health-care system.

A Systemic Perspective on Cancer

As a result of rapid advances in technology, Western medicine is investigating cancer at the molecular level. The objective is to develop treatments with the highest specificity, no matter whether the treatment is drugs or physical means. The ultimate aim is to eradicate cancer cells with minimal side effects.

Adhering to its central belief, Chinese medicine is still largely looking at cancer from a macroscopic, systemic perspective. Diagnosing emphasizes assessing the imbalance of the mind/body system rather than examining microscopic, pathological cancer growth. It is believed that rebalancing and strengthening the mind/body network can help resolve the cancer.

Modern pharmacological studies show that some Chinese herbs have anti-cancer effects, especially those in the "heat dispelling and detoxification" category.[7] Herbs like bai hua she shi chao (*Hedyotis diffusa Willd*) and *ban zi lian* (*Scutellaria barbata Don*) are frequently used in herbal formulas for cancer patients. Nevertheless, these herbs most often play a secondary role in the formula. The primary treatment objective is still rebalancing the system. Killing cancer cells is a secondary aim only. According to Chinese medicine theory, overusing "heat dispelling and detoxification" herbs can damage health. As such, a milder, systemic-oriented, approach is preferred.

In Chinese medicine, cancer is viewed as a part of the clinical features of a syndrome representing an imbalance in the integrated whole. For example, stomach cancer may result from various systems imbalance, such as liver *qi* invading the stomach, stomach yin deficiency, stomach yang deficiency, *qi*-blood stagnation, spleen *qi* deficiency with phlegm accumulation, etc. Breast cancer may result from liver *qi* stagnation, blood stagnation, spleen *qi* deficiency with phlegm accumulation, etc. Colon cancer may result from damp heat in the large intestine, spleen and kidney yang deficiency, liver and kidney yin deficiency, etc. Because the system imbalance will change as the disease progresses, the syndromatic diagnosis will be revised from time to time. Toward the end stage, the imbalance will most often be a deficiency, such as yin deficiency, yang deficiency, *qi* deficiency, blood deficiency, etc. As such, treatments will need to be adjusted accordingly. The focus will be more on tonifying rather than actively detoxifying by means of strong herbal medicine.

Most cancer patients receive conventional Western medicine treatments, such as chemotherapy and radiotherapy. According to the holistic perspective of Chinese medicine, the treatments are part of the total environment that interacts with the patient. As such, the effect of the medicine on the overall balance in the system needs to be taken into account. Radiation is a form of extreme yang that can damage the yin, blood and moisture.[8] In contrast, chemotherapy is often a form of extreme yin that can damage the yang and *qi*. An important role of Chinese medicine is to help patient keep the system in balance when receiving chemo- or radiotherapy.

System imbalance can be manifested in many ways, and cancer is only one manifestation. A Chinese medicine practitioner puts the greatest emphasis on the subjective discomfort of the patient and makes the disease diagnosis based on that. Therefore, the disease diagnosis sometimes can be unrelated to the primary disease — cancer. For example, when a breast cancer patient presents with sleeping disturbance and is keen to have treatment for it, the Chinese medicine diagnosis will be insomnia. Interestingly, the syndromatic diagnosis is often the same as that of the primary disease: breast cancer, or liver *qi* stagnation. This is consistent with the belief that cancer is only one clinical manifestation of the underlying system imbalance. As such, the overall treatment direction will be the same, i.e., destagnation of liver *qi*, though the exact prescription will differ reflecting the different primary complaints, either sleep disturbance or cancer growth.

Chinese Medicine as Adjunctive Cancer Treatment

Chinese medicine plays the role of adjunctive cancer treatment by performing two major functions: (1) potentiating conventional chemo- and radiotherapies, and (2) reducing the adverse effects of conventional treatment. There is evidence that patients who receive combined Chinese and Western medicine treatments have better a response to the disease and a higher rate of survival than patients who receive Western treatment alone. For example, randomized controlled trials investigating the benefits of combined treatments have been conducted on patients with liver cancer [12,13] and nasopharyngeal carcinoma.[14]

Potentiating conventional chemo- and radiotherapies

There is increasing evidence suggesting that Chinese herbal medicine and acupuncture can potentiate conventional chemo- and radiotherapies.[15–19] This is achieved mainly through two mechanisms: (1) improving host resistance and (2) modifying tumour physiology. Many *qi*-tonifying herbs, such huang *qi* (*radix Astragalus membranaceus*), *dang shen* (*radix Codonopsis pilosula*) and *bai zhu* (*rhizoma Atraclylodis macrocephalae*) can increase host resistance through stimulating the immunological function. The mechanisms include increasing CD4/CD8 ratio, phagocytic activity and lymphocyte transformation. Most of them also have anti-inflammatory and hepatoprotective effects. Although *ren shen* (*Panax ginseng*) is a powerful *qi*-tonifying herb, it is less often used in clinical practice because it is expensive. Therefore, *ren shen* (*Panax ginseng*) is usually substituted by *dang shen* (*radix Codonopsis pilosula*).

Blood stagnation is a common syndrome in cancer patients. This classical view mirrors modern pathological findings that blood supply and circulation are poor in most malignant tumours. Cancer cells that survive in a low oxygen tension environment are found to be more resistant to chemo- and radiotherapies.[20,21] Blood destagnation herbs have been shown to potentiate conventional treatments.[22] These herbs commonly used include *tao ren* (*Prunus persica*), *hong hua* (*Carthamus tinctorius*), *dang gui* (*Angelica sinensis*) and *dan shen* (*Salvia miltiorrhiza*).

Flow of *qi* and blood in the meridian network through stimulating the appropriate acupuncture points. Treatment by acupuncture is again based on Chinese medicine syndromatic diagnosis. The primary objective is to facilitate self-healing through restoring balance in the system.

Animal and clinical studies suggest that acupuncture can moderate the immunological functioning of cancer patients.[23–26] Acupuncture has been shown to increase T-lymphocyte proliferation, increase NK cell activities, activate the complement system, and increase OKT4 cell counts. Animal experiments show that acupuncture can inhibit the growth of transplanted breast cancer. The main acupuncture points used are those facilitating spleen functions. According to Chinese medicine theory, the main functions of the spleen are the formulation of *qi* and blood, and the transportation and synthesis of vital materials inside the body.

The effects of acupuncture on tumour physiology and response to conventional treatments are relatively less well understood. There are studies on electro-chemotherapy, and some preliminary evidence of its benefits over chemotherapy alone has been shown.[27] The benefits may be bought about through a local effect in modulating blood flow, releasing cytokines, or neurological reflexes which adjust the balance between the sympathetic and parasympathetic nervous systems.

Reducing Adverse Effects of Conventional Treatment

Another important function of Chinese medicine as adjunctive treatment is reducing the adverse effects of conventional treatment, especially on immune or myelosuppression and gastrointestinal distress. Chemotherapy, and sometimes radiotherapy as well, can induce myelosuppression, which leads to a severe drop in immunological functioning. Sometimes the condition can be so bad that the treatment has to be suspended or stopped. This is extremely morale defeating to the patient. Chinese medicine is very helpful in preventing such situations from happening. *Qi*-tonifying herbs are helpful in maintaining host resistance. In particular, *huang qi* (*radix Astragalus membranaceus*) is most commonly used.

Gastrointestinal distress such as nausea, vomiting and loss of appetite is common, stubborn and morale damaging. Nowadays, potent anti-vomiting drugs can solve part of the problem. Chinese medicine can further enhance the patient's appetite, general well-being and sense of control. From the perspective of Chinese medicine, most chemotherapy is extreme yin that can damage yang. Spleen yang deficiency is the commonest syndromatic diagnosis underpinning gastrointestinal distress. The representative herbal formula dealing with the syndrome is *bu zhong yi qi tang*. *Huang qi* (*radix Astragalus membranaceus*) is the key herb and is assisted by other *qi*-tonifying herbs, *qi*-regulating herbs and meridian-guiding herbs. For more rapid symptom reduction, stomach-harmonizing and reverse-flow rectifying herbs are usually added into the base formula.

Acupuncture is an alternative treatment for reducing nausea and vomiting induced by chemotherapy. It is simple, has few side effects and has been shown to increase the anti-emetic effect of drugs.[28–30] The evidence of its efficacy is so clear that the US National Institute of Health (NIH) Consensus Development Conference in 1997 declared: "acupuncture is a proven effective treatment modality for nausea and vomiting" . P6, located at the wrist, is the commonest acupuncture point used. Applying acupuncture to P6 is relatively easy. Stimulation of this point may be done more conveniently with a small transcutaneous nerve stimulation (TENS), which is worn like a wristwatch.

Enhancement of Total Well-being

In late-stage cancer, Chinese medicine can play a useful role in maintaining and enhancing the total well-being of patients. This is achieved through three major mechanisms: (1) providing a sense of control and continuity of treatment when conventional treatments stop, (2) reducing symptoms in late-stage cancer, and (3) enhancing physical and mental health. Furthermore, milder tonifying herbs are safe and often used in everyday Chinese cooking. Preparing tonifying herbal soup for a patient is a powerful means of expressing care and concern. This helps facilitate the communication between the patient and significant others.

Providing a sense of control and continuity of treatment

Going through cancer treatments like chemo- and radiotherapy is a stressful experience because of the medical procedures and strong side effects. Coming to the end of treatment, however, does not necessarily lead to psychological relief, as one would normally expect. On the contrary, many cancer patients experience a strong sense of uncertainty, purposeless and loss of control when active treatment stops. Patients feel as if they cannot do anything further about the cancer, except wait for it to return. This often leads to anxiety and depression. Continuation with treatment using Chinese medicine can fill in this latent period nicely, because Chinese medicine is personalized and flexible.

From a holistic perspective, Chinese medicine can deal with any subjective complaint of the patient, including complaints whose cause is unclear and those that cannot be neatly categorized according to a disease classification system. The reason is that system imbalance can be assessed and determined even when diagnosis is unclear. Based on Chinese medicine syndromatic diagnosis, a prescription can be made to restore the balance in the body. Depending on the presenting problems, additional herbal medicine or acupuncture treatments can be included for more focused symptom reduction.

Acupuncture may also be rendered. Enhancement of immunity is often one of the key objectives. Acupuncture points commonly used include LI 4, LI 11, St 36, Sp 6, Sp 10, P 6, UB 20, GB 39 and GV 14.[6] If the patient has just received a course of radiotherapy, yin is often damaged. Nurturing yin will then be a key objective. If the patient has just received a course of chemotherapy, yang is often damaged. Nurturing yang will then be a key focus instead.

Reduction of Symptoms in Late-Stage Cancer

Pain is a common symptom in late-stage cancer. Effective pain management can greatly enhance the quality of life of patients. According to Chinese medicine theory, there are two general causes of pain: (1) stagnation of *qi* or blood and (2) lack of sufficient nurturing.[10] The two can easily be assessed and differentiated through standard Chinese medicine diagnostic methods through observing, hearing and smelling, interviewing, taking the pulse and touching. Locating the exact position of pain is important, because it tells what organ systems and meridian channels are involved. Based on Chinese medicine syndromatic diagnosis, treatments can be prescribed accordingly.

For stagnation, the main intervention strategy is destagnation, which may include smoothing the liver *qi*, calming the liver, and blood destagnation. Herbs commonly used include *chuan lian zi* (*Melia toosendan*), *bai shao* (*Paeonia lactiflora*), *gan cao* (*Glycyrrhiza uralensis*), *chen pi* (*Pericarpium Citrus reticulata blanco*), *qing pi* (*Citrus reticulata*), *tao ren* (*Prunus persica*) and *hong hua* (*Carthamus tinctorius*). Representative formulas include *yi quang jian* (*decoction for nourishing liver and kidney*) and *shao yauo gan cao tang*.

For *qi* and blood deficiency, the main intervention strategy is tonifying *qi* and blood. Common *qi*-tonifying herbs include *huang qi* (*radix Astragalus membranaceus*), *dang shen* (*radix Codonopsis pilosula*) and *bai zhu* (*rhizoma Atraclylodis macrocephalae*). Common blood-tonifying herbs include *dang gui* (*Angelica sinensis*), *chuan xiong* (*Ligusticum wallichii*), *bai shao* (*Paeonia lactiflora*) and *shu di huang* (*prepared Rehmannia glutinosa*). Representative formulas are *bai zhen tang* and *shi quan da bu tang*.

Fatigue, loss of appetite and decrease in body weight are common in late-stage cancer. According to Chinese medicine theory, these are often related to deficiency in spleen *qi* or yang.[8,10] As such, treatment will focus on tonifying spleen *qi* or yang accordingly. Herbs commonly used include *huang qi* (*radix Astragalus membranaceus*), *dang shen* (*radix Codonopsis pilosula*), *bai zhu* (*rhizoma Atraclylodis macrocephalae*) and *gan cao* (*Glycyrrhiza uralensis*). The representative formula is *bu zhong yi qi yi tang*.

Difficulty in breathing is also common. This is often a result of deficiency in lung *qi*, spleen *qi* or kidney yin and yang. Chinese medicine treatment is prescribed, depending on the syndromatic diagnosis.

Another common and disturbing symptom is dehydration. According to Chinese medicine theory, dehydration in end-stage cancer is often a result of *qi* and yin deficiency. A classical formula dealing with such a situation is *sheng mai shan*, which is composed of *ren shen* (*Panax ginseng*), *mai dong* (*Ophiopogon japonicus*) and *wu wei zi* (*Schisandra chinensis Baill*).

Enhancement of Physical and Mental Health

Physical health and mental health are closely connected and cannot really be managed separately. In a holistic care regime, effective management of physical symptoms is only half of the complete intervention. The other half concerns the management of mental health problems. In cancer, mood disturbances are common. Ng and his colleagues at the Centre on Behavioral Health, The University of Hong Kong[31] conducted a mental health survey at a modern Chinese medicine specialist clinic in Hong Kong and found that the prevalence of common mental disorders among oncology patients on the first consultation was 40.0%. In face of a life-threatening disease, intense sadness and anger, for example, are common among cancer patients. If not managed properly, extreme emotional states can affect compliance with physical treatments, as well as the overall well-being of the patients.

From the perspective of community psychiatry, treatment for common mental disorders should ideally be provided for by the physician-in-charge. Excessive sadness and even depression are common among cancer patients. In Chinese medicine, the disease category corresponding to depression is stagnation. The difference in naming disease clearly reflects very different emphases on the clinical manifestation of the disorder. Western medicine focuses on the mood that is lower than normal. As such, elevation of mood is the key treatment objective. In Chinese medicine, the focus is on the fluidity of bodily and emotional processes that became sluggish. As such, destagnation is the key treatment objective. Destagnation can be facilitated through herbal medicine and acupuncture, as well as non-physical treatments such as traditional health exercises and psycho-social-spiritual counselling. Herbal formulae commonly used include *chai hu shu gan san* and *shao yao san*. In acupuncture treatment, acupuncture points on the liver and gall bladder meridians are often used for destagnation of liver *qi*.

Excessive anger in cancer patients is also commonly seen in clinical practice. They may be angry with themselves, with family members or close relatives for having done something wrong so that the patients contracted the disease. They may be angry with health-care professionals for failing to provide the best medical service for them, or even angry with God or a higher power for being unfair to them. According to the emotion-organ interconnectedness theory in Chinese medicine, excessive anger will lead to hyperactivity of liver *qi* which, following the liver and gull balder meridians, will lead to a cluster of symptoms like loss of appetite, indigestion, stomach ache, lateral chest pain, redness of face and eyes, dizziness, sleeping disturbances, etc. The resulting system imbalance is overactive liver and weakened spleen. As such, the key treatment strategy is to calm the liver and tonify the spleen. Supplementary treatment is tranquillizing the emotional state. The representative herbal formula is *chai hu shu gan san*. Acupuncture points commonly chosen are on the liver, gull bladder and heart meridians.

Case Examples

Case 1: Disorganization and reorganization after having colon cancer

Mr A, male 35, was a rising star in a big multinational company. He was diagnosed with colon cancer two years ago when he was in England heading the company's sub-office there. The abnormal growth was successfully removed by surgery. Subsequent pathological evaluation indicated that the cancer was in the early stage, and Mr A was told that the prognosis was good. Physically, Mr A recovered rapidly and took up his usual social roles in a month. Psychologically, however, he developed a strong sense of fear and purposelessness. His career was virtually everything and had kept him going in the past. Now, he felt that success in his career was something very illusive. He did not have a substitute life goal for it. Going through the cancer treatment process was stressful. However, the completion of the treatment left him with a strong sense of uncontrollability and unpredictability. He was used to being the master of his life.

After about a year of struggling in a rather disorganized state, he requested a transfer back to Hong Kong, in the hope of having better family support there. His request was quickly approved. Advised by parents and friends, he began to have Chinese medicine treatment in Hong Kong. His primary motive was to reduce the chance of relapse. The Chinese medicine practitioner performed an assessment on Mr A, with emphasis on formulating a syndromatic diagnosis, although attention was also paid to the subjective complaints. The system imbalance was assessed to be "liver repressing spleen". A primary aetiological factor was emotion — excessive repression of anger. According to the system and mind/body connection theories of Chinese medicine, anger repression could lead to liver qi stagnation, which subsequently might repress the spleen. A cluster of symptoms could result, for example bowel symptoms, sleeping problems and emotional disturbances. With reference to the syndromatic diagnosis, the treatment direction was therefore to "calm the liver and strengthen the spleen". Chinese herbal medicine and acupuncture treatment were prescribed. Improvement over the presenting symptoms was noticed quickly. More importantly, Mr A regained a sense of mastery and control over his own health.

Adhering to the holistic tradition of Chinese medicine, attention was also paid to Mr A's psychosocial well-being. His feelings of purposelessness, fear and disorganization were heard. His wish to reprioritize life goals was acknowledged. After about a year of regular consultations, Mr A arrived at a new harmonized balance in life. He abandoned his promising career in the multinational company in preference to working in his father's small family business, so that he could have more time with his loved ones as well as time for himself. He developed a sharp awareness of the importance of wellness

— physical, psychosocial, and spiritual. He lived a healthy lifestyle and devoted himself to help others through participating in charity work. More importantly, he could live with the unpredictability of a relapse.

Case 2: *Quality end of life*

Ms B, female 45, was diagnosed with stage III/IV cancer of the ovaries three years ago. She had surgical removal of the abnormal growths and then a course of chemotherapy. Although the cancer marker dropped to a normal level, she knew that recurrence of the disease was likely. Chinese herbal medicine treatment gave her practical and psychological help during this period. The focus was on strengthening her health after going through the invasive treatment. With improved physical and psychological health, she began to really plan for her remaining life, especially with her loved ones — husband, a teenage son, parents, siblings, nieces and nephews. As a result, they moved home to a location convenient for more extended family contacts.

About half a year later, she had a relapse. Then, she was put on numerous courses of chemotherapy in the hope of containing the cancer growth. Chinese herbal medicine played an instrumental role in supporting Ms B to withstand and complete these treatments through reducing the side effects, maintaining her physical health and boosting morale. Also, Ms B was taught to practise qigong. Her quality of life had been reasonably well maintained for over two years. During that period, she had a good time with her loved ones. All of them had enough time to plan for her leaving, psychologically and practically.

In the last month of life, Ms B was so frail that she had to be cared for in the palliative medicine ward. Though physically weaker every day, she remained mentally fit until the very last moment. She valued and enjoyed the time with family members and relatives. As her lung function got worse, she could hardly speak. Love and concern were powerfully expressed by means of touch and massage. Her ability to swallow also became limited eventually. Her herbal tonic soup was delicious to her tongue, body and soul. Love and sayings of traditional wisdom were constantly whispered in her ears. She passed away peacefully.

Incorporating Chinese Medicine into Conventional Cancer Care Protocols

There is emerging evidence that Chinese medicine can play an important role in the supportive care of cancer patients. Integration of Chinese and Western medicine treatments can enhance a patient's survival and quality of life. In Chinese communities, it is the hope of many cancer patients and their family members to have Chinese medicine treatment along with conventional Western medicine treatment. However, such an integrative treatment approach can rarely be found in hospitals, except in mainland China. Therefore, patients can only seek Chinese medicine treatment quietly, without informing their oncologist. Such secretive action is certainly not desirable from a patient management point of view.

To improve the integration of Chinese medicine into Western oncology clinical care, a number of goals need to be accomplished. Firstly, a proper professional registration system of Chinese medicine practitioners is needed, to ensure a high degree of consistency in clinical competence. Such a system is already in place in mainland China, Hong Kong, Taiwan and a number of countries in the West. Secondly, Western medicine practitioners need to be better informed about the role of Chinese medicine in cancer care. Understanding can help reduce ungrounded suspicion and resistance toward Chinese medicine. Thirdly, in order to formally incorporate Chinese medicine into conventional protocols, many more clinical studies are necessary. Because there are so many different types of cancer and clinical scenarios, the volume of research work is tremendous. The involvement of as many oncology teams as possible will be most essential. Fourthly, cancer patients and their family members should have explained to them the benefits and limitations of Chinese medicine in cancer care so that they can make informed decisions in seeking medical treatments. Such information should be evidence-based. Exaggerated claims and overcharging of fees need to be prevented. Fifthly, appropriate funding for Chinese medicine is necessary. Many cancer patients cannot afford the continuous treatment when they have to pay for it themselves.

To conclude, there is convincing evidence to encourage good quality clinical trials for further evaluating the efficacy of Chinese medicine into cancer care and developing standardized clinical protocols. I am hopeful that a future integrated approach will enhance cancer patients' total well-being.

15

Providing End-of-Life Care: Enhancing Effectiveness and Resilience

Peter Wing Ho LEE and Tracy Tak Ching KWAN

Introduction

On several occasions during training workshops with health-care professionals, Lee was asked: "How can I be really helpful, involved and caring towards my patients, yet at the same time not be (emotionally) affected or feel bad in any way when they die?"

Kwan made the following observations:

My ICU [intensive care unit] patient just passed away. I had to perform post-mortem care. This patient of mine, a "man" with a human name moments before, now became a lifeless "it"— a mass of flesh. The pale white body felt cold. I removed all lines and tubes and gave "it" a quick wash. I tied tags on "its" big toe, making sure "it" was correctly identified — the last remaining bit of dignity and individual recognition. A colleague came to help me wrap up the body. The only words we exchanged were about how heavy "it" was. The cart came and off "it" went. Case closed, everything carried out smoothly in a seemingly calm and professional manner.

A lady in ICU was involved in a motor vehicle accident. The elderly couple was strolling hand-in-hand along the road. A speeding car hit the wife but left the husband untouched. The wife was rushed to ICU and pronounced dead on arrival. After basic procedures were completed, the husband and other family members were allowed into the unit. Curtains were drawn around the bed to provide privacy. Beyond the curtains, it was busy and business as usual. Subdued sobbing and wailing escaped through the curtains. The cries of agony and pain were, however, clearly suppressed, apparently as the family did not wish to "disturb" the rest of us. Despite trying to continue with our busy professional duties, we could hear them. For a split second, the bustling in the busy ward came to a halt. The staff looked at each other. We didn't know what to do next, despite that similar incidents had happened so many times before. The awkwardness was broken — luckily — when a nurse at the far end started to resume her work, and others promptly followed with a sigh of relief.

One expects intense emotions accompanying deaths in ICU. Yet surprisingly (or not so surprisingly), many staff members are not used to "seeing" (registering) intense expression of emotions. Emotions and how to handle them is not well covered in clinical training, as the core concerns of medicine are heroic life-saving measures to prevent and postpone death. Intense emotions do not fit well with the prevailing medical culture and are sometimes regarded as unbefitting the demeanour of "a true professional". Illich and Clark, however, were highly critical of the futile "medicalization of the dying" ethos.[1-2]

Working in end-of-life care may be the single most emotionally hazardous and personally taxing task there is in the hospital setting. It is difficult for professional care-givers to find their place in the patient's sufferings. It is doubly hazardous, as no formal channels for mourning and grief are sanctioned, as if feelings can easily be controlled with an on-off switch. End-of-life care is also potentially the most unforgiving task, as there is no second chance. Having someone "die in our hands" somehow reflects a degree of ineptitude. After all, there seems nothing professionals can do to help the poor patient and the family members to buy more time for each other. To be confronted with a dying person and the family members could be an intensely helpless experience. Kirchberg, Neimeyer and James noted that counsellors working with death and human losses experienced higher levels of personal distress than those engaged in other areas of care.[3] Many may choose not to confront death at all. The pervasive air of professionalism and emphasis on efficiency allows the "professional" to be immune to intense feelings and maintain a distance from the recurrent anguish and suffering of the patients. The professional care-giver manages to preserve a precarious emotional equilibrium and carries on with routine business yet strategically losing sight of the patient as a person and the patient's afflictions.

The opposite spectrum of terminal care may be equally taxing. While enthusiastic practitioners try their best to care, they pay a high price. The initial phase of engagement with a dying patient and the family members is one of the most difficult of all initial clinical encounters. It is a tightrope manoeuvre for the professional to successfully gain entry into the patient's system, to be non-intrusive yet not detached, involved yet not too involved, so that clinical decisions and therapeutic input can best be provided. The patient frequently presents with seeming aloofness yet simmers with poorly expressed fear, anger, uncertainty, blame, helplessness, and longing for life, wishing for freedom from pain and perhaps even miracles to happen. Without adequate preparation and a painstakingly built trusting rapport, expressions about death are ominous and offensive and may easily alienate the patient and family members. As the dying patient passes from initial resentment and non-acceptance to a languid resignation in accepting that time and life is running out, the health-care professional, like the family members, is often swept along by the roller-coaster fluctuation in the patient's physical state, mood, interpersonal and spiritual functioning. For the health-care worker, enduring the intensity of the patient's turbulent feelings while preserving one's own emotional composure can be trying and exhausting.

Intense anxieties may be generated in the health-care professionals, as medical technology proves ineffectual after all. Repeated brushes with death, albeit through someone else's experience, somehow increase one's sense of vulnerability and serve as sobering reminders of one's own mortality. Health-care professionals may also put themselves in the position of the patient, asking why they should *not* develop the same disease or predicament. There simply is no convincing answer. It is common to find health-care professionals becoming more sensitive to their own bodily signs and symptoms and periodically struck by feelings of fright when signs and symptoms similar to those of their patients are noted.

The Hazards of Death Encounters

Summation of all anxieties

Death is the summation of mankind's existential anxieties. Realistically, as mortals with human limitations, not all "professionals" are sufficiently equipped to face their own life concerns, not to mention confronting squarely and repeatedly death itself.

Dante Alighieri, in *The Divine Comedy*, summarized this well:[4]

Midway life's journey I was made aware
That I had strayed into a dark forest
And the right path appeared not anywhere
Ah, tongue cannot described how it oppressed
This wood, so harsh, dismal and wild, that fear
At thought of it strikes now into my breast
So bitter it is, death is scarce bitterer.

Confucian doctrines make little room for handling death

Death is inevitably veiled in mystery and the unknown. Confucian teaching, still influential today in Chinese societies, places emphasis on life and rarely on death. The overriding focus on living a good life and fulfilling one's duties allows little room for handling death, incapacitation, and enforced dependency at the end stage of life. Professionals indoctrinated with Confucian teaching may find themselves at wit's end when faced with the challenges of caring for a dying individual.

The blinkers inherent in medical training

Medicine has largely chosen to portray itself as heroic and "life-saving". This image has been noted even among medical students.[5] Medical students are inadequately trained to handle the scenario when a patient can no longer be saved, and when they can no longer maintain their "heroic" act. In a survey of 592 European physicians, despite variations across countries, fewer than fifty percent of the subjects reported having ever been taught about care of the dying during medical training, and less than twenty-five percent felt sufficiently prepared for the task.[6] Through his training contacts in China, Peter Lee noted among Chinese physicians a common practice of not informing patients of their diagnosis and prognosis, particularly in end-stage diseases, as it was thought that patients "do not need" to know.

The International Code of Medical Ethics says, "A doctor shall always bear in mind the obligation of preserving human life".[7] When life withers beyond the professional's reach, the goal and vision of medicine is challenged. Death or the "end stage" is shunned. The changing focus in palliative medicine does a great job of removing the catastrophe from death and normalizing it. However, death is still taboo and seldom talked about openly, even within the professional realm. As long as medicine confines its focus to cure and healing, death signifies failure.[8-9]

The aching heart bearing the patients' aches and suffering

More of Kwan's reflections:

> I stood at the bedside of Mr C, a 40-year-old gentleman with terminal cancer. He had always impressed me as being confident, hopeful and strong-willed. Now, he just lay there, eyes staring into space. Weak and gasping for air, we both knew he was dying. Seeing him in this state was highly unsettling. An inner voice urged: "Do something", so I asked if there was anything I could do for him. He pointed to his blanket. I arranged it. We fell into silence. Before I left, I told him I would visit again. However, I knew this would be our last meeting. I used to be capable of cheering him up with encouraging words and confident professional advice. Now I asked myself, ashamed and helpless, "Was that all you could do — fix his blanket?" Face to face with death, I feel belittled and insignificant.

Sister Teresa noted that even in the busiest ward, patients could remain intensely alone. For those afflicted with intolerable pain (be it physical, psychological or spiritual), death may come as an opportunity for timely relief or closure. Approaching the end may even be palatable for some who see the rest of life as being nothing but dire pain, burden, isolation, and aloneness. Professionals, too, feel robbed of their self-hypnotized sense of omnipotence and are powerless to do anything anymore. After all, how can one cheat death when life is held hostage?

Caring for patients at the stage of imminent death is challenging, as palliative care workers are "forced to confront humanity in the face of powerlessness and hopelessness, vulnerability, and loss".[10] In the "can-do" culture, solve the problem, cure the disease, ease the pain and relieve the suffering are the prime objectives. "Nothing can be done" seems too harsh to accept, as it signifies loss of control and defeat, and a "boxer's punch" to ego's stomach.

Professionals withdraw, under-help, and use avoidance as an attempt to reduce their own pain and sense of ineptitude. At the same time, demoralization — despair with one's helplessness[11]— may generate compensatory practices leading to over-identification with the patient, over-help, pathological grief, and over-involvement. To counter helplessness, some professionals may become excessively involved with an unthinking "flight into action". Yet, ill-considered excess can be equally damaging, as it blurs the demarcation between personal and professional involvement and undermines the therapeutic relationship.

Some "professionals" may try to fool themselves into feeling better by reasoning that perhaps it is the patients who should toughen up, pull themselves together and be brave. After all, the layperson's test of the toughness of a tyre is to kick it hard to see how well it stands up. The simple truth, however, is that no one needs to be brave and foolhardy in tolerating suffering when rightly, effectively and patiently, such suffering stands a good chance of being removed and lessened.

The trauma of repeated goodbyes

Terminal care is emotionally challenging in that the professional has to face death repeatedly. At times, it might feel as if nothing is worth the effort, as eventually the patient will die. The professional is also forced to learn to bid goodbye and to say it with as much peace of mind and as little regret as humanly possible. It takes years, if not decades, of professional and personal maturation for someone to effectively learn to accept the inevitable impermanence of existence, that of the patient as well as one's own, and to learn that, when life cannot be sustained, effort in augmenting quality in the remaining human life is never wasted. Parsons put it nicely in the novel *Man and Boy*: "you have to learn to let go … (*this is*) part of what it means to love someone. … If you love someone then you don't just see them as an extension of yourself. You don't just love them for what's in it for you".[12] To be compassionate and loving demands at the same time one's ability to form deep attachments as well as the fortitude to let go.

The solitude of those who meddle with "white affairs"

Chinese regard any matter associated with death as "white affairs" (白事). Meddling with "white affairs" is regarded as ominous, creates bad luck and increases vulnerability and weakness. Talking about such matters is not welcome.[13] People may take tremendous offence if a person should attend a ceremonial banquet wearing a white flower in the hair, signifying the recent death of a family member. One of the social responsibilities of those in mourning is to stay away from mainstream society so that ill luck would not be passed on. One simply does not see "white affairs" as being in synchrony with good or prosperous happenings. Even within family and close relationships, there is no "appropriate opportunity" to talk about one's encounters with death. For professionals who work with terminally ill persons, such taboos often block the otherwise available means of emotional and social support. Even simple ventilation of intense feelings after the death of a patient under their care may not be allowed, as the topic is not welcome. Although one can easily strike up a cordial conversation about job and career aspirations, those working in the field of terminal care are exempt and barred from such luxuries.

Striking the delicate right balance

Chinese health-care workers in end-of-life care are sometimes seen as emotionally tough or worse, numb, or "different". Otherwise, one questions how anyone could stay in this business for long. Indeed, it takes great patience and sensitivity to attain the right balance in achieving therapeutic goals while not alienating the patient and family members. Chinese value relational and harmonious interdependency rather than fulfillment of individualistic needs.[13–15] Instead of a sole focus on advancement of personal needs, the professional needs to be aware that a patient's needs are intricately intertwined with the needs of the family members. Chinese tend to be more reticent in matters of feelings and worries. Expressions of emotion or saying goodbye are often subdued and difficult for most Chinese confronting the death of a loved one. Yet, the health-care professional is conscious that not saying or doing what ought to be said or done may lead to later regret. Utmost care needs to be exerted in not hurrying the process. Particular caution needs to be exercised in any direct discussions about death, especially when the patient or family members do not initiate it. For example, any discussions about funeral arrangements are very delicate and may be considered highly unfilial of children to mention in front of their dying parent. The professional's role in facilitating communication between patient and family is important yet fraught with difficulties in view of the delicate balance between doing right versus wrong, or doing too much too soon versus doing the right amount at the right pace and time. Mulder and Gregory cautioned rightly: "I could harm or heal in the quality of time I spent with patients and their families".[16]

Heal Thyself: Enhancing Effectiveness and Resilience

The professional care-givers need to be reminded of the Chinese saying, "to achieve the best result in one's endeavour, one needs to first sharpen the right tools" (工欲善其事，必先利其器).

In end-of-life care, there are simply no "right tools" external to the care-giver. Modern medicine does an increasingly better job in pain and symptom control. Good simple nursing care facilitates physical well-being. However, no amount of injections or modern technology could take the place of the right person with the right heart* in facilitating comfort and a good death.

The right heart, however, needs to be healthy and well nurtured to be of greatest use. Professionals' well-being is of paramount importance for their calling to be well answered. Hence, a few areas (by no means exhaustive) that are deemed important and promising in promoting the professional's well-being are highlighted below for consideration.

Realistic death perception

Prominently displayed in a Hong Kong cemetery is the proclamation: "tonight my body reverts to dust; one future morning, yours will face the same destiny". An advertisement for a luxurious watch reads something like: "you don't own it (the watch), it's just on loan to be passed onto the next generation". Although the idea that one's longevity is shorter than that of a watch may seem unwelcome, the message does serve as a good reminder of one's limited time and place on earth.

To not be bullied by death, death has to be regarded as a fundamental and inevitable condition of life. The Buddhist sees "birth, aging, sickness and death" as the four fundamental sufferings of the human condition. Death is unavoidable yet may not be "the ultimate end". Buddhist philosophy notes: "all things put together come apart sooner or later". Death does not mean ceasing to exist. Even in death, nothing is lost. Death may just be a transition from one form of existence to another.[17]

Within the rich tradition of Chinese thinking are ample resources to help the professional worker figure out how best to relate to death. It has been

---

* In other words, the emotive heart, which is the source of compassion, love, good will and empathy.

mentioned earlier that Confucian principles provide little in the way of preparing one for death. Looking closer, however, Confucian teachings echo a fundamental principle for consideration: if one fulfils one's life functions, there is no fear of death. This emphasis on leading a good life and fulfilling one's duties as a person to oneself, one's family and one's country is seen as good enough preparation for eventual death.[18] Likewise, in the *Analects*, one is reminded, "If you are ignorant about living, how could you know anything about death?"[19] (不知生，焉知死？ [論語 · 先進篇]). Death is further regarded as being not as important as how and for what one dies (死有輕於 鴻毛，重於泰山).

The Daoist Lao-tzu urged one not to fear death or, more specifically, the death of one's body. He stated: "The reason for my difficulties/ailments is that I have a physical body. When I become free of this body, what more sufferings would I have?"[20] (吾之所以有大患者，為吾有身，及吾無身 ，吾有何患？ [道 德經 · 十三章])

Chuang-tzu, on the death of his wife, commented: "originally there was no birth. Not only was there no birth, there was no body … *Qi* changed and form came into being. Form changed and gave rise to life. Now life changes and death ensues. This is in line with the progression of the four seasons".[20] When death is regarded as a natural part of the living universe, death comes only naturally! （察其始而本無生，非徒無生也而本無形 ， 非徒無形也而本 無氣。 雜乎芒芴之間，變而有氣 ，氣變而有形 ，形變而有生 ，今又變而之 死 ，是相與為春秋冬夏四時行也 。 [莊子 · 至樂]）

Many Chinese feel that it is futile to meddle with death. A survey on Chinese seniors' perspectives of end-of-life decisions highlighted a strongly held view that the future is predetermined, including the timing of life and death.[13] However, although Chinese folk belief advocates not talking about or meddling with death, elderly Chinese people do show obvious acceptance by preparing for their own death through openly announcing their choice of burial place, clothes they would like to wear, ornaments they prefer, and type of coffin they wish to be buried in. Indeed, in burial services for the elderly, one sometimes sees smiling faces of family members who regard the burial as a "happy funeral", as the elderly person is seen to have fully lived life and arrived at the suitable age for departure. The concept of heaven and hell is prevalent. Whether or not one reaches heaven or descends into hell depends on what one does in life. Instead of fearing death, one is cautioned through early socialization to fear one's bad deeds.

Professional workers should not feel guilty or ashamed in approaching death of their patients. The death of a patient is not a personal failure. The professionals fail only when they willingly (or unwittingly) allow their anxieties and emotional blinkers to diminish the quality of their care. The professionals fail when the patients die in a miserable state of want of care and human connectedness.

Emotional management

How can one be fully effective in end-of-life care of patients and not feel bad afterwards? Undoubtedly, one is saddened when a patient one cares much for dies. A degree of mourning and grief is healthy and inevitable. However, if the professionals can satisfy themselves that, in the encounter, they have enriched the life of another human being, and provided, in whatever small way, a degree of comfort, warmth and security, then there need be no regrets. Instead, one should take solace in knowing that the encounter turned out to be benevolent and useful. The professional should be open to any show of gratitude and appreciation and be comforted by the fact that there is no greater gift to offer the patient beyond a compassionate presence. Gratitude inspires joy. To realize that one has served as a positive stimulus for a dying fellow human being is perhaps the most anyone could expect.

It may be comforting to realize that human suffering, however heart wrenching to witness, can often be soothed and lessened through simple human compassion combined with the best of medical technologies. The Dalai Lama noted rightly that, instead of shying away from the sufferings of other people, compassion is best cultivated through developing one's ability to be "empathetic and connected", and to have "a sense of closeness with others".[21] Suffering of the heart, soul and body is amenable to significant degrees of relief under skilful hands and a patient and loving heart.

Sadness and longing may linger for varying periods. There is no "normal" time limit for grief to be completed.[22] However, affirming that some good had been imparted to the patient often leaves the professional with a sense of nostalgia yet peaceful satisfaction and fulfilment. Over time, fond memories of human beings one had served, and served well reminds one that meaningful deeds had been accomplished. The Dalai Lama noted: "inner tranquillity comes from the development of love and compassion. The more we care for the happiness of others, the greater is our own sense of well-being. Cultivating a close, warm-hearted feeling for others automatically puts the mind at ease and opens our inner door. It helps remove whatever fears or insecurities we may have and gives us the strength to cope with any obstacles we encounter".[21]

Periodic self-reflection is useful and brings about clarification and understanding of a care-giver's thoughts and feelings. During self-reflection, one needs to watch out for extreme feelings of anger, undue guilt, bitterness, preoccupation, despair, futility, hypercritical scepticism, emotional blandness, and apathy. When professionals become aware of being bogged down by negative affect, it is important firstly to examine their philosophy of care and what they had set out to achieve. Finding or restoring meaning to one's work adds inner strength and enables the professional to weather any turmoil. Through self-reflection, unrealistic goals are abandoned. Readjustment of therapeutic aims and acceptance of one's basic human condition is crucial. There may also be problems of dissatisfaction stemming from the physical and interpersonal working environment, sense of incompetence, and other sources of life stress. Instead of allowing oneself to wallow in and be entrapped in increasing bitterness and frustration, it is important to take positive action to change the situation for the better, realizing at the same time that the world is neither perfect nor created to fit one's needs.

Spiritual management

Seldom does one see the need to care for the spiritual being of patients more than at the stage of dying. In face with death, one is confronted with unanswerable questions. What does death feel like? Is death the very end of being, or does one "go somewhere" else? If there is an afterlife, what would it be like? However well prepared one might feel, death's arrival inevitably arouses awe and humility.

When confronted with problems beyond their ability to solve, people commonly look beyond themselves for answers. Confronting death, it is natural to expand the quest for understanding beyond the physical world into the supernatural and spiritual realms. There may be some truth in the belief that one is closest to God (regardless of religious affiliation) at the moment of death. Spirituality is using one's presence, through God (or a Higher Being), to rise above oneself and feel the power that is beyond one's own. In this sense, spirituality is egoless. The spiritual dimension of palliative care does not necessarily dictate a religious understanding. Approaching the end stage of life may prompt some individuals to embark on a philosophical search for their reason for "being".[23] It is common for health professionals to be approached by terminally ill patients with life's fundamental questions: its origin, meaning and destination. Enhancing one's own spiritual awareness is useful in helping patients complete their spiritual quest for understanding life itself.

Effective care

Emotional well-being and resilience in dealing with obstacles is strengthened when the professionals feel proud and are happy with what they do. Effective care can alleviate stress. The feeling of a job well done is uplifting and boosts one's spirit and emotions. Remen spoke of restoring a sense of service to medicine as "a work of the heart and soul", which at the same time humbles and warms one's spirits.[24]

A healthy heart with compassion has to be nurtured and anchored on solid and realistic principles. The fundamental principle is realistic goal setting.

Professional care-givers need to be clear about what they aim to achieve in end-of-life care. Nager stated: "... his [the care-giver's] task is not limited to healing and reconstruction, sometimes merely requires discriminatory restriction to palliation and accompaniment".[25]

End-of-life work requires commitment, appropriateness, effectiveness, a sense of responsibility, and taking positive action. Sontag, in *Regarding the Pain of Others*, cautioned, "Compassion is an unstable emotion. It needs to be translated into action, or it withers. The question is what to do with the feelings that have been aroused, the knowledge that has been communicated. People don't become inured to what they are shown...because of the quantity of images dumped on them. It is passivity that dulls feeling".[26]

The best care can only be provided when care-givers are pure and single-pointedly focused. Effective care has to be tampered with concerns about oneself as little as possible. During moments of care, to worry about one's performance and correctness is itself a drain on the professional's caring resource. The professional's egoistic worries shift the focus away from the patient. Ideally, there should be no time or place for "I" or "me" at the moment of care. Evaluation and reflection in highlighting areas of improvement should be left for later review, when alone or with other professionals. Instead of fretting about not saying the right words, not doing the right and expected chore, or what others might think, it is best to allow oneself to enter freely and wholeheartedly into a voyage of discovery. A discovery not of one's personal theories, wants, desires, or failings, but simply and plainly what this patient needs, desires, and what can be done now to help fulfil the patient's last wishes and bring about as much physical, spiritual and emotional comfort as possible.

During moments of care, previously learnt theories on care or dying should be put aside. Theories on someone else's needs or the dying process are irrelevant as far as THIS human person one is caring for is concerned. To categorize is not to understand. The professionals have to exert utmost caution not to force on patients and their family members their own theories of what they need or should need during these precious moments of life. Humility and open mindedness are vital. One needs to nurture the capacity to risk "not-knowing" and "not-controlling", and simply make oneself available and open. One needs to listen without even arguing or refuting in one's heart. One needs to find out with a clean state of mind so that, as much as possible, one allows oneself to be awed by the intricacies and uniqueness of this person's inner world. One should count oneself fortunate to be inspired by someone else's wisdom of a lifetime.

In line with fulfilling the patient's needs, an awareness of the limited time the professional and the patient have is important so that goals and positive action can be put in order of priority. When death is imminent, there is always too little time to do everything. Left with little control over when death will happen, the professional needs all the more to be mindful of the all-powerful NOW and help patients taste the fullness of what at this moment is meaningful and gratifying. The quest is to do the utmost good of the utmost importance for/to/with this particular patient at this very moment — for the "next time" may never come.

Heeding early signs of distress and "browning out"

The concept of burnout is familiar to health-care professionals. The classic signs originally proposed by Maslach and Jackson are emotional exhaustion (feeling depressed, trapped, or hopeless), physical exhaustion (feeling tired or rundown and not recovering), and mental exhaustion (feeling worthless, disillusioned, resentful).[27] However, such signs are clearly the product of a prolonged accumulation of stress and dissatisfaction. By the time such signs become obvious, the health-care worker would have been professionally and personally hampered for a long time. It is thus important to heed the earlier warning signs of difficulties.

The concept of "browning out" is probably more important to watch out for in maintenance of the care-giver's everyday well-being.[28] Common signs of impending trouble in fulfilling the professional mission include losing efficiency, losing initiative, losing interest, feeling stressed more often than usual, getting easily tired, having somatic ailments (e.g., headaches, stomach problems), losing weight, having trouble sleeping, experiencing more frequent changeable or low moods, easily angered or frustrated , becoming more suspicious than usual, becoming more inflexible, becoming more critical of one's own and others' competencies, working more but feeling one is getting less done, and losing one's sense of humour and enjoyment of things.

Interpersonal harmony and support

It is vitally important to realize that as social animals, the professionals are inevitably affected by what others do and say to them, or how others regard them. In stressful surroundings, the availability of even one colleague to whom one can relate to and discuss concerns, thoughts and feelings without undue defence can work wonders. In the process of caring for the patients, the professionals should not forget that their colleagues, as well as themselves, also require care, appreciation and respect. A sure way to gain respect and care is to provide them first. Communication should be tactful but, as far as possible, open. An ounce of suspicion and doubt, left unresolved, quickly grows into mountains of fear, angst and paranoia. Particularly when emotionally and physically exhausted, negative affect can easily take a strong hold and eat away one's morale and faith in other human beings.

In the work setting, supervisors need to be particularly aware of their vital role, not only in affecting the quality of care provided to patients but also the health status of their staff. It has been said, and rightly so, that supervisors can be the single biggest source of stress as well as the most soothing of stress buffers, depending on how the supervisory role is carried out. Except for a small minority, it is probably safe to regard all staff as being good-natured and ready to improve, given the trust and opportunity to do so. Criticism should be made with respect and a constructive attitude. Covey stresses the importance of achieving shared vision and values in any work setting.[29] The supervisor's role is to serve as a model which inspires trust. Staffs function best when enabled to feel that they could be as important if they do what they do right, no matter what it is. Leadership is creating an environment that people want to be part of.

Have a life beyond the hospital

An enriched and fulfilled life involves more than work itself. It is important that the professional care-giver be able to derive gratification and joy from diverse aspects of life outside work. Maintaining close family relationships, developing and maintaining cordial friendships, leisure-time pursuits, hobbies, physical activities, interests in growth and self-improvement are high on the agenda for leading a continuingly meaningful and gratifying life. It is important that possibilities and potential are kept open as one progresses in life through finding and providing interpersonal support, resonance, emotional catharsis, gainful guidance and insight from own experiences, and through opportunistic problem resolution.

Professionals need to nurture their sense of humour and acceptance of things when they can or cannot change. Chinese wisdom points to a calm acceptance of all things to come, noting that most things are perhaps not what they seem, as in the fable of the man who lost his horse. A summary of the fable from the ancient Chinese classic *Hua Nan Zi*[30] goes like this: A man lost his favourite horse. Subsequently, not only did the horse return, she brought along a herd of beautiful horses. He rejoiced and his friends congratulated him on his good fortune. His son mounted one of the horses, fell, and broke his leg. A war broke out, and all young and fit men were recruited into the army. Many men died in battle. The man's son escaped the war because of his broken leg.

（ 夫禍福之轉而相生，其變難見也。近塞上之人，有善術者，馬無故亡而入胡，人皆弔之。其父曰：「此何遽不為福乎？」居數月，其馬將駿馬而歸，人皆賀之。其父曰：「此何遽不為禍乎？」家富良馬，其子好騎，墮

而折其髀，人皆吊之。："此何遽不為福乎？"居一年，胡人大入塞，丁
壯者引弦而戰，近塞之人，死者十九，此獨以跛之故，父子相保。故福
之為禍，禍之為福，化不可極，深不可測也。 [淮南子・人間訓])

It is important to nurture the professional's capacity for joy and
playfulness. A person who cannot play is deprived of the joys of making and
creating and is hampered in the capacity to feel alive and be alive. In learning
to come to terms with one's life conditions, one needs also to nurture a non-
blaming attitude, finding meaning, living one's life with faith, and cherishing
what one has.

One may also consider developing a cautious sense of adventure, bearing
in mind that life is always larger than one's belief system. Holden cautions
that: "risks must be taken because the greatest hazard in life is to risk nothing
… The person who risks nothing, does nothing, has nothing, is nothing".[31]
Instead of being constrained by anxieties, one may well be reminded that
"everyone dies, but not everyone lives".[32]

Concluding Remarks

At some point, beyond skills and wisdom, the best that a care provider could
offer is probably raw humanity and compassion. In the face of death, when
not too physically incapacitated, a patient probably has myriad of changing
feelings, concerns and awareness: fear of what is to come, of pain, of being
forgotten, sadness over impending separation from loved ones, prized
possessions, cessation of pleasure and joy, regrets for past hurts, failings, and
grief, unfulfilled wishes, anxiety and loneliness of having to leave alone.

The humanity that can be offered by the care-giver probably includes the
courage to allow patients to share their gloom, anxiety, and sadness; the
wisdom to offer alternative but realistic perspectives; the kind gift of patience
and time to listen, talk, and empathize; the compassion to laugh and cry with
the patient, to connect and resonate, and the composure to restore hope and
dignity when called for.

Gregory notes, however, "The cost of this journey is high because it means
being exposed to one's own suffering, woundedness and grief. Yet, it is one's
own experience of suffering that enables one to be compassionate and share
in the plight of another. Such caring through presence is a gift, a privilege,
and is necessarily approached with humility; both care-givers and those who
suffer are enriched through caring moments".[33]

The privilege bestowed on the end-of-life care professional is the ability
to see enough of death to fully appreciate life. To best take stock of his
privilege, however, the professional worker has to stay on course to continually
fortify mind, body and soul. Continual learning and personal growth from

one's experiences, from the wisdom of the experiences of other care-givers, and from listening to one's heart and calling is mandatory. It may not be easy to maintain one's equanimity witnessing life's harsh realities. The key, however, may be the very acceptance of life's certain impermanence. When down and out, cheerfulness and optimism may be just around the corner; at wit's end, the solution may come by morning's sunrise.

16

Care for Chinese Families with Patients Facing Impending Death: Nurses' Perspectives

Amy Yin Man CHOW, Jess Shuk Fun LO, Wendy Wai Yin LI and Carmen Yuek Yan LAI

Introduction

The hospital is an amazing place where most of us are born. It is supposed to be the place for quick fixes when we are injured or sick. Advanced medical technology can save lives and relieve human suffering most of the time. Yet, this miracle place may fail us when patients die. Though death is a certainty of life, not every one of us acknowledges this fact. After hearing the bad news[1-4] of a life-threatening illness or injury, the family and patients have to face and prepare for impending death. The time between hearing the bad news and death is the most precious moments in one's life. Nurses are usually around the patients and families during that crucial period. They play a significant role in helping the family to use this valuable time. When the families do not properly use this special time, they might have great regrets during bereavement.

There were 34,316 deaths in Hong Kong in the year 2002. The first three causes are cancer, heart disease and cerebral vascular diseases, accounting for 11,658, 4,069 and 3,218 deaths respectively. Although the majority of the deceased were elderly people, 8,096 were under the age of 65, about 23.6% of the total death rate in 2002.[5] As most deaths in Hong Kong take place in hospitals, nurses are in close touch with the families of patients who are confronting death. This chapter focuses on what nurses can do to help families cope with death. The principles in psychosocial support in palliative and end-of-life care are being adapted in acute settings and are called a CDE model (explained later).

Deaths in Hospitals

In Hong Kong, the majority of deaths take place in hospitals. Even people who appear to have died from a sudden illness, accident, or fatal injury are still sent to the accident and emergency rooms (A&E). A declaration of death will take place in the accident and emergency room if resuscitation fails, or in intensive care unit (ICU) if the patient dies there. Thus the family members have to digest a lot of bad news within a short time. Different family members express shock and grief differently. Some resort to shaking the deceased or slapping the face, hoping to wake the person up. They might scold the dead body loudly, blaming him or her for not taking good care of him or herself. Some may cry or yell, banging their head against the wall or performing other self-destructive acts to combat the numbness and pain. Sometimes, the bereaved might even faint after receiving the news of the death. Some resort to religious actions such as kneeling and praying loudly for resurrection, or bargaining for recovery. Lastly, some may direct their frustration to health-care professionals, including verbal complaints, scolding, cursing or even aggression. The family might not be cooperative with standard procedures, especially the last office.* They perceive sending the deceased to the mortuary as the final farewell. Nurses are torn between the regular demands of their duty in the wards and the special needs of bereaved family members.

There are also anticipated deaths in the hospitals. There is a period between breaking the bad news and the actual death. The length of this time varies. During this time some patients might be recipients of end-of-life care. As Lo[6] describes in Chapter 11 of this book, the palliative care team cares for the physical and psycho-spiritual needs of both patients and their families. Other patients might spend this period in the acute ward, with a focus on cure and rehabilitation. Death is an occasional event only. The usual nursing care required in these wards is mainly treatment oriented. In such an atmosphere, the family members are usually unprepared to face impending death, though they are well informed about that possibility. Death is still considered "sudden", and they have similar responses to those in the accident and emergency room.

There are other more complex cases of deaths in hospitals. Firstly, some patients might be clinically dead but are sustained by life-support devices. Before the announcement of death, a discussion on the question of withdrawing or withholding the life-support device takes place. Different family members might have diverse views on withdrawing life support from the dying family member who is in vegetative state. The case of Terri Shiavo[7-9] in the United States shows that the disagreement between the parents and the husband over withdrawing the feeding tube caused enormous pain in the family. Similar cases occur in our hospitals every day. Secondly, the death might be an unexpected outcome of presumably good events. Stillbirths and deaths from complications of delivery are two examples. Though Hong Kong has a very low rate of stillbirth, around 5 per 1000 births,[10] the scarcity of the incident

---

* Last office is the nursing procedure of cleaning and tidying up the deceased before sending the body to the mortuary.

makes the bereaved family members all the more shocked. At the same time, most nurses are not well prepared to handle this type of incident. Thirdly, the deaths might happen during a medical procedure. Death on the operating table (i.e., during surgery) is not uncommon. The surgery is expected to cure the patient, but he or she dies. Sometimes, even if the death has nothing to do with professional negligence, the doctors and nurses can easily become scapegoats. Bereaved family members might launch formal complaints through available channels, as an expression of their inability or refusal of accepting the death of their loved ones. In extreme cases, family members may use violence, take legal action, and go public via the mass media, advocacy organizations of patients' rights, or even political parties. The process is taxing for the families as well as for the medical team. Fourthly, there are cases, though rare, of suicides by patients during hospitalization. A review by Ho and Tay[11] found that significant numbers of people attempting suicide in hospitals used potentially lethal methods. Though they found that there were no particular peak hours for suicide attempts in hospitals; forty-one percent of suicides took place between midnight and 6:00 a.m. This is the time when fewer nurses are on duty. To most people, suicide is preventable and avoidable. Suicides in hospitals are perceived as negligence and a breach of duty of care. Again, complaints may follow.

In sum, deaths in hospitals are a common event. Each death generates very different familial and system responses. For the nursing staff in hospital wards, what are possible roles to play to relieve the suffering the patients and families in such situations?

Role of Nurses in Caring for Dying patients and their Families

The International Council of Nurses posted a position statement on nurses' role in providing care for dying patients and their families.[12] It affirms the unique role of nurses in offering compassionate care. There are extensive discussions on the role of nurses in caring for dying patients in end-of-life care and palliative care for both patients and family members.[13–16] The focus of care is not limited to physiological but holistic, including psychological, spiritual, and social aspects of the needs of patients and family members. Aside from technological nursing skills, communication skills are important. Volker highlighted the importance of the sense of control of the dying patient.[17] Despite a diagnosis of advanced cancer, patients still desire to live fully and remain actively involved in the personal decision-making process. Breitbart, Gibson, Poppito, and Berg proposed another domain — meaning and spirituality — as the focus of therapeutic intervention in end-of-life situations.[18]

Mr A is one of our ex-patients in his early thirties. He was diagnosed with cancer, shortly after he got married. He underwent three operations, hoping to remove all cancer cells. The tolerance of physical pain induced by the operations was not rewarded by a cure. The illness was finally pronounced incurable. After the bad news was delivered, his lips remained sealed. No words come out and no food was allowed in. Dying is uncommon in surgical wards. The whole team wanted to help, but Mr A seemed unreachable. Feeding him was relatively easy compared to reaching his heart. He occasionally spoke, but they were words of anger at anyone who came close. It would have been easy for professionals to hide from him, but tolerance and patience were used instead. He was asked to share his feelings whenever he wanted. He was greeted and invited to share everyday. With persistent care and concern, the anger that used to be the strong mask protecting the fragility was unveiled. He shared his guilt with his wife and his parents. As a Chinese man, he felt ashamed and pained at not being able to perform the role of a responsible husband and a filial son. The inability to face these unfulfilled roles forced him to block all communication. He died a short time later.

Chinese people tend to hide their intense emotions under anger. Tolerance is valued over expression of negative emotions. When confronted with death, it is common for dying patients to be angry. As Greenberg suggested, anger serves different functions. It can mask other emotions such as needs not being met and boundaries being invaded. Anger can also direct energy to fuel action against unfair treatment or injustice.[19] These descriptions seem to match that of a person facing impending death. Anger seems to be an appropriate response of dying patients, but we may mistakenly see it as manipulative behaviour or an attack on professional services. Without adequate knowledge in handling anger, professionals tend to use avoidance as the sole response. This is usually ineffective if it creates further frustration and misunderstanding. With encouragement and patience, professionals can help patients to appreciate the source of their anger and then direct the energy towards completion of unfinished businesses in the remaining time. In caring for Mr A, we did not focus our care on the physiological side. We gave more attention to the psychological and emotional aspects. With patience and care, he was courageous in exploring the meaning of illness. In addition, we worked with the family. The crucial task of nurses in working with families with dying patients is to facilitate communication between the patients and family members. As Chinese are mostly unable to communicate intimate messages such as "I love you", "I am proud of you" and "I forgive you" openly and freely, the nurses can foster effective communication of appreciation of each other, as this is the final chance for family members to do so before the death of the loved one.

Non-verbal communication through acts of providing care before death is also important. In some cases, we can offer opportunities to the family member to stay with and care for the dying patient. Mok *et al.*, in a study of family carers of terminally ill patients, found that having a chance to participate in caring for the patient is an act that shows love and responsibility. The family felt much better, as their relationship of commitment was fulfilled.[20] According to Chan *et al.*, filial piety is a highly valued virtue, deeply seated in the mind of the Chinese.[21] Although nursing care is often seen as specialized physical care, it is also about training family members to provide appropriate physical care to the patient. As Lo[6] suggests, eating and enjoyment from food is a great concern in Chinese culture. Thus, the family might equate good physical care to the dying patients as offering good nutrition and liquids. Yet, as patients approach death, they have a diminishing interest or need for food and fluid intake.[22] Family members might feel a sense of failure if the dying patients take little food and soup. Nurses play an important role as educators in teaching the patients and family members other ways to show care and concern. Cleaning the patient's face and limbs with a warm towel, gently massaging the patient, giving sips of liquid for dry lips are good ways to foster communication and expressions of love.

Another patient, Madam B, a lady in her sixties, had a stroke and was in a coma when she was admitted to the medical ward. She had four children who are all married, and four grandchildren. The family gathered in the lift lobby everyday. They were usually the first to get to the ward and the last to go during visitation. They behaved like detectives doing a criminal investigation. They asked detailed questions and made notes every time they communicated with health-care professionals. They were well organized, and there was always one of them in the ward. Whenever Madam B's monitor showed any sign of irregularity, the family would be alarmed and request immediate action. Though it was quite stressful for the team to provide care for the patient with very close monitoring by the family members, the team understood their needs and feelings. The family members were allowed to stay in the ward, as long as it did not interrupt the ward routines. They were regularly offered information. The nurses also extended their care to the family members; for example, by offering a cup of tea at night and greeting the family. Although medical technology did not save Madam B's life of, her family members managed to take care of her and, most important of all, the whole extended family witnessed her peaceful death. After Madam B's death, the family expressed their gratitude to the professionals. They said that they thought that they needed to fight with the health-care professionals for their mother's rights but were surprised to find out that health-care professionals were actually on their side. They were very anxious for fear of not being able to witness the moment of death, an important cultural expectation as a filial obligation, and were glad to have been there when Madam B died. Though they had tears in their eyes, the loss of their mother was bearable.

The family is the unit of care in the philosophy of palliative care, but this can also be applied to all patients, including Madam B's family. Although Mrs B's children appeared strong, knowledgeable and independent, they were still fragile when confronted with the death of their mother. With greetings or a cup of tea, the family members were empowered and they felt that a warm professional team supported the journey of care. Their initial hostility and mistrust of the medical team decreased, which prevented unnecessary conflicts between family members and hospital staff. It helped the family members to retain a relatively positive memory on the last days of life of the family member.

The reactions of the family members also change over time. At the moment of admission, they tried hard to deny and postpone the impending death. After a few days of reality testing, they became more prepared for the death. Moreover, when death did not happen as scheduled, they sometimes seemed to be disappointed and longed for death to take place because they were tired of taking care of Madam B, though the feeling might then be replaced by guilt and self-blame for their "evil" thoughts. Thus in caring for the family, we have to watch out for their emotional responses and respond accordingly.

Also, witnessing the death of one's parents is taken as the children's responsibility in traditional Chinese culture. Having no son to witness the death is a curse, as the reincarnation process would be aversely affected. Thus Chinese family members willingly shoulder this filial obligation, and there is strong anxiety that they may miss the moment of death. Such fear and anxiety may be converted to anger and hostility toward health-care professionals. Because of this cultural sensitivity, the team tries to inform the family at critical moments, a gesture that the family greatly appreciates, though false alarms can also be frustrating. The reassurance that they will be called at a critical moment relieves the burden of staying at the hospital while leaving children unattended at home. Sometimes, even when the family members arrive after the death, the team would still offer them adequate time to stay with the deceased. The team facilitates communication with the deceased and encourages them, saying, "Hearing is the last sense that goes. You can try to talk to him close to his ears. He might still be able to hear what you say".

In a study of death metaphors among Chinese, Cheung and Ho[23] found that three of the ten highly rated themes are interpersonal. When people thought about death, they thought about the separation from their loved ones. Dying patients may face death more peacefully if they understand that the needs of their family members will be taken care of. Thus, care for the family is an indirect way of care for the patients.

The last office or attending to the body after death is another crucial aspect in end-of-life care. The care for the patient is continued after death, through our gentle attention to the body. The act comforts the grieving family, too.[22] Involvement of the newly bereaved family members in the last office can be considered a valuable chance for them to contribute in the final caring procedures of their loved ones. In the past, the body of the deceased was usually naked and wrapped in a piece of white cloth before being sent to the mortuary in public hospitals. Now, the family members are allowed to dress the deceased. Having the deceased properly dressed, family members would feel much better, as the deceased would not feel cold and humiliated. In addition, a clean and tidy physical condition is one of the important elements of good death for Chinese.[24] A cross-sectional survey was done on the perception of sixty-seven bereaved persons, to measure their perception of helpful acts by nurses in the A&E unit in Hong Kong. Li, Chan and Lee[25] found that the first five most helpful acts are as follows: 1. providing written information about what to do following a death, 2. giving the family the opportunity to view the body in the ward, 3. respecting individual customs and religious procedures following death, 4. giving information about the severity of the patient's condition as early as possible, and 5. giving the family the opportunity to touch or hold the body. In sum, the chance to view the body and to receive information are valued aspects of care. Buckley and Joynt[26] extensively reviewed the literature on life-support care for critically ill patients in the ICU in Hong Kong. They found that the proportion of patients who die in ICU is comparable to that in the West. They also found that the family members wanted to participate in the decision-making process and at the same time expected to receive comprehensive information and care from competent medical staff. Along with information and the opportunity to view the body, as Li, Chan and Lee[25] suggested, participation in decision-making is crucial.

There is more awareness on the topic of death in other places like ICU,[27-29] A&E[25], obstetrics,[30-31] paediatrics,[32] and the neonatal ward.[33-34] Caring for families who experience stillbirth is a unique experience. From a qualitative study in exploring the roles of health-care professionals in helping grieving families of stillbirths, Saflund, Sjogren, and Wredling[30] identified six qualities that are considered crucial in the grieving process. They are 1. support in confusion, 2. support in meeting with and separating from the baby, 3. support in bereavement, 4. explanation of the stillbirth, 5. organization of the care, and 6. understanding the nature of grief. These findings match well our experiences in Hong Kong. The abrupt turn of a happy event (birth of a child) to a tragedy (death of the child) is so confusing for the families. Usually the grandparents and other relatives are gathered around the labour room, waiting to have the first sight of the newborn. Disclosing bad news is not an easy task for grieving parents; thus, support from nurses in carrying out the task is important in reducing their stress. In Hong Kong, a few patients share the postnatal ward. In order to reduce the stress from triggers induced by other mothers who are happily nursing their newborn babies, we usually place the grieving parents in a side ward or in the gynaecology ward. There is a changing attitude towards viewing the dead baby. Before the seventies, removal of a stillborn baby before the parents could see him or her was the usual practice in the West. Yet the guidelines published by the Royal College of Obstetricians and Gynaecologists in 1985 recommended nurses to encourage parents in viewing and holding their stillborn babies.[31] There was debate over the effects of seeing and holding their stillborn babies,[35–39] but the conclusion was that there may be individual variations and nurses should be sensitive to and respectful of the choice of the parents.[40] In Hong Kong in the past, not many parents wanted to see the baby. Recently, the number of requests by parents to see and to spend time with the stillborn baby is growing. We heard in the follow-up contacts that some grieving parents regretted not seeing their stillborn baby. We will not actively persuade them to see the baby after the stillbirth, but we should explain to them their rights and the availability of such an option. They can see the baby, the photograph, or both. We usually give them some time (around ten to fifteen minutes) to discuss this and decide. To those who plan to spend some time with the stillborn baby, we suggest bringing the clothing originally prepared for the baby on discharge. Parents are encouraged to be involved in bathing and dressing the baby, just as other parents with surviving newborns, if they feel comfortable doing so. The baby will then be placed in the cot. The parents are allowed to take photos, videos, footprints and handprints as they wish. We always ask the parents whether they have a name for the baby.

In response to the simple questions, the parents share their expectations and dreams for the baby. If a name is given, we will then use the name whenever we refer to the baby. The parents mirror our actions with theirs. Their monologue, or imagined dialogue, with the baby then starts. Though the parents are in tears, their faces show satisfaction as well. As reflected in the follow-up contacts, these were the things that the grieving parents treasured most. If the deceased baby has elder siblings, we welcome them to join the process, with the consent of the parents. We then have to provide information, as siblings usually have many questions. Parents also find this communication helpful to them, as some of the questions the children raise are difficult for the parents to handle, in their state of shock and grief. Also, nurses have a unique role in helping the grieving mother anticipate grief when she begins to lactate and take on other tasks. A grieving mother said that she was not aware of the power of lactation. Her tears dropped as her milk started flowing, as if the breast was grieving too. Sometimes, the problem returns after several years. Because of the cluster system of hospitals, the family will be admitted to the same hospital as the one they lost their baby in. The mother may be delivering another baby, or other children are admitted to the paediatric ward. The previous negative experience will cloud the new experience with irrational fear and anxiety.

The CDE Model of Caring for Families Facing Impending Death

Based on the literature as well as practical wisdom gained from frontline nursing experiences, a CDE model of nursing care for dying patients and families is proposed. The CDE model follows a chronological frame of dying, the moment of death and the aftermath. C components contribute to the dying phase; D and E contribute to the moment of death and the aftermath respectively. Table 1 summarizes the components of the model.

C Components: Communication, Clarification and Care

Communication

During the dying phase, communication is of utmost importance. The communication pathways include those between and within the patient, the family and the medical team. The content of communication between patient and health-care team includes exchange of information, problem solving, decision-making, establishment of rapport and building of trust.[41] In addition, the communication between the patient and family member that involves unfinished businesses is of the utmost importance. The role of nurses is not only in direct communication but also in facilitating communication between patient and family. Sometimes, the dying patient wants to share with the family the end-of-life plans, like the funeral or burial arrangement, but finds it too difficult to talk face to face with the beloved family members. Though the message can be conveyed through the nurse, or through tape recorder or written format, the best way is to encourage the patient to communicate directly with the family members. Sometimes, the patient is too weak to communicate, and non-verbal means of communication, for example through physical touch, or facial expression, can be used.

Clarification

The second C is clarification. In the dying phase, the patient's condition changes drastically. Clarification of current information about the process and treatment will induce a sense of control. As well, information is the prerequisite condition for rational decision-making. As each individual and family is unique, clarification of the individual's needs helps to develop an individualized care plan. Furthermore, facing death is an emotionally overwhelming experience. Both the patient and family might be confused and respond in a disorganized way. Facilitating emotional responses can help the family understand their own needs better.

Table 1
The CDE Model

C components (The Dying Phase)	D components (The Death Moment)	E components (Aftermath Phase)
Communication – between patients, family members and the teams – unfinished business – end-of-life plans – alternative ways of communication: verbal and non-verbal. *Clarification* – information about process and treatment – information about choices – emotions felt by patients and families *Care* – holistic care – family-centred care	*Delivery of Messages* – right timing, right information, right means and right person – clear, precise, comprehensive and accurate *Discretion* – over routines: resuscitation, last office, and sending to mortuary – over rules: number of visitations, duration of stay with the body, and no children rule *Death Scene* – privacy – peaceful scene – individualized rituals	*Explanation* – procedures: organ donatioin, autopsy, claiming of body, and funeral – grieving experience *Expression* – of condolence – of grief, if any – privacy and space for family *Exploration* – preferences in handling the belongings of the deceased – risk factors

Care

The third C is care. This is holistic care that includes care for all of the physical, psychological, spiritual, social and emotional aspects. It is not only addressed to the patient but also to the family.

D Components: Delivery of Messages, Discretion, and Death Scene

Delivery of messages

At the moment of death, the pronouncement of death is considered to be very important to the Chinese family. The exact time of the death of the patient is believed to affect the fate of the deceased's reincarnation; thus the family is very concerned about their presence around the deathbed. Thus pronouncement at the critical moment, so that family members are present, becomes important. Though the certification of death is the duty of physicians, there is a growing trend for nurses to share the duties of announcing the death to the family. Delivering the notice of death is an art. The right timing, right level of information, right means and delivery to the right person affects how the family responds. The content of the message should be clear, precise, accurate and succinct.

Discretion

The hospital is a place with multidisciplinary teams serving people of different age groups and backgrounds. Rules and regulations are set up to facilitate coordinated care as well as to protect the patients and families. There are rules that restrict visitation to a specific time and to a small number of visitors each day. Though the rules were less stringent in the past, the team became more conscious of the regulations after the SARS epidemic and the continuous threat of avian flu in Hong Kong. Despite the respect for surveillance, relaxation of visitation rules will be very helpful to the family at the moment of death; for instance, allowing the family to spend more time and allowing a larger number, i.e., the whole family including the young children, to witness the death at the bedside. Such discretion in the routine of last office exercised by the hospital staff is often deeply appreciated. Invitation of family members to participate in the last office as well as involving them in transporting the deceased to the mortuary is also welcomed.

Death scene

Bereaved family members often recall the memories around the deathbed, after the death of a loved one. We try to offer privacy to the family around the moment of dying, by moving them to a side ward or a less congested wing of the ward. We hope that the family can retain a better memory of this final moment with the patient in a more spacious environment. Brief individualized rituals after the moment of death are allowed for the family, provided there is no disturbance to other patients in the ward.

E Components: Explanation, Expression, and Exploration

Explanation

Right after the death, there are procedures to explain to the family about the autopsy, claiming of the body and other related decisions to be made, like organ donation. Usually, a physician will be the one to explain these things to the family, but the family might not understand this information when they are in a state of shock right after receiving the news of the death. Nurses can pay a unique role in explaining the information again in detail when the family members are more prepared to receive it. The family members need to go back to the ward the day after the death to get documents for burial or the funeral. The family members might have a lot of queries around the death, after they have digested the news over night. Some of them even say that the other family members designated them as representatives to get the relevant information. We are then in the position to explain the information to them. Sometimes, we even give them a brief picture of the grieving experience, in order to help them to prepare for it. We will also give them information about bereavement services, if they need them.

Expression

Family members may struggle to share with the nurses their memories of the patient and feelings about the loss of the patient. They worry that it would disturb the nurses' routine work. This is comforting to the family and makes them more at ease in sharing their grief and loss. Expression of memories and feelings is the first step in working through grief. The family expresses gratitude to have the space for expression. Some might even express their wish to go back to see the bed where the patient died. If another patient is not occupying the bed, we will give them a chance to stay there for some time. Some of them will talk to the bed, as if the patient were there. Some of them will stand and look at the bed, preoccupied with their own thoughts. Some will touch the bed and hope to be reconnected to the deceased. The reaction to such an arrangement is appreciated most of the time.

Exploration

The last E is exploration. We treat ourselves as gatekeepers as well. We will explore the risk factors to the family members and refer them to appropriate services if needed. Bereavement is not only about the loss of a loved one; there are other losses, material or immaterial, as well. They might be facing acute practical or financial problems, conflicts with in-laws, health matters or difficulties in child care. Nurses as gatekeepers will involve the medical social worker for risky cases. As well as exploring their needs, exploring their wishes in handling the belongings of the deceased is also important. The patient might have some personal belongings when admitted to the hospital. In particular, those who are injured in accidents have wallets, watches, and eyeglasses stained with blood. We have to ask whether the family want to get the things back, cleaned or as they were.

Barriers in Working with Families Facing Impending Deaths

Death usually shocks and upsets the family, but sometimes it affects the staff too. As for the grieving families, clear guidance can be helpful to the staff in inducing a sense of direction in facing the confusing and unpredictable situations around death. The CDE model may be helpful to less experienced nurses or those with less experience in encountering death. Yet each individual is unique, and so is each death and each family. The CDE model should be applied with flexibility and sensitivity.

Even with a clear direction of what to do, we have barriers in caring for patients who are facing death. Through focus groups with hospital staff on matters of care for dying patients and their relatives, Main[42] identified five themes. They are: 1. being uncomfortable, 2. being left to cope, 3. having relatives as the problem, 4. putting patients before relatives, and 5. managing death and dying. Some of the informants shared difficulties in using the word "death" directly. Personal grief and bereavement experience can interfere with one's nursing experience. A nurse who works in medical ward once told us, "I was OK in working with dying patients in the past. I regard death is a natural process of all living creatures. Recently, my dad died of a cerebral vascular accident (CVA). I found myself experiencing extreme difficulty in facing the death of patients. When a male patient died, I saw the face of my father instead of the patient. Tears then fell uncontrollably. Headaches resulted as I heard the sound of crying and wailing of the bereaved family members. Transference is so powerful. Yet, I felt it was not possible for me to be exempted from my duties to dying patients. Fortunately, my supervisor offered me resources to work through my grief. Though it is still not an easy task to witness death, I can fulfil my duty with more sensitivity towards the bereaved family members". Though personal loss might make working with a grieving family more challenging, it might also broaden the understanding of the nurse towards the grieving family.

Caring for young dying patients is considered a difficult task for health-care professionals. Because these professionals are about the same age and have a similar background to the dying patients, it is easy to develop transference. The ability to develop empathetic understanding is relatively simple, but at the same time the vicarious suffering with the patients and their family members can strongly affect the professionals. Also, young patients are relatively unprepared to face death, as they have many unfulfilled goals and unfinished developmental tasks, like getting married or bearing children. They may have young children, young spouses and aging surviving parents. Emotionally, they are not equipped to face impending death, as even the thought of death seems remote. Psychologically, they may feel they have failed personally in not being able to fulfil filial obligations. These are all secondary and relational pains that might be stronger than the primary pain arising from death.

In addition, for a caring professional, the inability to relieve a patient's suffering is disempowering, both personally and professionally. Paradoxically, the way to work through the sense of helplessness is not by doing more but by simply and peacefully following the flow, like the Daoist belief of following the flow of nature, the Dao. The sense of peace one can attain through not struggling seems to be very powerful and can resonate with the patient. A sense of peace in facing adverse life events is not easy to achieve. One has to actively reflect on one's own life values as well as work through one's own unfinished businesses in life before being a peaceful carer for dying patients. Care-giver support in continuous education and clinical supervision will be helpful to health-care professionals in maintaining a calm mind. As suggested by Burgess,[43] death and dying is a taboo and sensitive topic so it takes a "fine-tuned antenna" from nurses to be sensitive to the existential questions raised by patients and families. The receptiveness of the antenna will be affected by the nurses' upbringing and cultural context. The uneasiness in using the word "death" and the belief about talking about death increasing the likelihood for it to occur are barriers that have to be worked through. For better preparation, nursing schools have incorporated into the curriculum courses on the element of death and dying.[44]

Conclusion

The role of nurses in acute wards is similar to that in cancer wards or hospice wards in caring for dying patients. The key difference is that nurses in ICU or A&E will have to operate within a narrow time frame. Breaking bad news, disclosure, preparing for death, communicating with the family, performing the last office, and offering bereavement support have to be carried out efficiently. Transference and a sense of helplessness are common and can be disempowering for nurses. Professional support and training in death and bereavement care should be offered to all nurses, as most deaths take place in non-hospice units.

Nurses need various interventions to help them work through their experiences of care for dying patients.[45] Nurses feel that the domains of care in handling relationships, resources, measurement, control of involvement, personal growth and reflection are core in their work with dying patients. Comprehensive and continuous training in the above areas will form a translucent web of support for nurses.

This is a summary of reflections by frontline nurses in acute settings in hospitals in Hong Kong. The goal of the reflections is to help professionals providing care for dying patients to appreciate the perspective of nurses in these settings. Professionals working in non-cancer and non-hospice wards also contribute significantly in the care of dying patients and their families.

Although we cannot perform miracles in bringing deceased patients back to life, we can assure the family of continuous bereavement support and create a peaceful memory of the process of death, through the simple and concrete steps of death preparation and the last office. Knowledge and competence in handling the death of patients can also reduce the sense of helplessness among professionals. Hospitals continue to be amazing venues of life and death, especially when death is handled adequately and effectively.

17

Walking a Tightrope: The Loss and Grief of Parents of Children with Cancer in Shanghai

Vivian Wei Qun LOU and Cecilia Lai Wan CHAN

Introduction

Childhood cancer is one of the ten leading causes of death among children in China. Blood-related cancers such as acute lymphobastic leukaemia (ALL) and acute nonlymphobastic leukaemia (ANLL) are the most common types.[1-3] It is estimated that there are around 13,000 to 15,000 new cases of blood-related cancer in China each year.[4] The treatment of and research on childhood cancer are both disappointing and encouraging. The disappointment stems from the majority of new cases not receiving proper treatment for various reasons, such as wrong diagnosis, poor treatment protocol at hospitals in mid-size cities or rural areas, and lack of financial support.[4-5] However, the standard of treatment in research paediatric hospitals or paediatric wards in large cities such as Beijing and Shanghai is high. At the Shanghai Children's Medical Centre (SCMC), a national referral centre of children's cancer, it was reported that the estimated five-year disease-free survival rate was seventy-five percent for ALL and forty percent for ANLL, rates that are comparable to international figures.[5-6] However, even children being treated in a paediatric hospital that can provide the most effective treatment protocol have their quality of life affected, and the threat of death is still high.[7]

Having a child being diagnosis of cancer is a traumatic experience for the family, which profoundly affects the parents in three ways: the financial burden, role stress and psychosocial adjustment.[8-10] However, grief is a socially constructed experience, and parents from different cultures may have different responses with regard to illness, dying and the death of a child.[11-12] There is no study that examines the experiences of the grief of parents in the context of China's one-child policy, as well as China's lack of health coverage and psychosocial oncological services. This chapter has taken the initiative in filling this gap by exploring the experiences of parents in Shanghai.

Social Contexts

Three systems in contemporary China might have a significant influence on the experiences of parents of children with leukaemia.[13–14] They are the one-child policy, the health-care policy, and the dominant medical approach in providing service. These factors contribute to parents' feelings of shock, powerlessness, ambivalence, *renqing* debt (人情債) (a sense of inferior feeling in front of relationship parties and a feeling of wish to conduct certain behaviour to fulfil the social norm of *renqing* between relationship parties in future) as well as financial debt, fear, helplessness, and isolation if their child has cancer.

The one-child policy and the parent-child bond

According to Confucian tradition, a child in a Chinese family is not only an individual but is also a symbol of family continuity.[15] When there is only one child in a family, all expectations of the parents are focused on that child. This single child will be expected to bring honour to the family's ancestors, to take care of the parents when they are old, and to fulfil the goals of the parents or the family.[16] Therefore, the parent-child bond is usually enmeshed: the parents might regard their children as their possession, and families honour collective existence such as interdependence and integrity between parents and the child.[15,17]

Health-care policy and childhood health care

In the past two decades, the health-care system in urban China has undergone a drastic reform, moving toward a fee-for-service model that has reduced government commitment by increasing individual responsibility.[18–21] There is no national policy on health-care insurance for children, and the needs of children who suffer from chronic or severe illness are largely neglected. How much will a standard treatment for childhood leukaemia cost? The estimated cost for a two-year period of medical treatment is more than US$25,000, and a family is required to pay a large deposit before hospitalization and treatment. This amount is larger than people's means, as the average annual household income in Shanghai is less than US$7,000.[22]

In Shanghai, the city with the highest average income in China, there are three possible sources of financial support for families of children with cancer: a parent's work unit, private medical insurance, and Shanghai municipal health insurance. However, each of these sources has certain restrictive eligibility criteria. Only parents who work in government-owned work units can obtain health-care support for their children, and there is an annual limit or ceiling on the percentage of the total cost that can be recovered. The existing private medical insurance is not very helpful in cases of chronic disease, because often it offers only a one-time lump sum compensation in case of a major illness. The Collective Fund of Hospitalization for Primary and Secondary School Students, established in 1991, pays for only a percentage of the medical cost. As of 2005, Shanghai is the only city in China that has established this health insurance scheme for major illness for children.

However, even if a family is eligible for each of the above three sources of financial support, only around half of the medical expenses will be recovered. The parents will need to meet the remaining costs through other means. Indirect costs caused by a parent's loss of income due to job disruption and other costs for complimentary alternative treatments will also need to be met. Although members of the extended family are willing to contribute some money, the estimated expenses may be so high and the trajectory of the illness so uncertain that the parents' feelings are very complex and ambivalent. It is therefore understandable that many parents in China discontinue their child's medical treatment for cancer at some stage of the treatment.[7,23]

Dominant medical approach in providing service, and neglect of psychosocial needs among parents

Almost all the literature on childhood leukaemia in Chinese children focuses on medical-related topics such as treatment protocol, survival rate, and prognosis.[4, 23–25] The literature on the psychosocial effects of the illness, such as behavioural changes, emotions and quality of life, focus on the patient (the child) instead of the parents.[6, 26–27] A treatment team in a paediatric hospital has no expertise in the psychosocial aspects of the illness. Hence, there are no formal services provided in a hospital to cater for the psychosocial needs of the parents, such as hospital adjustment, information about the disease and the treatment, skills training and coping with emotions.[28]

There are also no community-based support services available to help parents cope with the multifaceted stressors during the treatment, such as skills for home-based care, parent-child communication, and coping with complex feelings.[29–32]

Loss of a child and Chinese relational-oriented grief

From the attachment point of view, losing a child is a dual loss affecting both first- and second-class of relationships.[33] The first loss is parents' loss of their child. The parent-child bond is regarded as the most significant for developing a sense of safety and security for both the child and the parents.[34,35] An anticipation of loss of this parent-child bond might generate strong overcompensation. In addition, this kind of compensation behaviour may induce a loss of second-class relationships, such as those with friends and colleagues, because parents might have no time or energy to nurture these other relationships. In the long run, this might have a profound bearing on the parents' own development and well-being.[35]

Scholars argue that, while Chinese parents face the loss of the first- and second-class relationships, their grief experiences have unique characteristics. Despite individual-based responses such as feelings of shock, denial, and depression, Chinese people also showed relational-oriented reactions such as the family members committing to maintaining the family, taking care of each other, and fulfilling the unfinished business that the death leaves.[36-37]

Therefore, it is worth exploring the grief experiences of Chinese parents of children with cancer within the context of the one-child family, lack of financial support, and absence of psychosocial support services.

Method

As no study has been conducted on the loss and grief experienced by Chinese parents whose child faces a life-threatening illness, it is important for us to explore themes within the socio-economic context of China.[38] By using in-depth interviews, descriptions of the experiences of parents of children with leukaemia were collected. Meanings can then be generalized from their narratives and themes can be identified.

Sample

The participants were referred by medical doctors at SCMC, the biggest children's hospital and a key service provider to children with severe illness, including cancer, in Shanghai as well as in eastern China. It has forty-two beds for childhood blood-related cancer patients. During the period of study (December 2001 to February 2002), about sixty percent of the active cases of leukaemia (both ALL and NALL) were either in recurrence or had complications, so doctors recommend they not participate in the study. Ten parents were invited to participant in the study and eight were successfully interviewed: one father, one grandfather,# and six mothers. They ranged in

---

\# Since the child's father is physically handicapped in a serious way and her mother is divorced from her father, the child's grandfather played the parent's role instead.

age from twenty-seven to sixty; their mean age was thirty-nine. Their children were aged between three and twelve, and most suffered from ALL. The demographic characteristics of the participants and their children are listed in Table 1.

In-depth interview

A face-to-face interview is a good method for exploring complex feelings and experiences.[38] An unstructured in-depth interview was used in order to explore all aspects of the experiences of parents, from the time of the onset of the illness. The in-depth interviews were conducted at SCMC with at least one parent from each family, in February 2002. The interviews, which lasted one to two hours, were audio-recorded and transcribed.

Data analysis

The interview transcripts of detailed information provided by the parents were analysed thematically by identifying categories and themes. The authors of the present study independently identified both manifest and latent themes from the narratives of the participants.[39] This was followed by discussions about the meaning and phrasing of all the themes, which continued until consensus was reached.

Table 1
Characteristics of the Care-givers and Their Children (N=8)

Child					Primary Care-giver					
Case	Age	Sex	M[a]	Diagnosis	Sex	Age	Occupation	Education Level	Religion
1	5	M	5	ALL	F	31	Clerk	Junior Secondary	Buddhism
2	6	M	14	ALL	F	46	Retired	Junior Secondary	None
3	4	M	14	ALL	F	33	Accountant	College	None
4	4	F	2	ALL	M	60	Retired	Junior Secondary	None
5	3	M	7	ALL	M	27	Unemployed	Junior Secondary	Buddhism
6	12	M	2	ANLL	F	41	Clerk	Senior Secondary	None
7	7	M	10	ALL	F	34	Accountant	University	None
8	12	F	22	ALL	F	38	Accountant	College	Christianity

Note. [a] M = Months since diagnosis.

Results and Discussion

A metaphoric term, "walking a tightrope", was identified to represent the core social process of how Chinese parents of children with leukaemia experience loss and grief. One parent said:

> "The whole process, from seeking diagnosis, to making decisions about the treatment protocol, the treatment process, and rehabilitation, even in the future, is just like an acrobat walking a tightrope. If you can go through [the process], you've made it. If you cannot, you fall. You have only one chance. Hence, the whole process is extremely stressful ..."

The metaphor of walking a tightrope in this social context covers three main themes. First, the parents perceive that, in regard to their dreams and plans for the future, the family has moved from a wide road onto a path consisting of a tightrope suspended over a cliff. Second, the parents shoulder very heavy burdens, including financial, emotional, and the burdens of daily care and social stigma, while walking this tightrope. Third, the whole process of walking the tightrope is overwhelmingly lonely. To extend the metaphor further, they will fall to their death in the ravine below, along with their family members whom they are carrying on their back, due to uncontrollable factors. These three themes are discussed below.

Standing on a tightrope: the broken family dreams

All the parents were shocked by the diagnosis of their child's illness — a new life that was expected to grow is now confronted with the danger of death. The feeling of shock and the related feeling of denial were clearly expressed by the parents:

> "I could not accept the diagnosis when I heard it. My husband supported me as I almost fainted."
>
> "We still have not told my parents about the diagnosis but just said my son had a tumour. You know, they have only one grandson and I don't want them to worry too much. He is their only purpose in life ..."

In addition, when the parents were confronted with the possibility of losing their only child, they felt a strong sense of emptiness and hopelessness:

> "Since the diagnosis, my husband and I have given up our life goals. Before that, our child was the hope of our family. Now, our dreams are all broken."
>
> "I felt that the sky was falling. In the past, I had a happy family. My husband and I worked hard and tried to provide a good environment for our son's development. Now everything seems to have vanished. There is no future ..."

Such descriptions of their feelings seem to support the argument that responses to grief are not confined just to individuals but extend to the entire Chinese family.[36,37] The anticipated loss of the child and ensuing grief generated strong behaviours of attachment such as holding on, focusing all attention on the child and excluding all other matters, and possibly, overcompensation. In the words of two of the parents:

> "He is my only son. I felt extremely stressed and stay with him twenty-four hours a day. Even during the nighttime, I always try to keep myself half awake."

> "I will try my best to fulfil her needs — buy toys, for example. My feeling is complicated as I have no idea how long she could still say she needs new toys and good food ..."

Interestingly, anger was not a theme that emerged from the analysis of the interview transcripts; instead, there was a prevailing sense of helplessness, confusion, and loss of goals in life. One possible explanation for this is that anger tends to be repressed in Chinese culture, as negative emotions are not supposed to be expressed.[40]

Stepping forward: balancing burdens and resources

Because the cost of treatment for the child was so high, the family would have to make a major decision on whether to spend a huge amount of money on the treatment or give up treatment shortly after the diagnosis was confirmed. When the parents were informed of the cost of the treatment and were required to pay a deposit to the hospital, the feelings of ambivalence, uncertainty, helplessness, and powerlessness were overwhelming. As one parent stated:

> "It is too much to ask a family to pay such a huge amount of money at once. Over the long term, we could try our best to repay it. But within such a short period before the treatment, we really feel hopeless. I know some parents just give up because they are not able to pay the full cost of treatment at the very beginning."

Under such a financial constraint, the informal support network, including extended family members and relatives, became the most important resource through which families could seek help. Though borrowing money could lessen a family's financial difficulties, it induces a sense of shame and *renqing* debt besides financial debt on the family:

> "Even though relatives and friends said they would give me the money, I tell
> them that that I am borrowing it from them. One day, when I am able, I will
> return the money to them."

Although appealing for public donations through the mass media is an
alternative, taking this action caused ambivalence, too:

> "I am grateful to all those who helped my son. I only hope that his treatment
> is successful and he survives. If so, he could contribute to society when he is
> grown up. Otherwise [if he cannot survive], I shall feel very sorry. So my
> feeling is very complex."

The feelings of ambiguity became chronic and deep because of the
unpredictability of the progression of the illness. The sense of obligation and
regret grew as *renqing* debt accumulated with financial debts. Therefore, each
step was a challenge full of ambivalence:

> "This time, I borrowed money to pay for the treatment. But how about next
> time? ... continuous worry. How about infection? There is no accurate
> estimation of how much I need to pay; any other problems such as infection
> will mean extra cost to the overall medical expenses. If you say 200,000
> [yuan] is the ultimate amount, then we'll just try to earn/borrow it, but it is
> out of our control and seems like a bottomless valley ... I will never be able
> to repay this debt."
> "There is always a conflict. On the one hand, we hope that the money
> paid could save our child's life. On the other hand, we know that many factors
> are out of our control. Sometimes, I wonder whether the money might end
> up being spent for nothing [as the child might die]."

This dilemma surrounding the financial and emotional burdens is an
additional factor that may result in the parents' decision to give up treatment
before it is complete.[7,23]

Walking alone: fighting along a lonely path

Though the parents have far more responsibilities than if they were rearing a
healthy child, they basically have to fight the disease on their own, without
much support from formal or informal channels.

The families were satisfied with the medical treatment their children
received at SCMC, the professional excellence and compassionate attitude of
doctors and nurses, as well as the warm atmosphere in the ward. Parents
became knowledgeable about medication, treatment and home care, a finding
that is consistent with the literature.[41] Thus, they were able to assume a more

active role in the care of their child in hospital. However, no matter how kind the doctors or nurses could be, the parents were aware that they should not interfere with the medical treatment and nursing care. In the words of two of the parents:

> "The doctors want to help me and provide me with more information such as on bone marrow transplant. But they are very busy and I don't want to disturb them."
>
> "The doctors and nurses are very busy. I don't want to always bother them with my personal worries."

There is no medical social worker or clinical psychologist in the hospital. The parents received little psychosocial support from health-care professionals. Parents sometimes supported each other by sharing information and chatting during meal times or in the ward corridor. However, as the parents did not have a designated leader and were not organized into a group, and because every child had his or her own timetable for hospitalization, support from other parents was usually short term and confined only to the exchange of information and practical skills.

Moreover, childhood leukaemia is not very well understood among the public in China, so misunderstanding and social discrimination are common. For this reason, sometimes the parents felt that they were rejected by the community and chose to isolate themselves. As two of the parents put it:

> "My daughter was at kindergarten when she was diagnosed. The kindergarten asked us not to bring her back until she was totally cured. So she quit school and has stayed at home since the diagnosis for treatment and rehabilitation." [When asked about plans for primary education, the parents were at a loss, as discrimination against cancer patients is real and common.]
>
> "I rented a room near the hospital. Because of the chemotherapy, my son lost his hair. My landlord asked me what happened, and I just lied. So we seldom went out but just stayed in our room" [for fear that the landlord would ask them to move out, as some people might still regard cancer as being contagious].

The above quotations suggest that the families were extremely lonely while walking the tightrope. They underwent a chronic mourning process in response to the loss of their child's health and even life, as well as the loss of their family's social connections.

The socio-contextual factors contribute to the parental experience of loss and grief. The one-child policy, inadequate health-care financing and lack of psychosocial support in hospitals generate much stress and grief for parents in contemporary China. These experiences can be represented by the metaphor of walking a tightrope (Table 2).

Table 2
Summary of Findings — Walking a Tightrope

	Step On	Step Forward	
		Behavioural — Balancing	Feeling — Lonely
Individual level	Shock/denial Overcompensation	Unaffordable Ambiguity	Helpless Lack of support
Relational level	Broken family dreams and plans	Family shame *renqing debt*	Fear of disturbing others Isolated from the mainstream

Implications for Practice

Confronted with the stark fact of their only child having a life-threatening illness, parents' feelings of shock, fear, ambivalence, and hopelessness are profound. Most parents and care-givers are young adults. Prolonged stress, grief, and mourning can affect their physical health, mental health, productivity at work,[42–44] and subsequent quality of life, as well as their family and social relationships.[42,43] Therefore, the psychosocial needs of parents should be met, and a relationship-oriented, self-help, and networking approach intervention should be considered.

The literature suggests that social support has a positive effect on the mental health of care-givers.[45–46] The current study shows that care-givers cannot find formal support under the existing medical care system and that they are ambivalent about receiving support from informal networks because of *renqing* debt. Patients and parent support groups, mutual help activities as well as network interventions may help to generate resources for care-givers dealing with the same problems.

In addition, under the current medical care system, care-givers have virtually no control over medical and non-medical expenses. Even if doctors give a child an optimistic prognosis, the parents may still be forced to stop treatment due to a lack of money. This situation is heartbreaking not only for the family but also for professionals. In this regard, there is an urgent need to develop a relevant national policy on health insurance or financial aid for health care, especially for children, to reduce anxiety or uncertainty within the family. Medical professionals are also advocating changes in China.[4,7]

As a result of improved health insurance and universal coverage of health care, the quality of life of parents of children with cancer can be improved, and in turn the quality of life of the children can be enhanced. Thus, instead of a mere tightrope, the family will have access to a sturdier bridge to help them over difficult times.

PART THREE

BEREAVEMENT

18

Bereavement Care in Hong Kong: Past, Present and Future

Amy Yin Man CHOW and Cecilia Lai Wan CHAN

Introduction

Death marks a permanent separation from our loved ones. It hurts because we are socially, emotionally and psychologically attached to the deceased, and our loved one may feel like a part of us. His or her death is equivalent to the amputation of a limb from our body. It is an irreversible loss. As there is no Chinese term to describe bereavement, we use the literal translation of "the experience of losing a dear one" (喪親的經驗).[1] Death is a taboo subject that is also not frequently mentioned[2] and is always replaced by euphemisms. The absence of a Chinese concept of bereavement as well as the infrequent mention of the concept in daily conversation deters or even inhibits the development of bereavement care in Chinese communities.

Bereavement Care in Hong Kong: The Past

Informal support from family

Bereaved Chinese expected to be supported by their own informal support network as well as by elaborate funeral rituals.[3] As a result of the large number of families emigrating from Hong Kong to other countries in the 1990s and the rapid aging of the population, the size of the immediate and extended familial support network has shrunk. The informal support that the population depended upon in the past is not readily available now. The lack of preparation for death and inadequate social support can make the adjustment to bereavement more difficult.

Remedial care from professionals

Professionals often offer bereavement care during their daily contact with clients, patients or students. The first specialized bereavement care in Hong Kong was offered , since 1993 by a clinical psychologist and volunteers[4] of Nam Long Hospital, a cancer hospital. Influenced by William Worden's books *Grief Counseling* and *Grief Therapy,* [5-6] the term "bereavement counselling" is used interchangeably with "grief counselling". Like the concept of bereavement, there is no compatible Chinese term for the concept of "grief". The Chinese term *bei shang* (悲傷) is a direct translation of the literal meaning of "grief", yet the Chinese term means "sadness". The vast scope of emotions that are embraced by the English word "grief" is lost. The Chinese term for "bereavement counselling" is literally translated as *bei shang fu dao* (悲傷輔導).[6]

Bereavement care as extension of hospice care

Structured bereavement groups were run for bereaved family members of deceased patients in Nam Long Hospital. The aim of the groups was to facilitate the expression of emotions as well as foster mutual support. Three groups had been organized by the end of 1994.[7] Shortly after that, the professional team of Bradbury Hospice, the first independent hospice in Hong Kong, also set up a system of risk assessment for bereaved family members. The intervention includes sending condolence cards, making telephone contact, offering office interviews and home visits by the home care nurses who knew the family members well before the death of the patient. A medical social worker and a psychologist supported them. In the beginning of the 1990s, only bereaved family members of patients in these two hospices were specially privileged to have these teams of experts serve them.

We have tried to apply an integrated Eastern body-mind-spirit approach[8] into serving Chinese bereaved clients in 1995. The experience of the group was documented as Amy Yin Man Chow's master thesis[7] and reported in a television documentary.[9] Three more groups were organized in 1996, and the revised group programme was published in two manuals.[10-11] In designing the programme, we introduced a new Chinese term for bereavement, *shan bei* (善別), meaning "good separation". The term is now used by some health-care professionals in Hong Kong[1]. In 1996, Comfort Care Concern Group, a charitable organization promoting peer support in terminal care, invited William Worden to train professionals in grief counselling in Hong Kong. Bereavement care became more widely accepted as part of the integral psychosocial and palliative care. The Bradbury Hospice team produced the first booklet for grieving children in 1997.[12]

Community bereavement care

The Jessie and Thomas Tam Centre of the Society for the Promotion of Hospice Care, the first community-based bereavement counselling centre, was inaugurated in 1997.[1] Bereavement counselling services for individuals, groups and families were offered to the general public. The centre also runs a hotline, a resource library, public education and memorial programmes. The Hong Kong team was invited by hospices and hospitals in Macau, China, Malaysia, Taiwan and Japan to run workshops for health-care professionals. The Comfort, Care and Concern Group offered regular volunteer training to support bereaved persons and run bereavement counselling groups concurrently. The former director, Lawrence Chen, published a book on bereavement,[13] an excellent resource kit for local practitioners.

The oncology unit of Tuen Mun Hospital and Tsung Tsin College, with the support of the Quality Education Fund, started an EQ Student Ambassadors Project in 1998. The project trained secondary school students to serve bereaved children in Tuen Mun, a predominantly low-income district. The project was well received and was extended to five other schools in 2000. The Child and Family Bereavement Centre was set up in 2003 in Tuen Mun Hospital, to offer bereavement counselling for grieving families.[14]

Bereavement Care in Hong Kong: The Present

Integration of bereavement care into health and educational services

As a result of the growing awareness of the need for bereavement care in Hong Kong, more professionals are integrating bereavement care into their daily practice. In 2000, The Jessie and Thomas Tam Centre produced a manual for working with children.[15] Workshops for teachers on grief in children were run, and they were very well received. Coupled with the professional input of psychologists of the Education Department, the school system has developed a systematic approach to bereavement care for students in Hong Kong.

Since 1986, when it was formed, The Society for the Promotion of Hospice Care invited many international experts like Terese Brady, Malcolm and Dianne McKissock, Robert Neimeyer, Colin Murray Parkes, Margaret Stroebe, and Jenni Thomas, to train local professionals in bereavement care. The need for palliative and bereavement care has been well received in the twenty-first century.

As most deaths are among older adults, mostly bereaved persons are also adults. Therefore, district elderly community centres have incorporated bereavement care into their regular services. This care has come about because of several factors. People have been made aware of the concept of "hospice" and "life and death" through public education, school talks, and a "Late Life Forum" for patients and the general public. Large-scale research has been done, and publicity programmes on "good death" and "end-of-life decisions" have been carried out. The Society for the Promotion of Hospice Care has trained many professionals in the technical skills of palliative and bereavement care.

A number of innovative non-governmental organizations that serve a large number of elderly people, such as St. James's Settlements, the Hong Kong Society for the Aged (SAGE), Holy Carpenter's Social Service Centre, and the Tung Wah Group of Hospitals are developing their own models of bereavement support services for the community. Under the leadership of the district social work officer, a number of social service organizations and leaders of the funeral industry joined to apply for a community bereavement support project in the Hung Hom District, funded by the Community Integration and Social Inclusion Fund in 2004. St. James's Settlements runs a large volunteer programme to help single elderly persons with funeral arrangements and bereavement care. The experiences of palliative care in nursing homes, hospices and hospitals are also being consolidated into training packages for local needs.

As most deaths take place in hospitals, public hospitals recognize bereavement care as one of their core services to the families of their patients. Tuen Mun Hospital runs a volunteer bereavement care project in the accident and emergency unit. The medical and geriatric unit of Caritas Medical Centre runs a care for the bereaved project for bereaved elderly people. The Bereavement Care team of Kwong Wah Hospital is run by a group of enthusiastic nurses. The Society of AIDS Care offers bereavement counselling service for care-givers of people with HIV/AIDS.

Bereavement Care in Hong Kong: The Future

Within two decades, bereavement care in Hong Kong was transformed from ad hoc episodic services to standardized care in hospices and palliative care units in hospitals, as well as being integrated into regular services for different targets groups in a wide range of settings. It is hoped that bereavement care in Hong Kong will move towards evidence-based practice and indigenization of care.

Evidence-based bereavement care

It is commonly believed that bereavement care is helpful and essential for bereaved persons. This assumption was recently challenged by a few scholars.[16–18] Allumbaugh and Hoyt[16] applied meta-analysis on thirty-five studies of effectiveness of grief therapy. They found that, compared with other meta-analyses on other forms of psychotherapy, the effect of this meta-analysis is relatively small, implying that the effect of grief therapy on participants is minimal. Instead of doing quantitative analysis on the available study, Schut, Stroebe, Van den Bout, and Terheggen[17] analysed the studies qualitatively. They divided the studies into three groups: primary, secondary and tertiary preventive interventions. The effects of primary preventive interventions are found to be disappointing, as negative results are sometimes found in a number of studies. The effects of secondary preventive interventions are controversial. Most are found to have modest and temporary effects. Yet screening for high-risk groups as inclusion criteria seemed to yield better results. The effect of tertiary preventive interventions is found to be more positive and long lasting. Jordon and Neimeyer[18] reviewed studies on the effectiveness of grief therapy and concluded that the effect is generally found to be low. They postulated three possibilities for failure in finding significant effects: the assumption of universal need of bereavement care is not necessarily true, the present form of bereavement care is not the optimal one, and there are methodological problems with the studies concerned.

Bereavement care in Hong Kong is less advanced than that in the West. We do not have a validated and standardized measurement on bereavement reactions in our language. Studies in the area of bereavement are scarce. Yet, from the review studies of our forerunners in the West, we have gain insights into designing and delivering bereavement care. A few reflective questions should be seriously addressed:

1. Do all bereaved persons need bereavement care? If not, who needs more?
2. What form of care do they need? What is available and what is not?
3. Would different client groups (age, type of loss, Social Economical Status) need different forms of bereavement care? What are the criteria for triage?
4. What are the risk factors of complicated grief among the various target groups?
5. How do we measure the effectiveness of the service in a culturally relevant manner?

There are no quick and pat answers to the questions above. The answers have to be explored through rigorous research studies, experimentation and critical reflections by clinicians. Thus the mushrooming of diversified bereavement care without effective outcome evaluation, communication and coordination might be futile. Better collaboration between clinicians and researchers in filling the gaps in knowledge of bereavement care would be a good start.

Indigenous bereavement care

Grief and bereavement is believed to be shaped by a person's culture.[21-22] Experience and findings from the West might be a good reference, but there might be something unique among ethnic groups in the East. Stroebe, Hansson, Stroebe, and Schut[22] proposed that the concept of culture was not limited to ethnic groups but to gender and generations as well. The bereaved persons are the real experts that researchers could draw insights from. We may have to rely more on qualitative studies of persons with bereavement experiences.[23] There are attempts to develop local measurements of grief, such as Grief Reaction Assessment Form (GRAF),[24] but more has to be done before a comprehensive picture of bereavement among Chinese people can be mapped out. Western strategies of bereavement care may not be relevant to the needs of Chinese bereaved persons. Chow identified three discourses from her extensive experience of working with Chinese bereaved persons.[25] The discourses are the ambivalences in seeking help, expressing emotions and the continuing bond with the deceased.

Discourse of help seeking

There is a strong need to talk about one's bereavement experience. Sharing the experience with professionals would be safe, as professionals are strangers who know nothing about the family. Unfortunately, bound by the cultural restrictions prohibiting sharing family affairs with non-family members, bereaved persons experience strong ambivalence about seeking help from professionals, despite a great desire to do so. The no-show rate for the first interview is usually very high. Bereavement counsellors can make it easier for those seeking help by arranging an immediate interview, offering home visits, sending friendly reminders of the appointment time through telephone contact, and showing appreciation of the client's disclosure as helping the counsellor to help other bereaved persons. Counsellors can also use appropriate moments like Chinese festivals or special days such as anniversaries. These are strategies to help resolve the ambivalence about seeking help.

Discourse of emotional expression

Chinese people believe that excessive emotional expression is hazardous to the health.[26] Bereaved persons tend to inhibit emotional expression, even within the counselling session. Putting pressure on them to express their emotions may lead to early dropout. Chinese people somatize[27] or use body-related expressions[28] to describe their emotions. It is therefore helpful to discuss matters such as appetite, quality of sleep, and bodily pain as entry points to talk about emotions and physical well-being. Other projective means like drawing, poetry, singing songs with lyrics related to loss, and discussing characters in movies related to bereavement can also be helpful. The Chinese bereaved person will find it easier to address emotional needs through an indirect way, because direct discussion of feelings towards the deceased, especially negative ones, may give rise to a sense of guilt, as if the person has been disloyal to the family.

Discourse of continuing bond

The traditional practice of ancestor worship fosters the concept of a continuing bond with the deceased and with life after death. There is also a cultural belief that the bereaved should let go of the deceased so that he or she can be reincarnated. Bereavement counsellors design programmes similar to traditional rituals, such as setting birds or fish free, as a symbol of letting go while maintaining connections.[7,29] These rituals serve to symbolize the need of the bereaved in letting go of the pain attached to the bereavement while continuing communication through attaching letters to balloons and kites before they are released. Elderly persons usually find such culturally relevant expressions soothing, and will feel a sense of relief after performing the rituals. Discussion with bereaved persons about their dreams of the deceased is also effective in legitimizing their need for a continuing bond.

The above discourses can be converted into culturally relevant practices in working with Chinese bereaved persons. Further research on the efficacy of such practices will be necessary.

Chow, Chan and Ho[30] have made a preliminary attempt to explore the bereavement experience of Chinese persons in Hong Kong. In a cross-sectional study[31] of 292 Chinese persons who lost a spouse or parents within two years, it was found that about ninety percent did share their bereavement experiences with others. This seems contrary to the common belief that death is a taboo topic among the Chinese. In addition, the majority of the people in this group shared their bereavement experience with friends rather than family members. The findings refute the belief that Chinese share their bereavement experience, which is a family affair, only with family members. The study also found no correlation between the level of sharing with emotional levels and health condition. The traditional Chinese belief that sharing negative emotional experiences is a threat to health is not supported by the data. Thus, we can see that traditional ideas on Chinese bereavement might not necessarily be true. Thus, the design of bereavement care should be based on current research data instead of taking cultural ideas as given.

Coordinated multidisciplinary and multi-level bereavement care

There is no "one size fit all" approach to bereavement care. The Centre for the Advancement of Health suggested that there should be differentiation between care for bereaved persons with uncomplicated bereavement experience from care for those who are at risk and those experiencing complicated grief. Care for bereaved persons who experience uncomplicated bereavement may be unnecessary and sometimes not helpful. Care for bereaved persons at risk or for those experiencing complicated feelings of grief is more beneficial.[32] Instead of replicating one bereavement model for everyone, we should carefully assess needs and promote a continuum of care for people with different levels of needs and at different levels of risk.

Conclusion

Bereavement care started developing in Hong Kong less than two decades ago. It is just like an adolescent who is still searching for an identity. We can be adventurous and innovative while learning from experts from other parts of the world. With input from our predecessors, we shall venture into more systematic research and service provision, paving our path to adulthood in the giving evidence-based bereavement care service in Hong Kong.

19

When East Meets West: Implications for Bereavement Counselling

Brenda Wing Sze KOO, Agnes Fong TIN, Elaine Wai Kwan KOO
and Sze-man LEE

Introduction

Bereavement can be understood as a social construction.[1] It is shaped by our
current socio-cultural environment. A mourner constructs and makes sense
of grief within the cultural and social context. Therefore, in order to
understand one's grief, it is important to first understand the socio-cultural
environment. However, it should be noted that our environment is ever-
changing and we are always in a process of revising our thoughts and feelings.
Therefore, the following is not an attempt to simplify the characterization of
the Chinese culture or to imply a static cultural pattern. It serves to highlight
briefly a part of Chinese culture that may help us better understand the grief
of the Chinese mourners.

Theories and models of bereavement counselling come mainly from the
West. When adopting these theories and models in the context of Chinese
community, modifications are necessary in order to fit the Western framework
into the Chinese context. After some discussion about the Chinese culture and
its influence on grief, this chapter discusses the necessary implications and
modifications in using the Western models of bereavement counselling for
different types of loss in our Chinese population.

Chinese Culture and Bereavement

Recognizing the loss

Most literature on bereavement suggests that acknowledgement of the death
of the loved one is the indispensable first step in the mourning process.[2–7]
However, as death is still a taboo subject in the Chinese community, people
avoid the topic of death by using metaphors or covering up the fact of death
by representations of life.[8,9] An environment of avoidance inhibits the

mourners from openly and fully acknowledging their bereavement experience. In working with Chinese mourners, the care-givers may need to promote an open atmosphere in talking about the death through, for example, using the word "dead" or "die" directly.

Another important component in the initial process of grieving involves the understanding of death. Buddhist and traditional Chinese beliefs are particularly influential in the attribution of death in our local community. Life is often understood by the Chinese as a process of *yin* (因), or previous deeds, and *yuan* (緣), or chance of nature. The idea of *yin* and *yuan* is a significant cultural concept in understanding and acknowledging the inevitability of every events in life.[10] Other cultural concepts like *feng shui* (風水) may also play a significant role in helping the mourners to make sense of the death. Due to the uncontrollable and mysterious nature of death, care-givers need to be aware of and deal with the different attributions by the mourners, because these attributions may lead to a different sense of control or liability in causing the death, resulting in different feelings and thoughts. For example, an external attribution (the end of *yuan* with the deceased) may promote acceptance. But if the mourners attribute the cause of death to personal or internal reasons as the *yin*, it may result in emotional distress, such as feelings of guilt.

Reacting to the separation

When reacting to the reality of death, grief can be experienced and expressed in physical, psychological and behavioural dimensions.[11] To most mourners, grief is not a "disease" in the sense of a sickness or unhealthy condition of mind or body but a "dis-ease" to them.[12] They may not be at ease with their situations or with themselves, typically associated with a sense of being out of control due to the unusual experience of grief. This is particularly true for Chinese when they are less accustomed to expressing their emotions. When dealing with their emotions, the Chinese are expected to suppress rather than express their feelings.[13] Another reason for this restraint of expression is the concealment of private problems in order to save the "face" of the family. The Chinese may believe that family shame should not be revealed to the outsiders. The fate of individuals and that of the family is closely related.[14] One's honour means the honour for the family; likewise, an individual's shame would become the shame of the family. This belief may prevent people from freely expressing their own feelings or problems.

The process of engagement is therefore especially important for Chinese, so that they may try out the speed of engagement until they feel safe enough to express themselves. Care-givers also need to be aware of the unique and indirect way Chinese mourners communicate their emotions. Due to their underdevelopment of intra-psychic awareness, the Chinese tend to present any intra-personal issue from an inter-personal frame of reference[15] or through a somatic complaint.[13] It should be noted that mere catharsis of emotions is not helpful, especially for Chinese who consider keeping emotions under control and well balanced as the mature way of dealing with problems.[16] Care-givers therefore need to help the mourners to gain mastery and give meaning to their experience, so that a sense of control of their emotions can be maintained. A group experience is also helpful, in which the sense of universality can encourage the mourners to express their feelings by arousing a sense of commonality and understanding.

Recalling the deceased and maintaining a spiritual relationship

When bringing back memories, all aspects of the deceased and the relationship are reviewed, whether they are good or bad. The care-givers can help the mourners to memorize the appearance of deceased through reviewing the photos, video, poems or music that bear special meaning for the relationship. More and more research and clinical interviews suggest that physical death does not sever the connection of spiritual relationships.[17] Continuing bonds between the deceased and the mourners are a normal and healthy part of grieving.

Ongoing relationships with the deceased are common in Chinese culture. Visiting the grave during *Ching Ming Festival* or *Chung Yeung Festival* , and burning incense sticks or offerings to the deceased are well-accepted folk rituals among Chinese people. Mourners may also initiate other individual ways to maintain this sense of connection with the deceased.[18] Listening with a non-judgemental attitude, showing genuine interest as well as making meaning of these unique experiences are helpful in facilitating a spiritual and therapeutic relationship between the mourners and the deceased.

Adapting to and reinvesting in life

The well-defined roles and obligations in Chinese families may complicate the process of adaptation. Mourners may find it difficult to deal with the missing roles or obligations that the deceased used to perform. They may need to make more of an effort to learn to assume or reorganize these roles in the family. Taking different skills training courses and having joint sessions with family members for communication or negotiation may be helpful at this stage.

A healthy accommodation to the loss also requires the mourners to revise their assumptive world, self-identity and reinvest their emotional energy in other aspects of life, including any other emotionally gratifying persons, objects, beliefs or activities. However, the interdependent definition of selfhood by Chinese makes this process difficult. The Chinese word for "person" (人) is defined as a person in a two-person relationship (仁者，人也). It means that the self of any individual has to be defined through an interpersonal relationship.[15] There are social, cultural and moral expectations that define how an individual should behave in different contexts, roles and relationships. The ultimate life goal of Chinese people is therefore to perform well in their roles and fulfil their corresponding obligations. The loss of significant others would then threaten this self-concept which is originally built up through the relationships. The mourners may often lose their meaning in life, have lower self-esteem, and experience feelings of confusion, anxiety and helplessness.

Care-givers can introduce the ideas of self-care and self-actualization and encourage the mourners to explore own personal will, interests, desires and strengths. However, over-reliance on the Western ideas of independent selfhood without considering the unique features of Chinese culture may not be helpful. A well-balanced interpersonal relationship is still far more significant for most Chinese. It is therefore important to encourage a balance between an interdependent selfhood and an independent selfhood, which in turn coincides with the Chinese virtue of maintaining harmony.

Intervention for Different Types of Loss

Widows

Mrs A (aged 45) found her situation very helpless after the death of husband:

> "The label of 'widow'(寡婦) makes me feel that I am inferior to others. I dare not tell anyone that my husband has died ... My life is so chaotic now. I used to depend on my husband, and now I don't even know how to deal with the bills for electricity and water supply. How can I look after the family without my husband? I just can't find any meaning in life anymore."

The common self-image of women as shaped by traditional Chinese culture is one that is dependent, caring and motherly. Women are socialized to be dependent on men. Their self-identity is often defined by their important roles in the family as wife and mother. Therefore, the self-identity of a married woman, which used to be defined by the dependent and caring role of a wife, would be greatly threatened by the death of the husband. Many widows would experience feelings of self-doubt and meaninglessness. In addition to the loss of the self, the label of "widow" for Chinese women even creates a sense of stigmatization and shame. It is common for widows to be blamed for bringing bad luck to the family and causing the death. The well-defined and dependent role of wife in the family may also lead to the widow's difficulty in readjustment to daily life. She may find herself struggling to learn to perform the different tasks that used to be done by her husband. The emotion-oriented pattern of women may further intensify the sense of helplessness and anxiety when they now have to learn to solve various problems alone. The situation would be worse for those who used to perform the single role of homemaker, due to their weak support network.

1. Provide tangible support (like looking after young children, preparing meals, accompanying them on various appointments, procedures etc.), especially during the acute phase of mourning.
2. Help them to master and consolidate their grief experience, not just facilitate mere venting and catharsis of emotions.
3. Keep a balance between emotions and restoration, so that they can be supported in slowly moving to resume life at their pace without over-indulging in their grief.
4. Enhance their coping and problem-solving skills in dealing with daily life events.
5. Affirm any of the minor achievements accomplished and help them identify their strengths.
6. Encourage them to set daily plans and achievable goals.
7. Affirm their uniqueness, promote self-love and self-care.
8. Support the bereaved children when their mother is still burdened by her own grief and fails to fully perform her role as mother in looking after the children's emotions.
9. Encourage widows to join a bereavement group and other skills training groups, to enhance their social support as well as their coping with grief and daily life.

Widowers

Mr B (aged 50) has always tried to "solve" his grief for his wife:

> "How can I possibly cry before others or tell them that I so desperately miss my wife? I can only pretend to be okay. I try to keep myself busy so that I won't think of my wife. Work, work, work ... The feeling of loneliness is so intolerable that the only way is to keep away from it. Can you suggest any ways so that I can shorten this period of pain?"

Traditional views suggest that gender determines how people mourn and cope. Women would experience intense emotions and tend to express them through talking. Men would focus on cognition and tend to cope with their grief through mastering the environment. Their emotions are moderate in intensity, and feelings of loneliness, anger and guilt are predominant.

A recent study by Martin and Doka[19] suggests another view. They claim that grief may only relate to gender but not be determined by it. It is the style, not the gender, that matters. There are two types of griever: the intuitive and the instrumental. Men are more likely than women to be socialized as instrumental grievers who prefer to confront their losses internally, cognitively and behaviourally. The Chinese word for "widower" (鰥) vividly shows this behavioural dimension of the instrumental grievers. The ancient meaning of this word refers to the eyes of fish and the state of insomnia during which the person's eyes stay open and stare at the sky. This is demonstrated by the tendency of grieving men to immerse themselves in activities such as work, taking legal or physical action over the loss, rituals, physical exercise, engaging in risk-taking behaviour and pursuing new relationships.

1. Reframe counselling as a process of problem-solving and helping action for other family members.
2. Work on cognition and use intervention like cognitive behavioural techniques and problem-solving skills.
3. Psycho-educate bereaved people on the models of grief, to enhance a sense of mastery.
4. Help them to express their emotions in ways that are compatible with the male role.
5. Ask about "reactions" rather than "feelings".
6. Allow them to express themselves through idiosyncratic means like painting, writing, poetry or physical exercise.
7. Encourage them to get involved in any rituals that they find meaningful or do something for the sake of the deceased.

Young children losing parents

John (aged 7) suffered from intense feelings of fear after his father's death:

> "In the funeral, I have to wipe the face of father with towel (a traditional Chinese ritual called 買水). Father looked so horrible and it just didn't look like him. I was so frightened that I really didn't want to do it. But my uncle said that I was the eldest son and insisted that I do it. I am still very afraid now and dare not sleep alone at night."

When a parent dies, some widows or widowers report that they have difficulty in breaking the bad news to their young children.[20,21] The death of parents and the subsequent involvement like attending the parent's funeral are all strange, novel or even frightening experiences to most children. The emotions that they may experience include sadness, anger, anxiety or guilt, once they have acknowledged the death.[22] But due to their limited attention span, children usually grieve intermittently. They may feel the pain of the death at one moment and be able to distract themselves from the pain at the next moment. Unlike adults, children may not easily articulate their inner feelings through verbal expression because of their limited cognitive and language capacity. Their grief can be observed through daily living such as changes in sleep pattern and appetite, or regressive behaviour such as clinging to the care-giver or wetting the bed. Bereaved children would also need to face secondary losses like a drop in family economic status and less attention from the grieving parent. Maintaining a continuing bond with the deceased parent is a natural and normal phenomenon for children. They usually construct an inner representation of the dead parent and maintain an ongoing relationship with him or her.[23]

1. Support and coach the bereaved families in breaking the bad news to children.
2. Respect their choice in the degree of involvement in funeral and related rituals, and give corresponding preparation or support.
3. Be aware of and deal with the guilt caused by their egocentric and magical thoughts, in view of their limited cognitive development.
4. Deal with any re-grief phenomenon as their new capacities develop through age and begin to process the experience of death from a very different vantage point from before.[24]
5. Accept and normalize their feelings, to reduce their sense of loneliness.
6. Use play and rituals to facilitate expression of feelings.
7. Support the surviving parents in dealing with their grief so that they are more available to their children and their active coping can further help the children to accommodate to the loss. [22,25]
8. Remind the family to report the death to school personnel so that they can offer support to the children.

Adult children losing parents

Miss C (aged 38) felt regret for not treating her mother better before death:

> "I have not done enough as a daughter. I should have quit my job so that I could devote myself to looking after my mother during her last years. I should not lose my temper nor disobey her ... I am still single, and my mother was just like my partner who gives me emotional support, guidance, love and care ... "

It is a natural expectation that the parents precede their children in death. It is therefore anticipated that the death of parents should be the most readily accepted form of bereavement in adult life. Nevertheless, some adults find it difficult to deal with the loss of their parents, and others often neglect their grief. According to Confucian teachings on filial piety, it is the adult children's obligation to take care of their parents as a kind of repayment to them. Regret and guilt are common, as they find that they should have done more for their deceased parents. Some of them may still perceive the death of their elderly parents as unexpected and untimely when they believe that they have not done enough. Adults who remain single in middle age may often report greater difficulty in adaptation. They tend to be heavily interdependent with the parents in all aspects of life, particularly emotional support. The unclear boundary between self and others in the Chinese family may result in enmeshment between parents and children. The death would then involve the loss of a close relationship full of shared experiences. They need to deal with a number of issues relating to self and independence in addition to their adaptation to grief.

1. Acknowledge their grief, especially when it is often overlooked.
2. Encourage them to meet with those who have shared a similar experience.
3. Acknowledge the sense of guilt and regret as a reflection of their love for the parents.
4. Review the relationship objectively and help them to identify the good things that they have done for their parents.
5. Help them to accept guilt and regret as part of life, which may not be totally eliminated but may be transformed to other positive motivations in life.
6. Foster a sense of spiritual connection with parents through continuing in action their parents' teaching, advice or traditions.
7. Help them to establish a new sense of identity.

Elderly people

Mr D (aged 76) found his children did not understand his grief for his wife:

> "My children said that their mother has already lived her life, and I should be more accepting. They told me to be more active in the elderly centre and try not to think that much about her ... But how can I possibly do so? We were married for 55 years. I have spent half a century with my wife. How can I not remember her?"

A unique feature has been observed in people's responses to elderly bereavement: people tend to react from two extremes.[26] On one hand, people may assume that death should be expected in old age. This results in the belief that death should be well accepted in old age and may lead to an underestimation of their grief or under-reaction to their situation. On the other hand, people also tend to overreact to elderly bereavement by "infantalizing" elderly people, who are treated as vulnerable and incompetent. This may result in an overreaction to the situation and the elderly people are over-protected. These over-generalizing assumptions prevent people from understanding and responding to the real needs of bereaved elderly people.

The long-term relationship with the deceased and the many past memories mean that elderly people may need a longer time to grieve and adapt. The death of significant others may also trigger elderly people's grief over other losses in their life. The life of retirement and an "empty nest" imply the significant role of the spouse for interdependence in old age, and hence the death of the spouse might lead to a drastic change in everyday activities. Confrontation with one's own death and the deterioration of health may further complicate their adaptation to life without the spouse. Without a concrete and hopeful prospect of the future, bereaved elderly people have more difficulty moving on with life. All these conditions might contribute to a sense of meaninglessness in regard to their developmental task of achieving ego-integrity.

1. Do not make assumptions but try to understand individual needs.
2. Respect their choice to be involved in funeral and rituals, instead of trying to over-protect them or neglect their need to acknowledge the death.
3. Use different ways (symbolic means, artwork, reminiscence) to facilitate expression of feelings if they are not used to direct confrontation with emotions.
4. Make use of their own religious or traditional Chinese beliefs in the process of making meaning of the grief experience.
5. Enhance the social network and get community support (like home helpers and volunteers) to help their resumption of life without a spouse.
6. Resume daily routine activities at their pace.
7. Help them establish their own way of living instead of making assumptions and plans for them.
8. Allow time, follow their pace and provide continuous support.
9. Review life with them through storytelling and other activities of reminiscence to facilitate integration and making meaning of life.
10. Understand their perception and attitude toward death, and support them in making psychological and practical preparations for their future life and death.
11. Arrange joint interviews with other family members to stimulate mutual support and understanding.

Parents losing children

Mrs E (aged 56) thought it was impossible to accept the death of her 25-year-old son:

> "How can that happen to my son? I keep on asking God 'why'. I should die first, not my son, he is only 25 ... I really wanted to see my son once more at the funeral, but my relatives did not allow it. They said that 'the white-haired should not say farewell to the black-haired (白頭人不送黑頭人)' ... I

am also angry with my husband. How can he be so cruel and calm? I never saw him shed a single tear. "

The loss of children often leads to intense and long-lasting grief, irrespective of the child's age. The unique and lifelong nature of parent-child relationships contributes to the uniqueness of the loss of a child. Children are perceived as both the psychological and biological extension of parents. The death of a child hence further induces a series of secondary losses in addition to the physical loss. Examples include the loss of self projected onto the deceased children, loss of hope and loss of future carer in old age. The loss is even more drastic for Chinese when the deceased is the only son in the family. This implies further loss of cessation of the generation and the absence of a male child at the death of parents (無仔送終), both of which are of great importance in traditional Chinese families. The death also violates the lifelong role of parents as protectors and nurturers, resulting in intense feelings of guilt. The law of nature that the old should die before the young is violated by the death, resulting in a breakdown of the assumptive world and a strong need for an explanation of the cause of death. It is common to turn to premonitions, omens or, in the local Chinese context, some traditional superstitions in order to explain the death. The death may even affect the relationship between parents if they misunderstand the gender difference in the pattern of grieving.

1. Respect the parents' choice to be involved in the funeral and other rituals.
2. Allow time, facilitate a review of the facts and interpretations of the cause of death.
3. Facilitate expression of grief in appropriate amounts in regard to their intense emotions.
4. Support them in grieving over secondary losses at a gradual and manageable pace.
5. Address guilt and help them to understand guilt as the shadow of the endless love for their children.
6. Facilitate exploration and revision of the assumptive world by their own spiritual and religious beliefs.
7. Support them in continuing their parental roles through spiritual and self-enhancing ways as a continuing bond with the deceased.
8. Help clients to reinvest in life in the light of their parental roles and their continuing bond with their children.
9. Enhance mutual understanding among individual family members regarding their different grieving and coping patterns, and facilitate reorganization of roles.

Conclusion

Our Chinese culture has shaped our bereavement experience according to the social expectations and values placed on different roles or duties in the family. When adopting the Western models in supporting mourners in the local Chinese context, it is important to be aware of the influence of Chinese culture on the grief process and make necessary modifications in the intervention accordingly. The essence is to be culturally sensitive and maintain a balance between the two cultures, especially in the context of Hong Kong, where East meets West. In this way, the Chinese culture is not a compromise made in adopting Western counselling models. In fact, it provides a rich source of data that are very helpful in understanding and engaging with our clients, making meaning of the bereavement experience as well as establishing therapeutic rituals.

20

The Use of Structured Therapeutic Bereavement Groups

Agnes Fong TIN, Elaine Wai Kwan KOO and Sze-man LEE

Introduction

The Jessie and Thomas Tam Centre of the Society for the Promotion of Hospice Care, the first community-based bereavement counselling centre in Hong Kong, established in 1997, has adopted group work as one of the main intervention modalities in supporting bereaved clients. By understanding the conceptual framework of bereavement groups, as well as the grief process from an interpersonal and cultural perspective, this chapter discusses the working mechanism and the implementation of the bereavement group in helping bereaved people through their bereavement experiences. Group work has been found to be an important and effective modality in bereavement counselling. A structured bereavement group is a helpful means to guide bereaved people through the grief process and facilitate personal growth.

Therapeutic Effect of Bereavement Groups

Of the bereaved clients that we have served in the past seven years, about one-third have received group counselling. Table 1 shows the statistics on the number and nature of the groups that we have run. In order to assess the grief reactions of the group members both before and after the group, a twenty-one-item self-reported inventory called Grief Reaction Assessment Form (GRAF) was used. GRAF is a local assessment tool of grief reactions developed by Chan and Chow.[1] Members are asked to rate their grief reactions according to an eleven-point scale (0 = none, 1 = 10% ... 10 = 100%) both before and after the group, for comparison. Table 2 to Table 8 show the results of the pre- and post-score, which demonstrates significant improvement in many aspects of the members' reactions to grief.

Table 1
Statistics on Bereavement Groups

Item	Number
Total number of cases served	1643
Clients who have received group counselling	568
Total number of groups being run	57 (396 sessions)
Groups for widows	32 (224 sessions)
Groups for bereaved elderly people	7 (49 sessions)
Groups for bereaved adult children	6 (36 sessions)
Groups for widowers	5 (30 sessions)
Groups for bereaved children	5 (30 sessions)
Groups for bereaved parents*	2 (27 sessions)

*An open group format is used for bereaved parents' groups.

Table 2
Impact of Bereavement Group: Feelings

ITEM	Pre-group Score	Post-group Score	Number	t	Sig.
Anger**	4.0307	3.1963	163	3.684	0.000
Sadness**	7.5689	4.6886	167	11.894	0.000
Depression**	5.2050	3.0932	161	8.329	0.000
Loneliness**	7.1024	5.0000	166	7.869	0.000
Fear*	4.0848	3.2061	165	3.134	0.002

** p < 0.001   * p < 0.01

Table 3
Impact of Bereavement Group: Physical Sensations

ITEM	Pre-group Score	Post-group Score	Number	t	Sig.
Headache**	3.6905	2.6786	168	4.104	0.000
Chest pain**	4.000	2.6380	163	4.949	0.000
Fatigue**	5.1796	3.7784	167	5.280	0.000
Numbness	2.7305	2.5210	167	0.779	0.437
Back Pain	4.5939	4.3273	165	0.952	0.342

** p < 0.001

Table 4
Impact of Bereavement Group: Cognition

ITEM	Pre-group Score	Post-group Score	Number	t	Sig.
Missing the deceased**	8.8727	7.5152	165	6.546	0.000
Mental dullness**	5.3675	3.4217	166	8.116	0.000

** p < 0.001

Table 5
Impact of Bereavement Group: Behaviours

ITEM	Pre-group Score	Post-group Score	Number	t	Sig.
Nightmares	2.0854	1.7317	164	1.481	0.140
Loss of appetite**	3.8537	2.2195	164	6.642	0.000
Talking less**	4.8788	3.1939	165	5.772	0.000
Avoidance**	5.8810	4.6310	168	4.267	0.000

** p < 0.001

Table 6
Impact of Bereavement Group: Memories

ITEM	Pre-group Score	Post-group Score	Number	t	Sig.
Stay calm with memory	4.3537	4.7622	164	-1.314	0.191
Select happy memory*	4.7500	5.3688	160	-2.179	0.031

* p < 0.05

Table 7
Impact of Bereavement Group: Coping

ITEM	Pre-group Score	Post-group Score	Number	t	Sig.
Problem-solving	5.2654	5.6173	162	-1.572	0.118
Adaptation *	5.2750	5.8563	160	-2.728	0.007

* p < 0.01

Table 8
Impact of Bereavement Group: Overall Distress

ITEM	Pre-group Score	Post-group Score	Number	t	Sig.
Overall distress**	8.1173	6.6235	162	7.443	0.000

** p< 0.001

The use of Group Work in Bereavement Counselling

Grief is a response to the death of our significant other. It is normal and natural. Grief, as the reflection of love for the deceased, can be understood as a lifelong process, but the effect of grief on the individual is different or diminishes over time. People have their own unique grief experience and pace. As supporters of the bereaved, we cannot expect to remove or erase grief, but we can try to help and support the bereaved in accommodating it or adapting to it. Some bereaved people may even experience personal growth in going through their journey of grief.[2] It is therefore the task of the counsellor to help and support the bereaved to go through this grief process.[3]

Our selfhood is made up of reflected appraisals from others. Through interacting with people, we keep on learning about ourselves and modifying our selfhood through consensual validation from others. This idea of selfhood developed from an interpersonal framework forms an important foundation for the use of group work.[4] In fact, this "interdependent self" is a dominant feature among Chinese populations compared with the "independent self" in Western culture.[5] The experience of the bereaved can then be better understood by applying this interpersonal perspective. People do not grieve in a vacuum but in context. Our way of grieving may be adapted through interacting in interpersonal relationships, the social environment and our culture. This can be illustrated by the ancient Chinese word for "death" (死), which graphically shows not only the status of the deceased but also the grieving reaction of the bereaved.[6] It demonstrates that, from the Chinese perspective, death is understood as interpersonal. This interpersonal perspective of the bereavement experience in the Chinese culture perfectly matches the framework of group work. This explains why group work is uniquely effective in bereavement counselling, by making use of the influence of interpersonal interactions on an individual's bereavement experience and helping the bereaved to overcome any related obstacles through the grief process.

Understanding the Grief Experience of the Chinese from the Cultural and Interpersonal Perspectives

By adopting the group work approach, one has to first translate grief into interpersonal terms. When exploring the context of the grief experience in the Chinese population, it is observed that the traditional Chinese culture still has an important influence on people's grief. Death remains a taboo subject in the Chinese community. One should not say the word "death" because it would bring bad luck. A bereaved person, being in proximity to death, is better kept at a distance. Due to the avoidance of death by others, the bereaved often find they are not welcome or understood. This not only weakens their social support network, but they may also experience a sense of stigmatization or even victimization, resulting in further isolation and loneliness.

Chinese culture emphasizes relationships rather than self as such. The selfhood of any individual is often defined through interpersonal relationships and roles in relation to others. Each family member has a socially defined role and obligation in the family, according to the relationships. For example, a husband's duty is to work and earn a living, whereas a wife's duty is to stay at home and take care of the house. When the death of a significant other occurs, there is a drastic change in the relationships and performance of roles. Self-identity that has long been established as an identity of "WE" is shattered. The bereaved may also have difficulty readjusting when certain family roles and obligations that used to be performed by the deceased are now missing. Together with the stigmatizing experience of bereavement, a decline in self-esteem is common for the bereaved.

In dealing with emotions, the Chinese are expected to suppress rather than express their feelings. So, very often, the bereaved may indirectly communicate their feelings through references to interpersonal relationships or somatic complaints. The most common expression of sympathy for the Chinese when meeting a bereaved person are to encourage the bereaved to stop grieving and adjust to the change (節哀順變). This social expectation is in fact contradictory to the normal process of grieving. Meeting this expectation would enforce a state of incongruence on the bereaved, resulting in further emotional isolation.

Design of the Group

By understanding the familiar complications and obstacles in the grief process of the Chinese, the ultimate goal of bereavement counselling is to untangle these complications and clear these obstacles, to help the bereaved to go through the natural process.[3] Using group work as the intervention model is to take the interpersonal perspective in accomplishing this task. The objectives therefore include a) promoting a sense of normalization, b) facilitating expression of feelings, c) enhancing social support, and d) facilitating development of selfhood.

Our bereavement group is structured and time-limited, having six or seven sessions in total. We have implemented a homogenous group format in which clients of different ages and relationships to the deceased would form different groups. Examples of grouping include groups for widows, widowers, elderly people, children, adult children and parents. This homogenous grouping is important in ensuring a sense of commonality and universality in the group.

We cannot solely rely on the Western model in our work without considering the unique characteristics of our Chinese culture. One of the prominent examples is the difficulty of the Chinese to fully acknowledge an independent selfhood, a relatively alien idea to our culture. So, when providing counselling, the development of a new sense of self and reinvestment in life have to be facilitated in the light of the relationships with the deceased as well as with other family members. Traditional Chinese rituals and beliefs related to life after death also provide a very rich source for making meaning of the grief experience. A creative synergy of techniques from Western group work models taking into account elements of Chinese modes of emotional and cultural expression is necessary in our local context where East meets West.

Screening, Assessment and Follow-up

Pre-group interviews with potential group members are carried out before the group sessions, for assessment. These interviews are also important in helping the group leaders to understand the expectation of the members as well as to prepare and motivate the members for the group experience. Another significant function of the pre-group interviews is to screen for suitable candidates who can benefit most from the group. Candidates who have extreme grief reactions, unique grief experiences, mental illness and severe suicidal tendencies are not suitable for participating in groups. The group works best for those who are experiencing common obstacles in the grief process, as mentioned, and have already gone through the crisis or acute phase of bereavement. Group work cannot replace individual work. Individual counselling would be more appropriate for extreme or unique cases, or ones that need special attention.

After completing the group sessions, the members are invited to a post-group interview. The group leaders would evaluate the influence of the group on the members and assess the need for any further individual counselling. If no further follow-up service is needed, the members would be invited to join a mutual help group for the bereaved. In view of the relatively long-term need of the bereaved for readjustment, this mutual help group serves the purpose of providing continuous support from peers when specific professional intervention is less necessary. It aims at maintaining social support, facilitating resumption of life and empowering the members to transform from service recipients to peer supporters.

Group Process

The well-known therapeutic factors for group work, as proposed by Yalom,[4] include instillation of hope, universality, imparting information, altruism, corrective recapitulation of the primary family group, development of socializing techniques, imitative behaviour, interpersonal learning, group cohesiveness, catharsis and existential factors. These factors serve as the important framework by which the obstacles in the grief process as mentioned above can be cleared through the group process.

Recognize the loss

> "People just avoid talking about the death as if nothing has happened. I understand that it is out of their good intention to protect me from sadness. But they don't understand that it is my need to talk and express myself. I find a strong urge to tell others what has happened to me. Every time I am telling the facts, I realize that I am in fact telling and reminding myself about the reality of death. I think I am learning to accept the death through this process, a process of repeatedly exposing myself to, re-experiencing and retelling the reality ..." (Mrs A, aged 40, whose husband died in a traffic accident)

The group structure and content are designed in accordance with the process of grief. At the beginning of the process, the bereaved has to recognize the loss. This requires the death be acknowledged, confirmed and understood. Verbal discussion of the death and behavioural rituals like attending the funeral are the usual and normal ways for bereaved persons to go through this process more smoothly. However, as death is taboo and a stigma among Chinese, people often avoid the topic. The bereaved have learnt not to openly acknowledge their experience, due to the lack of validation from others.

In a bereavement group, the factor of universality acts as an important element in helping the members to legitimize their grief and realize that they are not alone. This sense of togetherness and being in the same situation breaks the taboo and weakens the stigma, so that the group can now act as an open and safe platform for members to share and acknowledge their bereavement experience.

React to loss, memorize and transform the relationships

> "People always try to comfort me and tell me not to cry. I have now learnt to suppress my emotions in front of others and cry only when I am alone when I take a bath. But my emotions fluctuate so much and the memory becomes so overwhelming that I think I am going crazy. It is very helpful and assuring to find that I am not the only one who has all these reactions. I now understand that I am normal and okay. I feel relieved by being able to express myself and cry freely with those who understand my pain." (Mrs B, aged 50, whose husband died of cancer)

When reacting to the loss, the bereaved would have to experience, identify and express their emotions. They would also remember the deceased and gradually transform the relationship with a sense of permanence and continuity. Although the deceased is physically absent, the bereaved would feel that they are still spiritually or emotionally connected. However, the lack of understanding, the expectation from others that they should control their emotions as well as the suppression of feeling as the usual coping pattern of Chinese discourage the bereaved from freely and normally expressing their emotions. The social expectation that the bereaved should stop grieving and let go in order to move on with life also hinders development of a healthy continuing bond with the deceased.

In the group, giving information about normal grief reactions help the members to justify and validate their feelings, so that they may feel "normal" with the expression of complex and unfamiliar emotions. The factors of universality and group cohesiveness promote a safe, trusting and understanding environment. The members would then feel comfortable enough to express their emotions and share their memories. Different means like art, writing, visual, psychosomatic or symbolic means are used in order to facilitate the communication of feelings in the group. Members are also encouraged to use letter writing and sharing of photos to go over their memories of the deceased. This open sharing of memories and love implicitly acknowledges the members' need to connect with the deceased, so that they can be helped in the group to find their own adaptive way for connection.

Readjust adaptively and reinvest in life

> "The greatest thing I've learned from the group is about 'courage'. Being a widow now, I find that I have to learn everything all over again: how to face others, how to tell my story and my feelings, how to interact with people and be myself etc. ... I have found that I am rebuilding my courage through this group process." (Mrs C, aged 34, whose husband died of cancer)
>
> "In the previous session, I saw Mrs X wearing a pair of earrings. She looked so nice with them. I suddenly realized that I have forgotten about myself for so long. So today, I am wearing my earrings as well. I think it's time that I should also look after myself ..." (Mrs D, aged 31, whose husband died of a heart attack)

At the later phase of the grief process, the bereaved would have to adjust to their lives and invest energy in other aspects of life. However, the death of the significant other may result in loss of self-esteem and diminished sense of self. Together with inadequate reassurance and validation from others, the adjustment process can be difficult.

In the group, the message of "I am neither alone nor the worst" is clearly delivered to the members by the mere presence of other members who have a similar experience. This message forms a good foundation for the members to re-establish their self-image and esteem. Through the interactions and comments given by people in the group, the members experience interpersonal learning. They have the chance to continue reflecting on and revising their understanding of self through the group process. Understanding and appreciation from one another in the group helps the members to relearn about themselves as individuals, not only in their role as spouse. Altruism is another important therapeutic factor, particularly for the Chinese, due to their emphasis on relationships. Members find themselves being comforted or assured through actively comforting and assuring others. This reciprocal process allows the members to slowly experience the change of identity from a victim of death to a helper for others. In order to learn to survive in their own environment in the absence of the deceased, the members need to develop new socializing techniques in accordance with the reality of death, any differences in the relationships with others and the newly developing sense of self. The group then provides a safe and understanding environment to practise these new social skills. Existential factors are also very significant for group members, all of whom have experienced the death of a loved one. This experience of death would definitely call for the search for meaning in life as against the meaninglessness that they are experiencing. Through sharing with members who are all experiencing the same existential conflicts in life, they are searching together in the group for their own meaning and answers to these existential questions. Last but not least, the instillation of hope by the sharing of the ex-clients being invited to the group, as well as the imitative behaviours through observing the improvements made by other individual members in the group process are catalysts for the members to move toward the restoration of a happy life. Through the work of these therapeutic factors, the group dynamics can then become a helpful means to enhance self-awareness and development of a new sense of self. This readjustment of selfhood can further facilitate the readjustment in other aspects of life.

Use of rituals

"The ritual is very insightful to me. I could really imagine that my husband was receiving my message when I saw the balloon flying into the sky until it disappeared. He will know how hard I have tried to survive without him and I can feel his support. The experience of releasing the balloon is such a relief to me. Somehow I realize that I have to let go of something in the past in order to move on, but I understand that my husband's love and support are always there for me." (Mrs E, aged 49, whose husband died of cancer, performed the ritual of releasing a balloon with a written letter/message from the bereaved to the deceased.)

"I felt peaceful and relieved when I saw the fish swimming away, as if it was really bringing my blessing to my wife. The fish seemed to be so enjoying being free in the water ... maybe I should also start my own life and try to enjoy it." (Mr F, aged 67, whose wife died of chronic illness. The bereaved talk to the fish aloud before it is set free. This is a ritual for those who are illiterate. This act of setting fish free is also an act of virtue in the Chinese culture.)

Rituals can provide powerful therapeutic experiences by acting as the means through which the thoughts and emotions of the members can be expressed and made concrete. Different ending rituals are often used in the groups to legitimize the continuous connection with the deceased and at the same time symbolize a reinvestment in life. Examples of rituals include flying a kite and releasing balloons for children or adults, and the traditional Chinese ritual of setting free the fish for elderly people. The learning gained through the group experience, which is often abstract, can be effectively made real and concrete by performing these rituals.

Process of Change

"People can never imagine my grief. They always wonder why I am grieving so much over the death of my mother, as they think it is such a natural process for old people to die. Their responses make me feel that my emotions are problematic and I am a problem …The feeling of being understood and accepted in the group is something that I cannot experience elsewhere. Their acceptance helps me to accept my emotions and myself more." (Miss G, aged 41, whose mother died of chronic illness)

"I can express my grief here. As a man, I can never tell others how sad I am or how much I miss my wife. Being with other widowers here, I don't need to pretend to be strong. I don't need to worry about how others would look at me when I cry. I feel more at ease in expressing my feelings." (Mr H, aged 38, whose wife committed suicide)

"The sense of togetherness gives me strength and energy to move forward. The death of my husband has made me feel totally lost, as if I have changed into a different person who is depressed, pessimistic, and lacks confidence … Through crying, laughing and interacting with other group members, I am able to gradually re-experience and find mySELF again …" (Mrs I, aged 30, whose husband died of cancer)

Through the way the therapeutic factors work in the group process, the members are helped to experience a process of change. At the time their connections with the deceased, the most significant relationship in life, are abruptly cut off by death, the bereaved are confronted by extensive loneliness and isolation. Through the group process, they can again experience a sense of connectedness with others, which acts as an important starting point from which the bereaved can learn to gradually restore their social life. From their usual pattern of suppression, the trustful and understanding group environment can provide bereaved members with assurance and confirmation that they can freely express their feelings and thoughts. Through interpersonal learning in the group, the old and shattered identity of "WE" that has been long established through the relationship with the deceased can also move to the development of a new sense of "I". There is a further validation from the group that the members can continue to maintain a bond with the deceased while going on with their adaptive life.

Conclusion

Death is an inevitable part of life. However, people may overcome their passive role as victims of bereavement and go on to active and meaningful lives. Losing our loved ones is an experience of pain and sadness, but it can also be a journey of personal learning and growth. As supporters of the bereaved, we try to be with and support them through this painful but also insightful process. A structured and time-limited bereavement group " … provided the members with the number of structured exercises that were to assist members in experiencing important elements in the bereavement process".[7] A structured bereavement group is like a guided tour through this journey of grief and personal growth. In addition to facilitating emotional catharsis, self-understanding, learning, growth and existential exploration become more important in this process. The group leaders, the tour guides in this journey, are then responsible for identifying these important checkpoints in the natural grief process and going together with the clients. The completion of the group does not mean the end of grief. The group only serves to support the bereaved in going through the most difficult time of grief and preparing them for the way ahead. The members continue to experience grief and learn to adjust to life, but they would be equipped with better self-understanding, social support, a sense of mastery, coping skills and confidence.

21

The Use of Volunteers in Bereavement Care

Eddie Ho Chuen CHAN

Introduction

Volunteer participation is widely developed in many sectors in Hong Kong. To volunteer is to give service willingly of one's own accord. Volunteers give their time, skills, thoughts and talents to contribute to the community, without any monetary reward. Volunteering is probably a feature of an affluent society, but it is also a mark of a society in which the people are lucky and want to give some of that luck by doing things for those who are less fortunate. Volunteers form an integral and enriching part of hospice palliative care all over the world.[1] Is this also the main reason why volunteers are involved in hospice palliative care? Larson[2] revealed in his survey of hospice volunteers that the following motivations are most frequently cited: "Because I enjoy helping other people", "Because of my values, convictions, and beliefs", "Because I consider myself to be a loving and caring person", "To learn how to help people who are terminally ill or dying", and "To help members of my community". Payne's study[3] reported similar reasons for becoming a hospice palliative care volunteer.

The Comfort Care Concern Group (CCCG, 贐明會) is a volunteer-oriented organization providing services for the bereaved and terminally ill. This chapter describes the involvement of volunteers in Hong Kong hospice palliative care, by sharing my practical wisdom.

Volunteering in Hospice Palliative Care in Hong Kong

Not much is documented about volunteer work in hospice palliative care. Chung[4] stated that voluntary work is closely related to the professional team providing care for patients and their families at the beginning of the hospice movement in Hong Kong in the 1980s. By donating their effort and concern, volunteers help ensure the smooth functioning of a hospice programme, both in the administrative area and in helping directly with the patients, families and significant others. By being directly involved in the programme, volunteers enhance community connections and encourage community awareness. By reviewing local hospice units and organizations, volunteers serve in the following four major categories of services:

1. Administrative support
2. Direct contact with patients or families (in wards)
3. Bereavement care volunteer
4. Member of the governing board of directors.

Bereavement Care Offered by CCCG

CCCG delivers comfort care services to people facing death and bereavement, via participation by volunteers, which is the major feature.

Volunteer training	Six-session training courses, one and a half hours per session. Content covers terminally ill and bereavement in physical, psychological and social perspectives, resources for the clients, techniques and skills in visitation. Those passing the interview as registered volunteers in CCCG can join any visitation group.
Befriending visitation Teams	CCCG provides befriending visitation for six hospice wards in six hospitals with thirteen volunteer teams. Home visit is by referral.
Individual and group grief counselling	Individual bereavement counselling and structured group counselling is given by social workers. Bereaved volunteers joining the group can facilitate the group process.
Funeral support	The bereaved are accompanied by volunteers for the following services: (a) confirmation of a funeral rite and date, (b) death registry, (c) body identification, (d) procedure for cremation, (e) participation in the funeral ritual, and (f) installation of the niche.
Phone consultation service	People call in to ask for information and advice from volunteers or social workers.
Widow-to-widow service (bereaved volunteer)	A group of volunteers receive proper professional counselling and screening and must be emotionally and psychologically ready to share their experiences with newly bereaved persons.
Community education	CCCG has a mission to promote to the public the proper attitude towards death, loss and grief. Volunteers periodically assist in promotional exhibitions, workshops and talks.

Recruitment, Training and Supervision

Recruitment

Various methods may be used for the recruitment of volunteers. The study by Payne[3] revealed that recommendation by word-of-mouth is invariably one of the best options. Roughly, at least one-fourth of volunteers are recommended by friends to join the course. Publicity in local newspapers, churches and other social organizations are regarded as fruitful avenues for recruitment. As Payne's[3] results show, volunteers from counselling or social work students are unreliable in committing their time. Even after training and practical experience, they still treat themselves as interns. Thus, they may not be motivated enough to be volunteers.

Doyle[5] claimed that poor selection of volunteers can lead to disruption, conflicts and harm to individuals and the organization. Hence, selection of the "right" volunteers is crucial. How important it is for time and care to be given to the selection procedure cannot be sufficiently stressed. What qualities might one be looking for in that "right" person? Being a hospice palliative care volunteer is a highly emotional job. The most important feature is personality — having maturity and sensitivity, being caring and empathic, together with patience, understanding and a sense of humour. There are various forms of selection for screening the applicants, e.g., an interview before or after certain training sessions, a completed application form prior to the interview, etc. In CCCG, all are welcome to the training session, but full attendance and a minimum age of twenty-one are the basic requirements of the interview.

Training

Training for those who want to be hospice palliative care volunteers is of vital importance. For volunteers embarking on becoming hospice palliative care workers, special training courses are needed. Basic training programmes include understanding the values and philosophy of hospice palliative care, emotional and psychological issues of death and dying, understanding and knowledge of the normal process of grief, techniques and skills in practice, and volunteering in the hospice palliative care-community approach. Theses programmes are run by internal staff or with the help of appropriate professionals from multidisciplinary teams. Adequate training of volunteers is essential. Volunteer training does not stop after the completion of basic training. Volunteers may experience various reactions and feelings of inadequacy. Therefore, the organization has to hold periodic meetings for sharing. Programmes also provide ongoing in-service training and education, which include hospice updates, skills training and working with difficult families or individuals, etc.

Successful interviewees will be registered volunteers in CCCG. A probationary period of six months of work on site, with the assistance of a mentor or supporter, is also valuable in giving further opportunity for volunteers to know if this work is right for them.

Supervision

Understanding volunteer help is extraordinarily demanding and does not always unfold naturally. Given deeply rewarding and supportive programmes, a commitment to caring has a cost — the flame of caring can flicker or go out. Supervising the volunteers in caring can inspire great acts of caring and lead to self-fulfillment. However, a bright flame is by virtue more easily extinguished. Comprehensive supervision must include individual supervision, case supervision and clinical supervision.[6] Volunteers have to attend mutual support meetings once every two months, and ongoing periodic in-service training sessions. Volunteers are also asked to attend appropriate team meetings.

Individual Supervision	The volunteer service coordinator (VSC) should be available and approachable for volunteers who suffer crises in their service as well as their lives, and support them.[5] In addition, the VSC should pay attention to the volunteer who has a bereavement history. In the experience, the reason why a volunteer feels sad after the first visit in the hospice palliative care unit comes from being in the environment where the loved one died.
Case Supervision	Case supervision in person or by phone is routine in following up on cases with volunteers. In CCCG, each case (bereaved or terminally ill) has two volunteers, to ensure mutual support in handling cases. Case supervision is a matter that is not dealt with while difficulties are emerging.
Clinical Supervision	To enhance the techniques that volunteers use, a social worker arranges visits accompanied by volunteers, to demonstrate case handling. At the same time, a social worker will observe the volunteers in the way they handle the visit. A

debriefing session is required after each clinical supervision; this is the best opportunity to evaluate the skills of the volunteers and appraise matters stimulated by the case. The use of clinical supervision is the most fruitful review of work for the volunteer as well as the social worker. However, it is the most expensive service for the volunteer, as it is very time-consuming.

Uniqueness of Services in CCCG

Bereaved volunteer service

Doyle[5] argued that help for the bereaved should be deeply rooted in the culture and community where bereavement is experienced. Volunteers are drawn from people from all walks of life with different experiences. "The widespread involvement of volunteers underlines the concept that grief is natural. Volunteers are ordinary people and carry none of the stigma attached to mental health services, counselling or therapy."[7]

In CCCG practice, bereaved volunteers come mainly from structured group counselling. A few come from the basic volunteer training courses. Chow[8] pointed out that clients from structured group bereavement counselling who shift their role from that of helpless recipient to volunteer can show transformation and growth. A bereaved volunteer meets with a newly bereaved client at our centre, upon request, and then arrangements are made by a social worker (because we encourage the bereaved person to reach out. Those in need are served by outreach services). Interviews, visits, phone calls, cards and letters will provide emotional support to those at the newly bereaved stage.

The requirement of a bereaved volunteer is to pass an individual assessment and show readiness to support the newly bereaved. Studies have shown that those who have the support of other widowed persons are better able to adjust to widowhood.[9] In this connection, the more bereaved people relate the experience of loss with a bereaved volunteer, the more they learn each time. Thus, bereaved volunteer work is also a part of the healing process for the bereaved volunteers.

Volunteer funeral support

Volunteer funeral support (VFS) service is a culturally sensitive service. It is a difficult job for volunteers to do, unless they have adequate support. Not everyone responds in the same way to tragedy, to the fear or prospect of death, and to bereavement itself. Some of these differences result from customs, and some seem to originate in traditional patterns of behaviour. Loss of a loved one can affect the physical, mental, social and psychological well-being of individuals.[10,11] However, the bereaved has to deal with the funeral within a short time.[8] In the following paragraphs, I share some cases helped by this service. Most are under the CSSA (Comprehensive Social Security Assistance) funeral grant (Only dead CSSA receiver will have funeral subsidy entitlement). In this context, the illustrated cases are not commonly found in general funeral cases.

In the Chinese society, white is the main colour tone of a funeral. In Chinese culture, white represents being colourless, unpleasant and without joyful, and it is called a "white event" (白事). It is perceived as associated with "bad luck" (associated with ghosts and death). In traditional Chinese society, a family placed white lanterns in front of the main entrance of the house to signify the death a family member. Nowadays, people do not do this because of limited space. Now, only a few places allow people to set candles at the entrance. Most people only realize a funeral is going to take place if the family reveals the event.

People do not like to tell others about a funeral in the family. Several reasons account for this attitude: (1) don't waste others' time; (2) don't waste others' money (in Chinese culture, people give "sympathy money" [帛金, 又 稱賻儀] to support the survivors after the funeral); (3) bad luck will pass to others; (4) Some widows were from China and had been in Hong Kong for less than a year, they had inadequate social support. With above understanding, people feel inappropriate and embarrassed to ask relatives/friends for support. They prefer seeking advice from the ones who do not know their background information but care about their sufferings; therefore, the bereaved feel free to chat with the volunteers about his/her loss.

> Mrs K's (36/F) husband died of lung cancer. She has three children aged eight, ten and twelve. Kifa and PM (the volunteers) were assigned to this family. "Without the help of volunteers, I think I couldn't have done it on my own ... .I'd never been to a funeral in Hong Kong.....They directed me step-by-step through the procedures," Mrs K said. Kifa recalled, "I'll never forget Mrs K fainting during the process of body identification because she cried so much. Then, we took her to the emergency room for medication".

In Hong Kong, most people ask for help from the funeral home, to reduce anxiety in handling complicated procedures and unfamiliar customs. However, most services are performed by a few funeral homes. Thus, not all bereaved persons can afford the expense. In addition, we help the bereaved steadily deal with their emotions during the process of handling the funeral. Thus, we believe that it is a healing process for the bereaved if they participate in the funeral process.

Madam Y's (63/F) husband died. She has no children. "She looked thin at the first meeting with her in the centre," said Tracy (the volunteer). "She felt alone in the funeral ritual held for her husband. We stayed with her in the funeral home and accompanied her to the cremation centre...I think we have showed our support. Madam Y delivered fruit and cakes to us after the funeral. I am sure our volunteers and staff will agree that these 'rewards' cannot be described in words.

All these factors, especially the cultural responses to the funeral, hinder bereavement care. Thus, CCCG set up a team of VFS to assist the bereaved tangibly by staying with them and providing an emotional outlet in the process of handling the funeral. The volunteers accompany the bereaved for: (a) confirmation of a funeral service and date, (b) death certificate, (c) body identification, (d) procedures for cremation, (e) participation for the funeral ritual, and (f) the installation of the niche. The following elaborates on these services.

This following explanation is based on the handling of a funeral and some wisdom that helped the bereaved handle the funeral alone.

1.   Confirmation of a funeral and date

Most people do not know how to start a funeral, but experience tells us that the first thing is to collect the death certificate issued by the hospital. Then a volunteer will accompany the bereaved to a funeral home to plan the funeral and prepare an estimation of the cost. Confirmation will be made the next day.

2.   Death registry

Before booking the date for cremation, the bereaved has to go to the death registry. To book the time of cremation, a true copy of the death certificate is required.

3.   Procedure for cremation

The date of the cremation is crucial. The date of burial depends on this date. The applicant books an unallocated normal session within fifteen calendar days from the day after the date of application. Once the booking is complete and a time is available, the bereaved can return to the funeral home to confirm and agree to the date, the cost and the format of the funeral.

4.   Identifying the body

The bereaved has to identify the body. Most of our bereaved clients have few relatives to support them in doing this, so the volunteers accompany the person during this procedure. Viewing a dead body is a very uncomfortable experience, even if the deceased is a loved one. The volunteers will stay behind to help the bereaved express their emotions and feelings. Noticeable concerns should be dealt with during this process. Therefore, an in-depth briefing before identifying the body should be made for the volunteers and the bereaved. The briefing should include noting that there will be a significant change of appearance, skin colour and smell because of refrigeration. Psychological preparation is also necessary. Afterwards, a debriefing session is necessary.

5. Participation in the funeral ritual

This item is especially necessary for people who do not have much family support. The presence of volunteers ensures a sense of security and reduces loneliness.

6. Installation of the niche

In general, this is the last step of a funeral process. Then, the volunteers direct the bereaved to the venue of the niche.

At the start of the VFS service, funeral cases were mainly referred from hospice palliative care units. In the past two years, in addition to terminally ill cases, sudden death cases have been referred to us.

More recently, elderly people or terminally ill patients have approached us to prepare their funeral before they die. This is an unusual social phenomenon in my practical experience. These people are not afraid of death, but they are afraid that no one will handle their funeral after death.

> Mr K (70/M) was terminally ill with liver cancer. We met him in the hospice palliative care unit. "I am worried that no one will take care of my body after death but will leave me alone … .I don't want my ashes in Sha Tau Kok," he said. (Sha Tau Kok is a public area for the ashes of unidentified people.)

This is a typical idea of a traditional Chinese person viewing the world after death by the experience of living life. People belief that, after death, they may still have a sense of feeling or be in another form of life.[12] Also, according to traditional Chinese culture, not having a son before one dies is regrettable. Therefore, with the follow-up services provided by the volunteers, the traditional elderly Chinese people will fulfil the unfinished business of those in the pre-death phase.

Conclusion

For the benefit of the bereaved, in addition to a careful selection of volunteers, adequate training and supervision, volunteering needs to be structured.[4,5] I believe that well-trained and well-supervised volunteers are effective in bereavement support.

22

The Day After: Experiences of Bereaved Suicide Survivors

Amy Yin Man CHOW

"A suicide seems to end the pain of the completer,
yet commences a lengthy agony of those who love him."

Chow, AYM

Introduction

Although suicide may appear to be an individual decision and action in ending one's life, the effect and the subsequent pain of bereavement on family members may be phenomenal. Suicide bereavement has a higher chance of eliciting complicated bereavement responses[1,2] than do other forms of bereavement. The focus of studies on suicide is mainly on attempters. Shneidman alerted the public to the needs of bereaved family members or friends of deaths due to suicide. He introduced a new term, "postvention", a combination of "prevention" and "intervention", to form a comprehensive working approach to suicide.[3] "Postvention" is the supportive intervention particularly designed for bereaved persons who lost a loved one through suicide, with the hope of reducing the after-effects of suicide so that bereaved survivors are able to live on productively and be less traumatized than they might be otherwise.[3]

"Postvention is prevention for the next decade and for the next generation ... [it] probably represents the largest problem and thus represents the greatest area for potential aid."[4] Firstly, survivors themselves are potential attempters. Evidence shows that risks among suicide bereavement survivors are usually higher than among their non-suicide bereavement counterparts.[5] Secondly, survivors who can openly share their pain of losing a loved one through suicide can be great teachers for potential attempters, who may not have considered the possible effect of their suicide on others. Thus, development of postvention should go hand-in-hand with prevention and intervention of suicide.

In Hong Kong, the development of suicide postvention is in its infancy. This chapter is an initial attempt to describe the path of suicide survivorship in a chronological sequence, in the following days, weeks and months after the suicide. Theory and practice, culturally relevant issues and practical guides are described.

Scope of the Problem

Shneidman estimated that there are at least six bereaved survivors for each suicide.[6] There were 1,107 reported deaths from suicide in Hong Kong in 2002,[7] leaving approximately 6,640 survivors grieving over the loss of a loved one. This may be an underestimation. Firstly, the total real suicide rate is underestimated by excluding the "sub-intentioned suicide" deaths that may have been classified as accidental or natural. Secondly, in addition to the immediate family members, people such as neighbours, colleagues, and friends are potentially affected, even though the effect due to the loss may generally be less severe than it is for the immediate family members. The advancement of video technology has made possible repeated broadcasts of suicide scenes and corpses, via the mass media. Vivid images stay with the audience as if they have actually witnessed the suicide. Spectators who are weak, depressed or have a similar background to that of the completers may find themselves vicariously traumatized by the event. Thirdly, the resolution of the trauma due to suicide bereavement usually takes years; thus, the real size of the affected population may be significantly larger than originally thought.

In this chapter, the term "survivor" is limited to immediate family members of the completer. The information in the chapter is based on information provided by survivors on their pain and gain throughout the process of bereavement.

Pain in Bereavement

Losing a loved one through death is a bewildering experience. Bereaved persons experience a wide range of unfamiliar reactions of intense emotions such as sadness, anger, guilt, anxiety, loneliness, helplessness and shock; physical sensations of tightness, over-sensitivity to noise, a sense of depersonalization and fatigue; sleep disturbances, appetite disturbances, absent-mindedness, withdrawal, yearning; as well as disbelief, confusion, preoccupation and sense of presence.[8] The mental and physical health status as well as mortality of bereaved persons are affected severely and adversely.[9]

Greater Pain in Suicide Bereavement

Losing a loved one through suicide is a devastating experience. Clinicians and researchers found that bereavement from suicide is more difficult than it is for death from other causes.[1,10–12]. Bailley *et al.*[1] found that suicide survivors, when compared with bereaved persons of other forms of death, experienced more frequent feelings of rejection, greater sense of responsibility, higher levels of shame and perceived stigmatization as well as more intense grief reactions. Van der Wal[13] and Jordon[5] extensively reviewed articles comparing suicide bereavement and that due to other types of death. Although both agreed that quantitative differences between these two types of bereavement were not statistically significant, qualitative differences were sufficiently evidenced.

As suggested by Jordon,[5] special themes include: 1. the struggle of the bereaved in questioning the meaning around the death; 2. guilt, blame, and responsibility for the death, as bereaved family members perceive a suicide to be preventable; 3. sense of abandonment or rejection, which might be followed by anger towards the deceased, as suicide is self-inflicted. In addition to the three themes, Van der Wal[13] postulated two further points: 1. concealment of the cause of death during contact with others and 2. fear of being susceptible to the same vulnerability or sharing similar problems with the deceased through heredity.[13]

Observations in Hong Kong

As the former director and a counsellor of a community-based bereavement counselling centre in Hong Kong, I have had extensive contact with suicide survivors. In my experience, the themes of suicide bereavement as given in Western literature are also observable in Hong Kong. Moreover, some themes are specific to the Chinese culture.

On the point of concealment of the cause of death during contact with others as raised by Van der Wal,[13] Chinese consider suicide as an act that is a loss of face (*tiu lien*, 丟臉) for the whole family. Losing face can induce a sense of discomfort, shame or embarrassment.[14] Thus, survivors would try to hide the death or cause of death as far as possible. Yet, if the newspaper reports the suicide of the family member, they have no choice but to feel *tiu lien* in facing friends and neighbours. From my clinical experience, I know that survivors try to explain the suicide by statements such as: "He died of [mental] illness". "She died of accident[al fall from height]." "He died of carelessness [in using drugs]." "He was possessed by an evil spirit. (撞邪)". Even in a counselling session, people used expressions such as "He choose to end his own life", or "He determined to end his life" instead of the simple word "suicide". Probably, the word "suicide" has negative connotations, whereas euphemisms are neutral and have the connotation of "self-choice" and "self-determination". Recently, there have been celebrities in Hong Kong who committed suicide. Some family members use the statement, "He died as [the name of the celebrity who committed suicide] did", to describe the cause of death of their loved one and to feel less embarrassed.

In addition to disclosing the cause of death, self-attribution of the death is a source of stress. While in a continuous search for meaning, it is hard for individuals to accept the suicide of a loved one without finding a convincing and sound reason. The Chinese have rich traditional beliefs on fate; thus, suicide survivors use the folk concepts of bad luck and evil spirits to explain the suicide. Sometimes, the suicide is interpreted as "repaying a debt", as the person or ancestors might have done something wrong in this life or in the previous life (前世孽). The person or the younger generation is expected to repay the debt. There is a common saying in Chinese: "Debts by the father should be repaid by the son" (父債子還). Thus in facing the suicide of adult children, parents usually blame themselves, as they might have been the cause of the suicide. This self-blame adds pain and guilt to the hurt in the bereavement of losing adult children.

Another commonly cited reason for suicide is that it is a result of possession by ghosts (撞邪) or being cursed (受咀咒). These beliefs reinforce a great sense of fear, as the family would be very scared that they could lose another member soon. In order to cope with this fear, they either request reallocation of the housing unit (if it is a public housing unit) or arrange special rituals to "purify" the house or give alms to reduce or resolve the curse. These rituals may be costly. Even after performing the rituals, the family may live under the shadow of death, worrying about revisitation by ghosts or the reactivation of the curse.

If the suicide takes place in a person's own home, the situation is even more complicated. Though the family might find it traumatic to stay in the unit where they witnessed or discovered the suicide, they cannot move to a new place if they have limited resources. It would be difficult to sell the unit to other people, as banks in Hong Kong will usually blacklist all housing units in which suicide has taken place and assign it a lower resale value. It will be hard to get a remortgage on the unit. The desire to change the living unit is not only to reduce the triggers of the pain of loss; it may be motivated by the desire to change geomancy (*feng shui*, 風水) which is believed to affect the total well-being of individuals living in a place.

Another perceived cause of suicide is a "clash of fate". Fate is determined by the time and date of birth according to traditional astrology. The fate of different persons may interact favourably or otherwise, leading to mutual benefit or conflict. The clash of fate is usually detected when a new member joins the family through birth or marriage. Thus the new member usually becomes the scapegoat. From a social and psychological perspective, the change in membership, like the birth of a child or a marriage, can be a stressor. Suicide might be related to the problem in adjustment to stressful family events, yet it may be understood as a clash of fate from a supernatural framework. Sometimes, the name of a person is considered to have affected the fate of another family member. I have worked with families that changed the names of the surviving bereaved members, usually a child. They hope that the bad luck will not be continued. Unfortunately, the imposed change of name is another experience of loss for the child, as the child's personal identity (in school) ends with the sudden death of a beloved family member as well.

The Bereavement Experience

In order to develop a better understanding of the experience of suicide survivors, the experience is described chronologically from the day after, the month after, and then the year after.

The Days After

Right after the suicide, the survivors are challenged by many unfamiliar tasks. This is an active process that the suicide survivors have to work through.

Discovering the suicide

Suicides as a result of jumping from a height, hanging, or burning by charcoal are usually discovered by family members and close friends. Witnessing the process (in the case of jumping) or seeing the corpse is a great trauma in itself. The unprepared encounter of such an unusual heartbreaking event can leave a permanent scar on the survivors.

> Mrs A told us, "My 5 year-old daughter was the first one to discover my husband's body hanging in the bathroom. We'd just returned from the market and she needed to go to the bathroom. When she opened the door and unexpectedly saw the body, she screamed loudly and wet her pants. I was very scared, too. Yet, the first thing in my mind was to rescue him ... I tried very hard to untie him but was unsuccessful. It was my elder son who was calm enough to call the police. Since then, my daughter dares not open any doors and is extremely scared when she goes to the bathroom".
>
> Mr B said, "My wife gave me a big kiss, and then jumped out of the window. I was slow to respond at that time. The scene kept replaying in my mind a thousand times a day. I wish I had been quicker to grab her hands and prevent this incident from happening ... I feel so guilty!"

The experience of suicide survivors whose loved one died of carbon monoxide poisoning through burning charcoal can be traumatic. Contrary to the popular belief that charcoal burning leaves a full corpse with no obvious wounds, the body of completers may be seriously burnt.[15] The survivors who discover and see the burnt corpse would have a negative image of the deceased loved one. Moreover, the trigger of loss may be stored in the form of the memory of the smell. One survivor said that her daughter reacted hysterically to the smell of burning meat at the BBQ in her school outing. Her memory of the smell of the death scene was triggered and retrieved.

Receiving the bad news

Even if the survivors are not the first to discover the suicide, the moment they receive the news is traumatic. The news is usually given through a telephone call from the police. Many survivors said that they would be very anxious whenever the telephone rang. When they received the bad news at night, they would have difficulty sleeping. Some reported nightmares and waking up at a similar time every night, as if their biological clock had set an alarm for that specific time.

Breaking the news to other family members

The police or hospital staff usually notify the next-of-kin only. The responsibility of breaking the sad news to other family members will then fall on the survivors. Repeating the bad news of the suicide of their loved one is very painful, and facing the repeated question of "why" is even more heartbreaking. Firstly, the survivors might still be in a state of disbelief and find it difficult to say the word "suicide". Secondly, suicide is still perceived as an improper act; thus, telling others about the suicide of the loved one seems to be disgraceful and disloyal. Thirdly, the survivor might worry about the questions and comments of other people about not being able to care for the completer. Lastly, survivors are also concerned about the effects on the receivers of the bad news.

> Mrs C. said, "My heart was broken when I knew my husband had killed himself. The next minute I knew that I needed to calm down. My children were at school at that time. What should I say to them? Would there be negative effects if I told them the truth? They adore their father like a hero. Would they follow their father's act when learning the truth? As a wife, should I say something bad about my husband to the children?"
>
> Mrs D said, "The first problem that popped into my mind was how to tell my aged mother-in-law about the death of my husband. She is so old

and has heart problems. How could she stand the news? My husband was the meaning of her existence. Would she collapse? She would definitely blame me for not informing her at once, yet she would also blame me for not being able to take care of him!"

Viewing the corpse

After receiving the bad news, what the survivors long to do is to see the deceased. The survivors usually describe this process as the most painful experience. In situations like jumping from a height in the neighbourhood or in their own house, the first viewing of the body is usually done on the spot as a procedure of identification. The body is usually seriously deformed. Seeing their loved one lying without any signs of life is an absolute shock. Witnessing the injuries and physical disfigurement of the completer induces great pain for the survivors. The physical pain of the completer is actually converted into deep psychological and spiritual pain for the survivors.

> Mrs E explained, "When I saw the deformed face of my son, who jumped from the house, my heart was crushed. It should have been very painful when he fell to the ground. He used to care so much about his appearance; he would be very upset to see his face smashed in the fall. When I saw the broken legs, I felt so sad. Even when he died, he became a 'crippled' ghost … "

Sometimes, the survivors identify the body in a hospital. They are usually not informed about the death of the completers until they reach the hospital. Throughout the journey to the hospital, they are usually very anxious. They worry that they will lose their loved one, but they hope for the best. Once they reach the hospital and see the lifeless body, all their hopes are gone. They wanted to seize the last chance to share all the unfinished businesses with the completers yet were numbed and shocked by the unfamiliar environment and situation. At the same time, practical issues came to mind, questions like "How can I break the bad news to others?" "How am I going to live without him?" "How can I manage all the logistics and funeral arrangements?" A suicide catches survivors unprepared. The heavy demands and lack of preparation cause heavy stress to the survivors.

Even if the corpse is not deformed, the appearance can also be traumatic to the survivors. The corpse whose eyes or mouth are open is usually perceived to have unfinished business. The presence of nostril or ear discharge is perceived as great suffering before the death. Negative images of the corpse are coupled with the shock and refusal to accept the death. Flashbacks of the corpse in identification are frequent and bring great pain.

If the completers are found to have no signs of survival, they will be sent to the Public Mortuary instead of a hospital. A forensic autopsy, to explore the real cause of death, will be performed. The corpses are usually not cleaned or tidied up, to avoid damage of clues or any other relevant information. When the offer is made to survivors to view the body of their loved one in this condition, the bloodstains, bruises, and body fluids usually shock them.

> Mrs F told us, "When I was called to identify my husband in the Public Mortuary in the middle of the night, I was extremely scared. I had never been to such a place! ... . When I went there, I could see only a pool of flesh and blood. How could I verify that it was him! I really thought that it wasn't. It must be a thief who had stolen my husband's clothing and belongings ... . Then I recognized his hands, the hands I used to hold every night. They were no longer warm and caring ... The image of the flesh and blood popped up in my mind from time to time. I wish I could press an erase button to wash it away from my mind, but I can't".

The family is usually asked to view the corpse a second time upon claiming the body. After a day or more in the mortuary, the corpse will appear thinner, paler and colder, due to dehydration and cessation of blood circulation. The survivor will interpret this as a sign of hunger or of the deceased feeling cold. Guilt and blame will then surface at not being able to protect the deceased.

Police investigation

As suicide is an unnatural form of death, a police investigation is necessary to establish the real cause of death. The survivors can understand the necessity of such investigation procedures, but at the same time, the connotation of suspicion of "murder" or "negligence" can be hard to bear. Also, facing a suicide is an extremely emotional event; yet offering information to the police is a purely cognitive process. The survivors usually find it hard to switch between the "heart" and the "mind" to switch. In addition, the recall of events prior to the suicide helps them to notice warning signs that they had overlooked. The process of giving information is thus agonizing and quilt inducing.

In addition to verbal information, the police might need information like a suicide note, diary, letters, photographs etc. These materials are the treasures of the survivors but have to be taken away by strangers. This induces a sense of double loss: losing both the person and the links to their memories.

Decision of organ donation

The completers of suicide are usually potential organ donors, as their organs, especially the cornea, are healthy and undamaged. The coordinators of organ donation usually approach the survivors and explore the possibility of consent to organ donation. This decision has to be made within a short period, as the organs will soon deteriorate. This is usually a difficult decision. Some survivors find it a relief to have the organs donated, as it is considered a good deed that will accumulate merit for the deceased in heaven. Also, it seems that the deceased's body can continue to live in this world. Yet at times, the good-intended decision is spoiled by other peoples' comments like, "Do you want him to be a blind or heartless ghost?" or "He suffered a lot upon his death already. How cruel you are to let others hurt her again by cutting out her organs!"

Handling of reporters

A suicide is especially newsworthy if the completer is from a particular background, such as a professional or a well-known person. Reporters then usually try their best to obtain as much information about the completer, the stories behind the suicide and the suicide itself. The proper way to get information is usually by interviewing the survivors. Thus the reporters usually gather in the hospital, mortuary or home of the survivors to get an opportunity for an interview and photos. The survivors are numb with digesting the sudden and shocking departure of their loved one; thus, the zealous intrusion from the press is usually perceived as annoying. The miscommunication sometimes results in unnecessary conflict, which adds strain on the survivors.

Receiving the bad news again through the mass media

The survivors are usually ambivalent about reading the newspaper about the news of the suicide of their loved one. They usually worry about the report being very negative, especially if they have had previous conflicts with reporters. It is common to find report of suicide in newspapers. On a day when there is no special news, a report of a suicide might become front-page headlines. The style of presentation, scope and focus of the report may vary according to the management and professional standards of the editors of the paper.

> Mr G said, "I was so unprepared to see a photo of my son's deformed body on the front page of the newspaper. His eyes were still wide open! You can't image how painful it is when a loved one's photo is publicized in such a way. I wished I could buy all the newspapers and burn them!"

When survivors are reluctant to be interviewed, reporters then try to get information from other sources like neighbours, colleagues or classmates. The information given by secondary informants is incomplete. Some unethical reporters even mislead the ignorant informant to believe that they are police officers; thus, the informant is led to believe that giving information is a duty rather than a choice.

> Mrs H said, "I was shocked to find that our wedding photo was in the newspaper. Also, the report contained a lot of details. Neither my son nor I had agreed to an interview by the press after my husband's suicide. I then asked my domestic helper. She told me that she had given a similar photograph to a man who claimed to be a policeman. Also, she had spent an hour providing information. How angry I was when I discovered this! Fortunately, our family relationship was good all along. They could not make a terrible story".

The Hong Kong Jockey Club Centre for Suicide Research and Prevention of the University of Hong Kong has raised the attention of media professionals on the topic. Meetings, forums and workshops were arranged for discussion on the ethical consideration in reporting of suicide in the mass media.[16] There has been much improvement after the promotion of ethical standards, as defined by WHO, among reporters.

Funeral arrangements

The funeral is the time for bereaved family members to gather to commemorate the deceased. It is also a time for mutual support. Yet the elaborate funeral rituals may be used as battlefield of power and control. Hidden conflicts among family members over money and relationships may surface. Special rituals like chanting are believed to help to settle the spirit of the suicide completer. Disagreement over the rituals used may reflect individual needs. The guilty survivors who find themselves responsible for the suicide would prefer to perform as many rituals as possible, as a way of compensation and relieving guilt. The angry survivors who perceive suicide as abandonment would think that the completer did not deserve these costly rituals.

In addition to the tension within the family, decisions on who to invite to the funeral is a source of stress. The first two questions raised by those invited will be "When did it happen?" and "How did he or she die?" The "when" question is easy to handle but not the "how". To avoid embarrassment and shame, survivors usually limit the list of those invited. However, on the day of the funeral, when they see that the funeral halls of others are filled with people and that of the completer is empty, they would feel sorry for the completer.

In some religions, suicide is considered a sin. Survivors sometimes find it embarrassing and shameful to hold the funeral in their church. Some even keep it a family secret and do not tell their friends in the church. The strong emotional, social, spiritual and tangible support from the church cannot be materialized, as they are excluded.

The Weeks After

Weeks after suicide, the necessary procedures and the funeral are completed. Support from relatives and friends begins to fade, and everything is expected to return to normal. This is the commencement of the painful bereavement journey. The natural defence of numbness, weakness, pain and complex emotions surface. Survivors have more time to think about the whole event. Making sense of the death is one of the key tasks of the bereaved. It is not easy to formulate the whole picture of precipitating events and what was on the mind of the completer; thus, the process of making meaning is very difficult. The survivor may be locked in asking repeated questions of "why".

The unanswered "whys"

Incompleteness induces a sense of discomfort. The survivors would keep on searching for reasons for the suicide. As no one except the deceased knows the real answer, the process of searching seemed to be never ending. Usually, the approach in finding answers is through systematic recall of memories with the deceased. The survivors try hard to recall each and every moment, to find clues. Usually, they come up with more questions than answers.

Detective mode of thinking

If the survivors find no satisfactory explanation for the questions of "why", they might try to view the situation from different perspectives: "Could it be homicide rather than suicide?" or "Is he haunted by an evil spirit?" These modes of thinking externalize the cause to uncontrollable factors to reduce self-blame as well as anger towards the deceased. However, fear and a sense of insecurity may also result.

A "cocktail" of emotions: the sense of abandonment

Some bereaved persons perceive death as a form of abandonment by the deceased. Suicide is the only direct self-inflicted way of death, so the sense of abandonment is even higher. The survivors will perceive suicide as rejection: rejection of the care and concern of the survivors, rejection of facing problems together with the survivors, rejection of commitment in caring for the survivors and other family members as well as rejection of building the future with the survivors.

The sense of anger

A sense of abandonment is usually followed by anger. Anger is a normal reaction towards unfair treatment or injustice. The survivors, after handling all the necessary but unfamiliar procedures in arranging the funeral, investigation and death registration, have to adjust to a new future without the deceased. All this further fosters a sense of blame and injustice.

> Mrs J said, "He has chosen a comfortable way to escape from his problems by passing the 'ball' to me. How can I take care of a two young children and at the same time support the whole family? The loan shark keeps on disturbing me and asking me to repay the debt ... Ay! I have already sold everything valuable for him to pay his previous debts. His funeral was actually supported financially by my maternal family ... The loan shark still disturbs me ... It's unfair. It is my husband who borrowed the money. I did not spend a cent of it. Go to his grave and ask him. Don't come to me! Sometimes, I wish to kill myself so that I can go and scold him. I wish I had never met this guy and married him!"

The sense of sorrow

After venting anger towards the deceased, the survivors naturally talk about the good and sweet memories of the deceased. When the survivors are confronted with the reality that they will have to continue their life without the deceased, they will develop a sense of loss, sorrow, regret and grief. They mourn not only the loss of the deceased as a person but also their own life without the deceased.

> Mr K told us, "Even though life before my wife's death was a terrible experience, I miss her very much. She was very charming when I first met her. She was a good wife and mother. Only when she got the [mental] illness, she lost control. It's not her fault. Every night when I go to bed, I sense the emptiness. I miss her companionship, I miss her voice, even though she was always complaining ... "

The sense of guilt and regrets

Through repeatedly going over the details of interaction before the suicide, it is common for survivors to find things that could have been done to prevent the suicide. The survivors blame themselves for unspoken words of care, not noticing clues, and of untaken action. At the same time, they are guilty for the cruel words that hurt the deceased and the insensitive attitude in responding to the deceased's cry for help. They regret their mean words, non-action or negligence that caused the suicide. This belief is strengthened through suicide notes.

> Mrs L said, "I deserve punishment. I am the one who killed my husband. He was not feeling well and I cruelly scolded him. I told him angrily that he should kill himself and not burden the family anymore. He just followed my advice. He had been ill for years but never ever thought of giving up. It's my curse that killed him ... I feel very sorry. I wish I could go back to that time. I would definitely change what I said ... Actually, I love him so much. I don't want to see him lying there and do nothing. I just want to motivate him! ... Ah, he even said in the suicide note that he hopes his departure can free us from the burden! It's really me who had caused his death".

The sense of fear

After a death in family, other family members usually feel the fragility of life. The sense of insecurity fosters hypersensitivity to potential loss of other family members. When another family member has signs of illness or emotional disturbance, the survivor will worry that another death will occur. It is common to see a recently widowed parent over-disciplining the children. This is driven by an irrational fear of loss and accident.

Another source of fear is the new and extra role expectation. After the suicide, the survivor has to live without the completer. The previous roles and responsibilities will fall on the shoulders of the survivor. As the death is so sudden, no transition was possible. The survivor then has to bear the pain of grief and to learn new tasks and take on new responsibilities.

> Mr M said, "After the suicide of my wife, her role as homemaker immediately fell on my shoulders. For a man, going to the market is not an easy task. I felt so uneasy as I have to compete over a fresh fish with a homemaker. She looked at me in a disrespectful way. What would happen if my colleague saw such an incident? Everyone says that I can have a domestic helper. But when I planned to do so, my mother-in-law seriously objected. She thought that the maid would have an affair with me ... Another headache is how to provide care for my daughter. Yesterday, she asked me to tie her hair. I never learnt how to do that. She then threw a temper tantrum! One thing that scares me the most is that she wanted to go to the washroom when we went out. How can I let her go to the ladies' room on her own? She is only four. Yet she refused to go to the men's room".

Fear can also be developed from uncertainty. As suicide might be regarded as a sin, survivors may worry that the afterlife of completer will be difficult or that the person will have to face punishment in hell. Those that hold traditional Chinese beliefs might see suicide as a result of bad luck, punishment from heaven or possession by evil spirits. They might be afraid that such negative fate will be continued and the tragedy will repeat itself on other family members.

The Months and Years After

Months after a suicide, the survivors can usually resume most of their routines, like going back to work or to school. Yet, their emotions are still confused despite regaining a better control than they had in the previous months. Emotional outbursts are usually less intense and less frequent. The major concern in this period is usually social and interpersonal isolation as well as prolonged grieving.

The frequent triggers of pain

Physical rehabilitation seems to have a linear relationship with time. People who use the approach that "time heals" in consoling bereaved persons think psychological and social rehabilitation of bereavement also follows this pattern. In fact, the rehabilitation is in spiral form, having cycles of ups and downs. Triggers activate these cycles. Rando[11] called these triggers "subsequent temporary upsurges of grief" (STUG) reactions precipitants. She has classified them into three groups:

1. Cyclic

    These triggers are repeated annually on occasions such as birthdays and festivals, or monthly such as the same day of the suicide every month, or weekly, or daily. It can also be a holiday reaction. In our observation, survivors are very disturbed during Mid-Autumn Festival and Lunar New Year, holidays that are supposed to be times of family gatherings. It can also be seasonal. Hong Kong survivors also told us that their mood is highly affected when the weather changes. This usually happens when they start to put away summer clothing and take out winter clothing. Then they feel that they have lost their loved one.

2. Linear

    Linear triggers occur as a consequence of reaching a particular time, age or state. This can be age-related. Child survivors sometimes find that, when they reach the age of the death of the parent, it is usually a time of turmoil. It can also be experience-related, such as special transitional stages including graduation, marriage, having a baby, getting a divorce, or retiring. The survivors usually have thoughts such as, "How different this event would be if he or she hadn't died!"

3. Stimulus cues

These cues occur with the triggers of stimuli. Cues can be based on a real memory like photographs or old clothing. They can also be symbolic reminders like the deceased's favourite movie star, or a uniform of the same school where the deceased child studied. The survivors also said that, whenever there is a report in the media about another suicide attempt, the pain is revisited. Cues can also be stimulated by the senses, such as a special song, the smell of perfume or the place where the person has been. Grief can then last for decades.

> Mrs N said, "On the day I witnessed my son's death, I was shocked. My senses came back when I heard the police siren. Since then, whenever I hear a siren, the pain returns. Yesterday, a boy in the lift with me was playing with a toy police car. When the siren was on, tears fell from my eyes. It scared the child and everyone else in the lift. I was in deep grief and very embarrassed!"

> Ms O said, "My mother committed suicide when I was five … The suicide seemed to be a shared secret that we rarely mentioned. Year after year, I kept it inside my heart as if it had never happened … When my own child reached the age of five, my suppressed emotions suddenly surfaced. The emotions were just like wild horses I had no control over. The idea of 'suicide' popped in and out of my mind as if it was a curse. Fortunately, with the support of my family members, the turmoil is over … You cannot underrate the power of your psyche!"

How Can We Help Suicide Survivors? The SUICIDE Model

The journey of the survivors is not smooth. What can someone who is caring for the survivors do?

Space and Safety

Suicide survivors will usually try to conceal the cause of death. The concealment is rooted in a sense of insecurity and fear of being discriminated against. Only when a trustful relationship is built, with empathetic understanding, will the survivors feel it is safe for them to share the experience. Forcing the survivors to face the reality of their loss is usually undesirable. During the first few days or weeks, they are usually preoccupied with procedures, cognitive obsessions of "why" and recalling details of the event. Personal space is crucial for these tasks of exploration and making sense of the event. The courage to share bloody and horror stories as well as endurance of outbreaks of extreme emotion, devotion to unconditional acceptance and respect despite the obsession with thousands of unanswered whys, patience to listen to repeated small details of events and memories, as well as staying calm in sharing the pain of a heartbreaking scene are important qualities in a suicide bereavement counsellor.

Use of multi-disciplinary effort

Various professionals are present in the journey of the survivors. At the very beginning, the police and health-care professionals are involved. Then the funeral directors, social worker, psychologists, pastors (priests, masters, etc., depending on the religion) and insurance professionals follow. When the survivors are children, schoolteachers or counsellors will also be involved. Thus an interdisciplinary approach and wide network are needed.

Information provision

It is unusual for someone to have information about funerals, burial, cremation, or death registration before a death takes place. After a death in the family, especially suicide, which is so sudden, survivors are usually numb. The ability to digest different information and make decisions is usually low. It is important for professionals to provide necessary information and lead survivors through crucial decisions systematically and with clarity and precision. Procedures (like claiming the body, the police investigation) in their respective disciplines should be re-examined and reviewed by the professionals concerned. A more user-friendly and survivor-oriented approach would definitely reduce unnecessary stress on the survivors.

Continuous effort

The grief experience is like an emotional roller coaster; it goes up and down with mood swings for years. A model of short-term professional intervention is appropriate for most cases, yet flexibility of reactivating case intervention during the cyclic or linear reactions will be necessary. Lay volunteers and supporters should focus on care and support in the first few weeks. The first month is the time of action and making meaning of the event. The need for support usually starts after the funeral; thus, for friends and relatives, support in the first few months after the funeral is also crucial.

Involvement of the family system

Bereavement affects the whole family. Even if only one family member needs support, we need to pay attention to silent grievers like the children and men. A father killed himself two years after his son committed suicide. Soon after the son's funeral, he took his wife and daughter to the bereavement counselling centre but did not admit his need for support. He was the silent griever who also needed help. Special communication skills and techniques should be developed to help these individuals. For survivors, temporal support from outsiders is not compatible with continuous support from their own family. Thus, strengthening the whole family should be the goal of intervention.

Debriefing and Desensitization

Witnessing suicide, directly or indirectly, is a great trauma for most people. The frequent flashbacks are disturbing. When a suicide has occurred in an institution, school, big shopping mall, home for elderly people, or a hospital, a large number of spectators or workers are affected. It is important that appropriate debriefing sessions focussing on strength and meaning are held to help people deal with the trauma of witnessing a suicide. The Method of Eye Movement Desensitization and Reprocessing (EMDR) is a common approach used by trauma workers.

Empowerment

Later, part of journey of the survivor is filled with a mixture of emotions, a sense of guilt and self-blame as well as prolonged grief. Empowerment intervention can facilitate an awareness of growth through pain, regaining a sense of control through enduring the suffering of the loss of a loved one and focusing on developing inner strength and appreciation of life. Many survivors form self-help groups and devote their time to helping other people with problems. Their experience of loss can be turned into a blessing for others in need. Through helping other people, survivors can transcend to a higher level of selflessness and redirect their energy into creative innovation towards a better world.

Conclusion

The suicide of an individual has ripple effects on their loved ones. The agony is multi-dimensional and long-lasting. As suggested by Schut *et al.*[17] and the

Centre for the Advancement of Health,[18] intervention for bereaved persons can take the form of a community health framework of prevention. The primary preventive interventions are open to those who are experiencing uncomplicated bereavement. Secondary prevention interventions are for those who are more vulnerable, and tertiary level is for those who are experiencing bereavement-related problems or complicated grief. Suicide survivors fall into the the secondary or tertiary level of interventions. Based on extensive reviews on available research, the Centre for the Advancement of Health[18] advocates psychotherapeutic intervention, as it can benefit the tertiary level and likely the secondary level. Empowering survivors and mobilizing them to help others would be a way out of their grief and self-pity.

23

Conclusion

Cecilia Lai Wan CHAN and Amy Yin Man CHOW

> Naturally, most of us would like to die a peaceful death, but it is also clear that we cannot hope to die peacefully if our lives have been full of violence, or if our minds have mostly been agitated by emotions like anger, attachments or fear. So if we wish to die well, we must learn how to live well: hoping for a peaceful death, we must cultivate peace in our mind, and in our way of life.
>
> *The Dalai Lama[1]*

Death Can be Transforming

We can learn about life through the death of our loved ones.[2] Knowing death reminds us of the treasures in life, the importance of relationships as well as our connectedness with people and nature. The journey of loss and grief can be a joyous one if we can cultivate a sense of awakened awareness of unpredictability and vulnerability, learning to be mindful with non-attachment and freedom, non-possessiveness and yet with compassionate loving-kindness towards self and others, true respect and genuine appreciation of life and beauty.

After going through the various chapters on death, dying and bereavement in Hong Kong, we can see that death among Chinese people is an interpersonal phenomenon. Reconstructing meaning towards culturally relevant growth and the process of transformation may be a move to good death and bereavement.

Death in Chinese: An Interpersonal Event

The Chinese pictogram of the word death consists of two parts: the griever and the deceased. Yet, the griever seems to be the key character and the deceased person is the backdrop. Thus Ho and Tsui [3] put forth the concept of the interdependence in death and grief, as described in Chapter 8. Their finding is consistent with clinical observations among the Chinese population. As shown in the case stories of Chapter 2, family members and friends are usually the focus of patients' primary concern throughout the path of death and dying. Yet, as Chinese, we might not know how to express ourselves and communicate with our family our fear and anxiety about death. Fight or flight, avoidance, denial, putting on a strong defensive front seem to be the more commonly used strategies to "protect" our family members from pain and grief. Yvonne Mak validated the suffering of family members of dying patients in Chapter 3. She suggested the importance of connectedness, as death is such an isolated and solitary process. For us to address the issues of death and dying in Chinese families, it would be a good start to address the interpersonal filial obligations and attachments. Professionals should also try to involve the family in the provision of care to the patients while not losing sight of their needs and stress as family members in anticipatory grief.

Death in Chinese: An Event That Is Professionally Guided

Most of the contributors in this book are professionals in hospice and/or psychosocial care. Health-care professionals are most visible during the processes of death and dying. Coupled with the traditional Chinese influence of respect for authority, many Chinese people surrender their decision-making to medical professionals when confronted with severe illness and death. In a cross-sectional survey on attitudes towards life-sustaining treatment of older persons in Hong Kong, Hui *et al.* found that if the seniors were mentally incompetent in making end-of-life decisions, 50% of the residents in homes for the aged and 23.9% of inpatients in geriatric wards would prefer doctors to make the decision for them, whereas 24.2% and 37.5 % respectively would prefer their relatives to decide for them.[4] Being highly respected, doctors and nurses are expected to provide solutions to all medical problems. When confronted with disappointing disease progression, the family members might naturally blame the professionals. Thus communication with patients and their family members to help them in facing the realities of death and dying would be an important area worthy of further exploration. Dissatisfaction and aggression directed towards doctors and nurses prevail after the death of the patient. Such hostility might be projected further onto other professionals like forensic pathologists, medical social workers, clinical psychologists and/or bereavement counsellors.

Another challenge in a highly professionalized service is the financial implications for the patients and their family members. The expenses in public health care are growing rapidly. As a result of a deficit budget in Hong Kong, medical expenses in the last five years are being cut. The biggest hospice, Nam Long Hospital, was closed in December 2003. Oncologists had found it difficult to refer patients to hospices, and the waiting time for home care was long. Further professionalization is not the solution. Death education, public awareness of advance directives and training of family members in palliative care is the path to help individuals and families experiencing the death of a loved one. The palliative home care service, as described by Faith Liu in Chapter 13, is a good reference for family care-givers in their care for a patient at home. It echoes the traditional Chinese concept of "filial piety" in faithfully providing hands-on care for parents and loved ones. With direct involvement in care provision, the family members will experience less regret and self-blame for "not doing enough" for the patient. In turn, this will result in fewer complicated bereavement problems when the patient dies.

Death of Chinese: Culturally Sensitive Intervention

The psychosocial and emotional processes of death, dying and bereavement in Hong Kong are similar to those described in Western literature. When Western medicine fails, patients may try other methods to seek a miracle cure. Worried about the disapproval from and feeling guilty for being disloyal to their physicians, patients often hide their use of alternative medicine. Better communication and collaboration between Western doctors and Chinese medicine practitioners can foster an open dialogue towards optimal and evidence-based palliative care for patients and their family members.

We discussed indigenous ways of supporting Chinese bereaved persons. The strategies of working with the ambivalence in Chinese bereaved persons might also be valid in other forms of counselling. The rituals of letting go of fish or birds, the use of movies to discuss inner feelings, care for somatic complaints to access emotional states, sharing with clients the dreams of the deceased may contribute to culturally sensitive practices.

Learning from Death, Dying and Bereavement

It has widely been established that finding of meaning contributes to adapting to trauma and loss, like the death of loved one or a diagnosis of cancer.[5] Davies *et al.*[6] have differentiated meaning into *making sense of the event* and *finding benefit* from the experience.[7] Chinese people, being pragmatic and down to earth, would certainly feel better if they could explain the situation (karma of cause and consequence) and identify benefits, such as learning new skills and growing spiritually, from the experience of loss and trauma.

Making Meaning of Illness

"My father is a lifelong smoker, so it is logical that he developed lung cancer." The son of a lung cancer patient told this to the oncology nurse. As he has accepted his father's cancer, he was ready to discuss the preparation of death with his parents and siblings.

"I had back pain and went for acupuncture. The needles were not properly cleaned, and I became a Hepatitis B carrier. I developed liver cancer five years later." Mr Chan, a liver cancer patient explained to the social worker how he developed this life-threatening illness. Once patients can make sense of the situation, they feel empowered to confront it. He lived for almost twelve years after his diagnosis, by religiously practising *qi gong* three times a day.

"He was wheelchair-bound and the lack of exercise may be the cause of his colon cancer." The wife of a patient with terminal colon cancer discussed how to help her husband with the attending doctor. She was an excellent care-giver and nursed her husband until he died a year later.

Patients and family members find comfort if they can develop a narrative to make sense of their illness or the death of a loved one. As soon as they stop asking "Why me?", they can mobilize their resources into active coping and problem-solving.[8]

There is increasing evidence of the relationship between attributing meaning and psychological or physical health. For example, the meaning that terminal patients ascribed to their pain affects the level of their perceived pain and depression.[9] Bereaved women who reported positive meaning have increased natural killer cell cytotoxicity.[10] The extent of meaning attribution and ability in cognitive restructuring were found to be related to the quality of life and self-esteem among cancer patients in Hong Kong.[11] A pessimistic explanatory style is significantly associated with mortality. Men with HIV/AIDS who found meaning showed less rapid decline in CD4 T-cell levels.[12]

The patients, family carers, and professionals would easily burn out and suffer from "browning out" when focusing on coping and trying hard to return to normality, as Peter Lee and Tracy Kwan describe in Chapter 15. If we can actively look for growth and transformation through the traumatic experience of loss and pain, not only would we be able to cope better; we can actually develop an emotional strength and spiritual peace in living every moment with the adverse experience.[13]

It is a big step forward if one can appreciate adversity and embrace pain. They are nutrients for spiritual transformation towards greater compassion and loving-kindness.[14] These changes brought about by self-reflection through the experience of suffering can produce long-term effects on the individual, as it is the deep structure of human existence that is being realigned. The physical well-being of individuals can change with the alteration of meaning as a result of body-mind-spirit holistic intervention.[15] The lens of viewing the world is replaced with a crystal clear and watchful glass that actively screens for the bliss, integrity and beauty of life and human nature.

> "There was a man we picked up from the gutter, half eaten by worms. After we had brought him to the home, he only said, 'I have lived like an animal in the street, but I am going to die as an angel, loved and cared for.' Then, after we had removed all the worms from his body, all he said, with a big smile, was: 'Sister, I am going home to God', and he died. It was so wonderful to see the greatness of that man who could speak like that without blaming anybody, without comparing anything. Like an angel — this is the greatness of people who are spiritually rich even when they are materially poor."
>
> *Mother Teresa*

Coping with death and dying is painful and traumatic for most people, yet we can learn to become more resilient. A traumatic life event, like the loss of loved one in death, may challenge our previous unquestioned life goals and purpose of existence.[16] When confronted with the inevitability of mortality, people will start to ask existential questions such as "What do I live for? How shall I spend the remaining part of my life? What is the meaning of my life?" This process of meaning reconstruction can help to reorder their priorities and to restructure their life along genuinely gratifying lines.[13]

> "Trials, temptations, disappointments — all these are helps instead of hindrances, if one uses them rightly. They not only test the fibre of character but strengthen it. Every conquering temptation represents newfound moral energy. Every trial endured and weathered in the right spirit makes a soul noble and stronger than it was before."
>
> *James Buckham*

If we can use the ritual of a mini life review every evening before we go to bed, to tell our loved ones how grateful we are to be surrounded by their love and be unconditionally accepted and forgiven, the shadow of regret can be removed and it will no longer daunt the bereaved persons after our death.

Leaving a Legacy

Many cancer patients devote themselves to helping others, building schools for orphans, raising money to help people with HIV/AIDS, dedicating their time and effort to helping other cancer patients. Cancer or a life-threatening illness serves as an alarm clock to remind us of the vulnerability of life. Knowing that life is limited by time, many cancer survivors focus on doing what they feel is important in their life.

The Chinese Cancer Web

A young woman of thirty found herself with terminal cancer with an unknown primary source of the tumour. She knew that her lifespan was limited. Chemotherapy was not helpful. She decided to try alternative methods of diet, meditation, exercise and doing meaningful projects to help others. She devoted herself to setting up a Chinese cancer web page to provide information in Chinese for other Chinese cancer patients who cannot read English. She travelled to Taiwan and mainland China to learn about the cancer support services there and put them onto her website. She was very proud of herself for having set up such a system and being of service in the new Internet age. She died peacefully three and a half years later.

Those who are resourceful can do more, whereas patients with less can also be doing great works of care. Cancer survivors and patients living with terminal illness continue to visit patients in hospitals and at home. Some boil tonifying soup for single elderly people or accompany patients to treatment sessions in the hospital. Others make woollen scarves for seniors living in institutions. The personal experience of death, dying and bereavement opens doors of spiritual growth and can broaden the horizon of awakening souls.

Maggie House

Mrs Maggie Keswick was diagnosed with an incurable cancer. She was shocked and wanted to get more information from the doctor. As she was overcoming her shock in the waiting room of the hospital, she was asked to leave, as another patient would need to use the facility. Maggie decided that she would set up a venue for cancer patients to obtain information and get the necessary support that is so crucial during the breaking of bad news and throughout the treatment process. Now, there are seven purpose-built and magnificently designed Maggie Houses in the United Kingdom serving a large number of cancer patients.

Maggie Keswick turned a curse into blessings. Her unfortunate cancer experience was transformed into an international movement of love and care for people with cancer. She became a miracle-maker because she made the decision to be a victor instead of a victim of illness and death. Maggie Keswick is not alone. There are large numbers of cancer survivors, locally and internationally, running magnificent projects of love and passion. The Shanghai Cancer Club is one of the outstanding examples of what patients can do.

The Shanghai Cancer Club

"Cancer turns a new page to my life ... I've found new meaning in life ... I have survived an incurable cancer for 25 years although the doctor only gave a prognosis of three months to live ... I am now a different person after the cancer experience, I devote my time in helping other cancer patients and serve as a teacher in the Cancer Rehabilitation School ... "

The Shanghai Cancer Club was founded by a group of cancer patients. It now runs three-weeks residential courses that combined the use of *qi-gong*, songs, journal writing, dance, movement, reading, group activities into holistic self care. It is running Cancer Support Services in hospitals and owns an eight storey building with hotel service for the three weeks residential course. They are daily events of *qi-gong*, monthly social gatherings and annual events of sports day and public education campaign. Cancer patients from all over the world is visiting the Shanghai Cancer Club and learning from them on their self-help cancer rehabilitation program.

There are now more than twenty mutual help groups for cancer patients and more than fifty groups for patients with other chronic and degenerative illnesses in Hong Kong. There are groups for stroke survivors, people with chronic renal failure, muscular dystrophy, lupus, rheumatoid arthritis, epilepsy, diabetes, heart problems, COPD, Parkinson's disease, and dementia. With the deep pain of loss and disablement, with wounds of hurt and humiliation, patients can become more loving and accommodating as people. They can touch others by reaching directly into their heart.

Death: The Tip of the Iceberg

This book is a snapshot of a fast-moving object. We have been able to capture only a small part of what death is really about. We have a better glimpse from the perspectives of health-care professionals and we learn about death from the clients we serve. They are our teachers. Still, it is the tip of the iceberg. Death is largely unknown to all of us. We have not included aspects of art, poetry, philosophy, theology, legal and policy perspectives. We are humbled by our own ignorance and must admit that there is much more that we do not know about death, dying and bereavement.

References

CHAPTER 1

1. Chan CLW. Death awareness and palliative care. In: Fielding R, Chan CLW, editors. *Psychosocial oncology and palliative care in Hong Kong: the first decade.* Hong Kong: Hong Kong University Press, 2000: 213–32.

2. Tang ST. Meanings of dying at home for Chinese patients in Taiwan with terminal cancer: a literature review. *Cancer Nurs* 2000: 23(5): 367–70.

3. DeSpelder LA, Strickland AL. *The last dance: encountering death and dying.* 6th ed. Boston, MA: McGraw Hill, 2002.

4. DeSpelder LA, Strickland AL. *The path ahead: readings in death and dying.* Mountain View, CA: Mayfield Publishing Company, 1995.

5. Fielding R, Chan LWC. *Psychosocial oncology and palliative care in Hong Kong: the first decade.* Hong Kong: Hong Kong University Press, 2000.

6. Cheung TF, Leung MY. 凝視死亡 [Gazing at death]. 香港：中文大學出版社, 2005. (In Chinese)

7. Bagley C, Tse JWL. *Suicidal behaviour, bereavement, and death education in Chinese adolescents: Hong Kong studies.* Aldershot: Ashgate, 2002.

8. Levine S. 如果只有一年：若只剩一年可活你要做些甚麼？[A year to live: how to live this year as if it were your last]. 臺北縣新店市：立緒文化事業有限公司，1999. (In Chinese)

9. Kübler-Ross E, Kessler D. 用心去活：生命的十五堂必修課 [Life lessons]. 台北市：張老師文化事業股份有限公司， 2001. (In Chinese)

10. Nuland SB. 死亡的臉 [How we die]. 臺北：時報文化，1995. (In Chinese)

11. Tashiro S. 從癌症體驗的人生觀 [The life view of experiencing cancer]. 香港：海嘯出版事業有限公司， 1997. (In Chinese)

12. Watanabe S. 人死了以後 [After death]. 臺北：東府出版社，1978. (In Chinese)

13. Deeken, A. 生命的終結：死亡之準備與希望 [The end of life: the hope and preparation for death]. 香港：海嘯出版事業有限公司，1997. (In Chinese)

14. Lin Q. 生死學 [Thanatology]. 臺北：洪葉文化事業有限公司, 2000. (In Chinese)

15. Wei C. 生死學概論 [Introduction to thanatology]. 臺北：五南圖書出版有限公司，2000. (In Chinese)

16. Lin Q, Zhang Y, Xu M. 生死學: 基進與批判的取向 [Thanatology: development and directions for critical judgement]. 台北市：洪葉文化事業有限公司，2004. (In Chinese)

17. Huang T. 死亡教育概論 I：死夭態度及臨終關懷研究 [Introduction to death education I: research on death attitude and palliative care]. 臺北市：業強出版社，1991. (In Chinese)
18. Huang T. 死亡教育概論 II：死夭教育課程設計之研究 [Introduction to death education II: research on curriculum of death education]. 臺北市：業強出版社，1992. (In Chinese)
19. So YP 死亡，別狂傲 [Death be not proud]. 香港：突破出版社，1981. (In Chinese)
20. Kuang TWJ. 活在死亡前 [Facing death]. 香港：突破出版社，1997. (In Chinese)
21. Society for the Promotion of Hospice Care. *A survey on attitudes towards death and dying among general public in Hong Kong.* Report submitted by Quality Evaluation Centre, City University of Hong Kong. Hong Kong: The Society for the Promotion of Hospice Care, 2002.
22. Chan CLW. Chinese culture and values in social work intervention. In: Envall NTTE, editor. *Social work around the world.* Scgwarztirstrasse, Switzerland: IFSW Press, 2000: 70–80.
23. Chan CLW. Death and awareness and palliative care. In: Fielding R, Chan CLW, editors. *Psychosocial and palliative care.* Hong Kong: Hong Kong University Press, 2000: 213–32.
24. Chan CLW. Grief and bereavement in a Hong Kong Chinese cultural context. In: Chan CLW, editor. *Innovative bereavement care in local practice.* Hong Kong: Jessie and Thomas Tam Centre, SPHC, 2000: 3–16.
25. Ho SMY, Wong KF, Chan CLW, Watson M, Tsui YKY. Psychometric properties of the Chinese version of the Mini-Mental Adjustment to Cancer (Mini-Mac) scale. *Psycho-Oncology* 2003; 12: 547–56.
26. Chan CLW, Palley HA. The use of traditional Chinese culture and values in social work health care related interventions in Hong Kong. *Health & Social Work* 2005; 30(1): 76–9.
27. Ho DYF, Fu W, Ng SM. Guilt, shame and embarrassment: revelations of face and self. *Culture & Psychology* 2004; 10(1): 64–84.
28. Albom M. *Tuesdays with Morrie: an old man, a young man, and life's greatest lesson.* London: Warner Books, 1997.

CHAPTER 2

1. Loke AY, Liu CF, Szeto Y. The difficulties faced by informal caregivers of patients with terminal cancer in Hong Kong and the available social support. *Cancer Nurs* 2003; 26(4): 276–83.
2. Lin CC, Wang P, Lai YL, Lin CL, Tsai SL, Chen TT. Identifying attitudinal barriers to family management of cancer pain in palliative care in Taiwan. *Pall Med* 2000; 14(6): 463–70.
3. Chan CLW, Chow AYM, Ho RTH. Transformation intervention: Facilitating growth after loss and grief due to cancer or bercavement. In: Heinonen T, Metteri A, editors. *Social Work in health and mental health: Issues, developments and actions.* Toronto: Canadian Scholars. Press Inc. 2005: 300–320.

CHAPTER **3**

1. Bolton G. *Reflective practice: writing and professional development.* London: Sage, 2002.
2. Yuen R, Mak Y *et al.* Chinese patients with advanced cancer requesting euthanasia. Asia Pacific Cancer Conference, 1999, HK.
3. Mak YYW. Meaning of desire for euthanasia in Chinese advanced cancer patients: a hermeneutic study. University of Wales College of Medicine, 2001.
4. Mak Y, Elwyn G. Use of hermeneutic research in understanding the meaning of desire for euthanasia. *Pall Med* 2003; 17: 395–402.
5. Mak YYW, Elwyn G, Finlay I. Patients' voices are needed in debates on euthanasia. *BMJ* 2003; 327: 213–5.
6. Mak YYW, Elwyn G. Voices of the terminally ill: uncovering the meaning of desire for euthanasia. *Pall Med* 2005; 19: 343–50.
7. Husserl E. *Ideas: general introduction to pure phenomenology.* New York: Collier, 1962.
8. Seymour J, Clark D. Phenomenological approaches to palliative care research. *Pall Med* 1998; 12: 127–31.
9. Broin V. The act of understanding and the possibility of a critical hermeneutics. Boulder, CO: University of Colorado, 1988.
10. Gadamer H-G. *Truth and method.* 2nd ed. New York: The Continuum Publishing Company, 1998.
11. Geanellos R. Hermeneutic philosophy. Part I: implications of its use as methodology in interpretive nursing research. *Nurs Inquiry* 1998; 5: 154–63.
12. Geanellos R. Hermeneutic philosophy. Part II: a nursing research example of the hermeneutic imperative to address forestructures/pre-understanding. *Nurs Inquiry* 1998; 5: 238–47.
13. Pascoe E. The value of nursing research of Gadamer's hermeneutic philosophy. *J Adv Nurs* 1996; 24: 1309–14.
14. Walsh K. Philosophical hermeneutics and the project of Hans Georg Gadamer: implications for nursing research. *Nurs Inquiry* 1996; 3: 231–7.
15. Munhall P. *Revising phenomenology: nursing and health science.* New York: National League for Nursing, 1994.
16. Schwartz M. *Morrie: in his own words.* New York: Dell Publishing, 1997.
17. Koch T. Establishing rigour in qualitative research: the decision trail. *J Adv Nurs* 1994; 24: 174–84.
18. Mak YYW. Suffering and healing: patient, professional and relative. Bradbury Hospice 10th Anniversary Seminar, March 2003, Queen Elizabeth Hospital, Hong Kong.
19. Cherny N, Coyle N, Foley K. Suffering in the advanced cancer patient: a definition and taxonomy. *J Pall Care* 1994; 10: 57–70.
20. Cassell E. The nature of suffering and the goals of medicine. *NEJM* 1982; 306: 639–45.
21. Kearney M, Mount B. Healing and palliative care: charting our way forward. *Pall Med* 2003; 17: 657–8.

CHAPTER **4**

1. Worden JW. *Grief counselling and grief therapy: a handbook for the mental health practitioner,* 2nd edn. London: Routledge, 1991.

2. Stephenson JS. *Death, grief, and mourning: individual and social realities.* New York: Free Press, 1985.

3. Rando TA. *Treatment of complicated mourning.* Champaign, IL: Research Press, 1993.

4. Bertman S. Communicating with the dead: an ongoing experience as expressed in art, literature, and song. In Kastenbaum RJ, editor. *Between life and death.* New York: Springer, 1979: 547–67.

5. DeSpelder LA, Strickland AL. *The last dance: encountering death and dying,* 6th edn. Boston: McGraw Hill, 2002.

6. Lai CT. Making peace with the unknown: a reflection on Daoist funerary liturgy. In Chan CLW & Chow AYM , editors. *Death, Dying & Bereavement: A Hong Kong Chinese Experience.* Hong Kong: The Hong Kong University Press. 2006: 87–92.

7. 道端良秀著；劉欣如譯．佛教與儒教 [Buddhism and Confucianism]．臺北：大展出版社, 1998

8. 徐吉軍，賀云翔．中國喪葬禮俗 [Chinese burial rituals and customs]．杭州：浙江人民出版社, 1991.

9. Chan CLW, Chow AYM, Ho SMY, Tsui YKY, Tin, AF, Koo BWS, et al. (In press). The experience of Chinese bereaved persons: A preliminary study of meaning making and continuing bonds. *Death Studies.*

10. Ho SMY, Chow AYM, Chan CLW, Tsui YKY. The assessment of grief among Hong Kong Chinese: a preliminary report. *Death Studies,* 2000; 26: 91–8.

11. Chan CLW, Mak J. Benefits and drawbacks of Chinese rituals surrounding care for the dying. In: Fielding R and Chan CLW, editors. *Psychosocial and palliative care.* Hong Kong: Hong Kong University Press, 2000; 255–70.

12. 萬建中．中國歷代葬禮 [Chinese burial rituals through the dynasties]．北京：北京圖書館出版社, 1998.

13. 王夫子．殯葬文化學：死亡文化的全方位解讀 [Cultural studies on burials]．北京：中國社會出版社, 1998.

14. Kutcher NA. *Mourning in late imperial China: filial piety and the state.* Cambridge University Press, 1999.

15. 張捷夫．喪葬史話 [Burial rituals in history]．台北市：國家出版社, 2003.

16. 張捷夫．中國喪葬史 [History of burial rituals in China]．臺北：文津, 1995.

17. Chan YK, Yin B. Mortality rate in Hong Kong: 1951–2000. *Conference on Death and the Life-world.* The Chinese University of Hong Kong, Hong Kong, 2002.

18. Hill AM. Chinese funerals and Chinese ethnicity in Chiang Mai, Thailand. *Ethnology* 1992; 31(4): 315–30.

19. Watson JL. The structure of Chinese funerary rites: elementary forms, ritual sequence, and the primacy of performance. In: Watson JL, Rawski ES, *et al.,* editors. *Death ritual in late imperial and modern China.* Berkeley: University of California Press, 1988: 3–19.

20. 周蘇平．中國古代喪葬習俗 [Burial Customs in Ancient China]．西安：陝西人民出版社, 1991.

21. Klass D. The inner representation of the dead child and the worldviews of bereaved parents. *Omega: Journal of Death and Dying* 1992–93; 26(4): 255–72.

22. Irigaray L. *To be two.* London: Athlone Press, 2000.

23. Rawski ES. A historian's approach to Chinese death ritual. In: Watson JL, Rawski ES, *et al.,* editors. *Death ritual in late imperial and modern China.* Berkeley: University of California Press, 1988: 20–36.

24. Rupp K. The price of death: the funeral industry in contemporary Japan. *American Ethnologist* 2002; 29(3): 719.

25. Giddens A. Living in a post-traditional society. In: Beck U, Giddens A, Lash S, editors. *Reflexive modernization politics, tradition and aesthetics in the modern social order.* Cambridge: Polity Press; 1994: 56–109.

26. Beck U. The reinvention of politics: towards a theory of reflexive modernization. In: Beck U, Giddens A, Lash S, editors. *Reflexive modernization politics, tradition and aesthetics in the modern social order.* Cambridge: Polity Press; 1994: 1–55.

CHAPTER 5

1. Kirkland R, Barrett T, Kohn L. Introduction. In: Kohn L, editor. *Daoism handbook.* Brill: Leiden, 2000: xi–xviii.

2. Goossaert V. The invention of an order: collective identity in thirteenth-century Quanzhen Taoism. *Journal of Chinese Religions* 2001; 29: 111–38.

3. Schipper K. Taoism: the story of the way. In: Little S, Eichman S, editors. *Taoism and the arts of China.* 1st ed. Berkeley, CA: University of California Press, 2000.

4. Lai CT. The Daoist concept of central harmony in the scripture of great peace (*Taiping jing*): human responsibility for the maladies of heaven and earth. In: Girardot N, Miller J, Liu XG, editors. *Taoism and ecology.* Cambridge, MA: Harvard University, Centre for the Study of World Religions, 2001: 95–112.

5. Schipper K. The Taoist body. *History of Religions* 1978; 17: 315–81.

6. Yu YS. "O Soul, Come Back!": A study in the changing conceptions of the soul and afterlife in pre-Buddhist China. *Harvard Journal of Asiatic Studies* 1987; 47: 363–95.

7. Wang C. *Lunheng* [論衡]. Beijing: Chunghua shuchu [中華書局], 1990.

8. Ge H. *Baopu zi neipian* [抱朴子內篇]. Beijing: Chunghua shuchu [中華書局], 1985.

9. Wu H. Art in a ritual context: rethinking mawangdui. *Early China* 1992; 17: 111–43.

10. Seidel A. Traces of Han religion in funeral texts found in tombs. In: Akizaki K, editor. *Dokyo to shukyo bunka.* Tokyo: Hirakawa, 1987: 21–57.

11. Poo MC. The concept of ghost in ancient Chinese religion. In: Lagerwey J, editor. *Religion and Chinese society.* Hong Kong: Chinese University Press, 2004: 173–91.

12. Kominami I. Kandai no sorei kennen [古代の鬼魂觀念]. *Toho gakuho* 1994; 66: 17–9.

13. Lin FS. Shilun Taiping jing di jibing guannian [試論太平經的疾病觀念]. *Bulletin of the Institute of History and Philology (Academia Sinica)* 1993; 62: 225–63.

14. Strickmann M. Disease and Taoist law. In: Strickmann M, editor. *Chinese magical medicine.* Stanford, CA: Stanford University Press, 2002: 1–57.

15. Wang M. *Taiping jing heijiao* [太平經合校]. Beijing: Chunghua Shuchu, 1960.

16. Cedzich A. Ghosts and demons, law and order: grave-quelling texts and early Taoist liturgy. *Taoist Resources* 1993; 4(2): 23–35.

17. Kamitsuka Y. Taibeikyo no shofu to taibei no riron ni tsuite [太平經の承負と太平の理論について]. *Nagoya daikyoyobu kiyo* 1988; A(32): 41–75.

18. Chen J. Taiping jing zhong de chengfu baoying sixing [太平經中的承負報應思想]. *Zongjiaxue yanjiu* 1986: 35–9.

19. Hendrischke B. The concept of inherited evil in the Taiping jing. *East Asian History* 1991; 2: 1–29.

20. Oxfeld E. "When you drink water, think of its source": morality, status, and reinvention in rural Chinese funerals. *Journal of Asian Studies* 2004; 63(4): 961–91.

21. Graham AC, translator. *Chuang-Tzu: the inner chapters*. London: Mandala, 1991.
22. Lai CT. Hong Kong Daoism: a study of Daoist altars and Lu Dongbin cults. *Social Compass* 2003; 50: 459–70.
23. Boltz J. Singing to the spirits of the dead: a Daoist ritual of salvation. In: Rawski ES, Watson RS, editors. *Harmony and counterpoint: ritual music in Chinese context*. Stanford, CA: Stanford University Press, 1996: 177–225.

CHAPTER 6

1. Benson T. The conservation of energy [monograph on the Internet]. NASA Glenn Learning Technologies Home Page. Available at: http://www.grc.nasa.gov/WWW/K–12/airplane/thermo1f.html [accessed 9 March 2005].
2. Morris R, Hardy E, editors. *Anguttaranikaya*, London: PTS, 1900.
3. Rhys DCAF. *Visuddhimagga*. London: PTS, 1920–21.
4. in S. 成佛之道 [*Path to Enlightenment*]. Xing Zhu: Zheng Wen Press, 1994.
5. Dhammananda KS. *What Buddhists believe*. Kuala Lumpur: Buddhist Missionary Society Malaysia, 2002.

CHAPTER 7

1. Hong Kong SAR Government. *Coroners Annual Reports* (1999–2003), Hong Kong: HKSAR Government Printers; 1999-2003
2. World Health Organization (WHO). *International Statistical Classification of Diseases & Health Related Problems (ICD-10)*. Second Edition. Geneva: World Health Organisation Press; 2004.
3. Hong Kong SAR Government. *Coroner's Ordinance. Cap Laws of Hong Kong*. Hong Kong: HKSAR Government Printers.

CHAPTER 8

1. Feifel H. Psychology and death: meaningful recovery. *American Psychologist* 1990; 45: 537—43.
2. Cicirelli VG. Personal meanings of death in relation to fear of death. *Death Studies* 1998; 22: 713–33.
3. Corr CA. Children's understandings of death: striving to understand death. In: Doka KJ, editor. *Children mourning, mourning children*. Washington DC: Hospice Foundation of America, 1995: 3–16.
4. Koocher GP. Childhood, death, and cognitive development. *Developmental Psychology* 1973; 9: 369–75.
5. Brent SR, Speece MW. "Adult" conceptualization of irreversibility: implications for the development of the concept of death. *Death Studies* 1993; 17: 203–24.
6. Kane B. Children's concepts of death. *Journal of Genetic Psychology* 1979; 134: 141–53.
7. peece MW, Brent SB. The development of children's understanding of death. In: Corr CA, Corr DM, editors. *Handbook of childhood death and bereavement*. New York: Springer, 1996: 29–50.
8. Nagy M. The child's theories concerning death. *Journal of Genetic Psychology* 1948; 73: 3–27.
9. Kastenbaum R. *The psychology of death*. 2nd ed. New York, NY: Springer, 1992.

10. Speece MW. The search for the mature concept of death: progress on its specification and definition. *The Forum* 1995; 6(1): 20–3.

11. Holcomb LE, Neimeyer RA, Moore MK. Personal meanings of death: a content analysis of free response narratives. *Death Studies* 1993; 17: 299–318.

12. Noppe IC, Noppe LD. Evolving meanings of death during early, middle, and later adolescence. *Death Studies* 1997; 21: 253–75.

13. Leming MR, Dickinson GE. *Understanding dying, death, and bereavement.* New York: Holt, Rinehart, & Winston, 1985.

14. McMordie WR, Kumar A. Cross-cultural research on the Templer/McMordie Death Anxiety Scale. *Psychological Reports* 1984; 54 (959–63).

15. Schumaker JF, Barraclough RA, Vagg LM. Death anxiety in Malsysian and Australian university students. *Journal of Comparative Family Studies* 1988; 22: 85–100.

16. Wilson BA, Ryan S. Working with the terminally ill Chinese-American patient. In: Parry JK, editor. *Social work practice with the terminally ill: a transcultural perspective.* London, UK: Charles C. Thomas, 1990: 145–58.

17. Kulber-Ross E. *Death: the final stage of growth.* New York: Simon & Schuster, Inc., 1975.

18. McLennan J, Stewart CA. Using metaphors to assess anticipatory perceptions of personal death. *Journal of Psychology Interdisciplinary and Applied* 1997; 131: 333–43.

19. Ho SMY, Shiu WCT. Death anxiety and coping mechanism of Chinese cancer patients. *Omega* 1995; 31(1): 59–65.

20. Riley JW. What people think about death. In: Brim O, Freeman H, Levine S, Scotch NA, editors. *The dying patient.* New York: Russell Sage Foundation, 1970: 30–41.

21. Pollio HR, Barlow J, Fine H, Pollio. *Psychology and the poetics of growth.* Mahwah: NJ: Lawrence Erlbaum and Associates, 1977.

22. Cheung WS, Ho SMY. The use of death metaphors to understand personal meaning of death among Hong Kong Chinese undergraduates. *Death Studies* 2004; 28: 47–62.

23. Relational counseling: an Asian perspective on therapeutic intervention. The 55th Annual Convention International Council of Psychologists, 1997, Graz, Austria.

24. Markus HR, Kitayama S. Culture and the self: implications for cognition, emotion, and motivation. *Psychological Review* 1991; 98: 224–53.

25. Ho SMY, Chow AYM, Chan CLW, Tsui YKY. The assessment of grief among Hong Kong Chinese: a preliminary report. *Death Studies* 2002; 26: 91–8.

26. Ho SMY, Ho JWC, Chan CLW, Kwan K, Tsui YKY. Decisional consideration of hereditary colon cancer genetic test results among Hong Kong Chinese adults. *Cancer Epidemiology, Biomarkers & Prevention* 2003; 12(5).

27. Furth GM. *The secret world of drawings: a Jungian approach to healing through art.* Toronto, ON: Inner City Books, 2002.

28. Templer DI. The construction and validation of a death anxiety scale. *Journal of General Psychology* 1970; 82: 167–77.

29. McLennan J, Stewart CA. Using metaphors to assess anticipatory perceptions of personal death. *Journal of Psychology Interdisciplinary & Applied* 1997; 131(3): 333–43.

30. Yang SC, Chen SF. A phenomanographic approach to the meaning of death: a Chinese perspective. *Death Studies* 2002; 26: 243–75.

31. Fowler J. Moral stages and the development of faith. In: Puka B, editor. *Fundamental research in moral development. Moral development: a compendium.* New York, NY: Garland Publishing, Inc., 1994: 344–74.

32. Noppe LD, Noppe IC. Ambiguity in adolescent understandings of death. In: Corr CA, Balk DE, editors. *Handbook of adolescent death and bereavement.* New York: Springer Publishing Company, Inc., 1996.

33. Davis SF, Bremer SA, Anderson BJ, Tramill JL. The interrelationships of ego strength, self-esteem, death anxiety, and gender in undergraduate college students. *Journal of General Psychology* 1983; 108: 55–9.

34. Mikulincer M, Florian V, Tolmacz R. Attachment styles and fear of personal death: a case study of affect regulation. *Journal of Personality and Social Psychology* 1990; 58: 273–80.

35. Sterling CM, Van-Horn KR. Identity and death anxiety. *Adolescence* 1989; 24: 321–26.

36. Harter S. Processes underlying adolescent self-concept formation. In: Montemayor R, Adams GR, editors. *From childhood to adolescence: a transitional period? Advances in adolescent development: an annual book series.* Thousand Oaks, CA: Sage Publications, 1990: 205–39.

37. Bowlby J. Attachment and loss: retrospect and prospect. *American Journal of Orthopsychiatry* 1982; 52: 664–78.

38. Stroebe M, Gergen MM, Gergen KJ, Stroebe W. Broken hearts or broken bonds: love and death in historical perspective. *American Psychologist* 1992; 47: 1205–12.

39. Meshot CM, Leitner LM. Adolescent mourning and parental death. *Omega* 1992–93; 26: 287–99.

CHAPTER 9

1. Yalom ID. *Existential psychotherapy.* New York: Basic Books, 1980.

2. Janoff-Bulman R. *Shattered assumptions.* New York: The Free Press, 1992.

3. Wheeler I. Parental bereavement: the crisis of meaning. Death Studies 2001; 25: 51–66.

4. Neimeyer RA. *Lessons of loss: a guide to coping.* Boston, MA: McGraw-Hill, 2002.

5. Abramovitch HH. "Good death" and "bad death": therapeutic implications of cultural conceptions of death and bereavement. In: Malkinson R, Rubin SS, Witztum E, editors. *Traumatic and non-traumatic loss and bereavement: clinical theory and practice.* Madison, WI: Psychosocial Press, 2000; 255–72.

6. Hsu MT, Hahn DL, Hsu M. A single leaf orchid: meaning of a husband's death for Taiwanese widows. *Ethos* 2003; 30(4): 306–26.

7. Mak MHJ. Awareness of dying: an experience of Chinese patients with terminal cancer. *Omega: Journal of Death and Dying* 2001; 43(3): 259–79.

8. Center for the advancement of health. Report on bereavement and grief research. *Death Studies* 2004; 28(6).

9. Chan WCH. Good life and good death: we need both for good bereavement. Paper presented at the 6th Asia Pacific Hospice Conference, Seoul, Korea; 16–19 March.

10. Nakashima M. *A qualitative inquiry into the psychosocial and spiritual well-being of older adults at the end of life.* [Ph.D. Thesis]. University of Kansas, 2002; 1–280.

11. The Analects (translated by James Legge). Available at: http://www.isop.ucla.edu/eas/documents/lunyu.htm

12. Chu C. Comparison of views on death between Confucianism, Mahism, and Taoism

(In Chinese). 1999. Available at: http://www.taoism.org.hk/religious-studies/9901/art11.htm.

13. Zheng XJ. *Good death and good end: Chinese views on death.* Kunming: Yunnan ren min chu ban she, 1999. (In Chinese)

14. Fu WX. *The dignity of life and death: from hospice psychiatry to modern thanatology.* Taipei: Ching Chung Publisher, 1993. (In Chinese)

15. Engel T. *The four noble truths,* 2000. Available at: http://www.nyimc.org/articles/truths.htm.

16. Lee PC. Understanding death, dying, and religion: a Chinese perspective. In: Parry JK, Ryan AS, editors. *A cross-cultural look at death, dying, and religion.* Chicago, IL: Nelson Halls Publishers, 1995; 172–82.

18. Chao CC. The meaning of good dying of Chinese terminally ill cancer patients in Taiwan. Presentation at 3rd Asia Pacific Hospice Conference, Hong Kong; 3–5 June 1999.

19. Chan C, Chow A. Palliative care and hospice care. Notes of Lecture 4 of the course: oncology, palliative and hospice care (SOWK 6035), 2003. Department of Social Work and Social Administration, University of Hong Kong.

21. Chan WCH. Search for meaning in life: a temporary perspective of bereaved older adults. Paper presented at the 11th Hong Kong International Cancer Congress; 10–12 Nov 2004, Hong Kong.

22. Glaser BG. Doing grounded theory: issues and discussions. Mill Valley, CA: Sociology Press, 1998.

23. Chan WCH, Chan HY, Chan FMY, Tin A, Chan CLW. Perceptions of good death: how does it affect end-of-life care decisions? Presentation at the 11th Hong Kong International Cancer Congress; 10–12 Nov 2004, Hong Kong.

24. Carr D. A "Good death" For whom? Quality of spouse's death and psychological distress among older widowed persons. *Journal of Health and Social Behavior* 2003; 44: 215–32.

25. Walter T. *On bereavement: the culture of grief.* Buckingham, UK; Philadelphia, PA: Open University Press, 1999.

28. Attig T. Meaning of death seen through the lens of grieving. *Death Studies* 2004; 28: 341–60.

29. Henderson JM, Hayslip B Jr, King JK. The relationship between adjustment and bereavement-related distress: a longitudinal study. *Journal of Mental Health Counseling* 2004: 26(2): 98–124.

CHAPTER 10

1. Chan KS. Two decades of palliative care. *Hong Kong Medical Journal* 2002; 8(6): 465–6.

2. Lam KK. Spiritual suffering and spiritual needs in palliative care. *Newsletter, Hong Kong Society of Palliative Medicine* 2002; 2: 4–6.

3. Chan, KS. Ethical decision-making at end of life care. Hospital Authority Convention, Hong Kong, 2000.

4. Pang MCS, Tse CY, Chan KS, Chung BPM, Leung WKA, Leung MF. Towards a methodology for the ethical analysis of treatment-limiting decisions in end of life care. Eighth Annual Qualitative Health Research Conference, Banff, Canada, 2002.

5. Pang MCS, Tse CY, Chan KS, Chung BPM, Leung WKA, Leung MF. From struggled

to prepared death: nurses' therapeutic use of self in patients near the end of life. First International Arts in Healing Institute, Florida, 2003.

6. Sham MKM. Hospice care — a paradigm shift in the care of cancer patients. *The HK Practitioner* 2002; 24(3): 143–6.

7. Hillier R. Palliative medicine — a new specialty. *BMJ* 1988; 297: 874–75t.

8. WHO. *Cancer pain relief and palliative care: report of a WHO expert committee.* Geneva, Switzerland: World Health Organisation, 1990.

9. Sham MKM, Wee BL. The first year of an independent hospice in Hong Kong. *Ann Acad Med Singapore* 1994; 23: 282–6.

10. Sham MK, Chung JPS, Humphries MJ. The hospice care programme at Ruttonjee Sanatorium — the first 2 years' experience. *Journal of Hong Kong Medical Association* 1989; 41(3): 288–91.

11. Sze FK, Chung TK, Wong E, Lam KK, Lo R, Woo J. Pain in Chinese cancer patients under palliative care. *Pall Med* 1998; 12(4): 271–7.

12. Sham MK. Pain control in patients referred to a hospice unit. 3rd Hong Kong International Cancer Congress 1996, Hong Kong.

13. Sham MK. Relieving dyspnoea in patients with advanced cancer. 3rd Asia Pacific Hospice Conference, Hong Kong, 1999.

14. Lo RSK, Woo J, Zhoc KCH, Li CYP, Yeo W, Johnson P, *et al.* Cross-cultural validation of the McGill quality of life questionnaire in Hong Kong Chinese. *Palliative Medicine* 2001; 15: 387–97.

15. Chan KS, Lam ZCL, Chun RPK, Dai DLK, Leung ACT. Chinese patients with terminal cancer. In: Doyle D, Hanks GWC, MacDonald N, editors. *Oxford textbook of palliative medicine.* 2nd edition ed. Oxford: Oxford University Press, 1998: 793–5.

16. Liang, SM 梁漱溟，中國文化要義 · [Themes in Chinese culture]. 香港，三聯書店，1987, 77–94. (In Chinese)

17. Lo RSK, Woo J, Zhoc KCH, Li CYP, Yeo W, Johnson P, *et al.* Quality of life of palliative care patients in the last two weeks of life. *Journal of Pain and Symptom Management* 2002; 24(4): 388–97.

18. Yeung EWF, French P, Leung AOS. The impact of hospice inpatient care on the quality of life of patients terminally ill with cancer. *Cancer Nursing* 1999; 22(5): 350–7.

19. Wills BSH, Wootton YSY. Concerns and misconceptions about pain among Hong Kong Chinese patients with cancer. *Cancer Nursing* 1999; 22(6): 408–13.

20. Chung TK, French P, Chan S. Patient-related barriers to cancer pain management in a palliative care setting in Hong Kong. *Cancer Nursing* 1999; 22(3): 196–203.

21. Chung JWY. Basic principles of pain assessment and evaluation. In: Yang JCS, Tsui SL, editors. *A guide to pain medicine.* Hong Kong: Hong Kong University Press, 2002: 13–32.

22. Chung JWY, Wong TKS, Yang YCS. The lens model: assessment of cancer pain in a Chinese context. *Cancer Nursing* 2000; 23(6): 454–61.

23. Sham MKM. Inhaled fentanyl in the control of dyspnoea in advanced cancer. 3rd Hong Kong International Cancer Congress, Hong Kong, 1996.

24. Tse DMW, Sham MMK, Ng DKH, Ma HM. An ad libitum schedule for conversion of morphine to methadone in advanced cancer patients: an open uncontrolled prospective study in a Chinese population. *Pall Med* 2003; 17: 206–11.

25. Thorsen AB, Yung NSY, Leung ACT. Administration of drugs by infusion pumps in palliative medicine. *Ann Acad Med Singapore* 1994; 23(2): 209–11.
26. Chan KS. Palliation for end stage COPD. *Current management of COPD.* Hong Kong: Hong Kong Lung Foundation Limited, 1999.
27. Thorsen AB, Chan KS, Yung SY, Sham HY, Cheung LW, Chan LN, *et al.* Caring for AIDS patients in palliative care setting. Asia Pacific Hospice Conference, Hong Kong, 1999.
28. Lam PT, Chu CM, Leung WS, Tse CY. Treatment received by patients dying of chronic obstructive pulmonary disease. Asia Pacific Hospice Conference, Hong Kong, 1999.
29. Chu WWC, Leung ACT, Chan KS, Wu YM, Leung DMY. A breakthrough in the end of life care in a nursing home in Hong Kong. *Journal of the Hong Kong Geriatrics Society* 2002; 11(1): 38–41.
30. Lo RSK. Quality of life in palliative care patients: a multi-centre study of profile, determinants and longitudinal changes from inpatient admission to death [Doctor of Medicine Thesis]. Chinese University of Hong Kong, 2002.
31. Lo RSK, Ding A, Chung TK, Sze KH, Woo, J. Pilot programme of clinical assessment of quality of life in palliative care unit in Shatin Hospital. 4th Hong Kong International Cancer Congress, Hong Kong, 1997.
32. Lo RSK, Woo J, Zhoc KCH, Li CYP, Yeo W, Johnson PJ, *et al.* Multi-centre study on palliative care patients' quality of care — preliminary results. Asia Pacific Hospice Conference, Hong Kong, 1999.
33. Lo RSK. Quality of life in palliative care. The First National Quality of Life Symposium, Guangzhou, People's Republic of China, 2000.
34. Lo RSK, Woo J, Zhoc KCH, Li CYP, Yeo W, Johnson P, *et al.* Determinants of QOL in 389 palliative care patients. Asia Pacific Hospice Conference, Osaka, Japan, 2003.
35. Kwok OL, Tse DMW, Ng DKH. Symptom distress as rated by advanced cancer patients, caregivers and physicians in the last week of life. *Pall Med 2005;19:228-233*

CHAPTER 11

1. National Institute for Clinical Excellence. Guidance on cancer services. *Improving supportive and palliative care for adults with cancer.* London, UK, 2004.
2. Ellershaw J, Ward C. Care of the dying patient: the last hours or days of life. *BMJ* 2003; 326: 30–4.
3. Lo RSK, Woo J. Palliative care in the elderly. *Reviews in Clinical Gerontology* 2001; 11: 149–57.
4. The SUPPORT Investigators. A controlled trial to improve care for seriously ill hospitalized patients. *Journal of the AMA* 1995; 274: 1591–8.
5. Lo RSK, Ding A, Chung TK, Woo J. Prospective study of symptom control in 133 cases of palliative care inpatients in Shatin Hospital. *Pall Med* 1999; 13: 335–40.
6. Lo RSK, Woo J, Zhoc KCH *et al.* Cross-cultural validation of the McGill quality of life questionnaire in Hong Kong Chinese. *Pall Med* 2001; 15: 387–97.
7. Lo RSK, Woo J. Palliative care in the elderly. *Journal of the Hong Kong Geriatric Society* 2000: 10: 16–24
8. Lo RSK. Quality of life in palliative care patients: a multi-centre study of profile, determinants and longitudinal changes from inpatient admission to death. (Doctor of Medicine Thesis), 2002, Chinese University of Hong Kong.

9. Lo RSK, Woo J, Zhoc KCH *et al.* Quality of life of palliative care patients in the last two weeks of life. *Journal of Pain and Symptom Management* 2002; 24(4): 388–97.

10. Ng K, Woo J, Kwan M *et al.* Effect of age and disease on taste perception. *Journal of Pain and Symptom Management* 2004; 28: 28–34.

11. Lo RSK, Au KM. Resuscitation decisions at the end of life: the final decisions. *The Hong Kong Society of Palliative Medicine Newsletter* 2002; March (1).

12. Lo RSK, Lai A, Cheng J *et al.* Continuous quality improvement programme for promoting multi-disciplinary patient-centred hospice care. *Hong Kong International Cancer Congress* 1996 (abstract).

13. Lo RSK, Cheng J, Lai A *et al.* Continuous quality improvement programme for promoting training of hospice staff and volunteers. *Hong Kong International Cancer Congress* 1996 (abstract).

14. Lo RSK, Cheng J, Au KM *et al.* Outcomes evaluation of palliative day/home care services. *Asia Pacific Hospice Congress* 1999 (abstract).

15. Cheung S, Lo RSK. Use of aromatherapy in palliative care. *Asia Pacific Hospice Congress* 2003 (abstract).

16. Lo RSK, Hui E, Cheng H, Woo J. Benefits of tai chi in palliative care patients. *Asia Pacific Hospice Congress* 2003 (abstract).

17. Hospital Authority Central Coordinating Committee on Palliative Care. *Guidelines on palliative care.* Available at http://www.ha.org.hk/hesd/nsapi/? MIval=ha_visitor_index&intro=ha%5fview%5ftemplate%26group%3dOSR%26Area%3dFNC.

18. Hospital Authority Central Coordinating Committee on Palliative Care: Quality Assurance Subcommittee. Communication with advanced cancer patients and their families: what is the current standard and is there any scope for improvement? *Hong Kong Hospital Authority Convention* 2004 (abstract).

19. Trent Hospice Audit Group. Palliative care core standards. A multidisciplinary approach, 2nd edition. University of Sheffield, UK, 1998.

20. Lo RSK, Woo J, Zhoc K *et al.* Influence of age on the quality of life of patients at end of life. *Journal of the American Geriatric Society* 2004; 52 (4): S214.

CHAPTER 12

1. Forbes K, Hanks G. The euthanasia debate and a new position paper from a task force of the EAPC: a helpful reappraisal, or a retreat into obfuscation? *Pall Med* 2003; 17: 92–3.

2. Materstvedt LJ, Clark D, Ellershaw J, Forde R, Gravgaard AMB, Muller-Busch HC, *et al.* Euthanasia and physician-assisted suicide: a view from an EAPC ethics task force. *Pall Med* 2003; 17: 97–101.

3. American Medical Association. Withholding or withdrawing life-sustaining medical treatment. *AMA Policy Finder* 1995–98; E–2.20.

4. British Medical Association. Withholding and withdrawing life-prolonging medical treatment: guidance for decision-making. *BMJ* 1999.

5. Canadian Medical Association. Joint statement on resuscitative interventions. *Can Med Assoc J* 1995; 153(11): 1652A–C.

6. Hospital Authority of Hong Kong. *HA guidelines on life-sustaining treatment in the terminally ill.* Hong Kong, 2002.

7. House of Lords Select Committee. Extracts from the Report of the House of Lords

Select Committee on Medical Ethics. In: Keown J, editor. *Euthanasia examined.* Cambridge University Press, 1995; 96–112.

8. Qiu RZ. Chinese medical ethics and euthanasia. *Cambridge Quarterly of Healthcare Ethics* 1993; 2: 69–76.

9. Qiu RZ, Jin DJ. Bioethics in China: 1989–1991. In: Lustig BA, editor. *Bioethics yearbook* 1992; 2: 355–77. Netherlands: Kluwer.

10. Rich V. Will the Chinese legalise euthanasia? *Lancet* 1995; 345: 783.

11. 馮秀雲. 安樂死的幾個法律問題. [Legal questions about euthanasia]. 中國醫學倫理學 1997; 54: 49–51.

12. Ware J, translator. *The sayings of Chuang Tsu: a new translation.* Taipei: Confucius Publishing, 1983; 210.

13. 董平，王曉燕 (Dong P, Wang XY). 道家生死觀下的臨終關懷諧析 [Caring for terminally ill patients: the Daoist perspective]. 中外醫學哲學 *Chinese & International Philosophy of Medicine* 1998; 1(1): 107–20.

14. 羅秉祥 (Lo P.C). 儒家的生死價值觀與安樂死 [Confucian values of life and death and euthanasia]. 中外醫學哲學 *Chinese & International Philosophy of Medicine* 1998; 1(1): 35–73.

15. 郭清秀，靳風林，耿洪剛 (Guo QX, Jing FL, Gen HG). 中國人有關安樂死的價值選擇 [Chinese values concerning euthanasia]. 中外醫學哲學 *Chinese & International Philosophy of Medicine* 1998; 1:1: 137–49.

16. Doyle D. The world of palliative care: one man's view. *J Pall Care* 2003; 19(3): 149–58.

17. Pang MCS. *Nursing ethics in modern China: conflicting values and competing role requirements.* Value Inquiry Book Series 140. Amsterdam-New York: Rodopi, 2003; 153–61.

18. 郭清秀，耿洪剛. 關於安樂死在我國可行性的調查報告. [Report on the feasibility study of euthanasia in China]. 醫學與哲學 1988; 6: 34–7.

19. World Health Organization. *Cancer pain relief and palliative care.* Technical Report Series 804. Geneva, 1990.

20. Harris J. Euthanasia and the value of life. In: Keown J, editor. *Euthanasia examined.* Cambridge University Press, 1995; 6–22.

21. 袁光榮. 醫學目的與安樂死. [The aim of medicine and euthanasia]. 中國醫學倫理學 1997; 56(32): 13.

22. 王兵，朱永熙. 畸形新生兒處置的調查與分析. [Survey on caring for disabled infants]. 醫學與哲學 1990; 10: 31–3.

23. 姚軒鴿，余德華. 關於安樂死道德評價問題的思考. [Ethical consideration of euthanasia]. 中國醫學倫理學 1992; 4: 23–6.

24. President's Commission for the Study of Ethical Problems in Medicine and Biomedical and Behavioral Research. *Deciding to forego life-sustaining treatment.* Washington: US Government Printing Office, 1983; 3.

25. Hui E. A Confucian ethic of medical futility. In: Fan R, editor. Confucian bioethics. *Philosophy and Medicine* 1999; 61: 127–63.

26. Blackhall L, Murphy S, Frank G, Michel V, Azen S. Ethnicity and attitudes toward patient autonomy. *Journal of the AMA* 1995; 274: 820–25.

27. Mitchell JL. Cross-cultural issues in the disclosure of cancer. *Cancer Practice* 1998; 6(3): 153–60.

28. Fan RP. Self-determination vs family-determination: two incommensurable principles of autonomy. *Bioethics* 1997; 11: 309–22.

29. Ho DYF. Selfhood and identity in Confucianism, Taoism, Buddhism, and Hinduism: contrasts with the West. *Journal for the Theory of Social Behaviour* 1995; 25(2): 115–38.

30. Tse CY, Chong A, Fok SY. Breaking bad news: a Chinese perspective. *Pall Med* 2003; 17: 339–43.

31. Pang MCS, Tse CY, Chan KS, Chung BPM, Leung AKA, Leung EMF, *et al.* An empirical analysis of the decision making of limiting life-sustaining treatment for patients with advanced chronic obstructive pulmonary disease in Hong Kong China. *Journal of Critical Care* 2004; 19(3): 135–44.

32. Tse CY, Tao J. Strategic ambiguities in the process of consent: role of the family in decisions to forgo life-sustaining treatment for incompetent elderly patients. *Journal of Medicine and Philosophy* 2004; 29(2): 207–23.

33. Callahan D. *The troubled dream of life.* New York: Simon & Schuster, 1993; 23–56.

CHAPTER 13

1. Medical Service Development Committee. *Medical Service Development Committee — service development and organization of hospice care in Hospital Authority.* Hong Kong: Hong Kong Hospital Authority, 2000. Available at: http://www.ekg.org.hk/html/gateway

2. Aranda SK, Hayman-White K. Home caregivers of the person with advanced cancer: an Australian perspective. *Cancer Nurs* 2001; 24(4): 300–7.

3. Serra-Prat M, Gallo P, Pacaza JM. Home palliative care as a cost-saving alternative: evidence from Catalonia. *Pall Med* 2001; 15: 271–8.

4. Cartwright A. Changes in life and care in the year before death 1969–1987. *J Public Health Med* 1991; 13: 81–7.

5. Government White Paper. *Caring for people — community care in the next decade and beyond,* CM 849. London: HMSO, 1989

6. Winkinson EK, Salisbury C, Bosanquet N, Franks PJ, Kite S, Lorentzon M, Naysmith A. Patient and carer preference for, and satisfaction with, specialist models of palliative carer: a systematic literature review. *Pall Med* 1999; 13: 197–216.

7. Hingginson I, Wade A, McCarthy M. Palliative care: views of patients and their families. *BMJ* 1990; 301: 277–81.

8. Lecouturier J, Jacoby A, Bradshaw C, Lovel T, Eccles M. Lay carers' satisfaction with community palliative care: results of a postal survey. *Pall Med* 1999; 13: 275–83.

9. Medical Service Development Committee. *Medical Service Development Committee — service development and organization of hospice care in Hospital Authority.* Hong Kong: Hong Kong Hospital Authority, 2004.

10. Weitzner MA, McMillan SC. The Caregiver Quality of Life Index-Cancer (CQOLC) scale: revalidation in a home hospice setting. *J Pall Care* 1999; 15(2): 13–20.

11. Mok E, Loke A, Lau T. Needs and support of informal caregivers of disabled dependents. (Chinese version) *The Hong Kong Nurs J* 1994; 68: 4–7.

12. Davis BD, Cowley SA, Ryland RK. The effects of terminal illness on patients and their carers. *J Adv Nurs* 1996; 23(3): 512–20.

13. Wong FKY, Liu CF, Szeto Y, Sham M, Chan T. Health problems encountered by dying patients receiving palliative home care until death. *Cancer Nurs* 2004; 27(3).

14. Doyle D. Domiciliary palliative care. In: Doyle D, Hanks GWC, Macdonald N, editors. *Oxford textbook of palliative medicine,* 2nd ed. Oxford: Oxford Medical Publication, 1999.

15. Loke A, Liu CF, Szeto Y. The difficulties faced by informal caregivers of patients with terminal cancer in Hong Kong and the available social support. *Cancer Nurs* 2003; 26(4): 276–83.

16. Kristjanson L. Families of palliative care patients: a model for care. In: Arande S, O'Connor M, editors. *Palliative care nursing: a guide to practice.* Melbourne: Asumed Publication, 2001.

17. Rose KE. Perceptions related to time in a qualitative study of informal carers of terminally ill cancer patients. *J Clin Nurs* 1998; 7(4): 343–50.

18. Chan WHC, Chang MA. Managing caregiver tasks among family caregivers of cancer patients in Hong Kong. *J Adv Nurs* 1999; 29(2): 484–9.

19. Lazarus RS, Folkman S. *Stress, appraisal and coping.* New York: Springer, 1984.

20. Chan WHC, Chang MA. Stress associated with tasks for family caregivers of patients with cancer in Hong Kong. *Cancer Nurs* 1999; 22(4): 260–5.

21. Nolan MR, Grant G, Ellis NC. Stress is in the eye of the beholder: re-conceptualizing the measurement of carer burden. *J Adv Nurs* 1990; 15: 544–55.

22. Ngan R, Cheng ICK. The caring dilemma, stress, and needs of carers for the Chinese frail elderly. *Hong Kong J Geronotol* 1992; 6(2): 34–41.

23. Mok E, Chan F, Chan V, Yeung E. Family experience caring for terminally ill patients with cancer in Hong Kong. *Cancer Nurs* 2003; 26(4): 267–75.

24. Mackenzie A, Holroyd E. Study of caring and caregiving in Chinese families in Hong Kong. *The Hong Kong Nurs J* 1994; 68: 8–11.

25. Ngan R. *The informal caring networks among Chinese families in Hong Kong.* Hong Kong: University of Hong Kong, 1990.

26. Raudonis BM., Kirschiling M. Family caregivers' perspectives on hospice nursing care. *J Pall Care* 1996; 12(2): 14–9.

27. Payne S, Smith P, Dean S. Identifying the concerns of informal carers in palliative care. *Pall Med* 1999; 13: 37–44.

28. Leung BK. Social issues in Hong Kong. Oxford: Oxford University Press, 1992.

29. Holroyd E. Provision of nursing care for Hong Kong families: future implications. *The Hong Kong Nurs J* 1993; 6(62): 23–6.

30. Hall AJ, Altmann D. Which terminally ill cancer patients in the United Kingdom receive care from community specialist palliative care nurses? *J Adv Nurs* 2000; 32 (4): 799–806.

31. Thomas R. Patients' perceptions of visiting: a phenomenological study in a specialist palliative care unit. *Pall Med* 2001; 15: 499–504.

32. Hinton J. Services given and help perceived during home care for terminal cancer. *Pall Med* 1996; 10: 125–34.

33. Lundh U. Family carers 1: difficulties and levels of support in Sweden. *Br J of Nurs* 1999; 8(9): 582–8.

34. Wallston KA, Burger C, Smith RA, Baugher RJ. Comparing the quality of death for hospice and non-hospice cancer patients. *Med Care* 1988; 26: 177–82.

35. Tang ST. Meanings of dying at home for terminal cancer patients in Taiwan. *Cancer Nurs* 2000; 23: 367–70.

36. Sham, M.K. Medical reasons for hospitalisation of advanced cancer patients during their last three days. *Hong Kong Med J* 2004; 10(6): 433–4.

37. Peruselli C, Giulio PD, Toscani F, Gallucci M, Brunelli C, Costantini M, *et al.* Home palliative care for terminal cancer patients: a survey on the final week of life. *Pall Med* 1999; 13: 233–41.
38. Cox K, Bergen A, Norman I. Exploring consumer views of care provided by the Macmillan nurse using the critical incidence technique. *J Adv Nurs* 1993; 18: 408–15.
39. Buckman R. (1993). Communication in palliative care: a practical guide. In: Doyle D, Hanks GWC, Macdonald N, editors. *Oxford textbook of palliative medicine*. Oxford: Oxford Medical Publication.
40. Tolle SW, Tilden VP, Rosenfeld AG, Hickman SE. Family reports of barriers to optimal care of the dying. *Nurs Research* 2000; 49(6): 310–7.
41. Liu FCF & Lam CCW. Preparing cancer patients to die at home. *HK Nurs J* 2005; 4(1): 7-14.

CHAPTER 14

1. World Health Organization. *WHO traditional medicine strategy*. Geneva: World Health Organization, 2002.
2. Eisenberg DM, Davis RB, Ettner SL, Appel S, Wilkey, S, Van Rompay M, et al. Trends in alternative medicine use in the United States, 1990–1997. *Journal of AMA* 1998; 280: 1569–75.
3. Adler S. Complementary and alternative medicine use among women with breast cancer. *Med Anthropol Q* 1999; 13: 214–22.
4. Chinese Medicine Council of Hong Kong. List of registered Chinese medicine practitioners. Available at: http://www.cmchk.org.hk. Hong Kong: Chinese Medicine Council of Hong Kong, 2005.
5. Lam TP. Strengths and weaknesses of traditional Chinese medicine and Western medicine in the eyes of Hong Kong Chinese. *Epidemiology and Community Health* 2001; 55(10): 762–5.
6. Wong R, Sagar CM, Sagar SM. Integration of Chinese medicine into supportive cancer care: a modern role for an ancient tradition. *Cancer Treatment Review* 2001; 27: 235–46.
7. Li PW. The application of Chinese medicine in cancer palliative medicine. *Chinese Journal of Cancer Pall Med* 2002; 1(1): 1–3.
8. Beinfield H, Korngold E. Chinese medicine and cancer care. *Alternative Therapies* 2003; 9(5): 38–52.
9. Wang HT, Chiu MS, Hong P. *Selected readings from the Inner Canon of Yellow Emperor*. Shanghai: Shanghai Science & Technology Publishing House (in Chinese), 2000.
10. Cai J. *Advanced textbook on traditional Chinese medicine and pharmacology* Vol. 1. Beijing: New World Press, 1995.
11. Li KK, Yang BF. Lecture notes of the Jin Kui Yao Lue. Shanghai: Shanghai Science & Technology Publishing House, 1999. (In Chinese)
12. Li W, Lien EJ. Fu-zhen herbs in the treatment of cancer. *Oriental Healing Arts Int Bul* 1986; 11(1): 1–8.
13. Zhang DZ. Prevention and cure by traditional Chinese medicine of the side effects caused by radio-chemotherapy of cancer patients. *Chinese Journal of Modern Developments in Traditional Medicine* (Chinese) 1988; 8(2): 114–6.

14. Li I, Chen X, Li J. Observations on the long-term effects of yi qi yang yin decoction combined with radiotherapy in the treatment of nasopharyngeal carcinoma. *Journal of Traditional Chinese Medicine* 1992; 12(4): 263–6.

15. Kang K, Kang B, Lee B, Che J, Li G, Trosko JE, et al. Preventive effect of epicatechin and ginsensoide Rb(2) on the inhibition of gap junctional intercellular communication by TP and H(2)O(2). *Cancer Lett* 2000 (152): 97–106.

16. Boik J. Emerging trends in cancer research: development of a mechanism-based approach. *Protocol J Botanic Medicine* 1997(2): 5–9.

17. Tode T, Kikuchi Y, Kita T, Hirata J, Imaizumi E, Nagata I. Inhibitory effects by oral administration of ginsenoside Rh2 on the growth of human ovarian cancer cells in nude mice. *J Cancer Res Clin Oncol* 1993(120): 24–6.

18. Wang JZ, Tsumara H, Shimura K. Antitumour activity of polysaccharide from Chinese medicinal herb, acanthopanax giraldii harms. *Cancer Lett* 1992 (65): 79–84.

19. Lao BH, Ruckle HC, Botolazzo T, Lui PD. Chinese medicinal herbs inhibit growth of murine renal cell carcinoma. *Cancer Biother* 1994(9): 153–61.

20. Fyles AW, Milosevic M, Wong R. Oxygenation predicts radiation response and survival in patients with cervix cancer. *Radiother Oncol* 1998(48): 149–56.

21. Brizel DM, Sibley GS, Prosnitz LR. Tumour hypoxia adversely affects the prognosis of carcinoma of the head and neck. *Int J of Radiat Oncol Biol Phys* 1997(38): 285–9.

22. Xu GZ, Cai WM, Qin DX. Chinese herb 'destagnation' series I: combination of radiation with destagnation in the treatment of nasopharyngeal carcinoma (NPC): a prospective randomized trial on 188 cases. *Int J of Radiat Oncol Biol Phys* 1989 (16): 297–300.

23. Zhou JQ, Li ZH, Jin PL. A clinical study on acupuncture for prevention and treatment of toxic side effects during radiotherapy and chemotherapy. *Journal of Traditional Chinese Medicine* 1999(19): 16–21.

24. Sato T, Yu Y, Guo SY, Kasahara T, Hisamitsu T. Acupuncture stimulation enhances splenic natural killer cell cytotoxicity in rats. *Japanese Journal of Physiology* 1996(46): 131–6.

25. Bianchi M, Jotti E, Sacerdote P, Panerai AE. Traditional acupuncture increases the content of beta-endorphin in immune cells and influences mitogen induced proliferation. *American Journal of Chinese Medicine* 1991(19): 101–4.

26. Petti F, Bangraz A, Liguroi A, Reale G, Ippoliti F. Effects of acupuncture on immune response related to opioid-like peptides. *Journal of Traditional Chinese Medicine* 1998(18): 55–63.

27. Sersa G, Stabuc B, Cemazar M, Miklavcic D, Rudolf Z. Electrochemotherapy with cisplatin: clinical experience in malignant melanoma patients. *Clinical Cancer Research* 2000(6): 863–7.

28. Dundee JW, Chestnutt WN, Ghaly RG, Lynas AGA. Traditional Chinese acupuncture: a potential useful antiemetic? *BMJ* 1986(293): 583–4.

29. Dundee JW, Ghaly RG, Fitzpatrick KTJ, Abram WP, Lynch GA. Acupuncture prophylaxis of cancer chemotherapy-induced sickness. *J Royal Soc Med* 1989(82): 268–71.

30. Lee A, Done ML. The use of nonpharmacologic techniques to prevent postoperative nausea and vomiting: a meta-analysis. *Anesth Analg* 1999(88): 1362–9.

31. Ng SM, Tso IF, Chan CLW. *A prospective study on user satisfaction, treatment efficacy, and incoming and outgoing pathways of patients of the Chinese Medicine Specialist Outpatient Clinic, Tung Wah Hospital,* Hong Kong. Hong Kong: University of Hong Kong, 2005.

CHAPTER 15

1. Illich I. Limits to medicine. Medical nemesis: the expropriation of health. London: Mariou Boyars, 1976.
2. Clark D. Between hope and acceptance: the medicalisation of dying. *BMJ.* 2002, 324: 905–7.
3. Kirchberg TM, Neimeyer RA, James RK. Beginning counselors' death concerns and empathic responses to client situations involving death and grief. *Death Stud* 1998; Mar/Apr, 22: 99–120.
4. Sinclair J [translator]. *The divine comedy of Dante Alighieri.* Oxford University Press, 1961.
5. Fielding R. Life in the fast lane: student life in the University of Hong Kong's new medical curriculum. *Med Educ* 2001; 35: 702.
6. Herzler M, Franze T, Dietze F, Asadullah K. Dealing with the issue 'care of the dying' in medical education — results of a survey of 592 European physicians. *Med Educ* 2000; 34: 146–7.
7. The International Code of Medical Ethics [database on the Internet]. Hong Kong: The Medical Council of Hong Kong. [Revised 2000 Nov; cited 31 Jan. 2005]. Available at: http://www.mchk.org.hk/draft.htm
8. Chan KS. Two decades of palliative care. *Hong Kong Med J* 2002; 8(6): 465–6.
9. Wear D. "Face-to-face with it": medical students' narratives about their end-of-life education. *Acad Med* 2002; 77(4): 271–7.
10. Katz RS, Genevay B. Our patients, our families, ourselves. *Am Behav Sci* 2002 Nov; 46(3): 327–39.
11. Kissane DW. Demoralization syndrome — a relevant psychiatric diagnosis for palliative care. *J Palliat Care* 2001; Spring; 17: 12–21.
12. Parsons T. *Man and boy.* London: HarperCollins, 1999.
13. Bowman KW, Singe PA. Chinese seniors' perspectives on end-of-life decisions. *Soc Sci Med* 2001; 53: 455–64.
14. Woo KY. Care for Chinese palliative patients. *J Pall Care* 1999; 15(4): 70–4.
15. Tse CY, Chong A, Fok SY. Breaking bad news: a Chinese perspective. *Palliat Med* 2003; 17: 339–343.
16. Mulder J, Gregory D. Transforming experience into wisdom: healing amidst suffering. *J Palliat Care* 2000; 16(2): 25–9.
17. Brazier D. *Zen therapy.* London: Constable & Robinson, 2001.
18. Qian M. *Ren sheng shi lun.* Hong Kong: Cosmos Books, 2003. (In Chinese)
19. Xu Z. *Bai hua lun yu.* Hong Kong: Joint Publishing, 2000. (In Chinese)
20. Lu Y, editor. *Dao de jing.* Hong Kong: Chung Hwa Books, 2003. (In Chinese)
21. Bunson ME, editor. *The Dalai Lama's book of wisdom.* London: Rider, 2000.
22. Martin JD, Ferris FD. *I can't stop crying: it's so hard when someone you love dies.* Toronto, ON: Key Porter Books, 1992.
23. MacLeod RD, Parkin C, Pullon S, Robertson G. Early clinical exposure to people who are dying: learning to care at the end of life. *Med Educ* 2003; 37: 51–8.

24. Remen RN. Physicians need to reclaim meaning in their working lives. *West J Med* 2001 Jan; 174: 4–5.

25. Nager F. Doctor and death. *Schweiz Rundsch Med Prax.* 2004; 93(5): 140–9.

26. Sontag S. *Regarding the pain of others.* New York: Farrar, Straus & Giroux, 2003.

27. Maslach C, Jackson SE. The measurement of experienced burnout, *J Occup Behav* 1981; 2: 99–113.

28. Greenberg JS. *Comprehensive stress management.* Boston, MA: McGraw-Hill, 1999.

29. Covey SR. *The 8th habit.* New York: Free Press, 2004.

30. *Hua Nan Zi* [database on the Internet]. Taiwan: Huafan University Department of Philosophy. c2004 [cited 16 Feb 2005]. (In Chinese) Available at: http://www. hfu.edu.tw/~bauruei/5rso/texts/2han/te23.htm

31. Holden R. *Happiness now.* Philadelphia, PA: Coronet Books; 1998.

32. Sachs A. Online famous quotes. [database on the Internet]. US: QuoteHead.com; c2004 [cited 16 Feb 2005]. Available at: http://www.quoteshead.com/ show_authors_quotes/a-g%7e—sachs/1/

33. Gregory D. The myth of control: suffering in palliative care. *J Palliat Care* 1994; 10(2): 18–22.

CHAPTER **16**

1. Buckman R. Communication skills in palliative care — a practical guide. *Neurologic Clinics* 2001; 19(4): 989–1004

2. Rabow MW, McPhee SJ. Beyond breaking bad news: how to help patients who suffer. *Western Journal of Medicine* 1999; 171(4): 260–3.

3. Fraisse P. Breaking bad news by the respiratory physician: a therapeutic process. *Revue Des Maladies Respiratoires* 2004; 21(1): 75–91.

4. Woolfson RC. Breaking the bad news. *Practitioner* 2000; 244(1608): 247–250.

5. Hospital Authority. Statistical report 2002/2003. Hong Kong: Hospital Authority, 2004.

6. Lo RSK. Dying: the last month. In: Chan CLW, Chow AYM, editors. *Death, dying and bereavement: the Hong Kong Chinese experience.* Hong Kong: Hong Kong University Press, 2006; 151–168.

7. Silverman H. Withdrawal of feeding-tubes from incompetent patients: the Terri Schiavo case raises new issues regarding who decides in end-of-life decision making. *Intensive Care Medicine* 2005; 31(3): 480–1.

8. Quill TE. Terri Schiavo — a tragedy compounded. *NEJM* 2005; 352(16): 1630–1633.

9. Annas GJ. "Culture of life" politics at the bedside — the case of Terri Schiavo. *NEJM* 2005; 352(16): 1710–5.

10. Hospital Authority. Statistical report 2002/2003, Hospital Authority, Hong Kong. Hong Kong, 2004.

11. Ho TP, Tay MSM. Suicides in general hospitals in Hong Kong: retrospective study. *Hong Kong Medical Journal* 2004; 10(5): 319–24.

12. ICN. Position statement on nurses' role in providing care to dying patients and their families, 2000.

13. Reimer JC, Davies B, Martens N. Palliative care — the nurse's role in helping families through the transition of fading away. *Cancer Nursing* 1991; 14(6): 321–7.

14. Fakhoury WKH. Quality of palliative care: why nurses are more valued than doctors. *Scandinavian Journal of Social Medicine* 1998; 26(2): 131–2.

15. Butcher M. A nurse's approach to palliative and terminal care of the cancer-patient. *Ear Nose & Throat Journal* 1983; 62(5): 262–5.

16. Briggs L, Colvin E. The nurse's role in end-of-life decision-making for patients and families. *Geriatric Nursing* 2002; 23(6): 302–10.

17. Volker DL, Kahn D, Penticuff JH. Patient control and end-of-life care part I: the advanced practice nurse perspective. *Oncol Nurs Forum* 2004; 31(5): 945–53.

18. Breitbart W, Gibson C, Poppito SR, Berg A. Psychotherapeutic interventions at the end of life: a focus on meaning and spirituality. *Can J Psychiatry* 2004; 49(6): 366–72.

19. Greenberg LS. Lessons about anger and sadness from psychotherapy. In: Greenberg, LS editor. *Emotion-focused therapy: coaching clients to work through their feelings.* Washington, DC: American Psychological Association, 2001: 229–40.

20. Mok E, Chan F, Chan V, Yeung E. Family experience caring for terminally ill patients with cancer in Hong Kong. *Cancer Nurs* 2003; 26(4):2 67–75.

21. Chan KS, Lam ZCL, Chun RPK, Dai DLK, Leung ACT. Chinese patients with terminal cancer. In: Doyle D, Hanks GWC, MacDonald N, editors. *Oxford textbook of palliative medicine.* 2nd ed. Oxford, New York: Oxford University Press, 1998; 793–796.

22. Berry P, Griffie J. Planning for the actual death. In: Ferrell BR, Coyle N, editors. *Textbook of Palliative Nursing.* New York: Oxford University Press, 2001: 382–94.

23. Cheung WS, Ho SMY. The use of death metaphors to understand personal meaning of death among Hong Kong Chinese undergraduates. *Death Studies* 2004; 28(1): 47–62.

24. The meaning of good dying of Chinese terminally ill cancer patients in Taiwan. 3rd Asia Pacific Hospice Conference, 3–5 June 1999, Hong Kong.

25. Li SP, Chan CWH, Lee DTF. Helpfulness of nursing actions to suddenly bereaved family members in an accident and emergency setting in Hong Kong. *Journal of Advanced Nursing* 2002; 40(2): 170–80.

26. Buckley TA, Joynt GM. Limitation of life support in the critically ill: the Hong Kong perspective. *Ann Acad Med Singapore* 2001; 30(3): 281–6.

27. Couden BA. "Sometimes I want to run": a nurse reflects on loss in the intensive care unit. *J Loss & Trauma* 2002; 7(1): 35–45.

28. de Araujo MMT, da Silva MJP. Communication with dying patients — perception of intensive care units nurses in Brazil. *J Clinical Nurs* 2004; 13(2): 143–9.

29. Kirchhoff KT, Conradt KL, Anumandla PR. ICU nurses' preparation of families for death of patients following withdrawal of ventilator support. *Applied Nursing Research* 2003; 16(2): 85–92.

30. Saflund K, Sjogren B, Wredling R. The role of caregivers after a stillbirth: views and experiences of parents. *Birth-Issues in Perinatal Care* 2004; 31(2): 132–7.

31. Hughes P, Turton P, Hopper E, Evans CDH. Assessment of guidelines for good practice in psychosocial care of mothers after stillbirth: a cohort study. *Lancet* 2002; 360(9327): 114–8.

32. Kaplan LJ. Toward a model of caregiver grief: nurses' experiences of treating dying children. *Omega — Journal of Death and Dying* 2000; 41(3): 187–206.

33. Albersheim SG. Life and death decision-making in the NICU: do parents, doctors and nurses see eye to eye? *Pediatric Research* 2004; 55(4): 56–62.

34. Yam BMC, Rossiter JC, Cheung KYS. Caring for dying infants: experiences of neonatal intensive care nurses in Hong Kong. *J Clinical Nurs* 2001; 10(5): 651–9.

35. Ambuehl E. Psychosocial care of mothers after stillbirth. *Lancet* 2002; 360(9345): 1601.
36. Brooks D. Psychosocial care of mothers after stillbirth. *Lancet* 2002; 360(9345): 1601.
37. Kersting A, Fisch S, Baez E. Psychosocial care of mothers after stillbirth. *Lancet* 2002; 360(9345): 1600.
38. McCabe A. Psychosocial care of mothers after stillbirth. *Lancet* 2002; 360(9345): 1600-1.
39. Matthews M, Kohner N. Psychosocial care of mothers after stillbirth. *Lancet* 2002; 360(9345): 1600.
40. Hughes P, Turton P, Hopper E, Evans CDH. Psychosocial care of mothers after stillbirth — reply. *Lancet* 2002; 360(9345): 1601-2.
41. Street JRL. Interpersonal communication skills in health care contexts. In: Greene JO, Burleson BR, editors. *Handbook of communication and social interaction skills in health care contexts*. Mahwah, NJ: Lawrence Erlbaum, 2003.
42. Main J. Management of relatives of patients who are dying. *J Clinical Nurs* 2002; 11(6): 794-801.
43. Burgess TA, Brooksbank M, Beilby JJ. Talking to patients about death and dying. *Aust Fam Physician* 2004; 33(1–2): 85-6.
44. Mok E, Lee WM, Wong FKY. The issue of death and dying: employing problem-based learning in nursing education. *Nurse Education Today* 2002; 22(4): 319-29.
45. Hopkinson JB, Hallett CE, Luker KA. Everyday death: how do nurses cope with caring for dying people in hospital? *International Journal of Nursing Studies* 2005; 42(2): 125-33.

CHAPTER 17

1. Cao JL. A survey on the causes of childhood death under five years old in Lian Yun Gang from 1997 to 1999. *Journal of Qiqihar Medical College* 2001; 22: 1320-1. (In Chinese)
2. The National Collaborative Group for Survey of Deaths of Children Under Five. A survey on deaths of children under the age of five years in China. *Chinese Journal of Pediatry* 1994; 32: 149–52. (In Chinese)
3. Wang YG. An analysis on causes of death of children from birth to fourteen years old in Xu Hui District Shanghai. *Shanghai Journal of Preventive Medicine* 1996; 8: 506–8. (In Chinese)
4. Hu YM. Setting up a medical centre for children with leukaemia. *China Oncology* 2002; 11: 8. (In Chinese)
5. Gu LJ. Increasing disease-free survival rate for childhood ALL by developing standardized treatment protocol. *China Journal of Haematology* 1999; 20: 341-2. (In Chinese)
6. The Leukemia & Lymphoma Society website: http://www.leukemia-lymphoma.org/all_faq.adp?item_id=9454. Retrieved on 2 April 2005.
7. Chen J, Gu LJ, Yao HY, Shen LX. Quality of life of twenty-two survivals of acute nonlymphobastic leukaemia. *China Journal of Pediatric* 2000; 38: 111-2. (In Chinese)
8. Stein RE. Reissman CK. The development of an Impact-on-Family Scale. *Medical Care* 1980; XVIII: 465-72.

9. Sawyer MG, Antoniou G, Toogood I, Rice, M, Baghurst PA. A prospective study of the psychological adjustment of parents and families of children with cancer. *Journal of Pediatric Child Health* 1993; 29: 352–6.

10. Sharan P. Mehta M, Chaudhry VP. Psychiatric disorders among parents of children suffering from acute lymphoblastic leukemia. *Pediatric Hematology and Oncology* 1999; 16: 43–7.

11. Blount RL, Davis N, Powers S, Roberts MC. The influence of environmental factors and coping style on children's coping and distress. *Clinical Psychology Review* 1991; 11: 93–116.

12. Rosenblatt PC. A social constructionist perspective on cultural differences in grief. In: Stroebe MS, Hansson RO, Stroebe W, Schut H, editors. *Handbook of bereavement research: consequences, coping and care.* Washington DC: American Psychological Association, 1991: 285–300.

13. Bronfenbrenner U. *The ecology of human development.* Cambridge, MA: Harvard University Press, 1979.

14. Bronfenbrenner U. Ecology of the family as a context for human development: research perspectives. *Developmental Psychology* 1986; 22: 723–42.

15. Wu DYH. Chinese childhood socialization. In Bond MH, editor. *The handbook of Chinese psychology.* Hong Kong: Oxford University Press, 1986: 143–54.

16. Bond MH, Hwang KK. The social psychology of Chinese people. In: Bond MH, editor. *The psychology of the Chinese people.* Hong Kong: Oxford University Press, 1986: 213–66.

17. Goodwin R, Tang CS. Chinese personal relationships. In: Bond MH, editor. *The handbook of Chinese psychology.* Hong Kong: Oxford University Press, 1996: 294–308.

18. Gong S. Health-care system for employers in state-owned enterprises: historical review and prospect. Internal report no. 4. Beijing: Social Development Department, Development Research Centre, State Council, 2004. (In Chinese)

19. Gong S. China's financial health input and the analysis of its performance since economic reform. Internal report no. 2. Beijing: Social Development Department, Development Research Centre, State Council, 2004. (In Chinese)

20. World Health Organization. World health report 2000 — health system: improving performance. Geneva: WHO, 2000. Available at http://www.who.int/whr2001. 2001/achives/2000/en/index.htm.

21. World Health Organization. *World health report.* Geneva: WHO, 2003.

22. Shanghai Statistics Bureau. *Statistical yearbook of Shanghai* 2001. Shanghai: Author, 2001.

23. Gu LJ, Yao HY, Xue HL, Zhao, HJ, Wang YP, Gu MY, et al. Initial and continuous intensive chemotherapy for childhood acute lymphoblastic leukaemia (ALL): the clinical results in treatment of 57 cases with XH-88 protocol. *Chinese Journal of Haematology* 1994; 15: 76–9.

24. Gu LJ, Sun GX, Lu XT, Tang JY, Wu MY. Suggested treatment protocol for childhood acute lymphocytic leukaemia (ALL). *Chinese Journal of Pediatry* 1999; 37: 305–7. (In Chinese)

25. Zhang YP, Zhang XC, Zheng CJ, Xu JH, Guo LC, Li CY, et al. Logistic regression analysis of risk factors in child leukaemia. *China Journal of Pediatry* 1999; 37: 625–8. (In Chinese)

26. Chen J, Gu LJ, Xu YP, Yao HY. A survey on psychological behavioural characteristics of children with leukaemia. In: Proceedings of the 1st National Symposium on

Psychosocial Oncology for Cancer Patients, 15–17 April 2002, Shanghai: 94–7. (In Chinese)

27. Fu XY, Meng F, Li CB, Liang AB, Xie XT, Mei Z. A survey on personality and behavioural problems among children with blood cancer. In: Proceedings of the 1st National Symposium on Psychosocial Oncology for Cancer Patients, 15–17 April 2002, Shanghai: 100–3. (In Chinese)

28. Shen NP, Xu LH. An exploratory study on parents stress, feeling of uncertainty and needs of parents who have children with leukaemia. In: Proceedings of the 1st National Symposium on Psychosocial Oncology for Cancer Patients, 15–17 April 2002, Shanghai: 105–9. (In Chinese)

29. Brown RT, Kaslow NJ, Madan-Swain A, Koepke KJ, Sexson SB, Hill LJ. Parental psychopathology and children's adjustment to leukemia. *Journal of the American Academy of Child and Adolescent Psychiatry* 1993; 32: 554–61.

30. Kazak AE, Penati B, Boyer BA, Himelstein B, Brophy P, Waibel MK, et al. A randomized controlled prospective outcome study of a psychological and pharmacological intervention protocol for procedural distress in pediatric leukemia. *Journal of Pediatric Psychology* 1996; 21: 615–31.

31. Wills BS. The experiences of Hong Kong Chinese parents of children with acute lymphocytic leukemia. *Journal of Pediatric Nursing* 1999; 14: 231–8.

32. Zhu YM. Psychosocial support for parents of children with cancer. In: Proceedings of the 1st National Symposium on Psychosocial Oncology for Cancer Patients, 15–17 April 2002, Shanghai: 1–4. (In Chinese)

33. Weiss R. Loss and recovery. In: Stroebe MS, Stroebe W, Hansson RO, editors. *Handbook of bereavement: theory, research and intervention.* Cambridge: Cambridge University Press, 1993: 271–84.

34. Bowlby J. *Attachment and loss vol. 1. Attachment.* London: Hogarth, 1969.

35. Bowlby J. *Attachment and loss vol. 2. Separation: anxiety and anger.* London: Hogarth, 1973.

36. Ho SMY, Chow AYM, Chan CLW, Tsui YKY. The assessment of grief among Hong Kong Chinese: a preliminary report. *Death Studies* 2002; 26: 91–8.

37. Tsui YKY. Other-focused grief. Paper presented at the 8th Hong Kong International Cancer Congress, September 2001, Hong Kong.

38. Tutty LM, Rothery M, Grinnell RM. *Qualitative research for social workers: phrases, steps, & tasks.* Boston, MA: Allyn & Bacon, 1996.

39. Denzin NK, Lincoln YS. *Strategies of qualitative inquiry.* London: Sage Publications, 1998.

40. Russell JA, Yik MSM. Emotion among the Chinese. In: Bond MH, editor. *The handbook of Chinese psychology.* Hong Kong: Oxford University Press, 1996: 166–88.

41. Jackson AC, Tsantefski M, Goodman H, Johnson B, Rosenfeld J. The psychosocial impacts on families of low-incidence, complex conditions in children: the case of craniopharyngioma. *Social Work in Health Care* 2003; 38: 81–107.

42. Helson R. Comparing longitudinal studies of adult development: toward a paradigm of tension between stability and change. In: Funder D, Parke R, Tomlinson-Keasey C, Widarman K, editors. *Studying lives through time: personality development.* Washington, DC: American Psychological Association, 1993: 93–119.

43. Ronka A, Kinnunen U, Pulkkinen L. The accumulation of problems of social functioning as a long-term process: women and men compared. International *Journal of Behavioral Development* 2000; 24: 442–50.

44. Lou VWQ, Shen NP, Zhao HJ, Shen GM. Mental health of parents of children with leukemia in China. World Federation for Mental Health Biennial Congress 2003; Melbourne, Australia 23–28, February.

45. Kupst MJ, Schulman JL. Long term coping with pediatric leukemia: a six-year follow-up study. *Journal of Pediatric Psychology* 1988; 13: 7–22.

46. Kupst MJ, Natta MB, Richardson CC, Schulman JL, Lavigne JV, Das L. Family coping with pediatric leukemia: ten years after treatment. *Journal of Pediatric Psychology* 1995; 20: 601–17.

CHAPTER 18

1. Chow AYM, Koo BWS, Koo EWK, Lam AYY. Turning grief into good separation: bereavement services in Hong Kong. In: Fielding R, Chan LWC, editors. *Psychosocial oncology & palliative care in Hong Kong: the first decade.* Hong Kong: Hong Kong University Press, 2000: 233–54.

2. Chan CLW. Death awareness and palliative care. In: Fielding R, Chan CLW, editors. *Psychosocial oncology & palliative care in Hong Kong: the first decade.* Hong Kong: Hong Kong University Press, 2000: 213–32.

3. Tong CK. *Chinese death rituals in Singapore.* London: RoutledgeCurzon, 2004.

4. hkacs.org.hk. Updates of events and review. In: Society HKACS, editor. Hong Kong.

5. Worden JW. *Grief counseling and grief therapy: a handbook for the mental health practitioner.* New York: Springer, 1982.

6. Worden JW. 悲傷輔導與悲傷治療 (李開敏譯) [Grief counselling and grief therapy]. 台北：心理出版社有限公司，1995.

7. Chow YMA, University of Hong Kong. The development of a practice model for working with the bereaved relatives of cancer patients: the single system study of the "walking through the road of sorrow" [M.Soc.Sc. Thesis]. University of Hong Kong, 1995.

8. Chan CLW, University of Hong Kong. Department of Social Work and Social Administration. *An eastern body-mind-spirit approach: a training manual with one-second techniques.* Hong Kong: Department of Social Work and Social Administration University of Hong Kong, 2001.

9. Ng Y, Siu D, 別矣吾愛 Goodbye, my love, videorecording]. Hong Kong: RTHK, 香港電台，1996.

10. Chan CLW, University of Hong Kong. Department of Social Work and Social Administration. *Therapeutic groups in medical settings.* Hong Kong: Department of Social Work, 1996.

11. Hong Kong Society for Rehabilitation. Community Rehabilitation Network. 長期病患者: 治療小組導師手冊 [*Therapeutic groups for the chronically ill and families*]. 香港: 香港復康會社區復康網絡, 1998.

12. Bradbury Hospice. 雨後陽光 [*Sunbeams after rain*]. Hong Kong: Bradbury Hospice, 1997.

13. Chen L, Chung C. Comfort Care Concern. *Bereavement counseling handbook: concepts and methods.* 2nd ed. Hong Kong: The Comfort Care Concern Group, 2002.

14. Tuen Mun Hospital. EQ Students Ambassador Project. Hong Kong.

15. Chow YMA, Koo WSB, Koo WKE. 孩子心, 善別路 [Little grieving hearts]. 香港: 善終服務會譚雅士杜佩珍安家舍, 2000.

16. Allumbaugh DL, Hoyt WT. Effectiveness of grief therapy: a meta-analysis. *Journal of Counseling Psychology* 1999;46(3):370–380.
17. Schut H, Stroebe M, van den Bout J, Terheggen, M. The efficacy of bereavement interventions: Determining who benefits. In: Stroebe MS, Hansson RO, Stroebe W, Schut H, editors. *Handbook of bereavement research: consequences, coping, and care.* 1st ed. Washington, DC: American Psychological Association, 2001: 705–37.
18. Jordan JR, Neimeyer R. Does grief counseling work? *Death Studies* 2003; 27(9): 765–86.
19. Cohen J. *Statistical power analysis for the behavioral sciences.* 2nd ed. Hillsdale, NJ: Lawrence Erlbaum Associates, 1988.
20. Murphy KR, Myors B. *Statistical power analysis: a simple and general model for traditional and modern hypothesis tests.* 2nd ed. Mahwah, NJ: Lawrence Erlbaum, 2004.
21. Rosenblatt PC. A social constructionist perspective on cultural difference in grief. In: Stroebe MS, Hansson RO, Stroebe W, Schut H, editors. *Handbook of bereavement research: consequences, coping, and care.* 1st ed. Washington, DC: American Psychological Association, 2001: 285–300.
22. Stroebe MS, Hansson RO, Stroebe W, Schut H. Future directions for bereavement research. In: Stroebe MS, Hansson RO, Stroebe W, Schut H, editors. *Handbook of bereavement research: consequences, coping, and care.* 1st ed. Washington, DC: American Psychological Association, 2001: 741–66.
23. Neimeyer RA, Hogan NS. Quantitative or qualitative? Measurement issues in the study of grief. In: Stroebe MS, Hansson RO, Stroebe W, Schut H, editors. *Handbook of bereavement research: consequences, coping, and care.* 1st ed. Washington, DC: American Psychological Association, 2001: 89–118.
24. Ho SM, Chow AY, Chan CL, Tsui YK. The assessment of grief among Hong Kong Chinese: a preliminary report. *Death Stud* 2002; 26(2): 91–8.
25. Chow AYM. 善別輔導:與喪親者共行的經歷 [Bereavement Counselling: the pathway with bereaved persons]. In: Chan CLW, Ho SMY, Fan FM, Wong AMP, editors. 華人文化與心理輔導模式探索 [*The exploration of the culture and model in psychotherapy of Chinese*]. 北京：民族出版社。 2002: 236–44.
26. Chan CLW. *An eastern body-mind-spirit approach: a training manual with one-second techniques.* Resource Paper Series No. 43. Hong Kong: Department of Social Work and Social Administration, The University of Hong Kong, 2001.
27. Cheung FM, Lau BWK, Waldmann E. Somatization among Chinese depressives in general-practice. *International Journal of Psychiatry in Medicine* 1981; 10(4): 361–74.
28. Tung MPM. Symbolic meanings of the body in Chinese culture and somatization. *Culture Medicine and Psychiatry* 1994; 18(4): 483–92.
29. Chow AYM, Koo BWS, Koo EWK, Lam AYY. Turning grief into good separation: bereavement services in Hong Kong. In: Fielding R, Chan CLW, editors. *Psychosocial oncology & palliative care in Hong Kong: the first decade.* Hong Kong: Hong Kong University Press, 2000: 233–54.
30. Chow, AYM, An update on bereavement research in Hong Kong. Paper presened at 10th Hong Kong International Cancer Congress, 19–21 November 19–21, 2003; Hong Kong.
31. Chow AYM. Social sharing experience by Chinese bereaved persons in Hong Kong. Paper presented at 27th Annual ADEC Conference, 31 March – 3 April 2005; Albuquerque, New Mexico.

32. Ayers T, Balk D, Bolle J, Bonanno GA, Connor SR, Cook AS, *et al.* Report on bereavement and grief research. *Death Studies* 2004; 28(6): 491–575.

CHAPTER 19

1. Rosenblatt PC. A social constructionist perspective on cultural differences in grief. In: Stroebe MS, Hansson RO, Stroebe W, Schut H, editors. *Handbook of bereavement research: consequences, coping, and care.* 1st ed. Washington, DC: American Psychological Association, 2001: 285–300.
2. Rando TA. *How to go on living when someone you love dies.* New York: Bantam Books, 1991.
3. Rando TA. *Treatment of complicated mourning.* Champaign, IL: Research Press, 1993.
4. Worden JW. *Grief counselling and grief therapy: a handbook for the mental health practitioner.* 2nd ed. London: Routledge, 1991.
5. Baker JE, Sedney MA, Gross E. Psychological tasks for bereaved children. *American Journal of Orthopsychiatry* 1992; 62: 105–16.
6. Baker JE, Sedney MA, Gross E. How bereaved children cope with loss: an overview. In: Corr CA, Corr DM, editors. *Handbook of childhood death and bereavement.* New York: Springer, 1996: 109–30.
7. Furman E. *A child's parent dies: studies in childhood bereavement.* New Haven, CT: Yale University Press, 1974.
8. Kwok YW. 郭于華，死的困惑與生的執著 [Confusion about death, attachment about life]. 洪葉文庫，台北, 1991.
9. Cheng HK. 鄭曉江，中國死亡智慧 [The Chinese wisdom in death]. 東大圖書，台北，1994.
10. Chan KS, Lam ZCL, Chun RPK, Dai DLK, Leung ACT. Chinese patients with terminal cancer. In: Doyle D, Hanks GWC, MacDonald N, editors. *Oxford textbook of palliative medicine.* 2nd ed. Oxford: Oxford University Press, 1998: 793–5.
11. Worden JW. *Grief counseling and grief therapy: a handbook for the mental health practitioner.* 3rd ed. New York: Springer Pub., 2002.
12. Corr CA, Nabe C, Corr DM. *Death and dying, life and living.* 4th ed. Belmont, CA: Wadsworth, 2003.
13. Tseng W-S, Lu QY, Yin PY. Psychotherapy for the Chinese: cultural considerations. In: Lin TY, Tseng WS, Yeh Y, editors. *Chinese societies and mental health.* Hong Kong: Oxford University Press, 1995: 281–94.
14. Ting HS. 丁曉山，中華全書百卷書 —傳統文化系列：中華家庭文化 [*The complete book of Chinese culture: the culture of families*]. 首都師範大學出版社，北京，1994.
15. Sun LK. 孫隆基，中國文化的深層結構 [Deeper structure of Chinese culture]. 集賢社，台北，1992.
16. Hsu J. Family therapy for the Chinese: problems and strategies. In: Lin TY, Tseng WS, Yeh Y, editors. *Chinese societies and mental health.* Hong Kong: Oxford University Press, 1995: 281–94.
17. Klass D, Silverman PR, Nickman SL. *Continuing bonds: new understandings of grief.* Washington, DC: Taylor & Francis, 1996.
18. Chan LWC. Grief and bereavement in a Hong Kong Chinese cultural context. In: Chan LWC, Ho SMY, Chow AYM, Tin AF, Koo BWS, editors. *Innovative bereavement care in local practice.* Hong Kong: Jessie and Thomas Tan Centre of SPHC, 2000: 3–16.

19. Martin TL, Doka KJ. *Men don't cry — women do: transcending gender stereotypes of grief.* Philadelphia, PA: Brunner/Mazel, 2000.
20. Chu DD. A death in the family: family readjustment at the death of a parent [M. S.W. Thesis]. University of Hong Kong, 1975.
21. Ho DYL. Bereavement and coping in widows following the loss of their husband [Unpublished M.S.W. Thesis]. The University of Hong Kong, 1992.
22. Worden JW. *Children and grief: when a parent dies.* New York: Guilford Press, 1996.
23. Silverman PR, Nickman SL. Introduction: what's the problem. In: Klass D, Silverman PR, Nickman SL, editors. *Continuing bonds: new understandings of grief.* Washington, DC: Taylor & Francis, 1996: 3–30.
24. Oltjenbruns KA. Developmental context of childhood: Grief and regrief phenomena. In: Stroebe MS, Hansson RO, Stroebe W, Schut H, editors. *Handbook of bereavement research: consequences, coping, and care.* 1st ed. Washington, DC: American Psychological Association, 2001: 169–98.
25. Christ GH. *Healing children's grief: surviving a parent's death from cancer.* New York: Oxford University Press, 2000.
26. Scrutton S. *Bereavement and grief: supporting older people through loss.* London: Edward Arnold, 1995.

CHAPTER 20

1. Chan CLW, Chow AYM. An indigenous psycho-educational counselling group for Chinese bereaved family members. *Hong Kong Journal of Social Work* 1998; 32(1): 1–26.
2. Schaefer JA, Moos RH. Bereavement experiences and personal growth. In: Stroebe MS, Hansson RO, Stroebe WG, Schut H, editors. *Handbook of bereavement research: consequences, coping, and care.* Washing DC: American Psychological Association, 2001: 145–68.
3. Rando TA. *Treatment of complicated mourning.* Champaign, IL: Research Press, 1993.
4. Yalom I. *The theory and practice of group psychotherapy.* New York: Basic Books, 1985.
5. Markus HR, Kitayama S. Culture and the self: implications for cognition, emotion, and motivation. *Psychological Review* 1991; 98: 224–53.
6. Ho SMY, Fan FM, Cheng NKC. 何敏賢、樊富珉、鄭躬貞. 香港華人的死亡及悲痛的互賴關係 [The interdependence of grief in Chinese]. 華人心理輔導理論與實踐研究, 2002.
7. Stone WN. Commentary on bereavement groups. *The International Journal of Group Psychotherapy* 1988; 38(4): 447–51.

CHAPTER 21

1. Saunders CM, Kastenbaum R. *Hospice care on the international scene.* New York: Springer Pub. Co., 1997.
2. Larson D. *The helper's journey: working with people facing grief, loss, and life-threatening illness.* Champaign, IL: Research Press, 1993.
3. Payne S. The role of volunteers in hospice bereavement support in New Zealand. *Pall Med* 2001; 15:107–15.
4. Chung LST. The hospice movement in a Chinese Society — a Hong Kong experience. In: Saunders CM, Kastenbaum R, editors. *Hospice care on the international scene.* New York: Springer Pub. Co., 1997: xii, 303.

5. Doyle D. *Volunteers in hospice and palliative care — a handbook for volunteer service managers.* New York: Oxford University Press, 2002.

6. Chan EHC. Candles for the bereaved. *Newsletter of Hong Kong Society of Palliative Medicine* 2004; 2004(2).

7. Relf M. Involving volunteers in bereavement counselling. *Eur J Pall Care* 1998; 2: 61–5.

8. Chow AYM, Koo BWS, Koo EWK, Lam AYY. Turning grief into good separation: bereavement services in Hong Kong. In: Fielding R, Chan CLW, editors. *Psychosocial oncology & palliative care in Hong Kong: the first decade.* Hong Kong: Hong Kong University Press, 2000: 233–54.

9. Parkes CM. *Bereavement: studies of grief in adult life.* 3rd ed. London; New York: Routledge, 1996.

10. Stroebe W, Stroebe MS. *Bereavement and health: the psychological and physical consequences of partner loss.* Cambridge: Cambridge University Press, 1987.

11. Chen L, Chung C, Comfort Care Concern. *Bereavement counseling handbook: concepts and methods.* 2nd ed. Hong Kong: The Comfort Care Concern Group, 2002.

12. Chan CLW, Mak JMH. Benefits and drawbacks of Chinese rituals surrounding care for the dying. In: Fielding R, Chan CLW, editors. *Psychosocial oncology and palliative care in Hong Kong: the first decade.* Hong Kong: Hong Kong University Press, 2000: 255–70.

CHAPTER 22

1. Bailley SE, Kral MJ, Dunham K. Survivors of suicide do grieve differently: empirical support for a common sense proposition. *Suicide Life Threat Behav* 1999; 29(3): 256–71.

2. Clark S. Bereavement after suicide — how far have we come and where do we go from here? *Crisis* 2001; 22(3): 102–8.

3. Shneidman ES. *Deaths of man.* New York: Quadrangle Books, 1973.

4. Shneidman ES. *Comprehending suicide: landmarks in 20th-century suicidology.* 1st ed. Washington, DC: American Psychological Association, 2001.

5. Jordan JR. Is suicide bereavement different? A reassessment of the literature. *Suicide and life-threatening behavior* 2001; 31(1): 91–102.

6. Shneidman ES. Prologue: Fifty-eight years. In: Shneidman ES, editor. *On the nature of suicide.* San Francisco, CA: Jossey-Bass, 1969.

7. Report on Hong Kong 2002 Coroner cases of suicide deaths. *Newsletter,* The Hong Kong Jockey Club Centre for Suicide Research and Prevention, The University of Hong Kong: Spring 2005, 6.

8. Worden JW. *Grief counseling and grief therapy: a handbook for the mental health practitioner.* New York: Springer, 1982.

9. Stroebe MS, Hansson RO, Stroebe W, Schut H. Introduction: concepts, issues in contemporary research on bereavement. In: Stroebe MS, Hansson RO, Stroebe W, Schut H, editors. *Handbook of bereavement research: consequences, coping, and care.* 1st ed. Washington, DC: American Psychological Association, 2001: 3–22.

10. Clark SE, Goldney RD. Grief reactions and recovery in a support group for people bereaved by suicide. *Crisis* 1995; 16: 27–33.

11. Rando TA. *Treatment of complicated mourning.* Champaign, IL: Research Press, 1993.

12. Seguin M, Lesage A, Kiely MC. Parental bereavement after suicide and accident: a comparative study. *Suicide and Life-Threatening Behavior* 1995; 25(4): 489–98.
13. Vanderwal J. The aftermath of suicide — a review of empirical evidence. *Omega — Journal of Death and Dying* 1989; 20(2): 149–71.
14. Bond MH, Hwang KK. The social psychology of Chinese people. In: Bond MH, editor. *The psychology of the Chinese people.* Hong Kong: Oxford University Press, 1986: 213–66.
15. Ho WS, Ying SY. Suicidal burns in Hong Kong Chinese. *Burns* 2001; 27(2): 125–7.
16. The Hong Kong Jockey Club Centre for Suicide Research and Prevention. Suicide and the media: recommendations on suicide reporting for media professionals. Hong Kong: Hong Kong Jockey Club Centre for Suicide Research and Prevention, The University of Hong Kong, 2004.
17. Schut H, Stroebe M, van den Bout J, Terheggen M. The efficacy of bereavement interventions: Determining who benefits. In: Stroebe MS, Hansson RO, Stroebe W, Schut H, editors. *Handbook of bereavement research: consequences, coping, and care.* 1st ed. Washington, DC: American Psychological Association, 2001:705–37.
18. Ayers T, Balk D, Bolle J, Bonanno GA, Connor SR, Cook AS, *et al.* Report on bereavement and grief research. *Death Studies* 2004; 28(6): 491–575.

CHAPTER 23

1. Dalai Lama. Foreword. In: Rinpoche S, editor. *The Tibetan book of living and dying.* New York: Harper, 1993: ix.
2. Schnedier JM. *Finding the way: healing and transformation through loss and grief.* Colfax, WI: Seasons Press, 1994.
3. Ho SMY, Tsui YKY. Interdependence in death and grief among Hong Kong Chinese. *Newsletter of Hong Kong Society of Palliative Medicine* 2002; 2002(1).
4. Hui E, Ho SC, Tsang J, Lee SH, Woo J. Attitudes toward life-sustaining treatment of older persons in Hong Kong. *Journal of the American Geriatrics Society* 1997; 45 (10): 1232–6.
5. Brady MJ, Peterman AH, Fitchett G, Mo M, Cella DA. A case for including spirituality in quality of life measurement in oncology. *Psychooncology* 1999; 8: 417–28.
6. Davies CG, Nolen-Hoeksema S, Larson J. Making sense of loss and benefiting from the experience: two construals of meaning. *Journal of Personality and Social Psychology* 1998; 75(2): 561–74.
7. Davies CG, Nolen-Hoeksema S, Larson J. Making sense of loss and benefiting from the experience: two construals of meaning. *Journal of Personality and Social Psychology* 1998; 75(2): 561–74.
8. Taylor SE. Adjustment to threatening events: a theory of cognitive adaptation. *American Psychologist* 1983; 38(11): 1161–73.
9. Barkwell DP. Ascribed meaning: a critical factor in coping and pain attenuation in patients with cancer-related pain. *Journal of Palliative Care* 1991; 7(3): 5–14.
10. Bower JE, Kemeny ME, Taylor S, Fahey J. Finding positive meaning and its association with natural killer cell cytotoxicity among participants in a bereavement-related disclosure intervention. *Annals of Behavioral Medicine* 2003; 25(2): 146–55.

11. Chan C, Leung P, Ho KM. Empowering Chinese cancer patients: taking culture into account. *Asia Pacific Journal of Social Work* 1999; 9(2): 6–21.

12. Bower JE, Kemeny ME, Taylor S, Fahey J. Cognitive processing, discovery of meaning, CD4 decline, and AIDS-related mortality among bereaved HIV-seropositive men. *Journal of Consulting and Clinical Psychology* 1998; 66(6): 979–86.

13. Neimeyer RA. *Meaning reconstruction and the experience of loss.* Washington, DC: American Psychological Association, 2001.

14. Lai CN. *Activate our self-healing potential.* Hong Kong: Buddhist Youth Association of Hong Kong, 2004.

15. Ho RTH. Psychophysiological effect of psychosocial interventions: an example of breast cancer patients in Hong Kong [Unpublished Ph.D. Thesis]. The University of Hong Kong, 2005.

16. Frankl V. *Man's search for meaning.* Boston, MA: Washington Square Press, 1984.

Index